MEDIA POWER IN POLITICS

Third Edition

MEDIA POWER IN POLITICS

Third Edition

Doris A. Graber
University of Illinois at Chicago

A Division of Congressional Quarterly Inc.
Washington, D.C.

Copyright © 1994 Congressional Quarterly Inc.

Printed in the United States of America

Book design: Naylor Design, Inc.

Library of Congress Cataloging-in-Publication Data

Media power in politics, 3rd ed.

   Includes bibliographical references.
   1. Mass media—Political aspects—United States.
2. Mass media—Social aspects—United States.
I. Graber, Doris A.
   HN90.M3M43   1993   ISBN 0-87187-785-6
   302.23- -dc20

                                93-30565
                                CIP

For Courtney and Alexander
who need the power of knowledge
to master their world

CONTENTS

TOPIC CORRELATION CHART

In addition to the six broad categories into which these essays have been divided, other groupings are possible. This chart lists twenty-eight major topics and the selections in which they are discussed, allowing readers to organize articles in whatever way best suits their purposes.

Agenda-setting   Part II and 17, 23, 26, 27
Attack journalism   16, 25, 29, 30
Audience roles   1, 2, 5
Communication theories   1, 2, 5, 8, 24
Comparative analysis   4, 9, 17, 18, 24, 25, 33, 35, 37
Controlling media   Part VI and 2, 28
Crisis coverage   4, 5, 9, 23, 24, 28-30, 35
Democracy and media impact   2, 3, 10, 12, 13, 15, 16, 33
Elections   Part III and 7, 21, 22
International politics   4, 5, 20, 27, 28, 35, 36, 37
Journalism ethics   6, 16, 19, 20, 25, 28, 29
Media effects   Part I and 7, 10-15, 18-22, 26, 27, 29, 31, 34, 35
Newsmaking processes   2, 4, 9, 15, 17, 19, 24, 25, 29, 31, 36
Policy making   Part V and 7, 8, 9, 20, 32, 35, 36
Politicians and media impact   Part IV and 2, 15, 16, 26, 32, 34, 35, 36
Protest group coverage   4, 24, 25, 28-30, 35, 36
Public opinion and media impact   5, 6, 7, 10, 11, 12, 20, 25, 29
Public relations   2, 15, 17, 18, 21, 22, 24, 25, 27, 28-31, 34, 35, 37
Reality distortions   3, 4, 5, 6, 12, 28
Research techniques
   case studies   4, 5, 8, 9, 16, 17, 20, 23-25, 27-31, 34, 35, 37
   content analysis, qualitative   8, 15, 16, 19, 29, 30, 35

PREFACE

The media are to blame!" "The media deserve the credit!" These have become common outcries in an era when television and newspapers and, to a lesser extent, news magazines and radio are perceived as major political forces. The scholarly and popular literature about media power continues to grow exponentially. Political communication is, indeed, a field in ferment. It has also become an intellectual thicket that students find difficult to traverse without some direction to landmark studies and major ideas and controversies. *Media Power in Politics* provides the guidance essential for students at all levels. That the book is now in its third edition is testimony to the need for such a volume and to its success in keeping political communication students familiar with cutting-edge research.

Media Power in Politics is a collection of articles, described fully in the Introduction, that may be used as primary reading for courses on mass media and politics, public opinion, political communication, and mass media and society. It is also suitable as supplementary reading in American government courses and in courses that focus on public policy formation. The book includes contributions by social scientists and media professionals, and because many of the academic authors have worked for media organizations, their theories, analyses, and recommendations are tempered by the realism that comes from practical experience. The selections span several social science disciplines, giving students the chance to view problems from an interdisciplinary perspective.

Media Power in Politics is divided into six parts, prefaced by introductions that outline major areas of media impact. A brief commentary precedes each selection, highlighting its principal contributions and introducing its author or authors. The articles follow the original text in all essential

matters. Deletions and editorial inserts are clearly marked. Footnotes have
been renumbered when necessary to maintain unbroken sequences, but
footnote styles have not been altered. Factual errors, such as erroneous
dates and misspelled names, have been corrected.

The thirty-seven selections reprinted in this book represent the work of
seventy-one authors. Many of them are nationally and internationally
recognized scholars; others have just begun careers that promise to earn
them distinction. I thank all of them for the contributions they have made
to understanding media and for their willingness to allow me to include
their work in this collection of readings. Thanks also are due to the many
publishers who consented to the use of selections that originally appeared
in their books and journals. For guidance in choosing essays that accomplish the goals set for this book, I am deeply indebted to Michael G.
Hagen of Harvard University, Jan Leighley of Texas A & M University,
and Silvo Lenart of Purdue University.

Preparation of a book of readings entails many tasks beyond selecting
and editing the contents and writing introductory comments. I am grateful
to the staff at CQ Press for handling these tasks ably and expeditiously.
Special thanks are due to CQ's capable acquisitions editors Brenda Carter
and Shana Wagger and to Barbara de Boinville, the nicest and best copy
editor that any author could hope to have. Book production has been
handled smoothly by Nancy Lammers, assistant director of the book
department, and Laura Carter, production editor. The concern and
friendship of the CQ crew, headed by David Tarr, have made my job a
pleasure. Last, but not least, the efforts of my research assistants,
especially Laurent Pernot and Leta Dally, and my proofreader, La Vonne
Downey, must be acknowledged. I thank them all.

Doris A. Graber

INTRODUCTION

How powerful are the mass media in shaping politics? No definite answers are in sight despite a great deal of research and informed speculation. The full scope of media power and the circumstances that make it wax and wane remain shrouded in mystery. Current investigations do shed light, however, on many factors that explain various aspects of media power. They provide some clues to the puzzling questions about when, where, and why media power peaks and when it reaches bottom. The literature exploring media power has been expanding so rapidly that it has become difficult for newcomers to the field to gain an overview of the substantive information and research approaches. This book of readings simplifies the task.

Media Power in Politics, third edition, analyzes mass media effects on the political system in general, and on its formal and informal components, such as Congress, the executive branch, and organized lobbies and protest groups. The interactions of the mass media with political institutions have brought about profound changes. Their nature and magnitude raise exceptionally provocative questions about the roles that a privately controlled profession—journalism—and the private mass media enterprise as a whole play and should play in government and politics.

Each of the six parts into which the essays have been grouped illustrates the influence of mass media on an important facet of U.S. politics. Part I deals with mass media effects in general. The selections in Parts II through V explore the influence of mass media on political opinions and preferences, on presidential and congressional elections, on participants within and outside the political power structure, and on the formation and implementation of domestic and foreign public policies. Part VI examines private and public efforts in the United States and abroad to control the impact of the mass media and to shape media offerings.

Certain principles guided the choice of specific selections. Most important among these were the significance and quality of the research and its ability to shed light on diverse aspects of media power. Several studies that compare media power in the United States with media power abroad have been included because comparisons bring media effects into sharper focus. To introduce readers to the intellectual origins and contemporary milestones in the field of media research, a few "classics" are also included. Clarity of presentation and ease of reading were other choice criteria.

While a concerted effort was made in this new edition to feature well-known media scholars from different social science disciplines, newcomers to the field and practitioners also have been given space. Twenty-two essays from the second edition have been retained in the current volume. For the fifteen new selections, the goal has been to include the most recent and thought-provoking scholarship. This thoroughly revised edition alerts readers to the latest developments in a rapidly growing, interdisciplinary area of study. It presents the work of political scientists, sociologists, communication researchers, and media practitioners.

To stimulate thinking about the processes for acquiring knowledge, along with thinking about substantive issues and public policies, several of the readings contain information about theories, research designs, and research methods. A number of essays explain and illustrate particularly well the procedures for content analysis. The introduction to Part I includes a brief description of this important media research technique. The footnotes and bibliographies in most selections provide ample leads to additional methodological explanations as well as other types of reading.

Readers should keep in mind that the excerpts were chosen with a specific purpose in mind: to assess the impact of the media on the political process. This was not necessarily the primary purpose of each of the authors. Therefore, the precise thrust of the original work cannot always be judged from the thrust of the excerpts presented here. Readers also must keep in mind that a price must be paid for trimming selections to hone the argument and accelerate its pace. Interesting methodological and factual details and arguments had to be omitted. The reward is a more succinct presentation of relevant information that allows the main arguments to emerge with greater clarity.

In addition to the six broad categories into which these essays have been divided, other groupings are possible. Guided by the topic correlation chart on page xi, readers may wish to focus on research trends or compare research techniques (for example, quantitative and qualitative content analysis or large- and small-scale surveys that use cross-sectional or panel approaches). Other research techniques presented in the book are intensive interviews and experimental studies.

The essays also can be used to study various aspects of the news-making process. All selections are relevant, but several address the topic explicitly. The study of news making raises questions about the effects of the television age on American democracy since public opinion, elections, and pressure groups have all been influenced by the medium. The media's role in crises is explored repeatedly. Finally, several essays offer comparisons among different countries or groups and comparisons among different types of media, thereby illustrating the value of comparative analysis.

The boundaries between the six parts of the book are flexible. For example, essays in Part I, which addresses the study of media effects, can be supplemented by selections from several other parts. The concept of agenda setting surfaces throughout the book, either explicitly or implicitly. Part VI, which discusses efforts to control media output, also sheds light on the reciprocal influence of the media and the executive branch, Congress, and pressure groups covered in Part IV. Similarly, discussion of media impact on public policy is not limited to Part V. Articles in other parts raise policy issues concerning the treatment of dissident groups, the regulation of various economic sectors, and child abuse. All of these selections broaden the picture sketched out in Part V.

The flexibility of *Media Power in Politics* springs from its rich content and from the variety of disciplinary viewpoints that are included. The importance of the issues raised by the media's role in contemporary politics and the fascination of exploring this new area in the study of politics have attracted many brilliant scholars. You are invited to sample their works in whatever order best suits your purposes.

I

PUTTING MASS MEDIA
EFFECTS IN PERSPECTIVE

This section puts research on mass media effects into historical and contextual perspective. Where have we been? Where are we going? In the first selection, Denis McQuail presents a broad overview of current theories, research, and knowledge about the influence of mass media on politics. He argues that the minimal effects myth of the 1960s has been exploded and that media research has entered a new phase, thanks to new theories and new research tools. Scholars now acknowledge that media can be powerful and take a broad view of the scope and variety of possible media effects. They realize the need to examine each type of effect separately as well as the context in which effects occur.

In a related vein Michael Gurevitch and Jay G. Blumler counsel that media effects are relative. Media influence is enhanced or diminished by the political power or weakness of other players in the political arena. The expectations that democratic theorists have about the functions of media in democratic societies must be tempered by the realities of power struggles.

In the next selection Walter Lippmann comments on the role presumably and actually played by the media in informing citizens. Like Gurevitch and Blumler, he notes the wide discrepancy between the role assigned to the media by democratic theory and the capabilities of the media in the real world. News is not truth. It is a tiny slice of reality removed from the context that gives it meaning. No study of the effects of news on public thinking would be complete without including at least a small portion of the wisdom of this modern political philosopher. His trenchant writings about public affairs spanned more than fifty years and continue to provide important insights into the media's impact on politics.

Walter C. Soderlund and Carmen Schmitt shed further light on the problem of conveying truth. The same situation reported by news media in various countries will give rise to very different images. The effects of the story will vary accordingly. Thus, it is not the situation itself that influences thought and action but the image that emerges when the facts are reported.

The Soderlund and Schmitt essay is the first of several selections that provide details about content analysis as a research technique. Content analysis assesses the media stimulus that produced or failed to produce a particular effect. The technique can be used informally, through reading or watching mass media stories and gleaning general impressions; or it can be used formally, through more elaborate procedures. In formal content analysis, researchers specify the features of the story that relate to their particular concerns. They then examine the story systematically to identify and record the presence or absence of these features. Soderlund and Schmitt, for example, recorded (*coded* is the technical term) whether stories about El Salvador were editorials, cartoons, or straight news stories and whether they appeared on the front or back page. They also noted to whom the stories were attributed, the specific issues and actors discussed, and whether the stories reflected positively or negatively on various political groups. Content analysis still is most commonly done manually because categorizations often require complex judgments, but it also can be done through computer searches of texts that judge the frequency and verbal context of words designating key concepts.

During the early phases of media effects research, investigators usually looked only for changes in behavior. When behavior remained stable, they declared that there had been no effects. But when research was broadened to include effects other than behavior, such as changes in attitudes or knowledge, large new areas of effects came into view. The selection by William C. Adams and his co-workers demonstrates how difficult it is to anticipate all effects of a media stimulus. Much work remains to be done to conceptualize all media effects and to build adequate methods of discovery into research designs.

In the final selection G. Ray Funkhouser and Eugene F. Shaw warn about the mischief media stories can create. Not only do news stories fail to capture reality, as Lippmann argues, but they are routinely dramatized to deliberately distort reality. Audience appeal has become more important than mirroring real life. The authors' concerns raise several perennial questions about media effects. Are the media harmful to America's political health? If they are, what, *if anything*, should media professionals, the government, or the public do in a society committed to press freedom?

1

THE INFLUENCE AND EFFECTS OF MASS MEDIA

Denis McQuail

Editor's Note

Questions about the effects of the mass media cannot be answered in broad generalities. Scholars have learned to ask about various types of effects, on various types of people and institutions, at various levels of society, under various conditions. Denis McQuail provides an overview of these contingencies in a diverse array of important media situations. In addition to discussing the general nature of mass media effects, McQuail traces the history of research findings produced by several kinds of investigations. His bibliography is an excellent starting point for review of the English language literature on media effects through 1976.

McQuail is a professor of sociology and mass communication at the University of Amsterdam in the Netherlands. He has taught at the University of Southampton, England, and at the University of Leeds. He has written several books on the sociology of mass communication. The following selection is from Mass Communication and Society, *ed. James Curran, Michael Gurevitch, and Janet Woolacott (Beverly Hills, Calif.: Sage Publications, 1979).*

The questions most insistently asked of social research on mass communication, and perhaps least clearly answered, have to do with the effects and social influence of the different mass media. The reasons for asking are understandable enough, given the amount of time spent attending to the mass media in many countries and the amount of resources invested in mass media production and distribution. Although much has been written by way of answer and a good deal of research carried out, it has to be admitted that the issue remains a disputed one—both in general about the significance of mass media and in particular about the likely effect of given

From *Mass Communication and Society,* edited by J. Curran, M. Gurevitch, and J. Woolacott, pp. 70-93. Copyright © 1979 by Sage Publications, Inc. Reprinted by permission of Sage Publications, Inc.

7

instances of mass communications. Inevitably, this discussion has to begin with some clarification of terms, since one of the perennial difficulties in the case has been the lack of communication between those who have investigated the question of media influence on the one hand and, on the other, the public, media producers and those concerned with public policy for the media.

Perhaps it should first be claimed that the question of effects is a somewhat unfair one, one rarely asked of comparable institutions like religion, education or the law which all in their way communicate to the public or to particular publics and where questions about effects as well as aims could well be asked. The mass media are highly diverse in content and in forms of organization and include a very wide range of activities which could have effects on society. To make the question not only more fair, but also more meaningful, we need to introduce a number of qualifications and specifications.

First, we can distinguish between effects and effectiveness, the former referring to any of the consequences of mass media operation, whether intended or not, the latter to the capacity to achieve given objectives, whether this be attracting large audiences or influencing opinions and behaviour. Both matters are important, but a different set of considerations relates to each. A second, though perhaps minor, point on which to be clear concerns the reference in time. Are we concerned with the past, or with predictions about the future? If the former, we need to be precise. If the latter, and often it is a prediction about what is going on now and its results which is a main concern, then some uncertainty is inevitable.

Third, we need to be clear about the level on which effects occur, whether this is at the level of the individual, the group, the institution, the whole society or the culture. Each or all may be affected in some way by mass communication. To specify the level meaningfully also requires us to name the kinds of phenomena on which influence may be exerted. We can investigate some phenomena at several levels—especially opinion and belief which can be a matter of individual opinion as well as the collective expression of institutions and societies. On the other hand to study the effect of the media on the way institutions operate requires us to look at the relationships between people occupying different roles and at the structure and content of these roles. Politics provides a good example, where the mass media have probably affected not only individual political opinions but also the way politics is conducted and its main activities organized. Political roles may have been changed, as well as our expectations of politicians, the relationships of followers to leaders, and even perhaps some of the values of political life. All this is a matter of historical change, much slower and less reversible than any influence on opinion, attitude or voting behaviour. Again it is clear that difference of level of effect is also related to different time spans. Changes in culture and in society are slowest to occur, least easy to know of with certainty, least easy to trace to their origins, most likely to persist. Changes affecting individuals are quick to occur, relatively easy to demonstrate and to attribute to a source, less easy to assess in terms of significance and performance. Hence we tend to find a situation in which the larger and more significant questions of media effect are most subject to conflicting interpretation and the most certain knowledge we have is most open to the charge of triviality and least useful as a basis for generalization. Perhaps one could usefully add a further set of distinctions which have to be made early on, whatever the level of analysis. This relates to the direction of effect. Are the media changing something, preventing something, facilitating something or reinforcing and reaffirming something? The importance of the question is obvious, but it is worth stressing early in the discussion that a 'no change' effect can be as significant as its reverse and there is little doubt that in some respects the media do inhibit as well as promote change.

The History of Research Into the Effects of Mass Communication

. . . [W]e can characterize the 50 years or more of interest in media effects in terms of three main stages. In the first phase, which lasts from the turn of the century to the late nineteen thirties the media, where they were developed in Europe and North America, were attributed considerable power to shape opinion and belief, change habits of life, actively mould behaviour and impose political systems even against resistance. Such views were not based on scientific investigation but were based on empirical observation of the sudden extension of the audience to large majorities and on the great attraction of the popular press, cinema and radio. The assumption of media power was also acted upon, as it were, by advertisers, government propagandists in the First World War, newspaper proprietors, the rulers of totalitarian states, and accepted defensively by nearly all as the best guess in the circumstances. It is not irrelevant that this stage of thinking coincided with a very early stage of social science when the methods and concepts for investigating these phenomena were only developing.

The second stage extends from about 1940 to the early 1960s and it is strongly shaped by growth of mass communications research in the United States and the application of empirical method to specific questions about the effects and effectiveness of mass communication. The influence of this phase of research is surprisingly great, given the rather narrow range of the questions tackled and relatively small quantity of substantial studies. Most influential, perhaps, were the studies of Presidential elections in 1940 and

1948 by Lazarsfeld (1944), Berelson [et al.] (1954) and the programme of research into the use of films for training and indoctrination of American servicemen undertaken by Hovland et al. (1950). An earlier and longer tradition of social-psychological inquiry into the effects of film and other media on crime, aggression and racial and other attitudes should also be mentioned (e.g. Blumler, 1933). In practice, a small number of much cited studies provided the substance for the general view of media effects and effectiveness which was generally being disseminated in social and political science by the end of the 1960s. Where there was research outside the United States (e.g. Trenaman and McQuail, 1961), it was in the same mould and tended to confirm rather than challenge the agreed version of media effects. Basically, this version affirmed the ineffectiveness and impotency of mass media and their subservience to other more fundamental components in any potential situation of influence. The mass media—primarily radio, film, or print at the time most research was conducted—emerged as unlikely to be major contributors to direct change of individual opinions, attitudes or behaviour or to be a direct cause of crime, aggression, or other disapproved social phenomena. Too many separate investigations reached similar negative conclusions for this to be doubted. The comment by Klapper (1960) in an influential view of research, that 'mass communication does not ordinarily serve as a necessary and sufficient cause of audience effects, but rather functions through a nexus of mediating factors' well sums up the outcome of the second phase. Of course, research had not shown the different media to be without effects, but it had established the primacy of other social facts and showed the power of the media to be located within the existing structures of social relationships and systems of culture and belief. The reversal of a prior assumption by scientific investigation was striking and seemed the more complete because the myth of media power was so strong and occasionally uncritical and naive. At the same time, it should be admitted that neither public anxiety about the new medium of television nor professional opinion in the field of advertising and mass communication was much changed by the verdict of science. In fact, hardly had the 'no effect' conclusion become generally accepted than it became subject to re-examination by social scientists who doubted that the whole story had yet been written.

The third phase, which still persists, is one where new thinking and new evidence is accumulating on the influence of mass communication, especially television, and the long neglected newspaper press. As early signs of doubts we could cite Lang and Lang (1959) or Key (1961) or Blumler (1964) or Halloran (1964). The case for re-opening the question of mass media effects rests on several bases. First of all, the lesson of 'no-effects' has been learned and accepted and more modest expectations have taken the place of early belief. Where small effects are expected, methods have to be more precise. In addition, the intervening variables of social position and prior audience disposition, once identified as important, could now be more adequately measured. A second basis for revision, however, rested on a critique of the methods and research models which had been used. These were mainly experiments or surveys designed to measure short-term changes occurring in individuals, and concentrating especially on the key concept of attitude. Alternative research approaches might take a longer time span, pay more attention to people in their social context, look at what people know (in the widest sense) rather than at their attitudes and opinions, take account of the uses and motives of the audience member as mediating any effect, look at structures of belief and opinion and social behaviour rather than individual cases, take more notice of the *content* whose effects are being studied. In brief, it can be argued that we are only at the start of the task and have as yet examined very few of the questions about the effects of mass media, especially those which reveal themselves in *collective* phenomena. Some of these matters are returned to later, and at this point it is sufficient to conclude that we are now in a phase where the social power of the media is once more at the centre of attention for some social scientists, a circumstance which is not the result of a mere change of fashion but of a genuine advance of knowledge based on secure foundations. This advance has been uneven and buffeted by external pressure, but it is real enough. . . .

The Evidence of Effects

In order to discuss the results of research into mass media effects in a meaningful way, it may be helpful to divide up the problem under a set of headings which in a composite way reflects the various distinctions which have already been mentioned: of level; of kind of effect and of process; of research strategy and method. Although the headings which follow do not divide up the field in a mutually exclusive way, they do separate out the main topics which have been discussed, and provide a basis for evaluating research evidence. Basically what is being indicated is a set of media situations or processes which have distinctive features and require separate evaluation. The most important media situations are: (1) the campaign; (2) the definition of social reality and social norms; (3) the immediate response or reaction; (4) institutional change; (5) changes in culture and society.

The Campaign

Much of what has been written about the effects or effectiveness of the media either derives from research on campaigns or involves predictions about hypothetical campaign situations. . . . The kinds of media provision which might fall under this heading include: political and election campaigns, attempts at public information; commercial and public service advertising, some forms of education; the use of mass media in developing countries or generally for the diffusion of innovations. We recognize the similarity of these different activities. The campaign shares, in varying degrees, the following characteristics: it has specific aims and is planned to achieve these; it has a definite time-span, usually short; it is intensive and aims at wide coverage; its effectiveness is, in principle, open to assessment; it usually has authoritative sponsorship; it is not necessarily popular with its audience and has to be 'sold' to them; it is usually based on a framework of shared values. The campaign generally works to achieve objectives which in themselves are not controversial—voting, giving to charity, buying goods, education, health, safety, and so on. . . .

. . . Rather than discuss evidence in detail, which space would not allow, a brief assertion of a general condition of effect is made, with some reference to a source or summarizing work which justifies the assertion. One set of relevant factors has to do with the audience, another with the message and a third with the source or the system of distribution. Amongst audience factors, an obvious primary condition is that a large audience should be reached. Second, the appropriate members of the audience should be reached, since size alone does not guarantee the inclusion of those for whom the campaign is relevant. . . . Third, the dispositions of the audience should at least be not antipathetic or resistant. Political campaigning is most subject to this constraint and there is evidence that the lack of strong disposition either way and a condition of casual attention may be most favourable to the success of mass propaganda. (Blumler and McQuail, 1968.) A part of this condition relates to the need for consistency with the norms of locality and sub-culture as well as the presence of broad societal consensus. Fourth, success is likely to be greater when, within the audience, the flow of personal communication and structure of relevant interpersonal status is supportive of the mass media campaign and its aims. (Lazarsfeld, [et al.] 1944; Katz and Lazarsfeld, 1956; Rogers and Shoemaker, 1971.) Fifth, it is important that the audience understands or perceives the message as intended by its originators (Cooper and Jahoda, 1947; Belson, 1967) and does not selectively distort it.

Factors to do with the message or content are also important. First, the message should be unambiguous and relevant to its audience. The factor of relevance and a parallel self-selection by the audience makes it likely that campaigns are most successful at reinforcing existing tendencies or channelling them into only slightly different pathways. Second, the informative campaign seems more likely to be successful than the campaign to change attitudes or opinions. (Howland et al., 195[0]; Trenaman and McQuail, 1961.) Third, in general, subject matter which is more distant and more novel, least subject to prior definitions and outside immediate experience responds best to treatment by the campaign. The essential point is that the receiver has no competing sources of information and no personal stake in resisting an appeal or disbelieving information. It is easier to form opinions and attitudes about events abroad than events at home, about unfamiliar than about familiar matters. Fourth, the campaign which allows some immediate response in action is most likely to be effective, since behaviour generally confirms intention and attitude, whether in voting or buying, or donating to a charity. Fifth, repetition can be mentioned as a probable contributor to effect, although this is a common-sense assumption rather than well demonstrated. As far as the source is concerned, we should mention first the condition of monopoly. The more channels carrying the same campaign messages, the greater the probability of acceptance. This is not easy to demonstrate and there are circumstances where an imposed monopoly invites distrust and disbelief. (e.g. Inkeles and Bauer, 1959.) But, in general, this condition is presupposed in several of the conditions already stated. Second, there is evidence that the status or authority of the source contributes to successful campaigning and the principle is applied in most campaigns whether commercial or not. The source of attributed status can of course vary, including the strongly institutionalized prestige of the political or legal system or the personal attractiveness of a star or other 'hero' of society or the claim to expert knowledge. Endorsement by an individual or institution embodying strong claims to trust and attachment can be crucial in a campaign. Third, there is a variable condition of affective attachment to a media source. There is evidence that loyalty and affective ties exist in relations to some media rather than others which may affect their ability to influence. (Butler and Stokes, 1969; Blumler et al., 1975.)

These factors are all important in the process of intentional influence. . . . If we accept the validity of these points we are already very far from thinking the mass media to be ineffective, [n]or can it be said that we have no certain knowledge of the effects of mass media.

The Definition of Social Reality
and the Formation of Social Norms

The topics we should look at under this heading are diverse and the processes involved equally so. Here we mainly consider the process of learning through the media, a process which is often incidental, unplanned and unconscious for the receiver and almost always unintentional on the part of the sender. Hence the concept of 'effectiveness' is usually inappropriate, except in societies where the media take a planned and deliberate role in social development. This may be true of some aspects of socialist media (see Hopkins, 1970) or of some media applications in developing countries. (Pye, 1963; Frey, 1973.) There are two main aspects to what occurs. On the one hand, there is the provision of a consistent picture of the social world which may lead the audience to adopt this version of reality, a reality of 'facts' and of norms, values and expectations. On the other hand, there is a continuing and selective interaction between self and the media which plays a part in shaping the individual's own behavior and self-concept. We learn what our social environment is and respond to the knowledge that we acquire. In more detail, we can expect the mass media to tell us about different kinds of social roles and the accompanying expectations, in the sphere of work, family life, political behaviour and so on. We can expect certain values to be selectively reinforced in these and other areas of social experience. We can expect a form of dialogue between persons and fictional characters or real media personalities and also in some cases an identification with the values and perspectives of these 'significant others.' We can also expect the mass media to give an order of importance and structure to the world they portray, whether fictionally or as actuality. There are several reasons for these expectations. One is the fact that there is a good deal of patterning and consistency in the media version of the world. Another is the wide range of experience which is open to view and to vicarious involvement compared to the narrow range of real experience available to most people at most points in their lives. Third, there is the trust with which media are often held as a source of impressions about the world outside direct experience. Inevitably, the evidence for this process of learning from the media is thin and what there is does little more than reaffirm the plausibility of these theoretical propositions. The shortage of evidence stems in part from a failure to look for it, until quite recently, and in part from the long-term nature of the processes which make them less amenable to investigations by conventional techniques of social research than are the effects of campaigns. . . .

A long list of studies can be cited showing the media to have certain inbuilt tendencies to present a limited and recurring range of images and ideas which form rather special versions of reality. In some areas, as with news reporting, the pattern is fairly inescapable; in others the diversity of media allows some choice and some healthy contradiction. What we lack is much evidence of the impact of these selective versions of the world. In many cases discount by the audience or the availability of alternative information must make acceptance of media portrayals at face value extremely unlikely or unusual. We should certainly not take evidence of content as evidence of effect. There is no close correspondence between the two and some studies show this. For example Roshier (1973) found public views about crime to be closer to the 'true' statistical picture than the somewhat distorted version one might extract from the content of local newspapers. Similarly Halloran's study of audience reaction to television reports of the 1968 demonstration shows this to have been rather little affected by the 'one-sided' version presented on the screen. Even so, there is enough evidence as well as good theory for taking the proposition as a whole quite seriously. The case of the portrayal of an immigrant, especially coloured, minority provides a good test, since we may expect the media to be a prominent source of impressions for those in Britain who have little or very limited personal contact with 'immigrants.'. . .

[T]he media are associated with a view of immigrants as likely to be a cause of trouble or be associated with conflict. It also seems that impressions attributed to the media as source show a rather higher degree of internal similarity and to be in general less evaluative than those derived from personal contact. The main contribution of the mass media is not, according to this study, to encourage prejudice (often the reverse) but in defining the presence of immigrants as an 'objective' problem for the society.

. . . [T]he terms 'amplification' and 'sensitization' and 'polarization' have been used to describe the tendency of the media to exaggerate the incidence of a phenomenon, to increase the likelihood of it being noticed and to mobilize society against a supposed threat. In recent times, it has been argued that this treatment has been allotted to drug-taking (by Young, 1973), to mugging and to left-wing militants. It is notable that the groups receiving this form of polarizing treatment tend to be small, rather powerless and already subject to broad social disapproval. They are relatively 'safe' targets, but the process of hitting them tends to reaffirm the boundaries around what is acceptable in a free society.

When the question of media effects on violence is discussed, a rather opposite conclusion is often drawn. It seems as if general public opinion still holds the media responsible for a good deal of the increasing lawlessness in society (Halloran, 1970), a view based probably on the frequency with which crime and violence is portrayed, even if it rarely seems to be 'rewarded.' It is relevant to this section of the discussion to explore this view. American evidence obtained for the Kerner Commission on Violence and reported by Baker and Ball (1969) shows there certainly to be much violence portrayed on the most used medium, television. It also shows that most people have rather little contact with real violence in personal experience. The authors chart the public expression of norms in relation to violence and also television norms as they appear in content and find a gap between the two. Thus, while public norms cannot yet have been much affected directly, the gap suggests that the direction of effects is to extend the boundaries of acceptable violence beyond current norms. In brief then, the authors of this study lend support to one of the more plausible hypotheses connecting crime and violence with the media—that the tolerance of aggression is increased by its frequent portrayal and it becomes a more acceptable means of solving problems whether for the 'goodies' or the criminals. It should not be lost sight of, even so, that most dependable research so far available has not supported the thesis of a general association between any form of media use and crime, delinquency or violence. (Halloran, 1970.) The discussion linking social norms with violence takes place on the level of belief systems, opinions, social myths. It would require a long-term historical and cultural analysis to establish the propositions which are involved. Nor should we forget that there are counter-propositions, pointing for instance to the selectivity of public norms about violence and aggression. It is not disapproved of in general in many societies, only in its uncontrolled and non-institutionalized forms. . . .

. . . It has already been suggested that the media help to establish an order of priorities in a society about its problems and objectives. They do this, not by initiating or determining, but by publicizing according to an agreed scale of values what is determined elsewhere, usually in the political system. Political scientists have been most alert to the process and the term 'agenda-setting' has been given to it by McCombs and Shaw (1972). They found the mass media to present a very uniform set of issues before the American public in the 1968 presidential election and found public opinion to accord in content and order rather closely to this pattern. The phenomenon had been noted earlier in election campaign studies, where order of space given to issues in media content was found to be predictive of changes in order of importance attributed to issues over the course of the campaign. (Trenaman and McQuail, 1961; Blumler and McQuail, 1968.) In one sense the media only record the past and reflect a version of the present but, in doing so, they can affect the future, hence the significance of the 'agenda' analogy. . . .

Given the sparseness of evidence, it is not surprising that we cannot so adequately state the conditions for the occurrence or otherwise of effects from the media in the sphere of forming impressions of reality and defining social norms. In particular, we are dealing with society-wide and historically located phenomena which are subject to forces not captured by normal data-collecting techniques in the social sciences. However, if we re-inspect the list of conditions associated with media campaign success or failure, a number will again seem relevant. In particular, we should look first at the monopoly condition. Here what matters is less the monopoly of ownership and control than the monopoly of attention and the homogeneity of content. Uniformity and repetition establish the important result of monopoly without the necessity for the structural causes to be present.

The more consistent the picture presented and the more exclusively this picture gains wide attention then the more likely is the predicted effect to occur. (cf. Noelle-Neumann, 1974.) We can suppose, too, that matters outside immediate experience and on which there are not strongly formed, alternative views will also be most susceptible to the level of influence spoken of. Further, we can think that here, as with media campaigns, a trust in the source and an attribution of authority will be an important factor in the greater extension of media-derived opinions and values. Other conditions of social organization must also be taken into account. It is arguable, but untestable, that circumstances of greater individuation and lower ties of attachment to intermediary groups and associations will favour an influence from the media. Finally, we might hypothesize that conditions of social crisis or danger might also be associated with strong short-term effects from the media on the definition of problems and solutions.

Immediate Response and Reaction Effects

To discuss this, we return to questions relating largely to individuals and to direct and immediate effects. We are concerned exclusively with unintended, generally 'undesirable,' effects which fall into two main categories. One relates again to the problem of crime and violence, another to cases of panic response to news or information, where collective responses develop out of individual reception of the media. . . .

. . . One school of thought is now convinced that media portrayals of aggression can provoke aggression in child audiences. (e.g. Berkovitz, 1964.) Another favours the view that the effect of fictional evidence is more likely to be a cathartic or aggression-releasing tendency. (Feshbach [and Singer], 1971.) Many experiments have been inconclusive and majority opinion seems inclined to the cautious conclusion that direct effects involving disapproved behaviour are rare or likely to occur only where there is a strong disposition in that direction amongst a small minority of the already disturbed. . . .

The possibility that information received from the mass media will 'trigger' widespread and collective panic responses has often been canvassed, but rarely demonstrated. The 1938 radio broadcast of Wells' *War of the Worlds* which involved simulated news bulletins reporting an invasion from Mars is the case most often cited in this connection mainly because of [research by Cantril *et al.* (1940)] after the event. An event with some similarities in Sweden in 1973 was investigated by Rosengren *et al.* (1976) and the results cast doubt on the thesis as a whole. It seems that in neither case was there much behavioural response, and what there was was later exaggerated by other media. Investigations of news transmission in times of crisis, for instance the studies by Greenberg of the dissemination of news of the assassination of Kennedy (Greenberg [and Parker], 1965) tells us a good deal more of the processes which begin to operate in such circumstances. Essentially, what happens is that people take over as transmitters of information and those who receive news seek independent confirmation from other media or trusted personal sources. The circumstance of solitary, unmediated, reception and response is unusual and short-lived. Shibutani (1966) reminds us that rumour and panic response are the outcome of situations of ambiguity and lack of information and, on the whole the mass media operate to modify rather than magnify these conditions.

In dealing with this aspect of potential media effects, more attention should perhaps be paid to various kinds of 'contagion' or spontaneous diffusion of activities. The situations most often mentioned relate to the spreading of unrest or violence. For instance at times during the late 1960s when urban violence and rioting was not uncommon in American cities it was suggested that television coverage of one event might lead to occurrences elsewhere. Research into the possibility (e.g. Pal[e]tz and Dunn, 1967) does not settle the matter and it remains a reasonable expectation that given the right preconditions, media coverage could spread collective disturbance by publicity alone. Political authorities which have the power to do so certainly act on the supposition that unrest can be transmitted in this way and seek to delay or conceal news which might encourage imitators. The imitation of acts of terrorism or criminality, such as hijacking, seems also likely to have occurred, although the proof is lacking and the phenomenon is different because of its individual rather than collective character. In many areas where there is no institutionalized prohibition there is little doubt that spontaneous imitation and transmission do occur on a large scale by way of the mass media. In the sphere of music, dress, and other stylistic forms, the phenomenon is occurring all the time. It is this which has led to the expectation that the media on their own are a powerful force for change in developing countries (Lerner, 1958), through their stimulation of the desire first to consume and then to change the ways of life which stand in the way of earning and buying. Research evidence (e.g. Rogers and Shoemaker, 1971) and more considered thought (e.g. Golding, 1974) have led to the realization, however, that facts of social structure and of social institutions intervene powerfully in the process of imitation and diffusion. Even so, we should beware of dismissing the process as a misconception or, where it occurs, always as trivial. It is at least plausible that the movement for greater female emancipation owes a good deal to widely disseminated publicity by way of mass media.

Consequences for Other Social Institutions

It was emphasized at the outset that the 'effects' of mass media have to be considered at a level beyond that of the individual audience member and the aggregate of individual behaviours. The path by which collective effects are produced is, in general, simple enough to grasp, but the extent to which effects have occurred resists simple or certain assessment and has rarely been the subject of sustained investigation or thought. As the mass media have developed they have, incontrovertibly, achieved two things. They have, between them, diverted time and attention from other activities and they have become a channel for reaching more people with more information than was available under 'pre-mass media' conditions. These facts have implications for any other institution which requires allocation of time, attention and the communication of information, especially to large numbers and in large quantities. The media compete with other institutions and they offer ways of reaching continuing institutional objectives. It is this which underlies the process of institutional effect. Other social institutions are under pressure to adapt or respond in some way, or to make their own use of the mass media. In doing so, they are likely to alter. Because this is a slow process, occurring along with other kinds of social change, the specific contribution of the media cannot be accounted for with any certainty.

If this argument is accepted, it seems unlikely that any institution will be unaffected, but most open to change will be those concerned with 'knowledge' in the broadest sense and which are most universal and unselective in their reach. In most societies, this will suggest politics and education as the most likely candidates, religion in some cases and to a lesser degree, legal institution[s]. In general we would expect work, social services, science, [and] the military to be only tangentially affected by the availability of mass media. Insofar as we can regard leisure and sport as an institution in modern society this should perhaps be added to politics and education as the most directly interrelated with the mass media. . . .

. . . The challenge to politics from media institutions has taken several forms, but has been particularly strong just because the press was already involved in political processes and because the introduction of broadcasting was a political act. The diversion of time from political activity was less important than the diversion of attention from partisan sources of information and ideology to sources which were more accessible and efficient, often more attractive as well as authoritative, and which embodied the rather novel political values of objectivity and independent 'expert' adjudication. As we have seen, it has increasingly seemed as if it is the mass media which set the 'agenda' and define the problems on a continuous, day to day, basis while political parties and politicians increasingly respond to a consensus view of what should be done. The communication network controlled by the modern mass party cannot easily compete with the mass media network. . . .

Changes of Culture and Society

If we follow a similar line of analysis for other institutions, it is not difficult to appreciate that we can arrive at one or more versions of ways in
which culture and social structure can be influenced by the path of development of media institutions. If the content of what we know, our way of
doing things and spending time and the organization of central activities
for the society are in part dependent on the media, then the fact of interdependence is evident. Again, the problem is to prove connections and quantify the links. The 'facts' are so scarce, open to dispute and often puny in
stature that the question is often answered by reference to alternative theories. For some, the answer may still be provided by a theory of mass society of the kind advanced by Mills (1956) or Kornhauser (1959) and criticized by Shil[s] (1975). Such a theory suggests that the mass media
encourage and make viable a rootless, alienated, form of social organization in which we are increasingly within the control of powerful and distant
institutions. For others, a Marxist account of the mass media as a powerful
ideological weapon for holding the mass of people in voluntary submission
to capitalism (Marcuse, 1964; Miliband, 1969) provides the answer to the
most important effects of the rise of the mass media.

A more complex answer is offered by Carey (1969), in his suggestion
that the mass media are both a force for integration and for dispersion and
individuation in society. Gerbner [and Gross (1976) see] the key to the
effects of mass media in their capacity to take over the 'cultivation' of images, ideas and consciousness in an industrial society. He refers to the
main process of mass media as that of 'publication' in the literal sense of
making public: 'The truly revolutionary significance of modern mass communication is . . . the ability to form historically new bases for collective
thought and action quickly, continuously and pervasively across the previous boundaries of time, space and status.' The ideas of McLuhan (1962
and 1964), despite a loss of vogue, remain plausible for some (e.g. Noble,
1975), especially in their particular reference to the establishment of a
'global village' which will be established through direct and common experience from television. The various theories are not all so far apart. A
common theme is the observation that experience, or what we take for
experience, is increasingly indirect and 'mediated' and that, whether by
chance or design, more people receive a similar 'version' of the world. The
consequences for culture and society depend, however, on factors about
which the theories are not agreed, especially on the character and likely
tendency of this version of reality. Similarly, the available theories are not
agreed on the basis of the extraordinary appeal of the mass media, taken in
general. Do they meet some underlying human needs? If so, what is the

nature of these needs? Alternatively, is the apparent 'necessity' of the media merely the result of some imposed and artificial want? Certainly, the question of what most wide-ranging consequences follow from the media must also raise the question of motivation and use.

The Social Power of Mass Media—A Concluding Note

It has been the intention of this whole discussion to make very clear that the mass media do have important consequences for individuals, for institutions and for society and culture. That we cannot trace very precise causal connections or make reliable predictions about the future does not nullify this conclusion. The question of the power of the mass media is a different one. In essence, it involves asking how effectively the mass media can and do achieve objectives over others at the will of those who direct, own or control them or who use them as channels for messages. The history of mass media shows clearly enough that such control is regarded as a valued form of property for those seeking political or economic power. The basis for such a view has already been made clear in the evidence which has been discussed. Control over the mass media offers several important possibilities. First, the media can attract and direct attention to problems, solutions or people in ways which can favour those with power and correlatively divert attention from rival individuals or groups. Second, the mass media can confer status and confirm legitimacy. Third, in some circumstances, the media can be a channel for persuasion and mobilization. Fourth, the mass media can help to bring certain kinds of publics into being and maintain them. Fifth, the media are a vehicle for offering psychic rewards and gratifications. They can divert and amuse and they can flatter. In general, mass media are very cost-effective as a means of communication in society; they are also fast, flexible and relatively easy to plan and control. . . .

The general case which can be made out along these lines for treating the mass media as an instrument of social power is sufficiently strong for many commentators to regard it as settled. In this view, all that remains is to discover not *whether* the media have power and how it works, but *who* has access to the use of this power. Generally this means asking questions about ownership and other forms of control, whether political, legal or economic. It is arguable, however, that we need to take the case somewhat further and to probe rather more carefully the initial general assumption. That is, we cannot assume that ownership and control of the means of mass communication does necessarily confer power over others in any straightforward or predictable way. . . .

. . . [M]ore attention should be given to the various structures of legitimation which attract and retain audiences and which also govern their attitudes to different media sources. There are critical differences between alternative forms of control from above and between alternative types of orientation to the media, both within and between societies. This is, as yet, a relatively unexplored area but meanwhile we should be as wary of trying to answer questions of power solely in terms of ownership as we should be of doing so in terms of 'effects.'

References

Baker, R. K. and Ball, S. J., 1969: *Mass Media and Violence*. Report to the National Commission on the Causes and Prevention of Violence.
Belson, W., 1967: *The Impact of Television*. Crosby Lockwood.
Berelson, B., Lazarsfeld, P. F. and McPhee, W., 1954: *Voting*. University of Chicago Press.
Berelson, B., and Steiner, G., 1963: *Human Behaviour*. Harcourt Brace.
Berkovitz, 1964: 'The effects of observing violence.' *Scientific American*, vol. 210.
Blumler, H., 1933: *Movies and Conduct*. Macmillan.
Blumler, J. G., 1964: 'British Television: the Outlines of a Research Strategy.' *British Journal of Sociology* 15 (3).
Blumler, J. G. and McQuail, D., 1968: *Television in Politics: its uses and influence*. Faber.
Blumler, J. G., Nossiter, T. and McQuail, D., 1975: *Political Communication and Young Voters*. Report to SSRC.
Blumler, J. G. and Katz, E. (eds.), 1975: 'The Uses and Gratifications Approach to Communications Research.' *Sage Annual Review of Communication*, vol. 3.
Butler, D. and Stokes, D., 1969: *Political Change in Britain*. Macmillan.
Cantril, H., Gaudet, H. and Herzog, H., 1940: *The Invasion from Mars*. Princeton University Press.
Carey, J. W., 1969: 'The Communications Revolution and the Professional Communicator.' In Halmos, P., (ed.), *The Sociology of Mass Media Communicators*. Sociological Review Monograph 13. University of Keele.
Cohen, S., 1973: *Folk Devils and Moral Panics*. Paladin.
Cooper, E. and Jahoda, M., 1947: 'The evasion of propaganda.' *Journal of Psychology* 15, pp. 15-25.
De Fleur, M., 1964: 'Occupational roles as portrayed on television.' *Public Opinion Quarterly* 28, pp. 57-74.
Etzioni, A., 1967: *The Active Society*. Free Press.
Feshbach, S. and Singer, R., 1971: *Television Aggression*. Jossey-Bass.
Franzwa, H., 1974: 'Working women in fact and fiction.' *Journal of Communication*, 24 (2), pp. 104-9.
Frey, F. W., 1973: 'Communication and Development.' In de Sola Pool, I. and Schramm, W. (eds.), *Handbook of Communication*, Rand McNally.
Galtung, J., and Ruge, M., 1965: 'The structure of foreign news.' *Journal of Peace Research*, vol. 1.
Gerbner, G. and Gross, L., 1976: 'The scary world of TV's heavy viewer.' *Psychology Today*, April.

Golding, P., 1974: 'Mass communication and theories of development.' *Journal of Communication*, Summer.

Greenberg, B. and Parker, E. B. (eds.), 1965: *The Kennedy Assassination and the American Public*. Stanford University Press.

Halloran, J. D., 1964: *The Effects of Mass Communication*. Leicester University Press.

Halloran, J. D. (ed.), 1970: *The Effects of Television*. Paladin.

Halloran, J. D., Brown, R. and Chaney, D. C., 1970: *Television and Delinquency*. Leicester University Press.

Halloran, J. D., Elliott, P. and Murdock, G., 1970: *Demonstrations and Communication*. Penguin.

Hartmann, P., 1976: 'Industrial relations in the news media.' *Journal of Industrial Relations* 6(4), pp. 4-18.

Hartmann, P. and Husband, C., 1974: *Racism and the Mass Media*. Davis-Poynter.

Hopkins, M. W., 1970: *Mass Media in the Soviet Union*. Pegasus.

Hovland, C. I., Lumsdaine, A. and Sheffield, F., 1950: *Experiments in Mass Communication*. Princeton University Press.

Inkeles, A. and Bauer, R., 1959: *The Soviet Citizen*. Harvard University Press.

Katz, E. and Lazarsfeld, P. F., 1956: *Personal Influence*. Free Press.

Key, V. O., 1961: *Public Opinion and American Democracy*. Knopf.

Klapper, Joseph T., 1960: *The Effects of Mass Communication*. Free Press.

Kornhauser, F. W., 1959: *The Politics of Mass Society*. Routledge.

Lang, K. and Lang, G., 1959: 'The Mass Media and Voting.' In Burdick, E. J. and Brodbeck, A. J. (eds.), *American Voting Behaviour*, Free Press.

Lazarsfeld, P. F., Berelson, B. and Gaudet, H., 1944: *The People's Choice*. Columbia University Press.

Lerner, D., 1958: *The Passing of Traditional Society*. Free Press.

McCombs, M. and Shaw, D. L., 1972: 'The agenda-setting function of mass media.' *Public Opinion Quarterly* 36.

McLuhan, M., 1962: *The Gutenberg Galaxy*. Routledge. 1964: *Understanding Media*. Routledge.

McQuail, D., 1970: 'Television and Education.' In Halloran, J. D. (ed.), *The Effects of Television*, Panther.

Marcuse, H., 1964: *One-Dimensional Man*. Routledge.

Mills, C. W., 1956: *The Power Elite*. Free Press.

Miliband, R., 1969: *The State in Capitalist Society*. Weidenfeld and Nicolson.

Noble, G., 1975: *Children in Front of the Small Screen*. Constable.

Noelle-Neumann, E., 1974: 'The spiral of silence.' *Journal of Communication*, Spring.

Paletz, D. H. and Dunn, R., 1967: 'Press coverage of civil disorders.' *Public Opinion Quarterly* 33, pp. 328-45.

Pye, Lucian (ed.), 1963. *Communication and Political Development*. Princeton University Press.

Roberts, D. F., 1971: 'The nature of communication effects.' In Schramm, W. and Roberts, D. F., *Process and Effects of Mass Communication*, University of Illinois Press, pp. 347-87.

Rogers, E. and Shoemaker, F., 1971: *Communication and Innovations.* Free Press.

Rosengren, K. E., 1976: *The Bäxby Incident.* Lund University.

Roshier, B., 1973: 'The selection of crime news by the press.' In Cohen, S. and Young, J. (eds.), *The Manufacture of News,* Constable.

Seymour-Urc, C., 1973: *The Political Impact of Mass Media.* Constable.

Shibutani, T., 1966: *Improvised News.* Bobbs-Merrill.

Shils, E., 1975: 'The Theory of Mass Society.' In *Centre and Periphery,* Chicago University Press.

Star, S. A. and Hughes, H. M., 1951: 'Report on an educational campaign.' *American Journal of Sociology* 55 (4), pp. 389-400.

Trenaman, J. and McQuail, D., 1961: *Television and the Political Image.* Methuen.

Weiss, W., 1969: 'Effects of the Mass Media of Communication.' In Lindzey, G. and Aronson, E. (eds.), *Handbook of Social Psychology,* 2d edn., vol. V.

Young, J., 1973: 'The amplification of drug use.' In Cohen, S. and Young, J. (eds.), *The Manufacture of News,* Constable.

2

POLITICAL COMMUNICATION SYSTEMS AND DEMOCRATIC VALUES

Michael Gurevitch and Jay G. Blumler

Editor's Note

Power is a relative concept in the realm of politics. How much power human institutions are able to wield hinges on competing players in the political game and on the tasks they need to perform with the resources they control. These players play multiple games simultaneously, which often forces them into strategies of uneasy compromise.

Michael Gurevitch and Jay G. Blumler outline the rules of the mass media game in democratic societies and point out how these rules must be modified in complex political and economic environments. Their analysis makes it clear that media power, like the power of other social institutions, must always be appraised in light of the historical and social context.

Michael Gurevitch is a professor of journalism and director of the Center for Research in Public Communication at the University of Maryland. Jay G. Blumler, a former director of the Center for Television Research at the University of Leeds in England, is associate director of the Center for Research in Public Communication at the University of Maryland. Both scholars have written extensively on political communication topics. This selection comes from Democracy and the Mass Media, *ed. Judith Lichtenberg (New York: Cambridge University Press, 1990), chap. 9.*

The American media system is presumably animated by certain democratic principles. Some of these concern the relationship of the mass media to government—for example, the proposition that, acting on behalf of the citizenry, the media should guard against abuses of power by officeholders. Others concern the relationship of the mass media to diverse opinion sources—for example, the proposition that the media should provide a ro-

From "Political Communication Systems and Democratic Values," pp. 269-287 in *Democracy and the Mass Media* by Judith Lichtenberg, © 1990, Cambridge University Press. Reprinted with permission.

bust, uninhibited, and wide-open marketplace of ideas, in which opposing views may meet, contend, and take each other's measure. Yet others concern the relationship of the mass media to the public at large—for example, the propositions that they should serve the public's "right to know" and offer options for meaningful political choices and nourishment for effective participation in civic affairs.

Yet, a glance at the world of the American media today reveals a landscape dominated by a few giant media corporations. These enterprises may be as remote from the people as are other powerful and dominant institutions in society. Their inner workings are rarely opened to voluntary outside scrutiny. And they seem committed to the presentation, not of a broad spectrum of ideas, but of mainstream opinion currents, whose flows are bounded politically by the two-party system, economically by the imperatives of private enterprise capitalism, and culturally by the values of a consumer society.

This essay deals with the tensions and disparities between the ostensibly democratic ideals that the mass media are supposed to serve and the communication structures and practices that actually prevail. We argue that such disparities undermine the capacity of the system to serve these democratic ideals. Our diagnosis rests on some broad assumptions that are stated, elaborated, and illustrated in the following sections.

Democratic Expectations of Media Performance

Democracy is a highly exacting creed in its expectations of the mass media. It requires that the media perform and provide a number of functions and services for the political system. Among the more significant are:

1. Surveillance of the sociopolitical environment, reporting developments likely to impinge, positively or negatively, on the welfare of citizens
2. Meaningful agenda-setting, identifying the key issues of the day, including the forces that have formed and may resolve them
3. Platforms for an intelligible and illuminating advocacy by politicians and spokespersons of other causes and interest groups
4. Dialogue across a diverse range of views, as well as between power holders (actual and prospective) and mass publics
5. Mechanisms for holding officials to account for how they have exercised power
6. Incentives for citizens to learn, choose, and become involved, rather than merely to follow and kibitz over the political process
7. A principled resistance to the efforts of forces outside the media to subvert their independence, integrity, and ability to serve the audience
8. A sense of respect for the audience member, as potentially concerned and able to make sense of his or her political environment

But it is no easy matter to achieve and serve these goals. At least four kinds of obstacles hinder their attainment.

First, conflicts among democratic values themselves may necessitate trade-offs and compromises in the organization and performance of the media. There are tensions, for example, between the principle of editorial autonomy and the ideal of offering individuals and groups wide-ranging access to the media. The aim of serving the public by catering to its immediate tastes and interests is likely to conflict with the aim of providing what the public *needs* to know. Media organizations are also confronted by the conflict between a majoritarian concentration on mainstream opinions and interests and the rights of dissident and marginal views to be heard.

Second, authoritative political communicators often appear to exist in an elite world of their own, distanced from the circumstances and perspectives of ordinary people. In fact, political communication could virtually be defined as the transmission of messages and pressures to and from individuals who are demonstrably unequal: the highly informed and the abysmally ignorant, the highly powerful and the pitifully powerless, the highly involved and the blissfully indifferent. Thus, the very structure of political communication involves a division between movers and shakers at the top and bystanders below, imposing limits on the participatory energy the system can generate.

Third, not everyone in the audience for political communication is a political animal, nor is obliged to be. On the one hand, a viable democracy presupposes an engaged citizenry; on the other hand, one of the freedoms the members of a liberal society enjoy is the freedom to define for themselves their stance toward the political system, including the right to be politically apathetic. As a result, political messages are doubly vulnerable. For one thing, they must jostle and compete for limited time and space with other, often more entertaining and beguiling, kinds of messages. They are not guaranteed a favored share of our attention. For another, their ultimate dependence on winning and holding the attention of a heterogeneous audience can inhibit the media from committing themselves wholeheartedly to the democratic task.

Fourth, the media can pursue democratic values only in ways that are compatible with the sociopolitical and economic environment in which they operate. Political communication arrangements follow the contours of and derive their resources from the society of which they are a part. Even when formally autonomous and sheltered by sacrosanct constitutional guarantees of a free press, they are part and parcel of the larger social system, performing functions for it and impelled to respond to predominant drives within it. In the United States, for example, media organizations are large business enterprises and first and foremost must survive (and if possible prosper) in a highly competitive marketplace. Their pursuit of their democratic role is inexorably shaped by that overriding economic goal. Politically, too, media institutions are linked inextricably to the governing institutions of society, not least because of their mutual dependence as suppliers of raw materials (government to media) and channels of publicity (media to government). In fact, a central issue in current research on the "agenda setting" role of the mass media is the degree to which they exercise a discretionary power to highlight certain issues for public attention, as against the degree to which they depend on the policy initiatives of the big power battalions whose activities and statements they report.[1]

Some Redeeming Features

However constraining such pressures and problems, symbolically at least, journalism in the Western liberal democracies does reflect the influence of democratic values.

For example, the news media provide a daily parade of political disagreement and conflict. In that way what appears regularly in the news is a standing refutation of the antidemocratic notion that there is some single valid social purpose for pursuit through politics and some single group that is entitled to monopolize power because it alone knows what that purpose is and how best to realize it. In addition, the existence of a free press enshrines the democratic concept of the political accountability of power holders to ordinary citizens. Much of what the press reports in political affairs can be thought of as designed to encourage audience members to judge how what the government has been doing relates to their interests, problems, and concerns. Similarly, a free press can be said to embody the notion of citizen autonomy. It implicitly stands for the assumption that readers, viewers, and listeners are offered material on the basis of which they can make up their own minds about who the "good guys" and the "bad guys" in politics are.

Beyond what it represents symbolically, the press in a democratic society can be seen as performing an indispensable, bridging function in democratic politics. Inevitably, an enormous gulf stretches between the political world and ordinary people's perceptions of it. Although political decisions may affect people's lives in many ways, from *their* perspective the political world often seems remote, confusing, and boring. What the press does, it might be argued, is to bring developments in this distant and difficult arena within the reach of the average person in terms that he or she can understand. Viewed in this light, certain features of political reporting may be regarded as enticements to become involved in political questions, ways of interesting the public in affairs for which they might feel little prior enthusiasm. So the crowd-pulling appeal of journalism, the tendency to dramatize, the projection of hard-hitting conflict, the use of sporting analogies to awaken a horse race-like excitement, are, in this view, inducements to become interested in and aware of political matters. Even the media's proclivity toward the dramatic may be applauded in this spirit. A dramatic story can be treated as a peg for more information about the wider political context in which it occurred.

Even the much criticized tendency of the press to trade in simple stereotypes can be viewed in this light. As Winfried Schulz has put it, "In order to make politics comprehensible to the citizen, it must first be reduced by journalists to a few simple structural patterns." [2] This, of course, echoes Walter Lippmann's classic observation on the role of the press as constructors of "pictures in our minds." [3] Personalization, the penchant for clear-cut issues, the tendency to reduce most political conflicts to only two sides of the argument—all might be thought of as aids to popular understanding.

Yet such a positive evaluation ignores three problems. First, surveys of what audience members actually glean from the news demonstrate that it is a highly inefficient mechanism for conveying information.[4] Second, there are few signs that media personnel seriously try to verify for themselves how much information and insight their audiences get out of news reports, with a prospect of changing their news-telling ways accordingly. Third, with many journalistic practices the means seem to have become the end. An election campaign is predominantly treated *as* (not like) a horse race.[5] Journalists and their audiences are more often stalled on the bridge than transported to a more enlightened land beyond it.

Systemic Constraints

. . . We will consider the role of [systemic] constraints at four different levels of the political communication system: the societal level, the interinstitutional level, the intra-institutional level, and the audience level.

The Societal Level

We have already suggested that the production and dissemination of political messages occur within a web of economic, political, and cultural subsystems, which exert "pressure" on the media to select certain issues rather than others as subjects for public attention; to frame their stories according to favored scenarios; and to give the views of certain groups and individuals privileged treatment and heightened exposure. Such pressures need not be applied overtly or deliberately. Indeed, our emphasis on political communication as a systemic product reflects our view that the reciprocal flow of influence between the media and other social institutions is a more or less "natural" and mutually accepted phenomenon, tending to reproduce the power relations and reciprocal dependencies that obtain between them. And it is the varying linkages between such institutions, including closer relations and more powerful dependencies in some cases and more remote links and lesser dependencies in others, that may result in various constraints on "communications for democracy."

We can examine media linkages to the *economic* environment via the structure of ownership and control and via the dynamics of supply and demand in a commercial marketplace. Researchers have paid some attention to the former, where current trends point to an increased concentration of ownership in fewer hands, as well as a process of conglomeration, placing media organizations within larger corporate structures controlled by nonmedia interests.[6] Owners of media outlets may leave editors free to follow their own political and professional leanings; yet the potential for influencing editorial policy is clearly present. . . .

Market mechanisms may threaten democratic aspirations when two or more media organizations compete for a large and heterogeneous mass audience. Such circumstances are likely to generate pressures to:

1. *Limit the amount of public affairs coverage, and shift its style from the serious and extended to the entertaining and arresting:* There is simply no way in which an hour-long news show could be ventured on American commercial network television, although local stations do offer such programs. These, however, constitute a mixture of "hard" and "soft" local news, sometimes bordering on "infotainment."
2. *Impose format rigidities on public affairs coverage:* Even in election campaigns, the nightly news shows on American network television cannot be extended beyond their twenty-two-minute ration; nor can their commercials be retimed to create room for longer and more coherent reports.
3. *Deal blandly with social issues in non-news programming:* Many advertisers have guidelines on acceptable and unacceptable program features for their commercials, enforced through a pre-screening of episodes to be aired.

Of course, *political* constraints on the media can take different forms, ranging from direct political controls, through overt political pressures to promote or suppress specific contents, to strategies for steering journalists toward favored stories and away from less favored ones, to a more subtle reliance on informal channels and contacts. Much has been said and written about this area,[7] and it requires little further elaboration, except to point out that ultimately the media's ability to withstand such pressures turns on their credibility for doing the sort of job they claim to be undertaking and for serving the audience properly.

Another form of political "control," however, is less often noticed. Powerful institutions in society *are* powerful at least in part because they can plausibly claim authority over the definition of the issues falling in their spheres. This is to imply not that critics are silenced but that they often have to make their case on grounds not of their own choosing. Thus, the police are perceived to be the authority on issues of law and order;[8] the Treasury and the Federal Reserve Bank, on the state of the economy; the Pentagon, on defense and military matters; and the President of the United States is the "primary definer" of what constitutes the "national interest." Not surprisingly, when journalists seek an authoritative perspective on a certain field of issues, they turn to those officials who are defined by their positions as authoritative sources.[9] Media professionals do not see this practice as a violation of the canon of objectivity, since the sources are consulted precisely for their presumed expertise and not merely as proponents of a certain point of view. Alternative definitions of social issues are then disadvantaged—either not represented at all, given short shrift, or labeled as "interested" and "biased."

Social systems also structure a pecking order of status and prestige, giving those higher up the ladder a better chance of having their affairs reported in line with their own perspectives. Thus, certain institutions are commonly accorded respect, even reverence, in the news—for example, the institutions of the presidency and the Supreme Court (though not necessarily the incumbents in these positions), and the British royal family. Some enjoy a benign neglect. Some evoke a mixture of symbolic deference and pragmatic exploitation (for example, the British Parliament).[10] Some mainly suffer the slings and arrows of straight news-values fortunes (often trade unions). Some can get attention only if they stir up trouble (e.g., political "terrorists"). Elsewhere, we have outlined a conceptual framework for analyzing news personnel's orientations toward social institutions, based on a continuum between more sacerdotal and more pragmatic approaches to institutional reporting.[11] We argued that social institutions that are regarded as the symbolic embodiment of the core values of their society tend to elicit portrayals of their activities as if "through their own eyes." Conversely, the treatment of institutions, groups, and individuals that represent less central values, or dissident and deviant values, is likely to be guided more strictly by journalists' news values.

The Inter-Institutional Level

In modern political communication systems mediated political messages are a subtly composite product, reflecting the contributions and interactions of two different types of communications: advocates and journalists. Each side is striving to realize different goals vis-à-vis the audience; yet it cannot normally pursue these without securing the cooperation of the other side. Politicians need access to the communication channels operated by media organizations, and they must adjust their messages to the demands of formats and genres that have been devised inside such organizations. Nor can journalists perform their task of political reporting without access to politicians for interviews, news, and comment. Thus, the practice of addressing citizens is something of a compromise for both groups of communicators. It is not merely that they have different goals. It is also that in order to proceed at all, they must work through and with the other side. And from this interwoven process three problems of democratic communication arise.

First, there is a potential for blurring institutional functions that ideally ought to be kept distinct. For their part, politicians start to think, speak, and behave like journalists—a tendency epitomized by presidential statements couched in one-liners designed to guide and ease the work of newspaper headline writers and to give television reporters pithy ten-second sound bites. For their part, journalists, despite their professional values, may be reduced to virtual channels of propaganda. This poses a dilemma for the media. When politicians can predict confidently which events and comments will ring reportorial bells, media professionals are deprived of opportunities to exercise their own judgment. (This line of self-criticism became especially visible in postmortem analyses of the media's role in the 1988 presidential campaign.) Yet the routines that open the media to such manipulation cannot be discarded or overhauled without much disruption and cost. Thus, reform of the political communication process is seriously hampered by professionally rooted inertia in the media and by the coziness of the relationship between journalists and politicians, which appears to accommodate both sides, notwithstanding its occasional rough edges and adversarial explosions. This problem, too, is increasingly recognized and discussed by journalists.

Second, striking strategic developments have occurred in recent years on the advocates' side of the political communication process. Because politicians and other would-be opinion molders are competing fiercely for access to exposure in the media; because in order to achieve this they must tailor their messages to the requirements of journalists' formats, news values, and work habits; and because this is thought to demand anticipatory planning, fast footwork, and a range of specialist skills—for all these reasons, a significant degree of "source professionalization" has emerged. By this we mean the ever deeper and more extensive involvement in political message making of publicity advisers, public relations experts, campaign management consultants, and the like.

Such "source professionals" are not only farsighted, assiduous, and gifted at fashioning messages for media consumption. They immerse jour-

nalists in what appears to be an increasingly manipulative opinion environment. Perceiving themselves to be "professionals" rather than "advocates," source professionals regard newsmaking as a power struggle rather
than a process of issue clarification. . . .

Third, faced with such developments, journalists become uneasy and
concerned to reassert the significance of their own contribution. In fact,
during an observation study we conducted at the headquarters of NBC
News during the 1984 presidential election campaign, producers and correspondents talked to us about their awareness of this problem and their
efforts to resolve the dilemma of reporting the activities of candidates without becoming extensions of their propaganda machines.[12] One device they
have developed for this purpose has been termed "disdaining the news." [13]
This involves attempts by reporters to distance themselves from the propagandistic features of an event by suggesting that it has been contrived and
should be taken with a grain of salt. . . .

Clearly such an approach has a potential for cultivating political cynicism
and mistrust among viewers and further undermining the contributions of
the media to the democratic process.

The Intra-Organizational Level

Significant constraints on the portrayal of social and political issues in
the media also stem from factors internal to the organization of journalism,
including relations between news media outlets and the values and
ideologies that guide media professionals in their work.

In liberal-democratic societies, the relationship between media organizations is characterized primarily by competition—to maximize audiences, to
be first with the news, or to scoop one's rivals in other ways. Thus, although competition for audience patronage is related directly to the media's economic goals, it is also rooted deeply in the professional culture of
Western journalism. This diverts attention away from the aim of serving
the audience toward the democratically irrelevant goal of beating the competition. One example in recent years is the competitive zeal that fueled
the coverage by the television networks and CNN of the highjacked TWA
plane in Beirut in 1985. Nationally that competition was geared to serve a
news-hungry public, eager for information about the crisis. It soon became
apparent, however, that when the reporting from Beirut ceased to carry
any "news" or to have any significant informational value, it was motivated
primarily by inter-network competition for the highest journalistic profile.
Whether the country, the audience, or, indeed, the hostages were best
served by this rivalry remained moot points.

Competition is only one force shaping the behavior of journalists. Professional values, such as objectivity, impartiality, fairness, and an ability to

recognize the newsworthiness of an event, also serve as influential guidelines when framing stories. At one level, such norms provide safeguards essential to a democratic media system. They prescribe that reporters should stand above the political battle, serve the audience rather than politicians with partisan axes to grind, and do so with due regard for all the interests at stake in an issue. But at another level, the routinized application of such values can have distorting consequences. Many writers have pointed out, for example, that the neutral stance enjoined by the values of objectivity and impartiality can lend implicit support to the more powerful institutions and groups in society and for the social order from which they benefit.[14] Instead of promoting a "marketplace of ideas," in which all viewpoints are given adequate play, media neutrality can tend to privilege dominant, mainstream positions.

Adherence to professional definitions of news values may also act as a powerful force for conformity, for arriving, that is, at a common answer, across an otherwise diverse set of news outlets, to the question, What is the most significant news today?[15] Widely shared and professionally endorsed definitions of news values may force journalists' hand in other ways. For example, during our election observation study at NBC, one reporter, assigned to cover Geraldine Ferraro, described to us how within thirty seconds of her selection by Mondale as his running mate she was typecast by news editors and producers as the "first woman Vice-Presidential candidate."[16] His own wish to report her in terms, say, of the compatibility of her campaign utterances with her voting record in the House of Representatives, was rejected by editors as not part of "the Ferraro story," and a later attempt to place the same item ran into the obstacle that by then the dominant theme of "the Ferraro story" had become her response to the issue of her family finances. Revealed here is how widely shared news values can severely constrain the range of options within which reporters themselves can deal with political issues and leaders. Clearly, such tendencies constrict the potential of the media to serve as a genuine "marketplace of ideas" or to transcend the boundaries of the social and political mainstream. . . .

The Audience Level

What role does the audience play in a democratic media system? Ideally, its needs and interests should be uppermost. In practice, the media promptly heed any sign of decided audience dislike or rejection of certain ways of addressing it—if, that is, the media's competitive goals are perceived to be at risk as a result. In that sense, the audience holds a sort of reserve veto power.

Such sensitivity to audience attitudes may be interpreted as reflecting the media's democratic impulses. Nevertheless, there are systemic reasons why the audience for political communication is vulnerable to neglect and misrepresentation. Of the three main elements in a political communication system—politicians, journalists, and audience members—it is the audience that, though most numerous, is least powerful, because least organized. Amid their preoccupations with the intricacies, problems, calculations, and subtleties of coping with one another, politicians and journalists are liable to lose sight of the ordinary voter's concerns and instead attempt to accommodate one another. Thus, audiences are "known" to the media primarily as statistical aggregates produced by ratings services and market researchers, and the media's orientation to their audiences is dominated by numbers. Three problems arise from these circumstances.

First, research suggests strongly that if useful information is to be effectively conveyed to people through the mass media, a sine qua non is sensitivity to what the audience wants or needs to know.[17] The system does not foster such sensitivity.

Second, an audience known mainly through numbers is open to oversimplification, stereotyping, even contempt. This is illustrated by the comment of a news executive we interviewed during our observation study at NBC in 1984, who said: "The only thing that viewers want to know about this election is who is going to win."

Third, this statement (taken in conjunction with other similarly pithy maxims about audience propensities that gain currency in the lore of media executives) illustrates a feature of widely held audience images that contributes to the entrenchment of the system: Authoritative communicators tend to dismiss the audience *as if it were capable only of absorbing what the system supplies.* A deeply conservative view of the audience is thus propagated, one that reinforces the communication status quo. . . .

Notes

1. Philip Tichenor, "Agenda-Setting: Media as Political Kingmakers?" *Journalism Quarterly* 59, no. 3 (1982); Michael Gurevitch and Jay G. Blumler, "Sources of Cross-national Differences in the Discretionary Power of the Mass Media: A Conceptual Introduction," in Holli Smetko et al., *The Formation of Campaign Agendas: A Comparative Analysis of Party and Media Roles in Recent American and British Elections* (Hillside, N.J.: Erlbaum, 1992).

2. Winfried Schulz, "One Campaign or Nine?" in *Communicating to Voters: The Role of Television in the First European Parliamentary Elections,* ed. Jay G. Blumler (Beverly Hills, Calif.: Sage, 1983).

3. Walter Lippmann, *Public Opinion* (New York: Harcourt Brace, 1922).

4. E.g., John Robinson and Mark R. Levy, *The Main Source* (Beverly Hills, Calif.: Sage, 1986).

5. Jay G. Blumler and Michael Gurevitch, "The Election Agenda-setting Rules of Television Journalists: Comparative Observation at the BBC and NBC," in

Semetko et al., *The Formation of Campaign Agendas.*

6. E.g., Graham Murdock, "Large Corporations and the Control of the Commu-
    nication Industries," in *Culture, Society and the Media*, ed. Michael Gurevitch et
    al. (London: Methuen, 1982); Ben Bagdikian, *The Media Monopoly*, 2nd ed.
    (Boston: Beacon, 1987).

7. See, e.g., Colin Seymour-Ure, *The Political Impact of Mass Media* (London:
    Constable, 1974); Jay G. Blumler and Michael Gurevitch, "Towards a
    Comparative Framework for Political Communication Research," in *Political
    Communication: Issues and Strategies for Research*, ed. Steven Chaffee (Beverly
    Hills, Calif.: Sage, 1975); Anthony Smith, ed., *Television and Political Life:
    Studied in Six European Countries* (London: Macmillan, 1979).

8. Steve Chibnall, *Law-and-Order-News* (London: Tavistock, 1974).

9. Stuart Hall et al., *Policing the Crisis* (London: Macmillan, 1978); Gaye
    Tuchman, *Making News: A Study in the Construction of Reality* (New York: Free
    Press, 1978); Mark Fishman, *Manufacturing the News* (Austin: University of
    Texas Press, 1980); Herbert Gans, *Deciding What's News* (New York: Pan-
    theon, 1979).

10. See Jay G. Blumler and Michael Gurevich, "Journalists' Orientations to
    Political Institutions: The Case of Parliamentary Broadcasting," in *Communi-
    cating Politics*, ed. Peter Golding et al. (Leicester: Leicester University Press,
    1986).

11. Ibid.

12. See note 5, above.

13. Mark R. Levy, "Disdaining the News," *Journal of Communication* 31 (1981).

14. Hall et al., *Policing the Crisis.*

15. Leon V. Sigal, *Reporters and Officials* (Lexington, Mass.: Lexington Books,
    1973); Timothy Crouse, *The Boys on the Bus* (New York: Random House,
    1973).

16. See note 5.

17. Kjell Nowak, "From Information Gaps to Communication Potential," in
    Current Theories in Scandinavian Mass Communication, ed. M. Berg et al.
    (Grenaa, Denmark: GMT, 1977); Robinson and Levy, *The Main Source.*

3

NEWSPAPERS

Walter Lippmann

Editor's Note

In this classic study Walter Lippmann shows how journalists point a flashlight rather than a mirror at the world. Accordingly, the audience does not receive a complete image of the political scene; it gets a highly selective series of glimpses instead. Reality is tainted. Lippmann explains why the media cannot possibly perform the functions of public enlightenment that democratic theory requires. They cannot tell the truth objectively because the truth is subjective and entails more probing and explanation than the hectic pace of news production allows.

Lippmann's analysis raises profound questions about the purity and adequacy of mass media sources of information. Can there be democracy when information is invariably tainted? Are there any antidotes? The answers remain elusive.

Walter Lippmann, who died in 1974, was a renowned American journalist and political analyst whose carefully reasoned, lucid writings influenced American politics for more than half a century. He won two Pulitzer Prizes, the Medal of Freedom, and three Overseas Press Club awards. In addition to books, he wrote articles for The New Republic, *the New York* World, *and the New York* Herald Tribune. *This selection is from* Public Opinion *(New York: Free Press, 1965). It was published originally in 1922.*

The Nature of News

. . . In the first instance . . . the news is not a mirror of social conditions, but the report of an aspect that has obtruded itself. The news does not tell you how the seed is germinating in the ground, but it may tell you when the first sprout breaks through the surface. It may even tell you what somebody says is happening to the seed under ground. It may tell you that the sprout did not come up at the time it was expected. The more points, then, at which any happening can be fixed, objectified, measured, named, the more points there are at which news can occur. . . .

Wherever there is a good machinery of record, the modern news service works with great precision. There is one on the stock exchange, and the news of price movements is flashed over tickers with dependable accuracy. There is a machinery for election returns, and when the counting and tabulating are well done, the result of a national election is usually known on the night of the election. In civilized communities deaths, births, marriages and divorces are recorded, and are known accurately except where there is concealment or neglect. The machinery exists for some, and only some, aspects of industry and government, in varying degrees of precision for securities, money and staples, bank clearances, realty transactions, wage scales. It exists for imports and exports because they pass through a custom house and can be directly recorded. It exists in nothing like the same degree for internal trade, and especially for trade over the counter.

It will be found, I think, that there is a very direct relation between the certainty of news and the system of record. If you call to mind the topics which form the principal indictment by reformers against the press, you find they are subjects in which the newspaper occupies the position of the umpire in the unscored baseball game. All news about states of mind is of this character: so are all descriptions of personalities, of sincerity, aspiration, motive, intention, of mass feeling, of national feeling, of public opinion, the policies of foreign governments. So is much news about what is going to happen. So are questions turning on private profit, private income, wages, working conditions, the efficiency of labor, educational opportunity, unemployment,[1] monotony, health, discrimination, unfairness, restraint of trade, waste, "backward peoples," conservatism, imperialism, radicalism, liberty, honor, righteousness. All involve data that are at best spasmodically recorded. The data may be hidden because of a censorship or a tradition of privacy, they may not exist because nobody thinks record important, because he thinks it red tape, or because nobody has yet invented an objective system of measurement. Then the news on these subjects is bound to be debatable, when it is not wholly neglected. The events which are not scored are reported either as personal and conventional opinions, or they are not news. They do not take shape until somebody protests, or somebody investigates, or somebody publicly, in the etymological meaning of the word, makes an *issue* of them. . . .

Let us suppose the conditions leading up to a strike are bad. What is the measure of evil? A certain conception of a proper standard of living, hygiene, economic security, and human dignity. The industry may be far below the theoretical standard of the community, and the workers may be too wretched to protest. Conditions may be above the standard, and the workers may protest violently. The standard is at best a vague measure. However, we shall assume that the conditions are below par, as par is understood by the editor. Occasionally without waiting for the workers to threaten, but prompted say by a social worker, he will send reporters to investigate, and will call attention to bad conditions. Necessarily he cannot do that often. For these investigations cost time, money, special talent, and a lot of space. To make plausible a report that conditions are bad, you need a good many columns of print. In order to tell the truth about the steel worker in the Pittsburgh district, there was needed a staff of investigators, a great deal of time, and several fat volumes of print. It is impossible to suppose that any daily newspaper could normally regard the making of Pittsburgh Surveys, or even Interchurch Steel Reports, as one of its tasks. News which requires so much trouble as that to obtain is beyond the resources of a daily press. . . .

If you study the way many a strike is reported in the press, you will find, very often, that the issues are rarely in the headlines, barely in the leading paragraphs, and sometimes not even mentioned anywhere. A labor dispute in another city has to be very important before the news account contains any definite information as to what is in dispute. The routine of the news works that way, with modifications it works that way in regard to political issues and international news as well. The news is an account of the overt phases that are interesting, and the pressure on the newspaper to adhere to this routine comes from many sides. It comes from the economy of noting only the stereotyped phase of a situation. It comes from the difficulty of finding journalists who can see what they have not learned to see. It comes from the almost unavoidable difficulty of finding sufficient space in which even the best journalist can make plausible an unconventional view. It comes from the economic necessity of interesting the reader quickly, and the economic risk involved in not interesting him at all, or of offending him by unexpected news insufficiently or clumsily described. All these difficulties combined make for uncertainty in the editor when there are dangerous issues at stake, and cause him naturally to prefer the indisputable fact and a treatment more readily adapted to the reader's interest. The indisputable fact and the easy interest, are the strike itself and the reader's inconvenience.

All the subtler and deeper truths are in the present organization of industry very unreliable truths. They involve judgments about standards of living, productivity, human rights that are endlessly debatable in the absence of exact record and quantitative analysis. And as long as these do not exist in industry, the run of news about it will tend, as Emerson said, quoting from Isocrates, "to make of moles mountains, and of mountains moles." ² Where there is no constitutional procedure in industry, and no expert sifting of evidence and the claims, the fact that is sensational to the reader is the fact that almost every journalist will seek. Given the industrial relations that so largely prevail, even where there is conference or arbitration, but no independent filtering of the facts for decision, the issue for the newspaper public will tend not to be the issue for the industry. And so to try disputes by an appeal through the newspapers puts a burden upon newspapers and readers which they cannot and ought not to carry. As long as real law and order do not exist, the bulk of the news will, unless consciously and courageously corrected, work against those who have no lawful and orderly method of asserting themselves. The bulletins from the scene of action will note the trouble that arose from the assertion, rather than the reasons which led to it. The reasons are intangible. . . .

Every newspaper when it reaches the reader is the result of a whole series of selections as to what items shall be printed, in what position they shall be printed, how much space each shall occupy, what emphasis each shall have. There are no objective standards here. There are conventions. Take two newspapers published in the same city on the same morning. The headline of one reads: "Britain pledges aid to Berlin against French aggression; France openly backs Poles." The headline of the second is "Mrs. Stillman's Other Love." Which you prefer is a matter of taste, but not entirely a matter of the editor's taste. It is a matter of his judgement as to what will absorb the half hour's attention a certain set of readers will give to his newspaper. Now the problem of securing attention is by no means equivalent to displaying the news in the perspective laid down by religious teaching or by some form of ethical culture. It is a problem of provoking feeling in the reader, of inducing him to feel a sense of personal identification with the stories he is reading. . . . In order that he shall enter he must find a familiar foothold in the story, and this is supplied to him by the use of stereotypes. They tell him that if an association of plumbers is called a "combine" it is appropriate to develop his hostility; if it is called a "group of leading businessmen" the cue is for a favorable reaction.

It is in a combination of these elements that the power to create opinion resides. . . . This is the plight of the reader of the general news. If he is to read it at all he must be interested, that is to say, he must enter into the situation and care about the outcome. But if he does that he cannot rest in a negative, and unless independent means of checking the lead given him by his newspaper exists, the very fact that he is interested may make it difficult to arrive at that balance of opinions which may most nearly approximate the truth. The more passionately involved he becomes, the more he will tend to resent not only a different view, but a disturbing bit of news. That is why many a newspaper finds that, having honestly evoked the partisanship of its readers, it can not easily, supposing the editor believes the facts warrant it, change position. If a change is necessary, the transition has to be managed with the utmost skill and delicacy. Usually a newspaper will not attempt so hazardous a performance. It is easier and safer to have the news of that subject taper off and disappear, thus putting out the fire by starving it.

News, Truth, and a Conclusion

The hypothesis, which seems to be the most fertile, is that news and truth are not the same thing, and must be clearly distinguished.[3] The function of news is to signalize an event, the function of truth is to bring to light the hidden facts, to set them into relation with each other, and make a picture of reality on which men can act. Only at these points, where social conditions take recognizable and measurable shape, do the body of truth and the body of news coincide. That is a comparatively small part of the whole field of human interest. In this sector, and only in this sector, the tests of the news are sufficiently exact to make the charges of perversion or suppression more than a partisan judgment. There is no defense, no extenuation, no excuse whatever, for stating six times that Lenin is dead, when the only information the paper possesses is a report that he is dead from a source repeatedly shown to be unreliable. The news, in that instance, is not "Lenin Dead" but "Helsingfors Says Lenin is Dead." And a newspaper can be asked to take the responsibility of not making Lenin more dead than the source of the news is reliable; if there is one subject on which editors are most responsible it is in their judgment of the reliability of the source. But when it comes to dealing, for example, with stories of what the Russian people want, no such test exists.

The absence of these exact tests accounts, I think, for the character of the profession, as no other explanation does. There is a very small body of exact knowledge, which it requires no outstanding ability or training to deal with. The rest is in the journalist's own discretion. Once he departs from the region where it is definitely recorded at the County Clerk's office that John Smith has gone into bankruptcy, all fixed standards disappear. The story of why John Smith failed, his human frailties, the analysis of the economic conditions on which he was shipwrecked, all of this can be told in a hundred different ways. There is no discipline in applied psychology, as there is a discipline in medicine, engineering, or even law, which has authority to direct the journalist's mind when he passes from the news to the vague realm of truth. There are no canons to direct his own mind, and no canons that coerce the reader's judgment or the publisher's. His version of the truth is only his version. How can he demonstrate the truth as he sees it? He cannot demonstrate it, any more than Mr. Sinclair Lewis can demonstrate that he has told the whole truth about Main Street. And the more he understands his own weaknesses, the more ready he is to admit that where there is no objective test, his own opinion is in some vital measure constructed out of his own stereotypes, according to his own code, and by the urgency of his own interest. He knows that he is seeing the world through subjective lenses. He cannot deny that he too is, as Shelley remarked, a dome of many-colored glass which stains the white radiance of eternity.

And by this knowledge his assurance is tempered. He may have all kinds of moral courage, and sometimes has, but he lacks that sustaining conviction of a certain technic which finally freed the physical sciences from theological control. It was the gradual development of an irrefragable method that gave the physicist his intellectual freedom as against all the powers of the world. His proofs were so clear, his evidence so sharply superior to tradition, that he broke away finally from all control. But the journalist has no such support in his own conscience or in fact. The control exercised over him by the opinions of his employers and his readers, is not the control of truth by prejudice, but of one opinion by another opinion that is not demonstrably less true. . . .

. . . It is possible and necessary for journalists to bring home to people the uncertain character of the truth on which their opinions are founded, and by criticism and agitation to prod social science into making more usable formulations of social facts, and to prod statesmen into establishing more visible institutions. The press, in other words, can fight for the extension of reportable truth. But as social truth is organized today, the press is not constituted to furnish from one edition to the next the amount of knowledge which the democratic theory of public opinion demands. This is not due to the Brass Check, as the quality of news in radical newspapers shows, but to the fact that the press deals with a society in which the governing forces are so imperfectly recorded. The theory that the press can itself record those forces is false. It can normally record only what has been recorded for it by the working of institutions. Everything else is argument and opinion, and fluctuates with the vicissitudes, the self-consciousness, and the courage of the human mind.

If the press is not so universally wicked, nor so deeply conspiring . . . it is very much more frail than the democratic theory has as yet admitted. It is too frail to carry the whole burden of popular sovereignty, to supply spontaneously the truth which democrats hoped was inborn. And when we expect it to supply such a body of truth we employ a misleading standard of judgment. We misunderstand the limited nature of news, the illimitable complexity of society; we overestimate our own endurance, public spirit, and all-round competence. We suppose an appetite for uninteresting truths which is not discovered by any honest analysis of our own tastes.

If the newspapers, then, are to be charged with the duty of translating the whole public life of mankind, so that every adult can arrive at an opinion on every moot topic, they fail, they are bound to fail, in any future one can conceive they will continue to fail. It is not possible to assume that a world, carried on by division of labor and distribution of authority, can be governed by universal opinions in the whole population. Unconsciously the theory sets up the single reader as theoretically omnicompetent, and puts upon the press the burden of accomplishing whatever representative government, industrial organization, and diplomacy have failed to accomplish. Acting upon everybody for thirty minutes in twenty-four hours, the press is asked to create a mystical force called Public Opinion that will take up the slack in public institutions. The press has often mistakenly pretended that it could do just that. It has at great moral cost to itself, encouraged a democracy, still bound to its original premises, to expect newspapers to supply spontaneously for every organ of government, for every social problem, the machinery of information which these do not normally supply themselves. Institutions, having failed to furnish themselves with instruments of knowledge, have become a bundle of "problems," which the population as a whole, reading the press as a whole, is supposed to solve.

The press, in other words, has come to be regarded as an organ of direct democracy, charged on a much wider scale, and from day to day, with the function often attributed to the initiative, referendum, and recall. The Court of Public Opinion, open day and night, is to lay down the law for everything all the time. It is not workable. And when you consider the nature of news, it is not even thinkable. For the news, as we have seen, is precise in proportion to the precision with which the event is recorded. Unless the event is capable of being named, measured, given shape, made specific, it either fails to take on the character of news, or it is subject to the accidents and prejudices of observation.

Therefore, on the whole, the quality of the news about modern society is an index of its social organization. The better the institutions, the more all interests concerned are formally represented, the more issues are disentangled, the more objective criteria are introduced, the more perfectly an affair can be presented as news. At its best the press is a servant and guardian of institutions; at its worst it is a means by which a few exploit social disorganization to their own ends. In the degree to which institutions fail to function, the unscrupulous journalist can fish in troubled waters, and the conscientious one must gamble with uncertainties.

The press is no substitute for institutions. It is like the beam of a searchlight that moves restlessly about, bringing one episode and then another out of darkness into vision. Men cannot do the work of the world by this light alone. They cannot govern society by episodes, incidents, and eruptions. It is only when they work by a steady light of their own, that the press, when it is turned upon them, reveals a situation intelligible enough for a popular decision. The trouble lies deeper than the press, and so does the remedy. It lies in social organization based on a system of analysis and record, and in all the corollaries of that principle; in the abandonment of the theory of the omnicompetent citizen, in the decentralization of decision, in the coordination of decision by comparable record and analysis. If at the centers of management there is a running audit, which makes work intelligible to those who do it, and those who superintend it, issues when they arise are not the mere collisions of the blind. Then, too, the news is uncovered for the press by a system of intelligence that is also a check upon the press.

That is the radical way. For the troubles of the press, like the troubles of representative government, be it territorial or functional, like the troubles of industry, be it capitalist, cooperative, or communist, go back to a common source: to the failure of self-governing people to transcend their casual experience and their prejudice, by inventing, creating, and organizing a machinery of knowledge. It is because they are compelled to act without a reliable picture of the world, that governments, schools, newspapers and churches make such small headway against the more obvious failings of democracy, against violent prejudice, apathy, preference for the curious trivial as against the dull important, and the hunger for sideshows and three legged calves. This is the primary defect of popular government, a defect inherent in its traditions, and all its other defects can, I believe, be traced to this one.

Notes

1. Think of what guess work went into the Reports of Unemployment in 1921.
2. From his essay entitled *Art and Criticism*. The quotation occurs in a passage cited on page 87 of Professor R. W. Brown's *The Writer's Art.*
3. When I wrote *Liberty and the News*, I did not understand this distinction clearly enough to state it, but *cf.* p. 89 ff.

4

EL SALVADOR'S CIVIL WAR AS SEEN IN NORTH AND SOUTH AMERICAN PRESS

Walter C. Soderlund and Carmen Schmitt

Editor's Note

In the previous selection Walter Lippmann pointed to the difficulty of capturing reality in news stories. Walter C. Soderlund and Carmen Schmitt demonstrate that the problem is even more complex than Lippmann described. Images of reality not only are inadequate, they also differ among media and vary from country to country. This essay compares and contrasts newspaper coverage in 1981 of the civil war in El Salvador. Audiences in Argentina, Chile, Canada, and the United States were apt to form quite varied images about this remote war and its international ramifications. Obviously, different media produce different worlds when journalists disagree about which political actors and actions deserve the spotlight and which should be regarded positively, negatively, or neutrally.

Aside from the substantive findings, this study is interesting because it compares major media in several countries that vary from one another in language and in cultural traditions. Despite these differences, and despite the use of disparate news sources, there are substantial similarities in coverage. It is also striking that the South American and Canadian papers depended predominantly on U.S. and European sources rather than on their own. By contrast, U.S. newspapers rarely relied on foreign sources, evidence of what the authors term "extreme parochialism."

At the time of writing, Soderlund was professor of political science at the University of Windsor, Canada. Schmitt, who holds a master's degree in communication studies from the University of Windsor, was a television journalist in Chile. The selection comes from "El Salvador's Civil War as Seen in North and South American Press," Journalism Quarterly *63:2 (Summer 1986): 268-74. One table has been omitted.*

Reproduced from *Journalism Quarterly*, vol. 63, no. 2, summer 1986, pp. 268-274, with permission of the Association for Education in Journalism and Mass Communication.

The way in which media interpret events involving international conflict is recognized increasingly as important in international relations.[1] El Salvador was, during the final months of 1981 (as of course it has continued to be), one of the most dangerous "hot spots" of a rekindled cold war: a Western hemisphere society ripped apart by a civil war that has attracted international participation.

This research reports on the "pictures of reality" regarding events in El Salvador as conveyed to readers by major newspapers in Argentina, Chile, Canada and the United States. What is reported by the press about El Salvador (or any other foreign crisis) is important because most of us are simply unable to evaluate independently such situations. Rather, we, of necessity, must depend on the media for most of our information. Thus, in a real sense, a great deal of what we "know" about a given situation is based upon media reporting.

In this particular study we examine press coverage of El Salvador over a 10-week period in the Fall of 1981. The major question which we seek to answer is whether media images of "reality" regarding El Salvador differ for readers of newspapers in four different countries, located on two different continents. The newspapers selected for study are: in Argentina *La Nacion* and *La Prensa*, in Chile *El Mercurio* and *La Tercera*, in Canada the Toronto *Globe and Mail* and the Ottawa *Citizen*, and in the United States the Washington *Post* and the New York *Times*.[2]

The sampling frame began with a date randomly selected in the first week of October and continued using a two-day skip interval, through to the end of the second week of December. Twenty-seven issues per newspaper were included in the sample. Each issue was examined in its entirety for items dealing with El Salvador. Items were coded as to (1) *Type of content:* front page news, inside page news, feature columns, editorials, and cartoons; (2) *source of content:* local staff and special correspondents, columnists, and the various wire services; (3) *thematic coverage:* specific issues and actors discussed; (4) *evaluative direction:* whether a given item reflected positively or negatively on five major domestic and international political actors, the FDR/FMLN [guerilla forces], the Salvadorean junta, the United States, Cuba and Nicaragua. Items were coded mixed if both positive and negative material was included, or neutral;[3] and (5) the extent to which a "cold war" mentality based on language was evident in reporting.[4]

Findings

Our content analysis research produced a data set of 160 news items dealing with El Salvador, broken down nearly equally between those appearing in the South American newspapers (78) and those in the North

American newspapers (82). In South America, Argentine papers led Chilean in coverage 42 stories to 36, while in North America, the American papers led the Canadian, 55 stories to 27.

With regard to type of content, . . . [w]hat is clear is that there was a lack of in-depth, analytical material on El Salvador, to place day-to-day events in a coherent framework. This deficiency was especially apparent in the South American papers.

. . . The role of the United States in the crisis was the leading issue reported on overall, surpassing its nearest competitor by well over a 10% margin. Also, in terms of internationalization, we see the roles of Nicaragua and Cuba figuring prominently. . . . Peace-making efforts on the part of Mexico and refugee problems along the Honduran border accounted for the presence of these countries' activities among the top 10 issues.

The domestic factors which found their way into press reporting were the role of the guerrillas, the role of the Salvadorean military, actual reports of military action, backgrounders on the scheduled March 1982 Constituent Assembly election, and analyses of the politico-military strategies of both the FDR/FMLN and the Salvadorean government. There was scarcely any attention paid to social or economic conditions within El Salvador. . . .

Table 4-1 shows . . . thematic coverage . . . broken down by country. . . . The role of the United States showed up in 73% of the news items appearing in American papers. It was also the leading theme in Canadian news coverage (52%), as well as the number two theme in Argentine reporting (58%). In Chile, the role of the United States was not as prominently featured, (fourth in rank order), appearing in only 28% of news items. Roles played by Nicaragua and Cuba also dominated American newspaper reporting, second and third in rank order. Canadian reporting on Nicaragua earned that nation's activities a fourth place on the rank order list, while Nicaragua occupied the fifth and sixth positions on the Argentine and Chilean agendas. Cuban activities likewise merited less attention in Canada, Argentina, and Chile, occupying the sixth, eighth and ninth positions in these nations' reporting.

The role of guerrilla forces received most coverage in Argentina, with the theme appearing in 64% of news items, and in Chile (47%). Clearly, this theme was less salient in Canada and the United States. Reports of military action were featured prominently in the Chilean press and noticeably absent in Canadian coverage. Canada was also low in reporting on the politico-military strategy of the FDR/FMLN, as was Chile. Chilean newspapers also seemed unconcerned with the role of Mexico. American newspapers featured proportionately less material on Honduras than did the papers of the other three countries.

Table 4-1   News Coverage on Major Issues Dealing with El Salvador,
by Country (percent)

Issue	Country				
	Argentina (N=42)	Chile (N=36)	Canada (N=27)	United States (N=55)	Cramer's V
Role of the U.S.	57.1	27.8	51.9	72.7	.33[b]
Role of guerrilla forces	64.3	47.2	37.0	25.5	.31[b]
Role of Salvadorean military	42.9	25.0	40.7	20.0	.22[a]
Role of Nicaragua	28.6	22.2	29.6	38.2	.13
Politico-military strategy of the junta	31.0	33.3	14.8	30.9	.14
Report of military action	28.6	41.7	11.1	20.0	.24[a]
Role of Cuba	23.8	11.1	18.5	36.4	.23[a]
Election of March 1982	26.2	13.9	25.9	20.0	.12
Role of Mexico	21.4	2.8	14.8	16.4	.19
Politico-military strategy of FDR/FMLN	16.7	5.6	11.1	18.2	.15
Role of Honduras	19.0	13.9	18.5	7.3	.15

Note: Columns add to more than 100% because of multiple coding.
[a] p<.05.
[b] p<.01.

Table 4-2 presents data which show the way in which major actors in the Salvadorean crisis were portrayed in South American and North American newspapers. On this dimension, we see evidence of major differences in treatment with respect to almost all the major participants. With regard to the Salvadorean junta, South American papers were mainly neutral, with equal percentages (22%) falling in the positive and mixed categories. Only 15% of material on the junta was negative. North American papers presented quite a different picture of the junta. Here 64% of reporting was negative, 28% neutral, while only 8% was positive. Considering just the balance between positive and negative categories, the junta had a positive balance of +7 in South American papers, but a negative balance in North American papers of −56.[5]

While evaluation of the FDR/FMLN was not exactly the mirror image of that of the junta, the trend was definitely toward the opposite

Table 4-2   **News Coverage Dealing with El Salvador Reflecting on Major Actors in the Crisis, by South American and North American Newspapers (percent)**

Issue	South America				
	N	Positive	Mixed	Negative	Neutral
Portrayal of junta	27	22.2	22.2	14.8	40.7
Portrayal of FDR/FMLN	13	15.4	15.4	61.5	0
Portrayal of United States	27	59.3	7.4	18.5	14.8
Portrayal of Cuba	11	0	9.1	90.9	0
Portrayal of Nicaragua	16	0	12.5	75.0	12.5

	North America				
	N	Positive	Mixed	Negative	Neutral
Portrayal of junta	25	8.0	0	64.0	28.0
Portrayal of FDR/FMLN	15	20.0	6.1	13.3	60.0
Portrayal of United States	48	2.1	2.1	16.7	79.2
Portrayal of Cuba	23	0	0	21.7	78.3
Portrayal of Nicaragua	24	0	0	20.8	79.2

direction. Thus in South American papers, negative reporting on the FDR/FMLN predominated, appearing in 62% of coverage. Positive and mixed categories each accounted for 15%. In the case of North American papers, neutral reporting predominated, but in the balance between positive and negative coverage, the FDR/FMLN had a positive balance of +7. The corresponding negative balance in South American papers was −47.

Perhaps the most startling finding of all deals with the evaluation of the American role in the conflict. In South American papers, approval of American involvement was apparent in very nearly 60% of reporting while only 19% was categorized as negative. Thus, there was a +41 positive balance of coverage regarding the American role. In the North American papers, by way of contrast, there was a decided lack of support for U.S. policy. While it is true that almost 80% of reporting was neutral, 17% was negative, while only 2% viewed American actions as favorable. This yields a negative balance regarding United States involvement of −15 on the part of North American papers.

Portrayals of Nicaragua and Cuba were consistent on each continent. In South American papers these countries were portrayed negatively, for the most part, with some mixed and neutral reporting. In North American papers, it was the neutral category which predominated, with the balance accounted for by negative reporting.

Country by country analysis on this dimension is difficult due to the very small N's in a number of the categories. However, with respect to the Salvadorean junta, Argentine newspapers were the most opinionated overall, with 25% of items coded in the positive category and 19% in the negative category. By way of contrast, Chilean papers were mostly neutral (64%). In North America, Canadian papers ran no material which reflected positively on the junta, while 13% of American press items did. However, both countries' reporting was highly unsympathetic to the junta, more than 60% of items in both Canadian and American newspapers reflected adversely on the junta.

The other actor on which we have a sufficient number of cases to do a country by country analysis is the United States. Here, both the Argentine and Chilean press reporting is overwhelmingly favorable, 67% and 63% respectively. Canadian reporting falls entirely in the neutral category, whereas in the United States, while most items were neutral (74%), the percentage of negative items (22%) far surpassed the positive items (3%). Thus it is clear that press criticism of American policy on El Salvador in North American papers was found in American, not Canadian newspapers.

Data in Table 4-3 show the source of Salvadorean news coverage. The various wire services provided the majority of news items. The American wire services included AP, UPI, and New York Times, and these accounted for 38% of total coverage. The European wire services included Reuters, EFE (Spain) and ANSA (Italian), and these provided 28% of total coverage. Local staff or special correspondents added another 25% of content, while American and Canadian columnists produced the balance of material.

Interesting variations, both by continent and country, are apparent in this distribution. South American papers were heavily dependent on the wire services for coverage of El Salvador; European services provided only slightly less copy than American. An interesting side point is that none of the Latin American press agencies provided any information to our sampled Argentine or Chilean newspapers. The North American papers were less dependent on wire services overall, with the largest single source of information coming from local staff writers or special correspondents.[6] North American columnists furnished approximately 15% of total material.

The country by country breakdown is perhaps more interesting. It shows a clearly different pattern of Salvadorean information flow into Argentina and Chile. Argentina was linked primarily to the American wire services while Chile was highly dependent on the European services. The Canadian-American comparison is also revealing. The Canadian newspapers

Table 4-3   Source of News Coverage on El Salvador (percent)

Source	Argentina (N=42)	Chile (N=36)	South America (N=78)	Canada (N=27)	United States (N=55)	North America (N=82)
Local staff/special correspondents	19.0	0	10.3	20.8	51.0	41.3
Canadian columnists	0	0	0	8.3	0	2.7
American wire services	54.8	36.1	46.3	33.3	27.5	29.3
American columnists	0	0	0	12.5	15.7	14.7
European wire services	26.2	63.9	43.6	25.0	5.9	12.0

were the most balanced of all regarding where information came from, while the American press showed evidence of extreme parochialism. Only 6% of Salvadorean news came from non-American employed sources. However, given that 51% of copy was written by special correspondents and local staff, there appeared to be both greater personal contact with events in El Salvador and greater personal expertise on the part of American writers. Nonetheless, the amount of non-American perspective present in the reporting of both American newspapers was small indeed. Perhaps what is most ironic, (and no doubt due to the two papers chosen in the United States, both of which rely very heavily on local staff and special correspondents), is that American newspapers appeared less dependent on American wire services than did the newspapers in the other three countries.

Our final question is the degree to which reporting on El Salvador was characterized by a "cold war" orientation. This orientation was operationalized by whether the item used language such as Communist, Marxist-Leninist, leftist, Soviet-backed or Cuban-backed. Overall, this Cold War orientation was present in 42.5% of Salvadorean related news items. The cold war orientation was most prominent in material written by American columnists (73%) and least evident in material provided by the European wire services (28%). Canadian columnists and American wire services used cold war frames in 50% of their material while 44% of Local Staff Special Correspondent material contained cold war descriptive terms.

Source of information is crucial in explaining both continent and country variations in the intensity of cold war preoccupation. While cold war orientation was marginally higher in North American papers (45% vs. 40% for South American papers), it is in the country by country analysis that major differences are seen. Specifically, Chilean newspapers presented by far the least amount of cold war-oriented material (25%), while the Argentine newspapers featured the most (52%). American and Canadian figures were 47% and 41% respectively. This pattern is no doubt a reflection of the extent to which Chile received its news from the European wire services, which of course, featured by far the least amount of cold war-oriented material.

Conclusions

First, with regard to volume of coverage, American newspapers featured more material on El Salvador than did the newspapers from the other countries. Even here, however, one story per day (usually on the inside pages) was not a particularly impressive amount of coverage. Salvadorean material had least salience for Canadian newspapers, with Chilean and Argentine newspapers occupying intermediate positions. However, with regard to the specific issues discussed relative to El Salvador, the degree of similarity was quite strong.

The major area where differences became evident was that of evaluation. Here we found, in general, that the South American papers portrayed the Salvadorean junta, and especially the United States, positively, while critical of the FDR/FMLN, Cuba, and Nicaragua. North American papers, on the other hand, were quite negative with regard to the performance of the junta and more positive than negative with respect to the FDR/FMLN. Involvement of all foreign actors was covered mainly in a neutral manner in North American papers, with almost no positive portrayals (even of American involvement), and a good deal of negative evaluation of all outside involvement.

Differences were also very apparent with respect to where Salvadorean news came from. In this case, country was more revealing than continent, as different patterns were seen in Argentina and Chile regarding the use of American or European wire services. Canada and the United States also differed, with Canadian information (which was heavily American in origin) balanced by local staff writers and special correspondents and the Reuters wire. American newspapers, as was pointed out, were singularly dependent upon American news sources.

Finally, with respect to cold war orientation, Argentina topped the list, the United States and Canada followed closely behind, while Chile trailed significantly. Again, the degree to which Chilean information came from European rather than American sources seems to explain this variation.

Overall, then, what we have is a situation where the impact of news flows on the reporting of factual information on El Salvador is somewhat ambiguous. American and Canadian readers were more likely to see the situation in "international" rather than "domestic" terms, but this was only a matter of degree. However, South American readers were given an essentially positive evaluation of the Salvadorean junta and United States efforts to support it against the FDR/FMLN backed by Nicaragua and Cuba, all of which were portrayed negatively. While the North American papers were more "international" in their portrayal of the crisis, they did not present this international involvement in a positive light. This was true whether the involvement was on the part of the United States or Nicaragua and Cuba. Also, little sympathy was shown for the Salvadorean junta.

Notes

1. See for example, Harold and Margaret Sprout, "Environmental Factors in the Study of International Politics," *Journal of Conflict Resolution*, 1:309-328 (1957); and Michael Brecher, Blema Steinberg, and Janice Stein, "A Framework for Research on Foreign Policy Behavior," *Journal of Conflict Resolution*, 13:75-101 (1969); Charles W. Kegley, Jr. and Eugene R. Wittkopf, *American Foreign Policy: Pattern and Process*, 2nd ed. (New York: St. Martin's Press, 1982).

2. *La Prensa, La Nacion* and *El Mercurio* are listed among the 20 most prominent papers in Latin America; see John C. Merrill, ed., *Global Journalism: A Survey of the World's Mass Media* (New York: Longman, 1983), p. 265, 275, 305; while the New York *Times*, the Washington *Post* and the *Globe and Mail* make the list of the world's 50 greatest newspapers; see John C. Merrill and Harold A. Fisher, *The World's Great Dailies: Profile of Fifty Newspapers* (New York: Hastings House Publishers, 1980), pp. 138-143, 220-230, 343-352.

3. These data must be interpreted with care. Positive or negative codes may not necessarily reflect media bias in favor of the actions or goals of a particular actor, but may indicate a factual situation that either favors or detracts from a particular actor.

4. In a post-study intercoder reliability test, an intercoder reliability coefficient of 81.6% was achieved. See Ole R. Holsti, *Content Analysis for the Social Sciences and Humanities* (Reading, Mass.: Addison-Wesley, 1969), p. 140.

5. These findings appear to challenge the charge leveled by Edward Herman in his book, *The Real Terror Network: Terrorism in Fact and Propaganda* (Boston: South End Press, 1982, pp. 139-199), that American media are reluctant to criticize the failings of America's dictatorial cold war allies.

6. Past research has shown, however, that local staff writers occasionally base their stories on wire service copy without indicating the ultimate source. Thus this finding may be less significant than it at first appears. Also, the wire services provided a smaller percentage of material on El Salvador to North American papers than they did on general regional news. See Schmitt and Soderlund, "Television and Newspaper Coverage of Latin American and Caribbean News," *Canadian Journal of Latin American Studies*, p. 61. It is clear that when a situation reaches crisis proportions, newspapers send their own correspondents to the scene, thus lessening the dependence on the wire services.

5

BEFORE AND AFTER
THE DAY AFTER:
THE UNEXPECTED RESULTS
OF A TELEVISED DRAMA

William C. Adams, Dennis J. Smith, Allison Salzman,
Ralph Crossen, Scott Hiebert, Tom Naccarato,
William Vantine, and Nine Weisbroth

Editor's Note

Just as Shakespeare's Hamlet urged his friend Horatio to welcome the unexpected because "there are more things in heaven and earth, Horatio, than are dreamt of in your philosophy," William C. Adams urges researchers to watch out for unanticipated media effects. Failure to detect effects may be due to failure to hypothesize them coupled with an unwillingness to go on intellectual fishing expeditions. This article describes unexpected effects from a broadcast about a fictional nuclear attack. It also demonstrates that political insights may flow as readily from fictional programs as from factual programs, a fact that political leaders know and attempt to control. Finally, the article suggests why some of the catastrophic effects anticipated by pundits and politicians did not emerge.

Adams is a professor in the Department of Public Administration at The George Washington University. He is a well-known, prolific writer about television coverage of domestic and international politics. His co-authors were students at The George Washington University at the time of writing. The selection comes from "Before and After The Day After: *The Unexpected Results of a Televised Drama," Political Communication and Persuasion 3:3 (1986): 191-213.*

On Sunday evening, November 20, 1983, over 80 million Americans watched *The Day After*, ABC's drama about the horror and devastation of nuclear war. It was one of the most widely watched and debated dramatic programs in television history.

Nuclear-freeze advocates such as the director of the Campaign Against Nuclear War praised the program as "a 7 million dollar advertising job for our issue." Some conservatives denounced the movie as "blatant political propaganda." Meanwhile, White House strategists worked to minimize

From *Political Communication and Persuasion* 3, no. 3 (1986): 191-213, Taylor and Francis, Inc., Washington, D.C. Reproduced with permission.

any damage the show might do to President Ronald Reagan's defense policies, and the Secretary of State was dispatched to present an immediate
televised response.

One television critic predicted that the movie, as a "shared national experience," would "touch our emotions, our attitudes and our hopes for the
future." He added:[1]

> No one will be able to forget it. . . . As has rarely happened in television history,
> a work of fiction has achieved the urgency and magnitude of live coverage of a
> national crisis. . . . The actual impact will probably be . . . a pervasive shading of
> popular attitudes toward nuclear weaponry in general and the Reagan adminis-
> tration's New Brinkmanship in particular.

The advance billing was that *The Day After* would be a compelling drama
that could create a "pervasive" shift in public attitudes. If this was to be a
turning point in the national consciousness, it was important to measure
the degree and character of that change.

Our study was designed to assess the effect of *The Day After* on a variety
of subjects, including attitudes toward the following: (1) defense spending,
(2) a bilateral nuclear freeze, (3) unilateral nuclear disarmament, (4) the
likelihood of nuclear war, (5) the severity of nuclear war, (6) personal
political efficacy on the issue of war and peace, and (7) the likelihood of
nuclear war under the presidency of Ronald Reagan or Walter Mondale.
We also appraised behavioral changes by examining public communication
to the White House, the Congress, the ABC network counseling services,
and antinuclear groups. *The Day After,* we discovered, produced a surprising pattern of reactions.

Methodology

On the evening of the broadcast, we conducted random nationwide telephone surveys both before and after *The Day After.* Working with Smith,
Berlin & Associates, a Washington polling firm, and several dozen student
volunteers, we surveyed a total of 928 people.

Our short questionnaire consisted of a dozen key attitudinal and demographic questions. Calling began about ninety minutes before the start of
The Day After in each time zone. We interviewed only those people who
said they were about to watch the program, and who were 17-years-old or
older. (Most 17-year-olds would be eligible to vote in November 1984.)
Thanks to the enormous audience, brief questionnaire, and intense public interest in the subject, we were able to complete 510 pre-test
interviews.

A separate post-test sample was surveyed to obtain post-test data that
would not be sensitized by the pre-test questions. Telephoning began the

minute *The Day After* ended in each time zone and continued for about 45 minutes. People who had not seen the drama were screened out.

The questionnaire was identical to that used for the pre-test, with the addition of an inquiry as to whether respondents had been watching the special "Nightline" discussions about the movie. Viewers were eager to describe their opinions and refusals were unusually infrequent (under 5 percent). We completed 418 post-test interviews.

Random selection of subjects resulted in pre-test and post-test groups that were highly similar in their demographic composition. No statistically significant differences were found between the two groups on any of the available variables (age, sex, education, region, and party identification). Scores of the pre-test group could thus serve as baseline measures against which to contrast the scores of their counterparts in the post-test group.

Attitude Stability:
Defense Policy, Nuclear War, and Efficacy

Those who had predicted that *The Day After* would produce at least a short-term bonanza in additional antinuclear sentiment among the general public were completely wrong. Even with our sizable sample, we were unable to detect even a trivial shift on key questions. There were no statistically significant changes on any of the questions about defense policy or nuclear war.

Defense Policy. Table 5-1 presents responses to the initial three questions. Opinions toward current defense spending were unchanged. Both before and after the movie, about 37-39 percent said too much was being spent, while about 16-17 percent said too little.

Three-fourths of those surveyed already favored a mutual freeze on nuclear weapons before they witnessed *The Day After.* There was no significant change afterward. Before the show, only 14 percent were opposed to a mutual freeze—about the same share as previous national surveys had found. After the show, the fraction was almost identical.

Just as Americans overwhelmingly supported a mutual nuclear freeze, they overwhelmingly opposed unilateral nuclear disarmament. In the pre-test, only 12 percent said they would unilaterally scrap all U.S. nuclear weapons; in the post-test, the proportion was 11 percent. Americans were opposed to one-sided nuclear disarmament by a ratio of about 8 to 1 prior to the program. The imagery of a nuclear holocaust did not dislodge that opposition.

Nuclear War. Many people had speculated that *The Day After* would, at a minimum, convince Americans of the terror and slaughter of a thermonuclear war. Others predicted its graphic depiction would also increase fears

Table 5-1   **Defense Armaments Attitudes Before and After** *The Day After*
(percent)

Question	Pre-test (N=510)	Post-test (N=418)
Do you think current U.S. government spending on the military and national defense is too much, too little, or about the right amount?		
Too much	38.6	36.7
Too little	16.3	17.2
About right	34.1	31.3
Uncertain	11.0	14.8
Would you support or oppose an agreement for both the U.S. and the Soviet Union to freeze nuclear weapons at current levels?		
Support	75.9	78.7
Oppose	14.3	13.2
Uncertain	9.8	8.1
Would you support or oppose a plan for the United States to scrap all U.S. nuclear weapons, regardless of what the Soviet Union does?		
Support	12.0	10.8
Oppose	81.2	83.5
Uncertain	6.9	5.7

that the movie was a premonition of a real future. We found no indication, however, of any alteration in attitudes about the severity or likelihood of nuclear war.

As shown in Table 5-2, those surveyed in the pre-test were just as pessimistic about their chances of surviving a nuclear war as were those who had seen the ABC program. Before the movie, 47 percent said they had absolutely no chance of living through a nuclear war. After the movie, the figure was 45 percent, a statistically insignificant difference.

Watching the atomizing of Lawrence, Kansas, also produced no shift in the proportion of those who thought a "full-scale nuclear war" was likely within the next ten years. Before the show, 45 percent said it was likely. Following the drama, 47 percent thought it was likely, a statistically insignificant difference.

Political Efficacy. Before *The Day After* was aired, some commentators guessed it might stimulate grass-roots participation in the nuclear freeze

Table 5-2   **Nuclear War Attitudes Before and After *The Day After* (percent)**

Question	Pre-test (N=510)	Post-test (N=418)
In your opinion, how likely is a full-scale nuclear war within the next ten years?		
Extremely likely	10.4	12.4
Somewhat likely	34.5	34.9
Somewhat unlikely	32.5	28.9
Extremely unlikely	16.1	15.8
Uncertain	6.5	7.9
If there were a nuclear war, what do you think would be your chance of living through it?		
A good chance	0.8	2.6
About 50-50	11.6	11.5
A poor chance	35.1	36.4
No chance at all	47.1	44.5
Uncertain	5.5	5.0

movement, while others supposed it would spread feelings of helplessness toward such colossal issues. The latter idea would be consistent with findings of Michael Robinson[2] and others that television messages often inflate the viewer's sense of frustration, confusion, and powerlessness.[3]

The Day After neither discouraged nor promoted feelings of personal political efficacy. . . .

Nearly two-thirds of those surveyed disagreed with the statement, "There is nothing I can do to influence war or peace," both before and after the drama. (Again, differences were not statistically significant.)

Subgroup Similarity

Having found none of the expected changes in the aggregate, we turned to an examination of major demographic and political subgroups. Perhaps *The Day After* was particularly powerful for younger adults (thought to have been especially vulnerable to its appeals), for women (often more dovish than men), or for Democrats and Independents (because Republicans may have heeded conservative warnings).

When controlling for age, education, sex, and party identification, however, the data still revealed no marked attitudinal shifts. . . . Attitudes toward defense spending, among all of the subgroups, were essentially unchanged. . . .

Attitudes before and after *The Day After* on six issues—defense spending, nuclear weapons freeze, unilateral nuclear disarmament, likelihood of nuclear war, severity of nuclear war, and personal political efficacy on the issue of war—were examined separately for all nine subgroups: men, women, college, noncollege, ages 17-29, ages 30 and over, Democrats, Independents, and Republicans. None of these 54 crosstabulations showed any significant pre-test-post-test differences. . . . Thus, there was no evidence that *The Day After* notably influenced any one subgroup more than it did the general population.

Warmongers and Presidents

Up to this point, we have seen consistency and stability in opinions. There was, however, one area in which we unexpectedly found a statistically significant fluctuation. That area was the image of Ronald Reagan.

Republican strategists had feared that the movie might boost pacifistic feelings and jeopardize President Reagan's military budget, foreign policy tactics, and even damage his reelection chances. . . .

As it turned out, there was a statistically significant shift on the subject of Reagan and nuclear war. In sharp contrast to the worry at the White House and the hopes of Democrats, the change was actually in Ronald Reagan's favor.

We asked the following question: "Do you think a major nuclear war would be more likely if the President were Ronald Reagan or Walter Mondale?" After television's vision of the apocalypse, the share of people pointing to Reagan as the more dangerous President declined significantly from 36 to 27 percent. As shown in Table 5-3 Mondale's proportion stayed virtually the same (17 to 15 percent). A large plurality of the respondents refused to accept the forced-choice alternatives; nearly 47 percent on the pre-test and 58 percent on the post-test refused to label either Reagan or Mondale as more likely to preside over a nuclear war.

Similar findings appeared in two *Washington Post* polls which asked if "Reagan's handling of foreign affairs is increasing or decreasing the chances for war"? Results from the poll of November 3-5 showed 57 percent saying Reagan was increasing chances of war. The poll taken the day following *The Day After* produced a major drop of 14 percentage points—only 43 percent remained critical of Reagan for increasing the chances of war.

Neither Reagan nor Mondale is mentioned in the script of the show. Why should there be a large drop in the proportion of people believing nuclear war is more likely under Reagan? Although the decreased criticism of Reagan was more pronounced among men, the college-educated, Independents, and those under 30, his ratings improved in every demographic subgroup.

We can suggest two explanations. It may well be that many of those who would have—perhaps casually—linked Reagan to nuclear war before *The*

Table 5-3   Nuclear War and the President (percent)

Question	Pre-test $(N=510)$	Post-test $(N=418)$
Do you think a major nuclear war would be more likely if the President were Ronald Reagan or Walter Mondale?		
Ronald Reagan	36.1	27.3
Walter Mondale	16.9	15.1
No difference (volunteered)	47.1	57.7

Note: p>.005

Day After might have seen that charge as excessive, overly partisan, and slanderous after being reminded of the slaughter and suffering that would soon follow any launching of ICBMs. Accordingly, they may have tempered their evaluations.

A second possibility is that the program may have artificially produced a version of the "rally-round-the-flag" effect often noted during international crises. In the wake of the movie's ersatz hostilities, some citizens may have been less willing to criticize the Commander-in-Chief.

In the post-test, nearly six out of ten respondents rejected the implicit premise of the question and denied that either Reagan or Mondale as President might be culpable for the onset of the kind of carnage they had just seen dramatized on television. Respondents sometimes volunteered that no American President would initiate such a conflict and that if war broke out, it would be due to the Russians or to circumstances beyond the control of the President.

All of this did not mean that Reagan was invulnerable on the campaign issues of peace. However, chalking up another score for unanticipated consequences of mass media messages, Reagan's problems in that area were not exacerbated by *The Day After* and appear to have been, at least temporarily, partially assuaged. . . .

Behavior

Except for the increased reluctance to link Ronald Reagan to nuclear war, there was no evidence of even minor movement in opinions toward defense policy and nuclear war. However, it is possible that *The Day After* reinforced the intensity of public sentiment and stimulated a zealous minority to action. Thus, rather than confine our analysis entirely to reported attitudes, we examined public behavior as well.

We investigated public responses toward (1) ABC and its affiliate stations, (2) the White House, (3) the Congress, (4) psychological counseling services, and (5) antinuclear groups, such as Ground Zero. If *The Day After*—though not changing opinions—did mobilize viewers into action, we should have ample measures of such behavior.

ABC and Affiliates. . . . Despite the controversy surrounding *The Day After*, there was no outpouring of telephone calls, pro or con, to ABC stations. Those who did call were disproportionately more critical of the program than was, according to our sample, the national viewing audience. At least as far as this small indicator of behavior goes, it suggests that *The Day After* stimulated its critics more than its proponents.

The White House. A modest response was also tallied at the White House. . . .
Within 24 hours after the broadcast, the White House got only 596 telephone calls. (Of these calls, 77 percent said they believed the President was "doing a good job" in this area.) By comparison, the White House recorded 4,592 calls following the President's October 26 speech on Grenada and Lebanon. . . .

Congress. . . . Pegging their campaign to the TV drama, a coalition of thirty groups opposed to nuclear arms sponsored television and newspaper ads promoting a toll-free number to call for "Nuclear War Prevention Kits." The kits stressed the importance and techniques of writing members of Congress. With these efforts added to an audience of over 80 million, what happened to Congressional mailboxes following *The Day After?*
We surveyed the correspondence staffs of 21 Senators and 30 Representatives, selecting a wide variety of officeholders from all parts of the country, and from the liberal, moderate, and conservative wings of both the Democratic and Republican parties. Most offices maintain records of mail trends, and we asked for comparisons of the mail received on defense policy, arms control, and nuclear war for the week before and the week after November 20. . . . The nearly unanimous response was that there was no outpouring of mail in the ten-day period following the program. . . .

Antinuclear Groups. One of the leading groups in the general antinuclear area was Ground Zero. Theo Brown, its director, told us his organization experienced an extremely small increase in mail in the period after November 20, and only a minor increase in donations.
Brown's own conclusion was that *The Day After* was too antiseptic, too apolitical, and, having been oversold in advance, too anticlimactic to be

influential. Nevertheless, Brown believed the program helped focus public attention on the subject, and saw that as its "greatest contribution." People in other antinuclear groups who consented to give us information told a similar story. . . .

Psychological Aid. Much was made in the press about the potentially disturbing consequences of viewing the drama. Concern was expressed that vulnerable individuals might be depressed and emotionally upset by the show. To check this final issue, we surveyed mental health hotlines.

Did people telephone hotlines to talk about their problems coping with the trauma of *The Day After?* A survey of long-established hotlines in the Washington, D.C., area found little or no reaction to the program. Psychologists and psychiatrists appear to have spent far more time talking to television station reporters than to disturbed patients.

Intensity, Inoculation, Enervation, and Ennui

Aside from the increased reluctance to link Reagan with nuclear war, *The Day After* produced no significant evidence of changed attitudes or behavior. It was neither the salvation nor subversion the left and the right had claimed it would be. Why did it have so little influence on its viewers?

There appear to be four possible explanations: First, the controversy surrounding the program might have "immunized" many viewers so that they would be on guard against new ideas. Second, the special *Viewpoint* discussion immediately following *The Day After* may have mitigated some of its influence. Third, attitudes may have already been so strongly held that they were unlikely to be swayed by a two-hour show. Fourth, *The Day After* may have been more soporific than shattering, and a dull show would hardly be unsettling, no matter how much Hollywood hype had preceded it.

Inoculation. The week leading up to the ABC broadcast had been filled with news stories about the controversial show. Jerry Falwell and Phyllis Schlafly led the attack. Mushroom-cloud cover stories were featured in magazines such as *Newsweek* and *TV Guide.* Television shows like *Nightline, Sixty Minutes,* and morning news shows featured defenders and detractors of the forthcoming spectacle. Antinuclear groups mobilized to profit from what they hoped would be a windfall of antinuclear outrage. In this atmosphere, many viewers might have set up extra perceptual barriers to resist being influenced.

To measure suspicions about *The Day After,* we asked the following question: "Do you think that the movie about nuclear war is going to be politically fair or do you think it will be mainly propaganda?" (Past tense was used in the post-test version.)

Attitudes toward the movie itself did change before and after its presentation. Only a modest plurality of 40 percent were willing to say in advance that they were confident the show would be fair. On the other hand, one-quarter of the audience said they expected the movie to be "mainly propaganda." Despite our forced-choice question, over one-third insisted they were reserving judgment—they would wait and see. . . .

After seeing *The Day After*, the proportion who said it was "politically fair" grew from 40 to 63 percent. At the same time, the share saying it was "propaganda" shrunk from 26 to 20 percent. The fraction who were undecided was cut in half, although 17 percent of the respondents still would not characterize the movie even after having seen it. . . .

These figures fall short of being a resounding endorsement, but they do show substantial movement toward considering the program fair. Probably, most or all of those who said they had just watched a propagandistic show had already decided so in advance; there was certainly no increase in their numbers after the show. Nonetheless, one-quarter of the audience was primed to expect a loaded political message, and about one-third was at least prepared to find it slanted ("wait and see").

To examine whether this wary viewership limited the persuasive effects of *The Day After*, we first threw out those who labeled the movie "propaganda" and looked for attitude change among the balance of the audience. Once again, . . . there were no statistically significant differences before and after the movie on any of the five defense and nuclear questions. Even among those presumably most open to the movie there were no signs of change.

We tried another variation on this approach. We separately analyzed the before-and-after responses of those who had called the movie "fair," "propaganda," or were undecided. Again . . . we were unable to find traces of opinion shifts. . . .

. . . [T]he broader finding here was that the movie's failure to induce attitude shifts could not be easily attributed to 100 million people all having their defenses up. The less skeptical portion of the audience gave even less hint of change than did the critics.

Nightline. If the conservative brigade did not torpedo the movie before it was shown, did Ted Koppel's platoon shoot it down immediately after it was shown? Consistent with national TV ratings, nearly three-fourths of those surveyed stayed tuned after the end of *The Day After* to watch a special *Viewpoint* edition of *Nightline*. They first heard Secretary of State George Shultz minimize the prospect of nuclear war. Then they heard an assortment of mostly former government officials debate deterrence theory and defense strategies. (Some wags called the discussion "more frightening" than the movie.)

Previous research has demonstrated that the "coda effects" of subsequent commentaries can blunt the effects of a televised documentary[4] and that "instant analysis" can also dissipate the mood and impact of a presidential address.[5] Might the *Viewpoint* discussion have similarly undercut the power of *The Day After?*

Contrasting the opinions of those who did and those who did not watch *Viewpoint* failed to uncover significant differences. . . .

Intensity. Neither conservative attacks on *The Day After* nor *Viewpoint* discussions of it explained the absence of opinion change. What then about that usual bulwark against change—intensely-held attitudes? A truism verified by decades of communication research is that strong, long-held opinions do not yield easily to change.

. . . [S]everal decades of public opinion polls suggest that Americans have a long-standing appreciation of the destruction and death that would result from nuclear war. They strongly endorse efforts for mutual U.S.-Soviet limits and reductions of nuclear arms. . . .

Americans have embraced arms control proposals as surely as they have acknowledged the dangers of nuclear warfare. Overwhelming and immediate public support greeted the idea of a nuclear freeze. Almost no matter how the question is phrased, 70 to 85 percent of the public will voice support for a mutual freeze on nuclear weapons.

. . . [T]hese past findings . . . indicate that Americans had not been oblivious to the threat of nuclear war and were historically sympathetic to arms control. In dramatizing the anguish of the aftermath of nuclear war, *The Day After* did not tell its audience anything new.

Ennui. Along with the factor of prior convictions, one other major explanation can be offered: *The Day After* was not as sensational and heartrending as its promotions had promised.

Given the magnitude of violence in popular entertainment and a decade of disaster movies, *The Day After* had tough acts to follow. Moreover, its depiction of the aftermath of World War III appeared to have been less horrible, less gruesome than many viewers had imagined. Some authorities also argued that the movie's images were optimistic compared to the likely consequences of a worldwide rain of nuclear warheads. ABC conceded as much with a printed coda stating that its scenario was "in all likelihood less severe than what would actually occur."

Communication Theory and Unexpected Effects

Much of the debate in political communication research continues to center on the "minimum effects" (or no effects) view versus the "substantial effects" (or at least "more than minimum effects") view.[6] However, the findings of this study of *The Day After* suggest that too little attention has been paid to oblique or corollary effects. Just because viewers do not accept the exact message or learn the particular lesson predicted by the researcher does not mean that no lessons have been learned.

By focusing on narrowly defined effects, researchers can miss the unexpected oblique influences of mass communication. And, by their nature, unexpected effects are difficult to study. The researcher may not contemplate many possible consequences, and other effects may seem too illogical or farfetched to merit study. The argument here is not just that many viewers may reach conclusions opposite those presented in the mass media. . . .

Beyond the matter of opposite reactions, viewers may frame the story in different terms, may see different issues at stake, and may draw verdicts on different questions than those assumed by the scholar. *The Day After* data showed an audience response that varied markedly from expectations. A "rally" effect had not been imagined; issues and potential main effects had been conceptualized in other ways. . . .

An audience may not share the researchers' agenda or world-view. More expansive methodologies are needed to capture communication reactions that may escape the range of most researchers' few narrow effects variables. And a study that is headlined "no effects" ought to more properly claim that no effects were found in specific areas.

Notes

1. Tom Shales, "Must Viewing for the Nation: Devastating Images of Horror," *Washington Post*, November 18, 1983, p. C1.
2. Michael J. Robinson, "Public Affairs Television and the Growth of Political Malaise," *American Political Science Review* 70 (June 1976): 409-432.
3. William C. Adams, "Why the Right Gets It Wrong in Foreign Policy," *Public Opinion* 6 (August/September 1983): 12-15.
4. Michael J. Robinson, op. cit.
5. David L. Paletz and Richard J. Vinegar, "Presidents on Television: Effects of Instant Analysis," *Public Opinion Quarterly* 41 (Winter 1977-78): 488-497.
6. William C. Adams, Allison Salzman, William Vantine, Leslie Suelter, Anne Baker, Lucille Bonvouloir, Barbara Brenner, Margaret Ely, Jean Feldman, and Ron Ziegel, "The Power of *The Right Stuff*: A Quasi-Experimental Field Test of the Docudrama Hypothesis," *Public Opinion Quarterly* 49 (Autumn 1985): 330-339.

6

HOW SYNTHETIC EXPERIENCE
SHAPES SOCIAL REALITY

G. Ray Funkhouser and Eugene F. Shaw

Editor's Note

Media are often credited with the power to bring the world's major happenings into the living rooms of average Americans. Funkhouser and Shaw warn that this is a dangerous illusion. The media do not mirror reality. Instead, they expose audiences to synthetic realities fashioned in ways that meet the media's needs. Media images present distorted views of the world that raise false expectations and generate social discontent and undesirable behaviors. The authors concede that it is difficult to prove causal linkages between the audience attitudes and behaviors that they decry and media images. Nonetheless, they contend that the evidence of media influence is persuasive.

At the time of writing, G. Ray Funkhouser was Senior Teaching Fellow in the Faculty of Business Administration, National University of Singapore. Eugene F. Shaw was Director of the Institute of Communication Research at Temple University. The Annenberg School for Communication of the University of Pennsylvania provided assistance for the research. The selection is from "How Synthetic Experience Shapes Social Reality," Journal of Communication *40 (1990): 75-87. All footnotes and one figure have been omitted.*

. . . Numerous authors in contemporary culture (e.g., 1, 2, 4, 12, 14, 15, 17) have commented on the ability of the media to shape portrayals of reality in ways that may in turn shape audience perceptions of *content*. This article explores another dimension of how media shape reality: Ubiquitous electric (motion picture) and electronic (television and computers) media manipulate and rearrange not only the content but the *processes* of communicated experience, thereby shaping how the audience perceives and interprets the physical and social reality depicted. We suggest that the sight/sound media accomplish this by operating (as Plato might say) at yet a *fourth* remove from reality, providing their audiences with "synthetic experience."

Throughout recorded history, the content of communications has been used to produce intended effects in audience opinion, attitudes, and behavior, for example by political manipulators who stage pageants or ritual displays of authority (e.g., 8, 10). But political discourse has never occupied a major portion of humanity's waking hours. The pervasiveness of electronic media today means that their effects may go far beyond shaping opinion or perceptions concerning specific issues, figures, or regimes, to the point of coloring entire cultural world views. . . .

The issue of the representation of reality thus has achieved new and important dimensions in twentieth-century Western culture. As Zettl (20, p. 9) suggests, "the surgeon who cuts into human beings with his scalpel, and we, who cut into human beings with highly charged, keenly calculated aesthetic energy, have an equally grave responsibility toward them." In this article we argue that synthetic experience represents a distortion of reality that poses serious consequences for the media audience and for society in general. . . .

Until the nineteenth century, for most people actual experience was limited to events occurring within the "natural sensory envelope"— the limits of the human nervous system to detect physical stimuli, governed by natural, physical processes. The development of symbolic communication—first of language and drawings, then writing, then printing—had permitted access to information without firsthand experience. Individuals thus could get word of events that occurred outside their sensory envelope, but this constituted symbolic information, not experience.

Within little more than one hundred years, beginning with steam locomotion, internal combustion, and electricity in the nineteenth century and continuing by the turn of the century with electric media (telegraph, telephone, and phonograph) and then motion pictures, radio, and television, technological developments created a quite different perceptual world from that in which human perceptual capabilities and the social institutions of Western civilization had evolved. Twentieth-century communication innovations—notably motion pictures, television, and computers and their allied technologies—differ crucially from all previous media and forms of communication. Introduced into one's sensory envelope, they appear to extend it beyond its natural limits. Unlike speech, writing, drawing, painting, and even photography, they let mass audiences perceive, as quasi-eyewitnesses, events that happened in other times or in other places, or that never really happened at all. These kinetic media possess an immediacy of experience not essentially different from viewing life through a one-way mirror. Moreover, they are accepted and credible; audiences tend to believe what they see on television (16).

Modern cinematic and data-manipulating techniques have made it possible to experience even "real events" in new ways. Altheide (1) notes:

> All mediated experience is different from what we would experience if we encountered the phenomenon first hand. This is due to the peculiar nature of an activity or event and the meaningful connection it has to those who are directly perceiving it; however, it is also due to the way the electronic media operate. The mass media are able to transform events occurring in one time and place into another time and place by employing formats (p. 19).

We wish to extend this line of reasoning to broader aspects of modern media and their impact on society, and to go beyond the abilities of the media to transform the nature of events through "formats." The following techniques, frequently used not only in commercials and entertainment but also in news and documentaries, are now commonplace to film and television audiences (whether or not every member actually is conscious of them):

- altered speeds of movement, either slow or fast motion
- reenactments of the same action (instant replay)
- instantaneous cutting from one scene to another
- excerpting fragments of events
- juxtaposing events widely separated by time or space
- shifting points of view, via moving cameras, zoom lenses, or multiple cameras
- combined sight from one source and sound from another (e.g., background music, sound effects, dubbed dialogue)
- merging, altering, or distorting visual images, particularly through computer graphics techniques and multiple-exposure processing
- manufacturing "events" through animation or computer graphics

Computers have vastly extended these capabilities, enabling media producers to easily (if expensively) create visual images and effects, alter photographic depictions, and merge, excerpt, and modify sight and/or sound into depictions with little or no connection to events that ever occurred—or even could occur—in reality (see, e.g., 19). Thus, as we become more dependent on electronic media for information and entertainment, our information environment is permeated not only with synthetic events but also with synthetic experience.

We contend that synthetic experience is qualitatively different from real experience. A "real experience," as we define it, physically originates within a person's natural sensory envelope—continuous sight, sound, smell, etc., arising from events occurring at their own paces in real time within the reach of the person's sensory capabilities. "Synthetic experience" results from perceptions that could not possibly originate within any person's natural sensory envelope. Prior to the age of electricity only real experience was possible. However, during the twentieth century the public has become accustomed to an information environment of real experience intermixed with absolutely *un*real, synthetic experience. Postman (15), p. 79, notes: "There is no more disturbing consequence of the electronic and graphic revolution than this: that the world as given to us through television seems natural, not bizarre."

Motion pictures provide synthetic experience, but even in their heyday they occupied at most several hours per week of an individual's time, and people self-consciously attended them as a recreational event. Television has become routine in the typical U.S. home, where it is estimated to be on for more than six hours a day (18). To that we must add time spent viewing videocassettes and using other electronic media at home and elsewhere. Watching a television broadcast or a movie is, of course, a "real experience" in that it takes place within one's natural sensory envelope. But the crucial distinction is whether the media-depicted events are mistakenly perceived *and stored* as real experience, rather than as authentic experiences of viewing unreal depictions that, in Plato's words, have as an antidote the knowledge of the situation's true nature.

The average child in the United States today is estimated to have spent more time in front of a television set than behind a school desk by the time he or she reaches maturity (see 13). Again, the issue is, are these television-derived perceptions erroneously interpreted and stored by the child as real experiences? Is the stored map of the world that the child constructs a compilation of the child's actual experiences in the real world? Or is that picture being systemically blurred by synthetic experiences delivered through electronic media?

Both real and synthetic events are increasingly presented to mass media audiences in the form of synthetic experience. As noted earlier, the human experience has been for eons a mixture of real and synthetic events. According to Goffman (7), even in the simplest acts of presenting themselves to others, people do a little synthesizing to improve the picture they want others to receive. Through the mass media, synthetic events have become more pervasive in modern life, and—the point we wish to emphasize—increasingly these synthetic events have been presented to audiences in the form of synthetic experience. However, through the mass media, synthetic events have become both more pervasive and more insinuatingly salient in modern life. . . .

For example, one's impressions of flowers may come from a flower garden in one's yard—an extended series of manifold real events and experiences. Alternatively, one may visit a "flower show," a synthetic event typically staged by commercial interests to stimulate business. A flower show provides a real experience of the pleasures of flowers but minimal experience of the effort and patience they can demand. In the spring, local television news may present a 30-second essay on local flowers in bloom, cutting from one garden or yard to the next in 10-mile leaps to show a variety of flowers at the peak of beauty over a period of weeks, with appropriately floral background music (e.g., "June is Busting Out All Over"). . . . At the same time, seed companies may present TV ads targeted to would-be gardeners. One such ad featured edited, stop-frame photography depicting flowers bursting from sprout to blossom in colorful "explosions" resembling fireworks, synchronized with music from the 1812 Overture. Staged and produced to maximize persuasive impact, such an ad offers perceptions of flowers based on synthetic events and synthetic experience (compared to which the petunias in one's window box seem decidedly subdued). . . .

. . . [W]hether a particular experience is perceived as real or synthetic depends a great deal on the person experiencing it. . . . However, . . . much of our present-day experience is completely different from that existing prior to the twentieth century. . . . In common with people of past ages, we still have real experiences of both real and synthetic events. But, unprecedentedly in history, a considerable portion of our sensory input now comprises . . . synthetic experiences of real and synthetic events. . . .

A number of hypotheses link the growing prevalence of synthetic experience with tendencies apparent in contemporary American life. Five are described here:

1. *Low tolerance for boredom or inactivity.* With so much of our experience now designed explicitly to engage our interest and/or to attract our entertainment dollar, we probably have become used to a heightened sense of excitement and activity. Both staged synthetic events and real events (for example, the news) are communicated to us as synthetic experience, more interesting for most people than viewing events as real experiences. Indeed, what would be the point of using electronic razzle-dazzle if doing so did not attract audience mention and enhance audience interest (11, p. 171)? It should be possible to document a cultural shift toward increased excitement-seeking that parallels the growth of electronic media.

2. *Heightened expectations of perfection and of high-level performance.* As more human experience finds its source in professionally produced offerings of the sight/sound media, more of our perceptions involve individuals who have been specially selected for their superior appearance, pres-

ence, and ability to do whatever it is they are doing. Normally only television's very best takes are shown to audiences. Hours of tape are shot to produce a single 30-second commercial.

The result is that a very high proportion of what we see is far smoother, more expert, and more polished than would be possible for anyone to experience as an on-the-spot observer, even of a professional performance. It is not at all surprising that children entering grammar school after spending several years watching "Sesame Street" are often well prepared for letters and numbers but not for spending the day with a real-life teacher. Many expect more expertise, slickness, and stimulation than these teachers can deliver. As Postman (15, p. 143) puts it: "We know now that 'Sesame Street' encourages children to love school only if school is like 'Sesame Street.' Which is to say, we know now that 'Sesame Street' undermines what the traditional idea of schooling represents."

The danger of unrealistic expectations is that lack of fulfillment can lead to disappointment, frustration, and dissatisfaction. How much of current social discontent may be attributable to inflated expectations fostered by commercial media images presented as synthetic experience? With television's "beautiful people" a ubiquitous comparison, how many can remain easily content with the mundane people, events, and possessions that constitute their lots in life?

3. *Expectations of quick, effective, neat resolutions of problems.* Drama, sports events, and entertainment of all kinds presented on television are compactly packaged and neatly tied up. A problem is posed, and within a short space of real time (usually a half-hour or an hour) it is resolved. Commercials typically dramatize quick and complete solutions to whatever problem the product is claimed to solve. Processes that in reality require hours, days, weeks, or even years are telescoped down to seconds. By contrast, real-life problems tend to be complex, unresolved, and ongoing. But as more of their perceptions originate in synthetic experiences of synthetic events, television audiences may find themselves increasingly frustrated and dissatisfied with the slow and incomplete solutions allowed by real life to the messy problems it poses. It may not stretch the point too far to suggest that some roots of our intensifying litigiousness (a uniquely American proclivity) may be found in this aspect of our communication environment.

4. *Misperceptions of certain classes of physical and social events.* Relatively few people personally witness during their lifetimes a serious automobile collision, a determined fistfight between adults, or a homicide. But the typical American television viewer or regular moviegoer is exposed to a host of these every week, staged as synthetic events and delivered as

synthetic experience, replete with slow motion and the excerpting out of actual pain, gore, and aftermath. Repeated exposure to these and similar depictions may tend to desensitize a viewer's natural, human reactions to what are in real life genuinely traumatic situations. An uncritical viewer also might come to perceive, for example, that slow-motion violence doesn't hurt, that crime usually involves clean, articulate people in well-defined situations, that police are hardly gun-shy, and so forth.

5. *Limited contact with, and a superficial view of, one's own inhabited environment.* Until the twentieth century the vast majority of people never traveled great distances, and so their only experience of the world at large was at best vicarious knowledge gained from verbal reports, stories, myths, rumors or artistic illustrations. On the other hand, they knew their immediate world intimately. Today the sight/sound media provide an easily accessed window to the outside world. But media depictions of "everyday life," plus the opportunity the media provide for avoiding involvement with it, leave us less in touch with the actualities of our own physical and social world compared to people of bygone times. We may have a far broader picture of the world than did our forebears. But our wider range of "facts" and perceptions may be largely false or distorted (see, e.g., 6, p. 179) because of our own predilection for synthetic events electronically presented as synthetic experience. This, coupled with a concomitantly impaired understanding and appreciation of our own immediate milieu, may leave us on balance more ignorant of reality than were citizens of pre-electronic ages. . . .

. . . [E]mpirical evidence on how manipulations of depicted processes affect audiences is still scarce. Indeed, this research area poses some daunting methodological challenges. . . . Research also has been hindered by a paucity of conceptual frameworks that lead to theoretical models, testable hypotheses, and measurable variables. . . . However, . . . we can hardly afford to disregard useful insights into important problems merely because they do not meet impossibly strict methodological criteria. Greater cross-validation of findings and more thorough mutual monitoring among scholars (3) would be appropriate strategies in studying the social effects of synthetic experience.

Empirical research on agenda-setting—the notion that mass media, by selection and emphasis of content pertaining to specific issues or topics, can cause changes in the importance the audience accords those issues or topics—has generally focused on some combination of three variables: systematic variations in mass media content, variations in the flow of events being reported by the mass media, and changes in public opinion (see, e.g., 5, 9, 17). We suggest the term "micro agenda-setting" for this ability of mass media, through emphasis on content, to influence public perceptions of the relative importances of specific issues.

The potential of electronic media to color, distort, and perhaps even degrade an entire cultural world view, by presenting images of the world suited to the agenda of the media (in the U.S. case, commercial interests), we might term "macro agenda-setting." This process involves analogous variables: systematic deviations of media depictions from observable, everyday reality; actual characteristics of everyday reality; and changes in public perceptions of physical and social reality. We suggest that the distinctions proposed here between real and synthetic events, and between real and synthetic experience, may provide a fruitful framework for the study of macro agenda-setting.

References

1. Altheide, David L. *Media Power*. Beverly Hills, Cal.: Sage, 1985.
2. Boorstin, Daniel J. *The Image: A Guide to Pseudo-Events in America*. New York: Harper Colophon Books, 1971.
3. Campbell, Donald T. "Can We Be Scientific in Applied Social Science?" In R. F. Conner, D. G. Altman, and C. Jackson (Eds.). *Evaluation Studies Review Annual*, Volume 9. Beverly Hills, Cal.: Sage, 1984.
4. Ettema, James S. and D. Charles Whitney (Eds.). *Individuals in Mass Media Organizations*. Beverly Hills, Cal.: Sage, 1982.
5. Funkhouser, G. Ray. "The Issues of the Sixties: An Exploratory Study in the Dynamics of Public Opinion." *Public Opinion Quarterly* 37, Spring 1973, pp. 62-75.
6. Gerbner, George and Larry Gross. "Living with Television: The Violence Profile." *Journal of Communication* 26(2), Spring 1976, pp. 173-199.
7. Goffman, Erving. *The Presentation of Self in Everyday Life*. New York: Doubleday, 1959.
8. Lasswell, Harold D., Daniel Lerner, and Hans Speier (Eds.). *Propaganda and Communication in World History*, Volume 1: *The Symbolic Instrument in Early Times*. Honolulu: University Press of Hawaii, 1979.
9. McCombs, Maxwell E. and Donald L. Shaw. "The Agenda-Setting Function of Mass Media." *Public Opinion Quarterly* 36, Summer 1972, pp. 176-184.
10. Machiavelli, Niccolò. *The Prince*. Baltimore: Penguin, 1961.
11. McQuail, Denis. *Mass Communication Theory* (2d ed.). Beverly Hills, Cal.: Sage, 1987.
12. Meyrowitz, Joshua. *No Sense of Place: The Impact of Electronic Media on Social Behavior*. New York: Oxford University Press, 1985.
13. Moody, Kate. *Growing Up on Television: The TV Effect: A Report to Parents*. New York: McGraw-Hill, 1980.
14. Nimmo, Dan and James E. Combs. *Mediated Political Realities*. New York:

Longman, 1983.
15. Postman, Neil. *Amusing Ourselves to Death.* New York: Viking Press, 1985.
16. Robinson, Michael J. and Andrew Kohut. "Believability and the Press." *Public Opinion Quarterly* 52, Summer 1988, pp. 174-189.
17. Rogers, Everett M. and James W. Dearing. "Agenda-Setting Research: Where Has It Been, Where Is It Going?" In James A. Anderson (Ed.). *Communication Yearbook* 10. Beverly Hills, Cal.: Sage, 1987.
18. United Media Enterprises Report on Leisure. *Where Does the Time Go?* New York: Newspaper Enterprise Association, 1983.
19. West, Susan. "The New Realism." *Science 84,* July/August 1984, 31-39.
20. Zettl, Herbert. *Sight, Sound, Motion: Applied Media Aesthetics.* Belmont, Cal.: Wadsworth, 1973.

II

SHAPING THE POLITICAL
AGENDA AND PUBLIC OPINION

The pace of media effects research, throttled by the minimal effects findings of the 1960s, began to quicken in 1972 with the publication of a seminal article by Maxwell E. McCombs and Donald L. Shaw in *Public Opinion Quarterly*. The article examined agenda setting—the ability of the media to focus public attention on a set of issues—rather than the ability of the media to influence audience attitudes. The original study, which examined the impact of media coverage of the 1968 presidential election, is now outdated. But it has sparked a spate of empirical research that demonstrates the media's power as transmitters of political information.

Examples of this scholarship are presented in the comprehensive review of agenda-setting research of Everett M. Rogers and James W. Dearing. They report major agenda-setting effects in various political domains, such as elections, public policy formation, and foreign affairs. Issues featured by the media became important to the public, while issues receiving little media coverage were unlikely to arouse public concern or to engender political action.

Most agenda-setting research begins after media have featured an issue and attempt to fathom the relation between media concerns and the concerns of various audiences. But how are media concerns aroused? What circumstances and efforts are required to attract media attention sufficient to catapult a particular issue into the spotlight of political attention and action? Barbara J. Nelson explores this question as part of her study of the emergence of child abuse as a social issue requiring political action. Whether similar patterns hold true for other social issues remains to be tested.

The study of news coverage of the 1987 stockmarket crash by Dominic L. Lasorsa and Stephen D. Reese illustrates how the same event, when viewed from diverse perspectives, can splinter agenda-setting effects.

Content analysis of the information transmitted by various media showed that the facts and interpretations transmitted by stories differed sharply, depending on the sources whose views were publicized. Accordingly, diverse agendas were set.

Benjamin I. Page, Robert Y. Shapiro, and Glenn R. Dempsey claim another important role for the media—shaping public opinion about a broad array of public policies. They examine changes in policy preferences expressed in public opinion polls covering eighty issues over fifteen years. Their sample of polls demonstrates convincingly that the intervening television news stories affected policy preferences. Like other scholars, the authors point out that contextual factors determine the degree and direction of news impact. The Page-Shapiro-Dempsey study illustrates how a major research venture, simultaneously involving many different issues over an extended time, can bring results when other, less ambitious studies fail to attain conclusive findings.

Most agenda-setting studies have combined content analysis of news media and interviews of media audiences to assess how well media priorities and audience priorities coincide. Shanto Iyengar took a different approach. To make certain that audiences actually have been exposed to the particular news stories whose influence is under investigation, and to eliminate extraneous influences on their thinking as much as possible, Iyengar designed a series of laboratory tests. Subjects were exposed to stories with carefully controlled content and subsequently were tested in the laboratory for various types of agenda-setting effects. The experiment reported in Iyengar's essay demonstrates that news stories can guide the way audiences think about the causes of various social problems. It remains an intriguing but unanswered question, however, to what extent the artificial laboratory setting influences the results.

The last selection answers some questions—and raises several more— about the ultimate effects of television news and entertainment programs on public thinking and the democratic process. George Gerbner, Larry Gross, Michael Morgan, and Nancy Signorielli discuss how popular entertainment programs affect the political thinking of people who spend four hours or more each day watching television. They also describe how television reality, although grossly distorted compared with the real world, becomes embedded in people's images of society.

7

AGENDA-SETTING RESEARCH: WHERE HAS IT BEEN, WHERE IS IT GOING?

Everett M. Rogers and James W. Dearing

Editor's Note

The authors explore research on media power in three different yet related realms. First, what have researchers learned, they ask, about setting the media agenda? Who decides what is important enough for mass media to publish? Second, what influence do published media messages have on the public's agenda of perceptions and attitudes? And third, how does the public's agenda of public policy concerns affect the issues public officials choose to address? In short, what can agenda-setting research tell us about who sets the media agenda, the public agenda, and the policy agenda?

The excerpts presented here concentrate on the conceptual schemes used for analyzing agenda-setting issues and on the main findings. Portions of the literature review have been omitted.

At the time of writing, James W. Dearing was a doctoral student, and Everett M. Rogers was the Walter H. Annenberg Professor of Communication at the Annenberg School for Communications at the University of Southern California, Los Angeles. A prolific writer on communication topics, such as the diffusion of innovations and organizational communication, Rogers was then collaborating with Dearing on a major study of agenda-setting. The selections come from "Agenda-Setting Research: Where Has It Been, Where Is It Going?" *in* Communication Yearbook 11, *ed. James A. Anderson (Newbury Park, Calif.: Sage, 1988), 555-94.*

Public sentiment is everything. With public sentiment, nothing can fail. Without it, nothing can succeed. Consequently, he who molds public sentiment goes deeper than he who enacts statutes and pronounces decisions. (U.S. President Abraham Lincoln, quoted in Rivers, 1970, p. 53)

Appreciation for the power of public opinion and the influence wielded by the press has continued since Lincoln's comment. Such concerns address the processes of influence by which American democracy functions. As Lincoln's comment shows, in the mid-1800s the earlier notion of classical democracy, whereby a government responds directly to the wishes of its public, with the mass media serving as a go-between, was being questioned. Later, political analysts like Key and Lippmann provided a new view of the democratic process: Elected political elites decide upon policies for the public, and the public can make itself heard through political parties, which serve to link policymakers with their constituents.

Many scholars now see omnipotent mass media systems as the mechanism linking the public with political policymakers. The media have usurped the linking function of political parties in the United States, creating what can now be thought of as a "media democracy" (Linsky, 1986). One method for understanding modern democracy is to concentrate upon mass media, public, and policy *agendas,* defined as issues or events that are viewed at a point in time as ranked in a hierarchy of importance. Agenda research, concerned with investigating and explaining societal influence, has two main research traditions that have often been referred to as (1) *agenda-setting,* a process through which the mass media communicate the relative importance of various issues and events to the public (an approach mainly pursued by mass communication researchers), and (2) *agenda-building,* a process through which the policy agendas of political elites are influenced by a variety of factors, including media agendas and public agendas. The agenda-setting tradition is concerned with how the media agenda influences the public agenda, while the agenda-building tradition studies how the public agenda and other factors, and occasionally the media agenda, influence the policy agenda.

An Overview

. . . [W]e prefer to utilize the terminology of *media agenda-setting, public agenda-setting,* and *policy agenda-setting.* We refer to the entire process that includes these three components as the *agenda-setting process* (Figure 1). We call the first research tradition *media* agenda-setting because its main dependent variable is the mass media news agenda. We call the second research tradition *public* agenda-setting because its main dependent variable is the content and order of topics in the public agenda. We call the third research tradition *policy* agenda-setting because the distinctive aspect

Figure 7-1:   Three Main Components of the Agenda-Setting Process: Media Agenda,
Public Agenda, and Policy Agenda

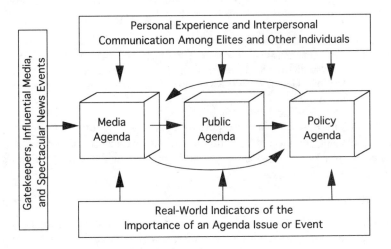

of this tradition is its concern with policy as, in part, a response to both the
media agenda and the public agenda. . . .

Media Agenda-Setting

The issue of the homogenization of the news into a set of topics addressed by all members of the news media was raised early by the Hutch-
ins Report (Commission on Freedom on the Press, 1947). This set of
topics was recognized as the media agenda. The question of who sets the
media agenda and the implications of that influence for society were initially explored by Lazarsfeld and Merton (1948). Lazarsfeld and Merton
conceived of the media issue agenda as a result of the influence that
powerful groups, notably organized business, exerted as a subtle form
of social control. "Big business finances the production and distribution of mass media. And, all intent aside, he who pays the piper
generally calls the tune" (Lazarsfeld & Merton, 1948, reprinted in
Schramm, 1975, p. 503). Similarly, Qualter (1985) argued that a commercially sponsored mass media system is operated by those in the ruling
class of society; therefore, the media cannot be expected to question the
socioeconomic structure of that society seriously. Ball-Rokeach (1985)
suggested analyzing the structural dependency organizing the relationship between the political system and the media, which she describes as
"cooperation based on mutuality of central dependencies" (pp. 491-
492).

The mass media softly but firmly present the perspective of the ruling class to their audiences. The result is consent and support (Schudson, 1986). This result is not a conscious objective of the media. Qualter (1985) stated:

> The media are far from being the sinister manipulators of the popular mind suggested by some conspiracy theories. Their major functions seem to be to support the system, to uphold conformity, to provide reassurance, and to protect the members of society from excessively disturbing, distracting, or dysfunctional information. (pp. x-xi)

These media functions are perpetuated through recruitment and the socialization of media elites, editors, and journalists. In this way, the traditions, practices, and values of media professionals shape the news agenda.

The Public Agenda

Understanding how public opinion is influenced by the content of the mass media has been an important concern of communication scholars tracing back to the writings of Robert E. Park, founder of the 1915-1935 Chicago School of Sociology (Rogers, 1986, pp. 76-80). Park, who has been termed "the first theorist of mass communication" (Frazier & Gaziano, 1979), expanded upon William James's (1896) notion of how people form an "acquaintance" with information by studying the role of newspapers in forming public opinion. Another seminal thinker on this relationship, and one more commonly credited, was Walter Lippmann, who wrote in response to Wallas's (1914) claim concerning the public's increasing dependence on the mass media. Early empirical research results, however, cast doubt on the mass media's power to bring about audience affects. Lazarsfeld and Stanton, in a series of studies on the effectiveness of radio campaigns, concluded that any effects of the mass media were considerably mediated by interpersonal relationship and by personal experience (Klapper, 1960). Social scientists interpreted Lazarsfeld's results as proof that the mass media had only weak effects.

Scholarly research on the agenda-setting process of the mass media stems most directly from the writings of Bernard Cohen (1963), who observed that the press

> may not be successful much of the time in telling people *what to think*, but it is stunningly successful in telling its readers *what to think about*. . . . The world will look different to different people, depending . . . on the map that is drawn for them by writers, editors, and publishers of the papers they read. (p. 13; emphasis added)

Cohen thus expressed the metaphor that stimulated both traditions of agenda-setting research described later in this chapter.

The Policy Agenda

Of direct importance to assumptions about democratic societies is the relationship of public opinion to policy elites' decisions and actions. Agenda-setting researchers who conceptualize policy information as a dependent variable want to know whether the agenda items that are salient to individuals in the public also become salient to policymakers. Occasionally, policy agenda-setting researchers investigate the extent to which the media agenda influences the policy agenda.

David Hume (1739/1896) was one of the first to propose a theory of government founded upon, and responsible to, widespread opinion. Hume extended the work of John Locke, who had posited several laws of human nature. The contribution of Hume was his theoretical development of the democratic society, the idea that widespread, supportive opinion alone was the justification by which a government is in power.

Early assessments reflecting on Hume's principle were optimistic (Dewey, 1927). Gradually, however, such optimism was replaced by skepticism, as empirical researchers began looking for evidence of a responsive government. Gabriel Almond (1950) was one of the first scholars of politics to attempt to understand the growing body of survey data and the course of foreign policy. Almond's pioneering emphasis, however, did little to explain how a transfer of opinion from public to policymakers (if indeed there was a transfer) happened. An explanatory mechanism of a policy-to-public transfer suggested by Katz and Lazarsfeld (1955) was a "two-step flow" of communication, whereby opinions in a society are first circulated by the media and then passed on via opinion leaders by interpersonal communication. This concept was expanded to a "four-step flow" by James Rosenau (1961) in his book *Public Opinion and Foreign Policy*. Rosenau played an important role in orienting policy research toward issue salience and agenda-setting: "We know practically nothing about why it is that some situations abroad never become the subject of public discussion, whereas others take hold and soon acquire the status of national issues" (Rosenau, 1961, pp. 4-5). Rosenau served another important function for later policy agenda-setting research by concentrating on the mass media and their relationships with policymakers.

Cohen's reviews (1973/1983) of the evidence supporting the hypothesis that foreign policymakers are responsive to public opinion concluded, "Our knowledge is partial, unsystematic, disconnected and discontinuous" (p. 4). "We are left with the unsatisfactory conclusion that public opinion is important in the policy-making process, although we cannot say with confidence how, why or when" (p. 7). . . .

Why are scholars so fascinated by agenda-setting? The main reason for interest by mass communication scholars is because agenda-setting research appeared to offer an alternative approach to the scholarly search for direct media effects, which had seldom been found in early mass communication research. Many of the agenda-setting publications by mass communication researchers stated or implied their main justification as an attempt to overcome the limited-effects findings of past communication research. . . .

Analysis of the Public
Agenda-Setting Literature

The basic conception of agenda-setting was a theoretical idea without much basis in empirical research until the study by McCombs and Shaw (1972) of the media's role in the 1968 presidential campaign. A sample of 100 undecided voters, as "presumably those most open or susceptible to campaign information," were identified and personally interviewed during a three-week period in September-October 1968. These voters' public agenda of campaign issues was measured by aggregating their responses to a survey question: "What are you *most* concerned about these days? That is, regardless of what politicians say, what are the two or three *main* things that you think the government *should* concentrate on doing something about?" (p. 178n). The number of mentions of each of five main campaign issues was utilized to index the public agenda.

McCombs and Shaw concluded from their analyses that the mass media set the campaign agenda for the public, or in other words, that the media agenda influenced the public agenda. Presumably the public agenda was important in a presidential election because it would determine who one voted for, although McCombs and Shaw did not investigate this consequence of the public agenda. . . .

Distinguishing Issues from Events

What is an *agenda?* It is a list of issues and events that are viewed at a point in time as ranked in a hierarchy of importance. The items on agendas of past study included (1) such *issues* as the war in Vietnam, Watergate, an auto safety law, unemployment, abortion, and drug abuse and (2) such *events* as the Sahel drought, earthquakes, and other natural disasters.

What is an issue? As Lang and Lang (1981) noted: "Without a clear definition, the concept of agenda-setting becomes so all-embracing as to be rendered practically meaningless" (p. 450). A rather wide range of issues have been studied in past agenda-setting research, and little care has been given to defining exactly what an issue is. Most typically, however, public agenda-setting scholars (e.g., McCombs & Shaw, 1972) have investigated general issues like inflation and the war in Vietnam rather than specific news events or media events like a hurricane or a nuclear power plant disaster.

An important step toward pruning the conceptual thicket of what constitutes an agenda item was taken by Shaw (1977), who distinguished between (1) *events,* defined as discrete happenings that are limited by space and time, and (2) *issues,* defined as involving cumulative news coverage of a series of related events that fit together in a broad category. Thus the drug-related deaths of Len Bias and Don Rogers, two young athletes, in 1986 were news events that helped put the issue of drug abuse higher on the national agenda, even though such "real-world" indicators of the drug problem as the total number of drug users in the U.S. population had remained fairly constant for several years. Our perspective is that events are specific components of issues. Both have been investigated in public agenda-setting research (McCombs, 1976), although we conclude that issues have been more often studied than events. The distinction is often difficult to make due to the conceptual confusion in the past regarding just what an issue and an event are. Further, the mass media often fit a news event into a broad category of a larger issue, as they seek to give the event meaning for their audience. For example, a news event like the 1986 *Challenger* explosion was interpreted by the U.S. media into the more general issue of NASA incompetence and the need for higher funding for the U.S. space program (American Association for the Advancement of Science, 1986; Miller, 1987). Similarly, a news event like the 1986 Chernobyl nuclear power plant [explosion] was interpreted by the U.S. media into the issue of the closed nature of Soviet society (and, yet more broadly, into the issue of U.S./Soviet international conflict).

Is it necessary for an issue to involve contention? Political science scholars in the policy agenda-setting tradition generally think so. For example, Eyestone (1974) stated: "An issue arises when a public with a problem seeks or demands governmental action, and there is public disagreement over the best solution to the problem" (p. 3). Similarly, Cobb and Elder (1971) stated: "An issue is a conflict between two or more identifiable groups over procedural or substantive matters relating to the distribution of positions or resources" (p. 82).

Further scholarly effort should be given to classifying the issues and events that are studied in agenda-setting research. Certainly, a rapid-onset news event like the 1986 U.S. bombing of Libya is markedly different from a slow-onset natural disaster issue like the 1984 Ethiopian drought. A high-salience, short-duration issue like the 1985 TWA hijacking is differ-

ent from such low-salience issues as the ups and downs of U.S. unemployment or from such long-duration issues as Japanese-U.S. trade conflict in
that an agenda item (such as in the case of an election issue) may influence the agenda-setting process, as Auh (1977) demonstrated.

Finally, agenda-setting research should recognize more clearly that each
agenda item influences other items on the media agenda and on the public
agenda. Today's top news story crowds out yesterday's. The salience of an
item on the agenda is "not just an absolute but to some extent a relative
matter" (Lang & Lang, 1981, p. 453). Issues compete for attention. Unfortunately, agenda-setting researchers have tended to treat each issue on
an agenda as if it were *not* dependent on the other items, which is a serious
oversimplification. "Some issues . . . very rarely share space on the same
agenda, while others quite regularly travel together" (Crenson, 1971, p.
163). One can appreciate the measurement and conceptual difficulties resulting from such interrelationships of agenda items.

Adding the Public Attitudes Link

Several studies raise the possibility that the mass media may be doing
more than just setting the public agenda. Weaver, Graber, McCombs, and
Eyal (1981), in a study of the 1976 presidential election, concluded that
the mass media affected *voter evaluations,* as well as cognitive images of
candidates. Davidson and Parker (1972) found a positive correlation between mass media exposure and public support for members of the U.S.
Congress. Mazur (1981) found negative correlations between amount of
mass media coverage and U.S. public support for fluoridation and for nuclear power:

> Detailed studies of a few technical controversies suggest that there is at least
> one simple effect of media coverage on attitudes which works in a reliable
> manner. When media coverage of a controversy increases, public opposition to
> the technology in question (as measured by opinion polls) increases; when
> media coverage wanes, public opposition falls off. (p. 109)

Can we then say that the mass media can change public attitudes, as
well as public cognitions (like the public agenda)? Becker and McLeod
(1976) proposed a model that suggested that public cognitions (the public
agenda) could be a direct effect of the mass media agenda, or an indirect
effect of mass media semantic content, mediated by public attitudes. Public attitudes, they suggested, could result either directly from mass media
semantic content or indirectly from the media agenda, mediated by public
cognitions.

A recent analysis of 12 field experiments on television news concluded
that public judgments as well as cognitions may result from mass media

agenda-setting. Iyengar and Kinder (1987) concluded that television coverage of U.S. presidential performance not only heightened viewer cognizance of the issues, but also set the standards (by highlighting some issues at the expense of others) by which presidential performance was then judged. The concept employed by Iyengar and Kinder (1987) to explain this power of the media is *priming*, defined by Fiske and Taylor (1984, p. 231) as the effects of prior context on the interpretation and retrieval of information. Iyengar and Kinder (1987) use the concept of priming to mean the changes in the standards that underlie the public's political evaluations. Iyengar and Kinder (1987) see priming as "a possibility at once more subtle and consequential than agenda-setting." They found considerable support for both public agenda-setting and priming hypotheses in their field experiments.

Priming, especially in its broader definition by Fiske and Taylor (1984), addresses the importance of both the mass media agenda and mass media semantic content in affecting public attitudes. If the mass media agenda "primes" readers and viewers by giving salience to certain events, these events are not merely made more salient to the audience. The mass media prime focuses on specific issues raised by a news event in the journalistic search for explanation. This selectivity forces these issues, not just the event, to the forefront of mass media coverage and of, perhaps, personal consideration. Moreover, these "event-issues" are prominently publicized by the media, not in an impartial way, but rather with positive or negative valences. Mass communicators may be "telling it like it is," but issues raised by the event retain their media intensity through positive or negative semantic content. An issue will not move through the priming sequence if it has not aroused public interest. As Downs (1972) observed, "A problem must be dramatic and exciting to maintain public interest because news is 'consumed' by much of the American public (and by publics everywhere) largely as a form of entertainment" (p. 42). Thus priming acts upon public attitude formation both through heavy media coverage (media agenda-setting), by showing people that the issue is important, and, in "successful" event-issues, by demonstrating a kind of entertainment value (semantic content).

Other Influences of the Public Agenda

The mass media are not the only influences on the public agenda, which is one reason the correlation of the mass media with the public's agenda of items is less than perfect. "Social processes other than mass communication also affect the public's judgment of an issue or person as important. For one thing, people talk to one another about social issues, and these conversations may play an important part in their judgments" (Wright,

1986, p. 155). In fact, McLeod, Becker, and Byrnes (1974) found that mass media content had a greater effect in forming the news agendas of individuals who participated in conversations about the topics on the media agenda, than for individuals who did not have such interpersonal communication. This finding is entirely consistent with the conclusions from research on the diffusion of innovations, where an individual's exposure to mass media channels often creates awareness of new ideas, but then interpersonal channels are necessary to persuade the individual to adopt the innovation.

Most scholars of agenda-setting seem to take a contingent view of the process: Agenda-setting does not cooperate *everywhere*, on *everyone*, and *always* (McCombs, 1976). Why might an individual's agenda *not* be influenced by the mass media agenda?

Low media credibility. A particular individual may regard the media in general, or the particular medium to which the individual is exposed, as low in *credibility* (defined as the degree to which a communication source or channel is perceived by an individual as trustworthy and competent). For instance, a Wall Street lawyer may regard the *National Enquirer* as less credible regarding international news than the *New York Times;* so when the lawyer reads a headline in the *Enquirer* about a new Soviet disarmament proposal, the medium's salience for this news item likely will not be accepted. The individual is informed about the news item by the media, but is not convinced that the item is important.

Conflicting evidence from personal experience or other communication channels about the salience of the issue or news event. Perhaps an individual hears the president of the United States pronounce in a televised address that America is experiencing a drug crisis, but this individual has recently heard CBS News's Dan Rather state that the number of U.S. drug users has remained constant for several years. Such conflicting statements in the media represent content about the drug issue, but are unlikely to raise that issue on the public agenda.

The individual holds different news values than those reflected by the mass medium or media. The individual's reaction to a newspaper headline might be to think, "How could they regard *that* as important news?"

An important step toward understanding why individuals have different issue agendas was taken by McCombs and Weaver (1973) by introducing the notion of a *need or orientation.* Any individual, when issue relevance is high and uncertainty is high, has a high need for orientation. This need leads to greater media exposure, which in turn leads to greater agenda-setting effects. Nevertheless, as McCombs and Weaver (1985) noted, "Such a limited three-part model is far from the full picture of the mass communication process" (p. 102). Future research should seek to understand more clearly the individual cognitive processes that are involved in the agenda-setting process at the individual level.

Assessing Causality

Agenda-setting research has generally found a positive association between the amount of mass media content devoted to an item and the development of a place on the public agenda for the item. The next step in establishing a causal relationship between the media agenda and the public agenda was to seek evidence for the expected time order; if the public agenda preceded media content, the latter could hardly cause the former. The expected time order of the two conceptual variables has been found in several post hoc studies. Funkhouser (1973a, 1973b) advanced the field of agenda-setting research by investigating a longer time period than in other studies; he utilized years as units of analysis for eight issues that emerged on the public agenda in the United States during the 1960s. The rank-order of these issues on the public agenda corresponded to their degree of mass media coverage.

Such media coverage did not correspond to the "real-world" severity of the agenda item; for example, in the case of drug abuse, mass media coverage began its decline well before the social problem began to become less serious, as indicated by "objective" indicators obtained from extramedia sources. When the mass media coverage of the issue and the real-world severity of the agenda item differed, the public agenda followed the degree of media coverage more closely. Overall, Funkhouser's analysis supported the media agenda moving toward public agenda relationship, although this support was limited to the particular era and issues that he studied (MacKuen, 1981, p. 24).

Real-world indicators are possible confounders of the media agenda moving toward public agenda relationships. A few studies support this view; for example, MacKuen (1981) found a direct influence of real-world indicators on the public agenda, without this relationship going through the media agenda. In contrast, Funkhouser (1973) generally found strong associations between the media agenda and the public agenda, and weaker associations between real-world indicators and either the media agenda or the public agenda. Unfortunately, relatively few agenda-setting scholars have included real-world indicators in their analysis. . . .

In only a few agenda-setting investigations were the researchers able to control the independent variable of the media agenda as it influenced the public agenda (the dependent variable). An example is a field experiment conducted by Iyengar, Peters, and Kinder (1982), in which families were paid to watch only special television news programs created by the investigators. When national defense was stressed in the television news programs constructed by the investigators, this issue became more salient to the families in the field experiment. A similar agenda-setting "effect" was achieved for the topic of pollution in a second field experiment, and for inflation in a third. . . .

. . . [T]here is undoubtedly a two-way, mutually dependent relationship between the public agenda and the media agenda in the agenda-setting process. Media gatekeepers have a general idea of the news interests of their audience, and this perceived priority of news interests is directly reflected in the news values with which media personnel decide the media agenda. A few studies, for example, Erbring, Goldenberg, and Miller (1980), have found a two-way relationship between the media agenda and the public agenda. This influencing of the media agenda by the public agenda is a gradual, long-term process through which generalized news values are created. In contrast, the influence of the media agenda on the public agenda for a specific news item is a more direct, immediate cause-effect relationship, especially when the public lacks alternatives (such as personal experience) that might influence their agenda. However, for general agenda issues like inflation, Watergate, and unemployment, where their priority on the public agenda is built up in a slow, accretionary process over many months or years, the nature of the media agenda moving toward public agenda relationship may be very gradual and indirect. Certainly there must be differences from agenda item to agenda item as to how rapidly they climb the public agenda.

If our present reasoning is correct, it is inappropriate to expect a one-way causal relationship of the media agenda on the public agenda. . . . More realistically, both the media agenda and the public agenda are probably mutual causes of each other. . . . Since there is a great deal of variance in the agenda items studied, some items probably can be expected to demonstrate linear, rather than circular, causality. . . .

The relative influence of the mass media in setting the public agenda for an agenda item depends greatly on whether the event is (1) of major importance or not and (2) a rapid-onset type versus a gradual, slowly developing topic. In a major, quick-onset news event, the importance of the news event is immediately apparent. Almost at once the news event jumps to the top of the media agenda and remains there for some time. The public usually has not other communication channels (such as personal experience) through which to learn of these news events. So the mass media would be expected to place the news event high on the public agenda quickly.

In the case of a relatively slow-onset news issue like a drought, the media often play an important role in "creating" the issue. Typically, the mass media discover the slowly developing news event through a particularly spectacular message about it, which serves as a "triggering device" (Cobb & Elder, 1983, p. 85) in setting the media agenda. In the case of the Ethiopian drought, a film report of a refugee camp at Korem by Mohamed Amin was shown by the BBC and then by NBC in October 1984. Immediately, other U.S. mass media began to feature this disaster as a major news issue, and rather quickly the public considered the Ethiopia drought an important issue. Relief activities by the U.S. government and by rock musicians (who attracted massive financial support from the public) soon followed. In this case, the mass media helped to "create" the news event, set the public agenda, and facilitate amelioration of suffering in Ethiopia through fund raising.

Much public agenda-setting research, especially the studies reported in the 1970s, involved a rather narrow range of political issues. This primary emphasis on political issues is understandable, in the sense that a great many media news events *are* political in nature. But much other news content is not directly political in nature, and these news events should also be included in agenda-setting research, in order to determine the generalizability of public agenda-setting across various types of media content. . . .

. . . For some agenda items, advertising must be very important. For example, the tremendous advertising campaigns for microcomputers in the 1980s by Apple, IBM, and other manufacturers certainly must have raised the American public's consciousness of computers. In recent years, microcomputers represented one of the most advertised products on U.S. television. Despite the obviously important role of advertising as an agenda-setter for certain issues, advertising's role in the agenda-setting process has received very little attention by communication scholars other than that given to political campaign spots. Exceptions are Sutherland and Galloway (1981) and Hauser (1986), who investigated how a consumer's agenda of products is affected by advertising.

In a sense, one of the strongest pieces of evidence of the media's agenda-setting influence may consist of the fact that issues and events that are completely ignored by the mass media do not register on the public agendas. As McCombs (1976) noted: "This basic, primitive notion of agenda-setting is a truism. If the media tell us nothing about a topic or event, then in most cases it simply will not exist on our personal agenda or in our life space" (p. 3). Unfortunately, it is extremely difficult or impossible for scholars to investigate such a "non-agenda-setting" process because of the problem of identifying news events or issues that are not reported by the mass media, which by definition cannot be measured by a content analysis of the media. . . . Perhaps public agenda-setting by the mass media only occurs in the case of transfixing issues and blockbuster events that receive very heavy media attention over an extended period of time. In any event, it is certainly dangerous to extrapolate intuitively from the present findings about agenda-setting for high-salience issues and events to those of much less salience. . . .

Critique of the Policy Agenda Literature

. . . Concomitant with interest in the public opinion-policy relationship has been interest in the influence that the mass media agenda has on U.S. foreign policy. As Cohen (1965) stated:

> The press functions in the political process like the bloodstream in the human body, enabling the [foreign policy] process that we are familiar with today to continue on, by linking up all the widely-scattered parts, putting them in touch with one another, and supplying them with political and intellectual nourishment. (p. 196)

In recent years, scholars often incorporate the media agenda, along with other variables, in research on policy agenda-setting. For example, Lang and Lang (1983, pp. 58-59) found that Watergate was an issue that required months of news coverage before it got onto the public agenda. Then, finally, Watergate became an agenda issue for action by U.S. governmental officials. In this particular case of policy agenda-setting, public agenda-setting by the mass media led to government action, and then policy formation.

Further exploitation of both the public opinion moving toward policymaker and mass media moving toward policymaker relationships was advanced by Cohen (1963), who concentrated on the agendas of elites responsible for foreign policy. Yet public opinion as a meaningful determinant of elite agendas was not clearly established in the way that communication scholars were able to replicate the media agenda moving toward public agenda link (e.g., stricter federal laws regulating campaign financing). So there may be various longer-range consequences of the mass media agenda than just forming the public agenda. But the main point of the Lang and Lang analysis of the agenda-building process for Watergate is that the mass media were only one element, along with government and the public, involved in a process through which the elements reciprocally influenced each other. Such multiple agenda-setting for an issue, with complex feedback and two-way interaction of the main components in the agenda-setting process, probably occurs in many cases. The media's influence upon policymakers might be expected to be greater for quick-onset issues when the media have priority access to information; alternatively, when policy elites control the information sources, they might be expected to set the media agenda.

An example of policy agenda-setting research that illustrates the impact of policy elite agendas upon media agendas is Walker's (1977) study of setting the agenda in the U.S. Senate. He commented:

> Once a new problem begins to attract attention and is debated seriously by other senators, it takes on a heightened significance in the mass media, and its sponsors, beyond the satisfaction of advancing the public interest as they see it, also receive important political rewards that come from greatly increased national exposure. (p. 426)

. . . In a recent study of mass media impact upon federal policymaking, Linsky (1986) concluded that the media are far more important than had previously been suggested. Out of 500 former government officials surveyed and 20 federal policymakers interviewed, 96 said that the media had an impact on federal policy. A majority considered the impact to be substantial. Linsky (1986) concluded that the media can speed up the decision-making process by positive issue coverage, as well as slow down the process by negative coverage. . . .

We conclude our review of policy agenda-setting research with three generalizations: (1) The public agenda, once set by, or reflected by, the media agenda, influences the policy agenda of elite decision makers, and, in some cases, policy implementation; (2) the media agenda seems to have direct, sometimes strong, influence upon the policy agenda of elite decision makers, and, in some cases, policy implementation; and (3) for some issues, the policy agenda seems to have a direct, sometimes strong, influence upon the media agenda.

Discussion and Conclusions

. . . What are the main theoretical and methodological lessons learned from the past 15 years of research on the agenda-setting process?

1. The mass media influence the public agenda. This proposition, implied by the Cohen (1963) metaphor, has been generally supported by evidence from most public agenda-setting investigations, which cover a very wide range of agenda items, types of publics, and points in time.
2. An understanding of media agenda-setting is a necessary prerequisite to comprehending how the mass media agenda influences the public agenda.
3. The public agenda, once set by, or reflected by, the media agenda, influences the policy agenda of elite decision makers, and, in some cases, policy implementation.
4. The media agenda seems to have direct, sometimes strong, influence upon the policy agenda of elite decision makers, and, in some cases,

policy implementation.

5. For some issues the policy agenda seems to have a direct, sometimes strong, influence upon the media agenda.

6. The methodological progression in agenda-setting research has been from one-shot, cross-sectional studies to more sophisticated research designs that allow more precise exploration of agenda-setting as a process.

7. A general trend in agenda-setting studies across the more than 15 years of their history is toward disaggregation of the units of analysis, so as to allow (1) a wider range of research approaches to be utilized and (2) a more precise understanding of the process of agenda-setting.

8. Scholars in the two main research traditions on the agenda-setting process, especially those studying public agenda-setting, need to become more fully aware of each others' research and theory, so that agenda-setting research can become more of an integrated whole (our analysis of the citations by the two research traditions shows there is little intellectual interchange in this direction). . . .

As pointed out elsewhere in this chapter, initial interest in research on the public agenda-setting process was stimulated by scholars who were questioning the limited direct effects of the mass media, and who thus searched for indirect effects. This expectation now seems to have been fulfilled: The media do indeed have important indirect effects in setting the public agenda. But how could the mass media have relatively few direct effects, and at the same time have strong indirect effects in setting the public's agenda? McQuail and Windahl (1981) stated:

> This hypothesis [agenda-setting] would seem to have escaped the doubts which early empirical research cast on almost any notion of powerful mass media effects, mainly because it deals primarily with learning and not with attitude change or directly with opinion change. (p. 62)

In other words, individuals learn information from the mass media about which agenda items are more important than others; this task is accomplished by the mass media, even though research shows these media are much less capable of directly changing attitudes and opinions. These general research results from agenda-setting research make sense in an intuitive way. Therefore, the theory of McCombs and Shaw (1972) that proposes the media agenda would influence the public agenda, drawn from the Cohen (1963) metaphor, has been largely supported by some 102 studies in the public agenda-setting tradition.

Here we see the main intellectual significance of agenda-setting research. No scholarly issue has been so important to the field of mass communications research as that of the research for media effects. The actual issue driving the mass communication field for the past 30 years or so has been this one: Why can't we find evidence for mass media effects? Agenda-setting research is viewed as important by many mass communication scholars because it has established that the media *do* have an indirect effect, public agenda-setting. This conclusion contains the germ of a lead for future research: Mass communication scholars should investigate indirect media effects on individual knowledge, rather than direct media effects on attitude and behavior change. Obviously, there are many other potential types of indirect media effects on knowledge than just agenda-setting. . . .

References

Almond, G. A. (1950). *The American people and foreign policy.* New York: Harcourt Brace.

American Association for the Advancement of Science. (1986). *Media coverage of the shuttle disaster: A critical look.* Washington, DC: Author.

Auh, T. S. (1977). *Issue conflict and mass media agenda-setting.* Unpublished doctoral dissertation, Indiana University, Bloomington.

Ball-Rokeach, S. J. (1985). The origins of individual media-system dependency: A sociological framework. *Communication Research, 12,* 485-510.

Becker, L. B., & McLeod, J. M. (1976). Political consequences of agenda-setting. *Mass Communication Research, 3,* 8-15.

Cobb, R. W., & Elder, C. D. (1971). The politics of agenda-building: An alternative perspective for modern democratic theory. *Journal of Politics, 33,* 892-915.

Cobb, R. W., & Elder, C. D. (1983). *Participation in American politics: The dynamics of agenda-building* (2nd ed.). Baltimore: Johns Hopkins University Press.

Cohen, B. C. (1963). *The press and foreign policy.* Princeton, NJ: Princeton University Press.

Cohen, B. C. (1965). *Foreign policy in American government.* Boston: Little, Brown.

Cohen, B. C. (1983). *The public's impact on foreign policy.* Lanham, MD: University Press of America. (Original work published 1973).

Commission on Freedom of the Press. (1947). *A free and responsible press.* Chicago: University of Chicago Press.

Crenson, M. A. (1971). *The un-politics of air pollution: A study of non-decision making in two cities.* Baltimore: Johns Hopkins University Press.

Davidson, R., & Parker, G. (1972). Positive support for political institutions: The case of Congress. *Western Politics Quarterly, 25,* 600-612.

Dewey, J. (1927). *The public and its problems.* New York: Henry Holt.

Downs, A. (1972). Up and down with ecology: The issue-attention cycle. *Public Interest, 28,* 38-50.

Erbring, L., Goldenberg, E. N., & Miller, A. H. (1980). Front-page news and real-world cues: A new look at agenda-setting by the media. *American Journal of Political Science, 24,* 16-49.

Eyestone, R. (1974). *From social issues to public policy.* New York: John Wiley.

Fiske, S. T., & Taylor, S. E. (1984). *Social cognition.* Reading, MA: Addison-Wesley.

Frazier, P. J., & Gaziano, C. (1979). *Robert E. Park's theory of news, public opinion and social control.* Lexington, KY: Journalism Monographs.

Funkhouser, G. R. (1973a). The issues of the sixties: An exploratory study in the dynamics of public opinion. *Public Opinion Quarterly, 37,* 62-75.

Funkhouser, G. R. (1973b). Trends in media coverage of the issues of the sixties. *Journalism Quarterly, 50,* 533-538.

Hauser, J. R. (1986). Agendas and consumer choice. *Journal of Marketing Research, 23,* 199-212.

Hume, D. (1896). *A treatise of human nature.* Oxford: Clarendon. (Original work published in 1739).

Iyengar, S., & Kinder, D. R. (1987). *News that matters: Agenda-setting and priming in a television age.* Chicago: University of Chicago Press.

Iyengar, S., Peters, M. P., & Kinder, D. R. (1982). Experimental demonstrations of the "not-so-minimal" consequences of television news programs. *American Political Science Review, 76,* 848-858.

James W. (1896). *The principles of psychology.* New York: Henry Holt.

Katz, E., & Lazarsfeld, P. F. (1955). *Personal influence.* New York: Free Press.

Klapper, J. T. (1960). *The effects of mass communication.* New York: Free Press.

Lang, G. E., & Lang, K. (1981). Watergate: An exploration of the agenda-building process. In G. C. Wilhoit & H. DeBock (Eds.), *Mass communication review yearbook 2* (pp. 447-468). Newbury Park, CA: Sage.

Lang, G. E., & Lang, K. (1983). *The battle for public opinion: The president, the press, and the polls during Watergate.* New York: Columbia University Press.

Lazarsfeld, P. F., & Merton, R. K. (1948). Mass communication, popular taste, and organized social action [Reprinted in W. Schramm (Ed.), *Mass communication* (2nd ed.)]. Urbana: University of Illinois Press.

Linsky, M. (1986). *Impact: How the press affects federal policymaking.* New York: W. W. Norton.

MacKuen, M. B., & Coombs, S. L. (1981). *More than news: Media power in public affairs.* Newbury Park, CA: Sage.

Mazur, A. (1981). Media coverage and public opinion on scientific controversies. *Journal of Communication, 31,* 106-115.

McCombs, M. E. (1976). Agenda-setting research: A bibliographic essay. *Political Communication Review, 1,* 1-7.

McCombs, M. E., & Shaw, D. L. (1972). The agenda-setting function of mass media. *Public Opinion Quarterly, 36,* 176-184.

McCombs, M. E., & Weaver, D. H. (1973, May). *Voters' need for orientation and use of mass communication.* Paper presented at the annual meeting of the International Communication Association, Montreal.

McCombs, M. E., & Weaver, D. H. (1985). Toward a merger of gratifications and agenda-setting research. In K. E. Rosengren, L. A. Wenner, & P. Palmgreen (Eds.), *Media gratification research* (pp. 95-108). Newbury Park, CA: Sage.

McLeod, J. M., Becker, L. B., & Byrnes, J. E. (1974). Another look at the agenda setting function of the press. *Communication Research, 1,* 131-166.

McQuail, D., & Windahl, S. (1981). *Communication models for the study of mass communication*. New York: Longman.

Miller, J. D. (1987). *The impact of the Challenger accident on public attitudes toward the space program* (Report to the National Science Foundation). Northern Illinois University, Public Opinion Laboratory.

Qualter, T. H. (1985). *Opinion control in the democracies*. New York: St Martin's.

Rivers, W. L. (1970). Appraising press coverage of politics. In R. W. Lee (Ed.), *Politics and the press*. Washington, DC: Acropolis.

Rogers, E. M. (1986). *Communication technology*. New York: Free Press.

Rosenau, J. N. (1961). *Public opinion and foreign policy*. New York: Random House.

Schudson, M. (1986). The menu of media research. In S. J. Ball-Rokeach & M. G. Cantor (Eds.), *Media audience and social structure* (pp. 43-48). Newbury Park, CA: Sage.

Shaw, E. F. (1977). The interpersonal agenda. In D. L. Shaw & M. E. McCombs (Eds.), *The emergence of American public issues: The agenda-setting function of the press* (pp. 69-87). St. Paul, MN: West.

Sutherland, H., & Galloway, J. (1981). Role of advertising: Persuasion or agenda setting. *Journalism Quarterly, 58,* 51-55.

Walker, J. L. (1977). Setting the agenda in the U.S. Senate: A theory of problem selection. *British Journal of Political Science, 7,* 433-445.

Wallas, G. (1914). *The great society*. New York: Macmillan.

Weaver, D., Graber, D. A., McCombs, M. E., & Eyal, C. H. (1981). *Media agenda-setting in a presidential election: Issues, images, and interest*. New York: Praeger.

Wright, C. R. (1986). *Mass communication: A sociological perspective* (3rd ed.). New York: Random House.

8

THE AGENDA-SETTING FUNCTION OF THE MEDIA: CHILD ABUSE

Barbara J. Nelson

Editor's Note

Among the perennial puzzles of human history, few are as intriguing as why ideas emerge and disappear. How do some issues capture public and legislative attention and become public policy while others perish without action? Research often points toward the mass media as the catalyst. Barbara J. Nelson's essay provides an interesting case study. She probes several major questions: how media decide that a state of affairs should be "news"; how they pursue a topic and frame it until large numbers of people are aroused and action is taken; and how and why media drop many topics after relatively brief spans of attention so that the pressure for action dissipates.

Besides its exposition of the role that media played in bringing the issue of child abuse to the fore, the essay is theoretically significant. It tests political economist Anthony Downs's theory of the "issue-attention cycle," which postulates that issues arise when intolerable conditions have come to public attention and fade when media coverage begins to bore the public or when solutions require economic redistribution. Nelson demonstrates that the predictions derived from the theory coincide only partly with what happened in the case of child abuse. Contrary to the theory, child abuse has remained a long-term interest of the media, and pressure for public action remains strong.

Nelson, at the time of writing, was a professor at the Hubert Humphrey Institute of Public Affairs at the University of Minnesota. Her scholarship in the public policy field has been recognized in many ways, including a Kellogg Foundation National Fellowship, a visiting fellowship at the Russell Sage Foundation, and major grants from Guggenheim and the National Academy of Sciences. The selection comes from "The Agenda-Setting Function of the Media:

From Barbara Nelson, *Making an Issue of Child Abuse: Political Agenda Setting for Social Problems*. Copyright © 1984 by The University of Chicago Press.

Child Abuse," in Making an Issue of Child Abuse: Political Agenda Setting
for Social Problems *(Chicago: University of Chicago Press, 1984), 51-75.
Several tables and footnotes have been omitted.*

What part did the media play in transforming the once-minor charity
concern called "cruelty to children" into an important social welfare issue?
We would expect the media's role to be very important, because the media
exist at the boundary between the private and the public. Their task is to
discover, unveil, and create what is "public." To do so they often wrench
"private deviance" from the confines of the home. In the case of child
abuse the media also helped to establish a new area of public policy. . . .

The "Issue-Attention Cycle"

In order to gain a full understanding of the media's role, we must examine how political issues are usually covered by the media, particularly how
and when coverage of an issue is sustained. Anthony Downs has presented
the most compelling description of the "issue-attention cycle" to date.[1]
Downs predicts that problems begin to fade from the media's and the public's attention when their solutions imply the necessity of economic redistribution, or when media coverage begins to bore an ever-restless public.

. . . [N]ineteenth-century coverage of the problem conforms to Downs's
formulation, but, perhaps surprisingly, twentieth-century coverage does
not. Rather than fading from prominence, child abuse has received constant, even growing, attention from the media. Careful investigation into
how and *why* the media covered child abuse at various times leads us to
revise Downs's issue-attention cycle. As we shall see, it appears that issues
can have a much longer attention cycle than previously supposed, a finding
which has important consequences, one of which is that political agendas
become increasingly crowded, a fact significant for the real and perceived
efficiency of government.

Just as there are many more issues, concerns, and conflicts than government can address, there are many more potential stories than the media
can report. The problem of deciding "what's news" is severe. Tom Wilkinson, Metro Editor for the *Washington Post,* has written that "the *Washington
Post,* like other large media outlets, receives approximately one million
words every day . . . [and] has the capacity to publish about 100,000
words—or 10 percent of the information received. Competition for this
space is fierce."[2]

. . . Downs suggests there is the pre-problem stage, where the objective
conditions of the problem are often more severe and pervasive than in the
second stage, called "alarmed discovery and euphoric enthusiasm." With
deadly accuracy, Downs notes that Americans have a touching blend of

horrified concern and wide-eyed, cotton-candy confidence which leads them to assert "that every problem can be solved . . . *without any fundamental reordering of society itself.*" [3] Government begins to try to solve the problem at this point. Soon, however, the initial enthusiasm for solving the problem gives way to the third stage, a more sober realization that significant progress will be costly not only in terms of money but also in terms of social stability. When the need for redistribution or social reordering seems to be part of the solution to a particular problem, Downs suggests that the cycle enters its fourth stage, where both the media and their audiences begin to lose interest. In step five an issue enters the "post-problem stage." Whatever response has been initiated by government becomes institutionalized. Once innovative and exciting programs become part of the business-as-usual processes of government. The issue retains routine coverage, but the public, hungry for novel news, implicitly demands a new set of issues.

Intuitively, Downs's description of the issue-attention cycle seems to be accurate. Certainly the cognoscenti of the media, the regular readers, listeners, and viewers, sense the pattern of the media's (and government's) attention to particular issues. Downs's formulation has not been put to the test, however. Indeed, it is difficult to do so because his objective was to sketch the overall pattern of the issue-attention cycle, not to specify its processes. By attempting to understand child abuse coverage in terms of Downs's formulation, we learn a great deal about what sustains media interest and coverage.

The Mary Ellen Case

Downs's issue-attention cycle aptly describes media, public, and governmental interest in child maltreatment at the point when the problem was "discovered" in 1874, and when the now-familiar Mary Ellen case tugged at the hearts of fashionable New York. It is fair to say that without media coverage of the Mary Ellen case, child protection might never have become institutionalized as a social problem distinct from the Scientific Charity movement's more general interest in reducing sloth, pauperism, and dependence on the public purse. Without a doubt the living and working conditions of many children during the Gilded Era conform to Downs's pre-problem stage. The misery of poverty and a tradition of legal and religious precepts supporting a father's right to raise a child as he saw fit probably made violence toward children fairly prevalent. The ideal of a protected childhood, which encouraged the recognition of child abuse as a social problem, was just beginning to develop.

It was the Mary Ellen case, however, which ushered in the second stage of "alarmed discovery and euphoric enthusiasm." [4] In the spring of 1874

the *New York Times*[5] and the other New York papers reported that Mary
Ellen Wilson had been chained to her bed and whipped daily with a raw-
hide cord by her stepmother. The *Times* was not yet governed by the motto
"All the News That's Fit to Print," which was adopted in 1897.[6] Nonetheless, the *Times* only rarely carried stories about cases of even such blatant
abuse as that suffered by Mary Ellen, and even when the *Times* did cover
such stories, it was in a tone much more moderate than that used by papers
with larger circulations such as the *New York Herald* and the *World*. In fact,
the *Times* covered only one other instance of a child similarly abused in the
two years prior to Mary Ellen's case.

Even Mary Ellen's story might never have become part of the public
record had not Henry Bergh [the founder of the American Society for the
Prevention of Cruelty to Animals] been informed of the abuse by "a lady
who had been on an errand of mercy to a dying woman in the house adjoin-
ing [Mary Ellen's]." [7] The ensuing trial of Mary Ellen's stepmother, who
received a one-year penitentiary term, and the decision about what to do
with Mary Ellen, who was eventually sent to the Sheltering Arms children's home, remained in the news through June of that year. As 1874
drew to a close, Mary Ellen's plight reemerged in the *Times*, this time as
the reason for the formation of the New York Society for the Prevention of
Cruelty to Children (New York SPCC), the nation's first charitable organization dedicated to identifying ill-treated children.

Of course, the Mary Ellen case was not the first instance of cruelty to
children to receive newspaper coverage. The bizarre brutalization of children and public horror over it always received a modicum of attention in
the press. The significance of the Mary Ellen case rests with its label—
cruelty to children—which like the later labels unified seemingly unrelated cases, and in the fact that it precipitated the formation of an organization whose purpose was to keep this issue alive.

The label "cruelty to children" and the Mary Ellen case did not, however, ensure sustained media attention. Two measures of the issue's rapid
decline from prominence can be garnered from the *New York Times Index*.
In the 1874 volume of the *Index* the entry "Children, Cruelty to" appears
for the first time. However, this subject entry disappears from the *Index*
beginning in July, 1877, and does not reappear until 1885, after which
time it occurs only infrequently until World War I. During the first three
years of recognition, the *Times* published fifty-two news articles it specifically categorized as dealing with "cruelty to children." But the deletion of
the cruelty to children subject heading did not signal the end of coverage
of the topic. By searching all the subject entries about children, articles on
child abuse cases and the activities of prevention societies can be found.
Most frequently, instances of abuse and neglect are classified under the

ignominious heading "Children, miscellaneous facts about." In the judgment of librarians of that period, cruelty to children ceased to be a problem
important enough to warrant special reference.

A century later, it is difficult to determine whether the issue's short tenure in the spotlight was indeed caused by the reason Downs suggests, i.e.,
that a meaningful response to the problem includes a major revamping of
society. Certainly, a concerted response to child abuse must include an
examination and reordering of economic and social arrangements—a protected childhood is not possible without it. . . .

. . . [A]fter the novelty of the Mary Ellen case wore off, newspapers and
professional journals gave the problem only sporadic coverage. Indeed, almost ninety years elapsed before the issue again took center stage in the
media, in the form of the now-famous article "The Battered-Child Syndrome" by [pediatrician] Dr. C. Henry Kempe and his associates, published in the July 7, 1962 issue of the *Journal of the American Medical Association.*[8] With the publication of this article, a tiny trickle of information
grew into a swollen river, flooding mass-circulation newspapers and magazines and professional journals alike. In the decade prior to the article's
appearance doctors, lawyers, social workers, educators and other researchers and practitioners combined published only nine articles specifically focusing on cruelty to children. In the decade after its publication, the pro-
fessions produced 260 articles. Similarly, mass-circulation magazines
carried twenty-eight articles in the decade after Kempe's article, compared
to only three in the decade before, two of which recounted instances of
bizarre brutalization.[9]

Even television displayed an interest in the problem. Although it is
harder to document this medium fully, it seems that child abuse was virtually absent from early television scripts, whereas after "The Battered-
Child Syndrome" appeared, soap operas and prime-time series alike created dramas based on the problem. The plight of Mary Ellen's fictional
brothers and sisters was first beamed into millions of households in episodes of *Dr. Kildare, Ben Casey, M.D.,* and *Dragnet.*[10]

These figures on the emergence of child abuse in the media suggest that
Downs's formulation of the issue-attention cycle needs to be amended.
Contrary to Downs's hypothesis, media attention to child abuse grew
steadily rather than declined, and the public has sustained a loyal interest
in what might on the surface be thought of as a small, even unimportant,
issue. Admittedly, Downs does not speculate on how long the issue-attention cycle takes to run its course. Nonetheless, findings so strikingly at
variance with the tenor of Downs's formulation deserve closer attention.

Four factors contribute to the continuing coverage of child abuse and
suggest that media attention to a host of issues can be more long-lived than

previously assumed. These factors include topic differentiation, issue aggregation, the link between the professional and the mass media, and the growing appeal of human interest stories (especially ones with a medical deviance twist).

First and foremost, coverage of abuse increased because stories about specific types of abuse were added to the earlier, more general reports. In other words, coverage increased because the general problem of abuse was differentiated into more narrowly defined topics such as the relationship between illegitimacy and abuse, or abuse within military families. Second, child abuse coverage increased because the issue was also linked with larger, more over-arching concerns, such as intrafamilial violence, which now includes abuse of a spouse, parent, or even grandparent. The scope of the problem is thus simultaneously decreasing and increasing.

Topic differentiation and issue aggregation are themselves explained by a third factor which encourages sustained media attention to child abuse. To a large extent the mass media carefully and consistently monitor professional and scientific journals in search of new stories. This symbiotic relationship is perhaps the most neglected factor contributing to ongoing media coverage of issues. Despite the lack of attention paid to it, the relationship between the mass media and professional outlets is well institutionalized, and serves both parties admirably, providing fresh stories for journalists and (for the most part) welcome publicity for scholars. Moreover, this relationship provides a regular source of "soft (i.e., interesting) news" about child abuse. Indeed, the fourth factor contributing to the durability of child abuse coverage is the fact that "soft news"—human interest stories—has been added to "hard news" stories, which have traditionally focused on child abuse cases as crime news. This last factor should not be confused with the first two. Soft news stories extend the range of story *types*, whereas differentiation and aggregation extend the range of story *topics*.

By investigating each of these factors we can show how media coverage both created the demand for, and was a product of, governmental action. The first three factors—differentiation, aggregation, and the relationship between the professional and mass media—can be considered together. These three factors are linked through the recognition that child abuse was initially a research issue, and that research on a problem has a life cycle of its own. This life cycle can greatly affect the prominence of an issue in the media.

. . . [P]hysical abuse was a research problem long before it was a public policy issue in the conventional sense. During the decade between 1946 and 1957 radiologists reluctantly pieced together evidence revealing that a fair number of children had bruises and broken bones, the cause of which could only be parental violence. This research, however, never crossed the bridge from scientific publications to the mass media. Indeed, not until 1960 did the Children's Bureau even mention these medical studies in its *Annual Report*. . . .

In 1962 the situation changed, however. Dr. C. Henry Kempe and his colleagues published "The Battered-Child Syndrome" in the AMA *Journal*. The article and its companion editorial caused a storm in medical circles and in the mass media as well. Indeed, the article and editorial are routinely used to date the rediscovery of abuse. In this instance, medical research and opinion did cross the bridge to the mass media, primarily through the vehicle of the AMA press release "Parental Abuse Looms in Childhood Deaths." [11] The message of the article and editorial was clear: Kempe and his co-workers had "discovered" an alarming and deadly "disease" which menaced the nation's children. The article was measured in tone and eminently professional, although its findings were later sensationalized through less careful retelling. But the editorial presented problems from the beginning.

The most important characteristic of the article is that it provided a powerful, unifying label in the phrase "the battered-child syndrome." Kempe purposefully chose the term to emphasize the medical, and downplay the criminal, aspects of the problem. . . .

. . . Like many professional associations, the AMA routinely issues press releases about important findings reported in its journal. This practice constitutes the first link in a chain which keeps mass media personnel abreast of medical, scientific, and technical developments. At the other end of the chain are the beat reporters who cultivate the sources behind the news releases. The chain, little studied in the policy-making literature but well institutionalized, transmitted Kempe's findings to journalists responsible for medical news.

Within a week of the news release, *Time* magazine summarized the article as the second feature in its "Medicine" section. . . . *Newsweek*, however, beat *Time* to the punch. In the April 16, 1962 edition of *Newsweek*, the findings of "The Battered-Child Syndrome" were reported.

. . . Together, *Time* and *Newsweek* informed millions of readers that a new "disease" imperiled the nation's children.[12]

If these two magazines informed a somewhat selective and small audience, the *Saturday Evening Post* and *Life* had more popular appeal. The *Post* published an article entitled "Parents Who Beat Children: A Tragic Increase in Cases of Child Abuse Is Prompting a Hunt for Ways to Select Sick Adults Who Commit Such Crimes" on October 6, 1962.[13]

Like the news magazine articles, the author of the *Post*'s article interviewed the medical experts. . . . But in the *Post* article, these interviews were juxtaposed with a recitation of the gory details of child abuse. . . .

In a double-barreled shot, photojournals and news magazines introduced child abuse to the American public. The articles can be considered the point at which an invisible problem became a public concern, and soon a major public policy issue. . . .

For the next twenty years, popular magazines began what seemed to be a campaign to publicize the problem. The *Readers' Guide to Periodical Literature* cites 124 articles published from 1960 through 1980. . . . [T] he articles cluster around significant research breakthroughs and political events. But the tempo of coverage was constant. Abuse has remained a staple in popular magazines as different as *Woman's Day* and *Scientific American*.

The durability of coverage was in part caused by new "events" (research or action) which continually revitalized interest. Thus Downs underestimated the extent to which his formulation assumed that individual or closely clustered events trigger the issue-attention cycle. Though every professional article did not get the recognition of "The Battered-Child Syndrome," over *1,700* articles on child abuse or related subjects have been published in professional journals over the last thirty years. Together they kept a steady stream of information flowing to beat reporters and issue partisans.

Once child abuse and neglect were adopted as policy issues, public funds supported much of the research reported in professional journals. The Children's Bureau spent over a million dollars between 1962 and 1967, and $160 million was authorized (though not all was appropriated) under [the Child Abuse Prevention and Treatment Act] and its reenactments through 1983. But public interest in child abuse was not limited to scientists and practitioners. The attention of the mass public was also engaged, quite deliberately in fact, by professionals who felt that government should take a greater responsibility for child protection. . . .

Newspaper Coverage

Newspaper accounts of abuse were extremely important in setting the government's and the citizenry's agendas. In the same year that "The Battered-Child Syndrome" was published, the Children's Division of the American Humane Association reviewed the major newspapers in forty-eight states to determine how many child abuse cases were reported by papers. They learned of 662 incidents, of which 178, or almost one-fourth, led to the death of the child.

. . . [W] hat had formerly appeared as isolated incidents of psychopathic behavior could now be understood as a patterned problem when over 600 cases were identified nationwide.

The 662 abuse cases found by the AHA typified newspaper coverage early in the issue's life. During the early 1960s, child abuse was covered as crime news and the press found stories of bizarre brutalization especially newsworthy. But as time went on, newspaper coverage began to include—even be dominated by—stories reporting research findings. Of course, there could not be any reporting on research when there was no research to cover. But it is the *addition* of research-related stories which accounts for the durability of child abuse articles in the *New York Times*. Space for research-based stories on abuse became increasingly available as the *Times* editorial staff decided to give more space to human interest stories, especially those with a medical or scientific slant.[14]

The crime-and-victims approach to covering child abuse cases always assured a minimum of coverage for the issue. Reviewing research on newspaper coverage of crime, Joseph R. Dominick found that "a typical metropolitan paper probably devotes around 5-10% of its available space to crime news. Further, the type of crime most likely reported is individual crime accompanied by violence."[15] Thus, even if the media should tire of reporting other aspects of child abuse, child-abuse-as-crime coverage will remain. Indeed, it was always present at some level; it merely lacked a label to unify seemingly unrelated events.[16]

But child abuse reporting is not merely crime reporting: it is crime reporting with an important twist. There is a certain unfreshness about the act of abusing a child which adds a sense of personal and social deviance to the existing criminality. If a person robs a bank, it's a crime; but if a child is beaten, it's something more. One obvious motivation for emphasizing the most unusual and extreme forms of abuse is that newspapers can then titillate their readers with stories that are unwholesome as well as violent. The penny press of the nineteenth century and its twentieth-century descendents made no bones about seeking out just this type of story. "Respectable" newspapers, on the other hand, feel the need to cloak the decision to run such articles behind a cloud of scientific justifications. Adolph Ochs, who bought the *New York Times* in 1896, perfectly captured the nuances of this perspective: "When a tabloid prints it, that's smut. When the *Times* prints it, that's sociology."

. . . [T]he reporting of child abuse follows a fairly consistent pattern in which unwholesomely criminal cases where the child survives are preferred to what might be considered the more serious, but somehow more routine, cases where the child dies. The titillation of bizarre brutality accounts in part for this pattern, but other factors also contribute to newspapers' apparent preference for this type of story. Part of this preference can be traced to the organizational needs of newspapers. From the perspective of news managers, more information unfolds in a case of brutality than in one where the victim dies. This fact in itself sustains coverage.

But factors more subtle than an editor's bent for sensationalism are involved in sustaining newspaper coverage of child abuse stories. Most importantly, the press enjoys playing an advocative role in maintaining cultural norms that protect children and defend the integrity of the home. These expressions are part of the Progressive Era values sustained by the media in general.[17] Additionally, abuse which results in death is murder, or at least manslaughter. Society has clearly defined sanctions which are invoked in cases of murder. No similarly straightforward response existed for child abuse in 1964. Under the doctrine of "the best interest of the child," there was a presumption that a child ought to remain at home unless the situation was hopeless. With only limited temporary shelter facilities available and permanent placement options restricted to foster care or—what was even less likely—adoption, an abused child was frequently returned to his or her parents. The implicit difficulty in determining what was a safe environment for a child and the common-law precedent supporting strong parental rights together created a tension in bizarre brutalization cases which led to sustained coverage of these cases. The bizarre brutalization of young girls may also account for the newspapers' continuing interest.

In a 1965 nationwide public opinion survey conducted by David G. Gil, newspapers were cited more frequently than other media as a source of information on physical abuse: 72.0% of Gil's respondents mentioned newspapers as an information source, 56.2% specified television, and 22.7% cited magazines.[18] The newspapers' tradition of reporting child abuse as crimes of bizarre brutalization helps to explain why approximately 30% of Gil's sample felt that parents or other abusers should be "jailed or punished in some other way." [19] Indeed, with the extremely brutal images provided by reporting abuse as a crime, we may do well to wonder why over two-thirds of those queried preferred a more therapeutic approach to dealing with abusers, believing close supervision or even leaving the abuser alone if the injury was not too serious (or not intervening at all) to be a sufficient response. The message of "The Battered-Child Syndrome," which portrayed abuse as medical deviance, was clearly in accord with more general attitudes defining social problems involving violence as psychological in origin.

Once child abuse was rediscovered as a social problem, newspapers began to cover cases more frequently and intensively. But not all the growth in the coverage of child abuse was a result of papers' interest in bizarre brutalization. As legislative response to child abuse grew, so did that type of newspaper coverage. Every state passed a child abuse reporting law between 1963 and 1967, and all amended and reamended their law several times, with each legislative action renewing newspaper interest in the problem. In addition, newspapers also began to run human interest stories on child abuse, in part aided by the now defunct Women's News Service, which provided feature stories on child abuse for the home, style, and fashion pages of subscribing newspapers. Local human interest stories focused on nearby programs to prevent or treat abuse, and special training sessions for county and state workers.

In deciding to investigate or publish a particular story, journalists quickly learn that "hard" and "soft" news are not accorded the same value. "Hard news," according to Gaye Tuchman, "concerns important matters and soft news, interesting matters." [20] Soft news does not have the "quickening urgency" which Helen MacGill Hughes asserts is the lifeblood of newspapers.[21] In other words, soft news is timeless and durable— although many would say insignificant—which means it appears at the back of a newspaper.

The special titillation of violent deviance accounts for the durability of child abuse as soft news. Newspapers usually feature such news in the portions of the papers devoted to women's interests. . . .

The role of human interest stories in sustaining newspaper coverage of child abuse can be seen by examining the *New York Times* stories in 1964 and again in 1979. The sixteen stories on child abuse published in 1964 split evenly between cases and legislative reports. Fifty child abuse stories made the *Times* in 1979. In that year the activities of various charitable groups and the results of numerous scientific research projects constituted *one-half* of the coverage. Cases, legislation, even criminal proceedings took a back seat to soft-news articles.

The pattern of newspaper coverage of abuse and neglect over the last thirty years is quite illuminating. Once again relying on the *New York Times Index*, we find that during the early 1950s child abuse stories were quite common, thinning to just a few stories a year until the late 1960s when coverage took a dramatic jump. . . . The sheer volume of coverage is remarkable. Between 1950 and 1980 the *Times* published 652 articles pertaining to abuse, certainly enough to keep the issue in the public's eye.

Of course, the media can lead the public to water, so to speak, but cannot always make it drink. The information was available to anyone who wanted it, but how many people read which articles (or watched which television programs) cannot be ascertained. And the information grew year by year, to an unprecedented volume, providing a climate of public awareness which initially encouraged elected officials to recognize the problem and ultimately caused them to maintain an interest in it.

In sum, we can say that child abuse achieved the public's agenda because the interest of a few pioneering researchers crossed the bridge to mass-circulation news outlets. Public interest was sustained and grew, however, because the media have both many *sources* of news and many *types* of audiences to whom they present the news. Through topic differentiation, issue aggregation, professional and mass-circulation linkages, and the growth in human interest newspaper reporting, child abuse remains a lively topic of media coverage. The public's interest in this newly recognized social problem prompted state legislatures into action. And act they did, out of humanitarian interest to be sure, but also from the recognition that child abuse was the premier example of no-cost rectitude. . . .

Would media attention decline if research funds continued to decline? I imagine so, but not quite for the reasons Downs proposed. Coverage may decline because there is less to report. There may be less to report because there is less research money spent. And there is less research money because of the conflicting values over the size of the budget and the role of the federal government in social programs. Conflicting values over the propriety of intervening in the family are not directly driving the budgetary decision making about federal child abuse legislation, although the social conservatives like the Moral Majority have raised these questions. In ways not evident during an era of plenty and growth, the issue-attention cycle may be significantly affected by larger macroeconomic and political concerns.

The downward spiral of decreasing research and media coverage may induce further programmatic and policy changes as well. The consequences of reduced research and coverage could include less public awareness and declining "demand" for public programs. In the long run, reporting of suspected cases to welfare offices might decline as well, the product of citizen apathy and fiscal difficulties in staffing reporting and service systems. A public convinced of bureaucratic unresponsiveness would be further discouraged to report. The great fear of advocates of public policy against abuse is that declining media coverage and declining reporting will be used to assert that the actual incidence of abuse is declining. . . .

Notes

1. Anthony Downs, "Up and Down with Ecology—'The Issue Attention Cycle,'" *Public Interest* 32 (Summer 1972): 38-50. See also Mark V. Nade, "Consumer Protection Becomes a Public Issue (Again)," in James E. Anderson, ed., *Cases in Public Policy Making* (New York: Praeger, 1976), pp. 22-34; and P. F. Lazarsfeld and Robert K. Merton, "Mass Communication, Popular Taste, and Organized Social Action," in W. Schramm and D. F. Roberts, eds., *The Process and Effects of Mass Communication* (Urbana, Ill.: University of Illinois Press, 1971), pp. 554-578.

2. Tom Wilkinson, "Covering Abuse: Context and Policy—Gaining Access," in George Gerbner, Catherine J. Ross, and Edward Zigler, eds., *Child Abuse: An Agenda for Action* (New York: Oxford University Press, 1980), p. 250.

3. Downs, "Up and Down," p. 39.

4. Ibid., p. 39.

5. In recounting the public's introduction to the problem we depend heavily on the accounts of the Mary Ellen case carried in the *New York Times*. This is a decision based on the exigencies of research, not on the *Times*'s stature during that period. . . .

6. Michael Schudson, *Discovering the News: A Social History of American Newspapers* (New York: Basic Books, 1978), p. 112.

7. The *New York Times*, April 10, 1874, p. 8.

8. C. Henry Kempe et al., "The Battered-Child Syndrome," pp. 17-24.

9. The figures reported here were derived by summing the articles listed under the appropriate headings in the following indexes. For the professional media: *Index Medicus*, the *Index of Legal Periodicals*, the *Social Science Index*, the *Humanities Index*, and the *Education Index*. Figures for mass-circulation magazines derived from the *Readers' Guide to Periodical Literature*. No reductions were made for the possibility of double counting.

10. For two perspectives on television's response to child abuse and other social problems, see Donn H. O'Brien, Alfred R. Schneider, and Herminio Tratiesas, "Portraying Abuse: Network Censors' Round Table"; and George Gerbner, "Children and Power on Television: The Other Side of the Picture," in Gerbner et al., *Child Abuse*, pp. 231-238, 239-248.

11. American Medical Association, "Parental Abuse Looms in Childhood Deaths," news release, July 13, 1962.

12. "When They're Angry . . . ," *Newsweek*, April 16, 1962, p. 74; and "Battered Child Syndrome," *Time*, July 20, 1962, p. 60.

13. Charles Flato, "Parents Who Beat Children: A Tragic Increase in Cases of Child Abuse is Prompting a Hunt for Ways to Select Sick Adults Who Commit Such Crimes," *The Saturday Evening Post*, October 6, 1962, pp. 32-35.

14. Harrison Salisbury, *Without Fear or Favor: The New York Times and Our Times* (New York: Time Books, 1980), pp. 558-560.

15. Joseph R. Dominick, "Crime and Law Enforcement in the Mass Media," in Charles Winick, ed., *Deviance and Mass Media* (Beverly Hills, Cal.: Sage, 1978), p. 108.

16. Gans's research on the content of the CBS and NBC nightly news and the news magazines *Time* and *Newsweek* shows that crime-and-victim news also forms a steady part of news offerings in these outlets. . . . Herbert Gans, *Deciding What's News* (New York: Pantheon, 1979), p. 13 from table 31.

17. Gans, *Deciding What's News*, pp. 203-206; and Schudson, *Discovering*, pp. 77-87.

18. David G. Gil, *Violence against Children* (Cambridge, Mass.: The Harvard University Press, 1973), p. 61, table 5: "Sources of Respondent's Knowledge

of the General Problem of Child Abuse during the Year Preceding the Survey." Respondents could mention more than one source.

19. Ibid., p. 66, table 10: "What Respondents Thought Should be Done About Perpetrators of Child Abuse."

20. Gaye Tuchman, "Making News by Doing Work: Routinizing the Unexpected," *American Journal of Sociology* 79, no. 1 (July 1973): 114.

21. Helen MacGill Hughes, *News and the Human Interest Story* (Chicago: University of Chicago Press, 1940), p. 58.

9

NEWS SOURCE USE IN THE CRASH OF 1987: A STUDY OF FOUR NATIONAL MEDIA

Dominic L. Lasorsa and Stephen D. Reese

Editor's Note

In their discussion of agenda setting, Rogers and Dearing noted that researchers have rarely focused on media agendas. Lasorsa and Reese supply part of the missing puzzle in their study of four national media: the New York Times, *the* Wall Street Journal, Newsweek, *and* CBS. *The authors' analysis of the stock market crash of 1987 shows that conventions about appropriate sources for stories and source solicitation of media coverage strongly influence whose views will be presented in news stories. While the rules and pressures are similar for all news channels, there are important variations in their choices of particular news sources. The predilections of the chosen sources are then reflected in the diverse facts and interpretations featured in each story.*

Besides its focus on story sources, the article illustrates several important trends in coverage. They include the efforts to tailor story appeal to particular types of audiences and the sparse attention usually given to the causes of important events.

At the time of writing, Dominic L. Lasorsa was Assistant Professor and Stephen D. Reese was Associate Professor of Journalism at the University of Texas at Austin. The article comes from Journalism Quarterly *67 (Spring 1990): 60-71.*

The national news media in the United States purport to work under the premise that within a news story they present an objective account of news events, giving fair treatment to those with differing positions. The press allows differing positions to be expressed by representative spokespersons. Source attribution, the attributing of positions to individual persons, preferably with their relevant organizational affiliations identified, is a fundamental practice of the press. This attribution serves important functions for the audience. It alerts the reader both to the expertise and the motives of the source. When critical readers "consider the source," they essentially make judgments about both the source's capacity to offer evidence and motivation in presenting it.

Audience members, however, cannot judge sources they do not hear. Thus, in addition to choice of stories, news media wield enormous gatekeeping responsibility in their selection of sources, which largely determines the way stories are framed. We consider this selection process an active one in two respects. Sources take an active part in promoting themselves into the news, and journalists actively choose sources based on their suitability to the story and to the audience. By examining the sources in news stories, we may learn much about who gains access to the press, how issues are framed, and how media differ in their source selection.[1]

October 1987 Crash

In this study, we focus on one major story, the Wall Street stock market crash in October 1987 and the debate over its causes and effects, and we examine how four major national news media—the CBS Evening News, *Newsweek,* the New York *Times* and the *Wall Street Journal,* used sources in their coverage of this story.

We have several reasons for choosing this particular story. First, it was an unexpected and largely ambiguous event, which resulted in many differing interpretations and questions. The crash combined taxes, trade, interest rates, deficits and political leadership into a dramatic national story. What caused the crash? What would be its effects?

Second, it was a "big" story. The *1988 Media Guide* called the crash the "most important story of the year." [2] The rapid plummet of stock prices on Oct. 19 was similar in magnitude, and instantly compared to, the great crash of 1929. This major story evolved over a few weeks time and was covered by all major news media, thus allowing comparisons across news channels. Metz provides a good in-depth look at how the business press covered the crash.[3]

Third, we believe that studies of media content should go beyond broad descriptions of news categories, such as "politics and government," "war and defense," and "economic activity," and focus on specific issues and events in order to add to our understanding of the dynamics of media coverage as it evolves over time and in historical context.

We assume that news sources have different organizational affiliations that help indicate their position in the power structure. The large majority of sources used in news stories are identified with particular organizations. "Average citizens" without organizational affiliations make their way into the news in times of personal triumph or tragedy (saving a child, dying in an accident) but they rarely appear in major news stories except as the "man in the street" reactor to news events.

The second assumption is that from these affiliations derive different primary missions. Organizations exist for different purposes and therefore have different agendas. For example, businesses, whether large corporations or small Mom and Pop outfits, have the primary mission of making money for their owners. Governments, whether federal, state, or local, have the primary mission of providing protection and providing services for their constituents. Academics, whether university- or institute-affiliated, have the primary mission of acquiring and disseminating knowledge. Lobbyists, whether for citizens or business groups, have the primary mission of influencing policy. Underlying these assumptions is our conviction that an analysis of sources is essential in understanding press coverage.

In his study of national news production, Gans gives close attention to the relationship between sources and journalists, describing it as a dance, with sources doing the leading more often than not.[4] Molotch and Lester share this source-centric view of news production, suggesting that powerful sources largely determine news by promoting "occurrences" into "events."[5] Descriptions of news content conceal who is saying what.

Who Are the Sources?

Who are the sources for news? Most often they are government officials and other elites—that is, the powerful. Gans notes that although sources can potentially include anyone, "their recruitment and their access to journalists reflect the hierarchies of nation and society."[6] He finds that network news and national newsmagazines are dominated by the "knowns," over half of which are government officials. Sigal draws a similar conclusion from his study of the New York *Times* and the Washington *Post*.[7]

We know the news is dominated by official sources and other elites, and we assume that they articulate their own interests. We know less about what these sources say. Do sources respond in a predictable manner based on their affiliation? To what extent do media use similar sources? Do mass and elite news stations differ in their use of sources?

One reason to examine source reliance is our concern that it is a major factor behind the phenomenon of "media convergence," a tendency for all the media to focus on the same story at the same time. Several factors underlie this process, including the herd mentality of the mainstream media as they look to each other for guidance.[8] Powerful sources represent another important influence: when national leaders speak, they often are able to amplify their voices through the tendency of the elite newspapers to cover them simultaneously.[9] . . .

The media may more often duplicate sources than stories. Prominent sources often range across a number of separate news stories. If Henry Kissinger appears in two stories the same day, one about aid to the Nicaraguan Contras and the other about guerrillas in El Salvador, the stories would differ but the source and corresponding point of view presumably would not.

Study Hypotheses

We test this media consonance notion as it relates to source selection. Based on the consonance literature, we hypothesize that:

1. The media will not differ in their use of sources with different institutional affiliations.

Of course, there is the possibility that source selection is largely irrelevant, for it matters only if different sources are saying different things. Because news sources have different organizational affiliations with different primary missions and perspectives, we expect them to focus on different aspects of the crisis and literally see—and report—different things.

Evidence for the effect of psychological factors on perception abound, including the effect of motivation,[10] prior experiences,[11] and attitudes.[12] Furthermore, regardless of perceptual differences that may exist among sources because of their organizational backgrounds, we know that some sources desire to persuade and may deliberately promote certain images and impressions over others. Indeed, this in some cases is the source's job. The result will be, we hypothesize, that different sources with different organizational affiliations will:

1. Differ in the degree to which they make statements about causes and effects of the crisis; and
2. Differ in the kinds of statements they make about the causes and effects of the crisis.

Method

Every story in the news sections of the New York *Times* and the *Wall Street Journal,* and every story in *Newsweek* and on the CBS Evening News during the month of October and November 1987 was examined for references to the stock market and Wall Street. To code the newscasts, abstracts of the CBS broadcasts were obtained from the Vanderbilt University *Television News Index and Abstracts.* These abstracts identify all sources used in a story. Television stories were defined as one or more reports under the major underlined story headings listed in the *Abstracts.* All stories which mentioned the stock market or Wall Street were coded in their entirety. This study, then, is based on a census, not a sample.

In each story, all sources were identified by the coder. Coders noted what, if anything, the source said about the causes and effects of the stock market crash. Each source was categorized according to his or her organizational affiliation. The seven broad organizational affiliations we used to categorize sources were:

1. *Business,* someone who was identified as representing, owning, or working for a large corporation or a small business;
2. *Government,* either federal, state, or local, including elected officials, appointees, and spokespersons;
3. *Academic,* someone representing either a university or policy institute;
4. *Wall Street,* without any more specific organizational citation; these include mostly brokers, traders, and investors;
5. *Lobbyists,* either citizens or business;
6. *Foreign,* and
7. *Unspecified.*

Each source in each story was examined for comments about causes of the crash. Their response was placed into one of 14 predetermined broad categories we thought responses might fall into, based on recollection of coverage at the time. Responses actually fell into only 13 of the 14 categories. No source mentioned the Federal Reserve System as a cause of the crash.

Each source also was examined for comments made about effects of the crash. As with the causes, mentions of effects were placed into one of 14 broad categories we thought responses might fall into. Again, responses actually fell into only 13 of the 14 categories; no source said the crash would affect mostly the wealthy.

Using our predetermined categorization scheme, an independent coder was used to code the data. A second coder was employed to double-code 13% of the data. Intercoder reliability, as measured by Cronbach's Alpha, was found to be acceptable (.86 for the affiliation measure, .80 for the causes and .78 for the effects).

Results

Individual stories varied widely in the number of unique sources cited. In the 167 stories analyzed, 1,022 sources were used, for a mean of 6.1 sources per story. The most sources employed in one story was 36. At the other extreme, 21 stories contained only one source. The 1,022 sources were not evenly distributed across the four media. As one might expect, the newspapers used more sources than did the broadcasts. About 45% (465) of the total number of sources cited in the four media appeared in the New York *Times.* See Table 9-1.

Table 9-1   **Frequency of Stories and Sources, by Medium**

| | Medium | | | | |
	Times	*Journal*	*Newsweek*	CBS	Total
Total stories	89	37	18	23	167
Total sources	465	257	189	111	1022
Mean sources per story	5.3	6.9	10.5	4.8	6.1
Maximum sources per story	36	22	31	15	36
Minimum sources per story	1	1	2	1	1

Sources did not speak much of causes. Four of five sources made no mention of causes of the crash, and only 2% of the sources quoted in a story cited more than one reason. The most commonly mentioned cause of the crash, cited by 21% of the sources, was the national debt, followed by computerized trading practices. See the last column of Table 9-2.

Sources talked considerably more about effects of the crash than they did causes. Four in 10 sources mentioned an effect of the crash.[13] Fifteen percent of the sources said the crash demonstrated the need for partisan cooperation to deal with the crisis, another 13% of the sources said they still were uncertain whether the crash would have serious effects or not, and 10% said the crash disproportionately would affect the health of small business. See the last column of Table 9-3.

Did sources with certain organizational affiliations tend to cite causes only, effects only, both or neither? We found that some sources with other organizational affiliations tended to mention effects but not causes. None of the lobbyist sources, nearly all representing business groups,[14] and only 9% of the business sources gave a cause for the crash, far less than any other groups. See the last row of Table 9-2. However, these lobbyist and business sources cited effects considerably more than did any other groups, 71% and 68%, respectively. See the last row of Table 9-3.

Table 9-2 shows that the organizational affiliation was related to causes cited. Business sources blamed the crash heavily on interest rates and, to a lesser extent, the national deficit. They also pointed to a generally "sick" economy, with no more specific cause mentioned. These sources also said the cause of the crash was unknown or uncertain. A quarter of them cited reasons for the crash other than the 14 we categorized.

Spreading the Blame

Government sources heavily blamed the crash on the national deficit and, to a lesser extent, computerized trading practices. Government

Table 9-2   **Causes of Crash Cited, by Source (percent)**

Cause[a]	Source						
	Business $N=8$	Government $N=45$	Academic $N=15$	Wall Street $N=85$	Foreign $N=10$	Unspecified $N=31$	Total $N=194$
Deficit	13	38	20	15	30	13	21
Computer	0	16	0	22	0	16	16
Trade	0	7	0	13	50	7	11
Interest	25	7	0	12	0	16	10
Unspecific	0	4	20	9	0	3	7
Policy	0	7	7	2	10	13	6
Unknown	25	7	20	2	0	0	5
Overvaluation	0	4	7	7	0	0	5
Partisan	0	7	7	2	0	7	4
Economy	13	0	0	1	0	0	1
Inequity	0	0	13	0	0	0	1
Speculation	0	0	0	0	0	3	1
Other cause	25	4	7	13	10	23	12
Total	9	31	20	17	28	18	20

Note: Cell entries are the percentages of the total number of causes cited by each source type. (No lobbyist source cited a cause of the crash.)

[a] The 13 causes are: 1) the national debt; 2) computerized trading practices; 3) the trade deficit; 4) interest rates; 5) unspecified causes: source says there are definite causes but leaves them unspecified; 6) presidential policy; 7) unknown or uncertain causes; 8) market overvaluation; 9) partisan politics; 10) a sick economy, with no more specific cause mentioned; 11) unequal wealth distribution; 12) wild speculation; and 13) other miscellaneous causes not listed above.

sources spread some of the blame over many of the other causes, as well, and only 4% cited reasons other than those we categorized.

Academic sources also cited a large number of reasons for the crash and they alone mentioned inequity in distribution of wealth as a cause. Sources identified only as from "Wall Street" without any more specific organizational affiliation heavily blamed computerized trading practices for the crash but they also spread the blame among a large number of sources, especially the national debt, the trade deficit, and lower interest rates.

Table 9-3 shows that the organizational affiliations of sources also makes a difference in what effects, if any, they cited. Many business sources were not sure if the crash would have serious effects but many said small business would suffer, and many others said real estate would suffer.

Forty percent of the government sources stated that the crash would prompt more cooperation between the President and Congress. Academic

Table 9-3   Effects of Crash Cited, by Source (percent)

Effect[a]	Business N=61	Government N=68	Academic N=39	Wall Street N=167	Lobby N=5	Foreign N=8	Unspecified N=48	Total N=396
				Source				
Partisan cooperation	2	40	13	11	0	25	15	15
Uncertainty	25	6	10	11	40	0	15	13
Small business hurt	23	2	10	9	0	0	15	10
Economic decline	5	6	8	10	0	13	15	9
Confidence down	8	3	26	8	0	0	4	8
Economic strictures	0	9	5	4	20	13	4	5
Speedy stabilization	2	7	0	7	0	0	2	5
Real estate hurt	16	0	0	2	20	0	4	4
Unspecified	2	6	0	1	20	0	2	2
Need taxes	0	6	0	1	0	0	2	2
Crash won't spread	0	2	5	1	0	0	2	1
Small investor shy	0	0	0	2	0	0	2	1
Other effect	18	15	23	34	0	50	19	25
Total	68	47	52	34	71	22	27	39

Note: Cell entries are the percentages of the total number of effects cited by each source type.

[a] The 13 effects are: 1) partisan cooperation: the crash will make national leaders cooperate more on economic matters; 2) uncertain effects: the crash may or may not have serious effects—we'll have to wait and see; 3) small business hurt: the crash will adversely affect small businesses; 4) economic decline: the general economy will worsen; 5) confidence down: public and investor confidence is or will be down; 6) economic stricture: constraints on the economy (e.g., credit tightening) will be instituted; 7) speedy stabilization: the crash was just a glitch in a generally sound stock market and the economy therefore quickly will stabilize or already has stabilized; 8) real estate hurt: real estate will be adversely affected; 9) unspecified effects: the crash may or may not have serious effects—we'll have to wait and see; 10) need taxes: the crash demonstrated the need for a wealth tax or other taxes; 11) crash won't spread: the crash was a serious market downturn, but it will not spread much thanks to market safeguards; 12) small investor shy: small investors will shy away from the market; and 13) other miscellaneous effects not listed above.

sources most often said the crash meant lower public and investor confidence and a consequent decrease in consumer spending, and a fair number

Table 9-4   Source Affiliations, by Medium (percent)

	Medium				
Source	Times N=465	Journal N=257	Newsweek N=189	CBS N=111	Total N=1,022
Business	9	7	9	12	9
Government	9	13	22	23	14
Academic	9	5	10	2	7
Wall Street	52	65	38	12	48
Lobby	0	1	2	0	1
Foreign	4	1	5	7	4
Unspecified	17	7	15	44	17

Note: Cell entries are the percentages of the total number of source types cited by the media.

also cited effects beyond those we categorized.

Since these are census data, sampling error is not relevant and a test of the statistical significance of the differences across these tables is inappropriate.[15]

Since sources with different organizational affiliations commented on different aspects of the crash (i.e., causes or effects), and made different comments about the causes and effects of the crash, the question emerges: Did different media rely on sources with different organizational affiliations? The answer is "yes." As Table 9-4 shows, the three print media relied heavily on sources whose organizational affiliation was given only as "Wall Street" (which included but were not limited to brokers, traders, and investors). In contrast, the CBS Evening News relied much less heavily on Wall Street sources and more heavily than the other media on government sources. *Newsweek,* however, also relied heavily on government sources, more so than did the newspapers. Academic sources were used rarely in the broadcasts and most heavily by *Newsweek.* Foreign sources were used most heavily by the network, which also used a large number of sources with organizational affiliations outside our categorization scheme.

Because sources with different organizational affiliations made different comments about the crash, and because the four media differed in the organizational affiliations of the sources they used, it follows that the messages in the different media about the crash's causes and effects should differ. This, in fact, was the case.

The most cited cause for the crash in three of the media was the national debt. For the *Journal,* however, that was one of the least cited causes; the

Table 9-5   Mentions of Causes of Crash, by Medium (percent)

	Medium				
Cause[a]	*Times* N=92	*Journal* N=47	*Newsweek* N=40	CBS N=15	Total N=194
Deficit	24	6	22	47	21
Computer	15	23	15	0	16
Trade	7	19	13	7	11
Interest	12	13	8	0	10
Unspecific	12	4	3	0	7
Policy	0	2	20	13	6
Unknown	4	13	0	0	5
Overvaluation	5	4	5	0	5
Partisan	7	0	0	13	4
Economy	0	0	3	2	1
Inequity	2	0	0	0	1
Speculation	0	0	0	7	1
Other cause	12	13	13	13	13
Total	47	24	21	8	100

Note: Cell entries are the percentages of the total number of causes cited by sources in each medium.

[a] The 13 causes are: 1) the national debt; 2) computerized trading practices; 3) the trade deficit; 4) interest rates; 5) unspecified causes: source says there are definite causes but leaves them unspecified; 6) presidential policy; 7) unknown or uncertain causes; 8) market overvaluation; 9) partisan politics; 10) a sick economy, with no more specific cause mentioned; 11) unequal wealth distribution; 12) wild speculation; and 13) other miscellaneous causes not listed above.

most cited cause in the *Journal* was computerized trading practices, followed by the trade deficit. The second leading cause of the crash, according to the *Times* sources, was computerized trading practices. According to the Evening News sources, it was presidential policy-making and partisan politics (a tie), and according to *Newsweek* sources, it was presidential policy-making. The sources also differed considerably in the diversity of opinion expressed about the causes. The Evening News sources made no mention of half of the causes of the crash. By contrast, the *Times* made mention of all three. See Table 9-5.

A similar pattern emerges in the citation of crash effects. The *Times* and the *Journal* sources most often cited uncertainty about the effects of the crash. *Newsweek* and the Evening News, however, cited partisan cooperation most often as an effect. That was the second-most mentioned effect of the crash in the *Times*. The second most-cited effect in the *Journal* was a general economic decline. According to *Newsweek* sources, it would be eco-

Table 9-6   **Mentions of Effects of Crash, by Medium (percent)**

Effect[a]	Medium				
	Times N=92	Journal N=47	Newsweek N=40	CBS N=15	Total N=194
Partisan cooperation	15	8	18	24	15
Uncertainty	16	17	4	9	13
Small business hurt	9	7	8	10	8
Economic decline	8	9	11	7	9
Confidence down	9	7	8	10	8
Economic strictures	3	0	17	0	5
Speedy stabilization	4	7	6	0	5
Real estate hurt	5	7	3	0	4
Unspecified	1	1	5	3	2
Need taxes	2	0	1	2	2
Crash won't spread	1	5	0	0	1
Small investor shy	2	0	0	0	1
Other effect	30	9	24	32	25
Total	46	19	20	15	100

Note: Cell entries are the percentages of the total number of effects cited by sources in each medium.

[a] The 13 effects are: 1) partisan cooperation: the crash will make national leaders cooperate more on economic matters; 2) uncertain effects: the crash may or may not have serious effects—we'll have to wait and see; 3) small business hurt: the crash will adversely affect small businesses; 4) economic decline: the general economy will worsen; 5) confidence down: public and investor confidence is or will be down; 6) economic stricture: constraints on the economy (e.g., credit tightening) will be instituted; 7) speedy stabilization: the crash was just a glitch in a generally sound stock market and the economy therefore quickly will stabilize or already has stabilized; 8) real estate hurt: real estate will be adversely affected; 9) unspecified effects: the crash may or may not have serious effects—we'll have to wait and see; 10) need taxes: the crash demonstrated the need for a wealth tax or other taxes; 11) crash won't spread: the crash was a serious market downturn, but it will not spread much thanks to market safeguards; 12) small investor shy: small investors will shy away from the market; and 13) other miscellaneous effects not listed above.

nomic strictures, and according to the Evening News the crash would result in a decline in public confidence and the suffering of small business (a tie). Again, the diversity of opinions expressed about the effects of the crash was lowest on the Evening News and highest in the *Times*. Sources on the Evening News made no mention of five possible effects of the crash; the *Times* mentioned them all. See Table 9-6.

Discussion

Since sources with different organizational affiliations said different things about the causes and effects of the crash, and since the media varied in their use of these sources, it is reasonable to ask whether audiences received a different picture of the causes and effects of the crash, depending upon the medium they relied on.

One of the more compelling findings of this study is the difference in the use of sources by the print media and the broadcast network. Table 9-4 confirms the fact that television relies more heavily on unattributed sources. Of those CBS sources with specified affiliations, which presumably were considered more important than sources left unspecified, government officials accounted for 23%. Table 9-5 shows the consequences of this reliance. Sources on CBS cited substantially different reasons for the crash than those in the print media. For example, the deficit was mentioned on CBS twice as much as in the other media, and CBS sources missed the computer angle entirely. These data appear to support the charge that television news, relative to the print media, presents superficial coverage using easily accessible, routine sources.

The notion then that the national media are all alike in the message they convey is contradicted here. The media give their audiences the same "story"—all the media extensively covered the crash—but that story differed significantly in sources used—and therefore in emphasis. . . .

Notes

1. Of course, journalists do not always reveal their sources. However, in this study we confine ourselves to examining identified sources.
2. Jude Wanniski, *The 1988 Media Guide* (Morristown, N.J.: Polyconomics, Inc., 1988) p. 21.
3. Tim Metz, *Black Monday: The Catastrophe of October 19, 1987 . . . and Beyond* (New York: William Morrow, 1988).
4. Herbert Gans, *Deciding What's News* (New York: Vintage, 1979), p. 116.
5. Harvey Molotch and Marilyn Lester, "News as Purposive Behavior: On the Strategic Use of Routine Events, Accidents and Scandals," *American Sociological Review*, 39:101-112 (1974).
6. Gans, *op. cit.*, p. 119.
7. Leon V. Sigal, *Reporters and Officials: The Organization and Politics of*

Newsmaking (Lexington, Mass: D. C. Heath, 1973).

8. Stephen Reese and Lucig Danielian, "Inter-Media Influence and the Drug Issue: Converging on Cocaine," in P. Shoemaker, ed., *Communication Campaigns About Drugs: Government, Media and the Public.* (Hillsdale, N.J.: Erlbaum, 1988).

9. Lucig Danielian and Stephen Reese, "A Closer Look at Inter-Media Influences on the Agenda-Setting Process: The Cocaine Issue of 1986," in P. Shoemaker, *op. cit.*

10. David C. McClelland and J. W. Atkinson, "The Projective Expression of Needs: I. The Effect of Different Intensities of the Hunger Drive on Perception," *Journal of Psychology*, 25:205-22 (1948).

11. H. H. Toch and R. Schulte, "Readiness to Perceive Violence as a Result of Police Training," *British Journal of Psychology*, 52:389-93 (1961).

12. Albert H. Hastorf and Hadley Cantril, "They Saw a Game: A Case Study," *Journal of Abnormal and Social Psychology*, 49:129-34 (1954).

13. Only 2 percent of the sources in a story gave more than one effect, and only 1 percent of the 1,022 sources cited three effects.

14. Only seven sources were lobbyists; one was for a citizens group and the rest were business groups.

15. For a discussion of this point, see Earl Babbie, *The Practice of Social Research*, Third Edition (Belmont, CA: Wadsworth Publishing Co., 1983), 426-7. Even though we dealt here with a census of stories, some researchers favor including statistical measures of significance as a guide for interpreting strengths of relationships. Most of our tables would have been considered statistically significant had we been dealing with a sample. The table numbers and associated Chi-square values and significance levels are as follows: Table 2, $X^2 = 121.6$, p is less than .01; Table 3, $X^2 = 170.8$, p is less than .001; Table 4, $X^2 = 163.6$, p is less than .001; Table 5, $X^2 = 83.0$, p is less than .001; Table 6, $X^2 = 125.5$, p is less than .001.

10

WHAT MOVES PUBLIC OPINION?

Benjamin I. Page, Robert Y. Shapiro,
and Glenn R. Dempsey

Editor's Note

Benjamin I. Page, Robert Y. Shapiro, and Glenn R. Dempsey believe that shortcomings in research design explain why many studies of media impact on public opinion do not detect substantial agenda-setting effects. The authors point out that most research designs focus on instant opinion formation about single events or classes of events, rather than opinions produced over longer periods of time by a multiplicity of media stimuli. Investigators seldom develop baselines that would allow them to assess opinions prior to news exposure. In cross-sectional studies, control groups are rarely as free from media exposure as the research demands. When the potency of media stimuli is measured, researchers usually fail to analyze the appeal of stories, their manner of presentation, and the sources who transmit the news.

Choosing a more realistic design, the authors examine media impact on a variety of opinions about public policy issues before and after audiences have been exposed to a wide range of news stories. The initial opinion and the pre-poll news stories furnish the baseline by which changes in opinion can be accurately assessed. To judge which factors make stories influential, stories were classified according to different content and format features that have a bearing on salience, credibility, and appeal. The findings reported in the essay demonstrate clearly that television news affects citizens' opinions about public policy issues. The influence varies, depending on the sources who advocate particular policies. News commentators' views were most influential, ranking ahead of the views of experts and high officials, such as popular presidents. Television news commentators have become powerful agenda setters for national public opinion.

At the time of writing, Page was the Frank C. Erwin, Jr., Centennial Professor of Political Science at the University of Texas at Austin; Shapiro was assistant professor of political science at Columbia University; Dempsey was a graduate student in political science at the University of Chicago. The selection comes from "What Moves Public Opinion?" American Political Science Review 81:1 (March 1987): 23-43. Several tables and notes have been omitted.

Rational Citizens and the Mass Media

. . . [N]ew information that modifies relevant beliefs can change the expected utility of policies for citizens. This should occur if five conditions are met: if the information is (1) actually received, (2) understood, (3) clearly relevant to evaluating policies, (4) discrepant with past beliefs, and (5) credible. (For related views of attitude change, see Jaccard 1981; Zaller 1985.)

When these conditions are met to a sufficient extent, new information should alter an individual's preferences and choices among policies. Further, if the conditions are met in the same way for many individuals, there may be a change in collective public opinion that shows up in opinion polls. For example, if many citizens' policy preferences depend critically on the same belief (e.g., "We must spend more on national defense because the Russians are overtaking us") and if highly credible, well publicized new information challenges that belief (e.g., U.S. military spending is reported to rise sharply and a CIA study concludes that Soviet spending has changed little since 1976), then enthusiasm for increased military spending may drop.

Since most people have little reason to invest time or effort learning the ins and outs of alternative policies (Downs 1957), we would not expect new information ordinarily to produce large or quick changes in public opinion. Indeed the evidence indicates that aggregate public opinion about policy is usually quite stable (Page and Shapiro 1982).

By the same token, however, for whatever they do learn about politics, most people must rely heavily upon the cheapest and most accessible sources: newspapers, radio, and television, especially network TV news. When news in the media reaches large audiences and meets our five conditions for many individuals, we would expect public opinion to change.

Television news often meets the exposure condition. Most U.S. families own television sets, and most tune in to network news broadcasts from time to time. Viewers may wander in and out; they may eat or talk or be distracted by children; but every day millions of U.S. citizens catch at least a glimpse of the major stories on TV news. Others see the same stories in newspaper headlines or get the gist of the news from family and friends. Over a period of weeks and months many bits and pieces of information accumulate.

The conditions of comprehension and relevance, too, are often met. The media work hard to ensure that their audiences can understand. They shorten, sharpen, and simplify stories, and present pictures with strong visual impact so that a reasonably alert grade-schooler can get the point.

Often stories bear directly upon beliefs central to the evaluation of public policies.

Credibility is a more complicated matter. Rational citizens must sometimes delegate the analysis or evaluation of information to like-minded, trusted agents (Downs 1957, 203-34). The media report the policy-relevant statements and actions of a wide variety of actors, from popular presidents and respected commentators, to discredited politicians or self-serving interest groups. News from such different *sources* is likely to have quite a range of salience and credibility, and therefore quite a range of impact on the public (see Hovland and Weiss 1951-52). The analysis of effects on opinion should allow for such variation.

News may also vary greatly in the extent to which it is or is not discrepant with past beliefs. If it closely resembles what has been communicated for many months or years, if it simply reinforces prevalent beliefs and opinions, we would not expect it to produce change. If, on the other hand, credible new information calls into question key beliefs and opinions held by many people, we would expect changes in public opinion. The extent of discrepancy with past news and past opinions must be taken into account.

We are, of course, aware of the curious notion that the contents of the mass media have only minimal effects (Chaffee 1975; Klapper 1960; Kraus and Davis 1976; McGuire 1985; but cf. Graber 1984; Noelle-Neumann 1973, 1980, 1984; Wagner 1983). This notion seems to have persisted despite findings of agenda-setting effects upon perceptions of what are important problems (Cook, Tyler, Goetz, Gordon, Protess, Leff, and Molotch 1983; Erbring, Goldenberg, and Miller 1980; Funkhauser 1973; Iyengar, Peters, and Kinder 1982; McCombs and Shaw 1972; MacKuen 1981, 1984).

We believe that the minimal effects idea is not correct with respect to policy preferences, either. It has probably escaped refutation because of the failure of researchers to examine collective opinion over substantial periods of time in natural settings and to distinguish among news sources. One-shot quasi-experimental studies (e.g., of presidential debates) understandably fail to find large, quick effects. Cross-sectional studies seek contrasts between media attenders and media "nonattenders" that hardly exist: nearly everyone is exposed either directly or indirectly to what the media broadcast (see Page, Shapiro, and Dempsey 1985a, 2-4). A more appropriate research design yields different results.

Data and Methods

Taking advantage of a unique data set in our possession, we have carried out a quasi-experimental study that overcomes several of the limitations of previous research. The design involved collecting data from many pairs of identically repeated policy preference questions that were asked of national survey samples of U.S. citizens; coding TV news content from broadcasts aired in between (and just before) each pair of surveys; and predicting or explaining variations in the extent and direction of opinion change by variations in media content.

Our design facilitated causal inferences and permitted comparison across types of issues and historical periods. The use of natural settings meant that all real world processes could come into play, including major events and actions, the interpretation of news by commentators and others, and the dissemination of information through two-step or multiple-step flows and social networks (cf. Katz and Lazarsfeld 1965). The examination of moderately long time periods (several weeks or months) allowed enough time for these natural processes to work and for us to observe even slow cumulative opinion changes. In addition, our measurement scheme permitted us to distinguish among different sources of news and to take into account the extent of news story relevance to policy questions, the degree of discrepancy between current and previous media content, and the credibility of news sources.

As part of our ongoing research project on public opinion and democracy, we have assembled a comprehensive collection of survey data on U.S. citizens' policy preferences. It includes the marginal frequencies of responses to thousands of different policy questions asked by various survey organizations since 1935. Among these data we have identified several hundred questions that were asked two or more times with identical (verbatim) wordings, by the same survey organization. (For a partial description, see Page and Shapiro 1982, 1983a.)

For the present research we selected 80 pairs of policy questions from the last 15 years (for which TV news data are readily available) that were repeated within moderate time intervals averaging about three months.

These 80 cases are not, strictly speaking, a sample from the universe of policy issues or poll questions but (with a small number of exceptions) constitute either a random sample of the available eligible survey questions and time points for a given survey organization or *all* the available cases from an organization. They are very diverse, covering many different kinds of foreign and defense ($n=32$) and domestic ($n=48$) policies. In nearly half the cases public opinion changed significantly ($p<.05$; 6 percentage points or more), and in a little more than half, it did not—nearly the same proportion as in our full data set of several hundred repeated items. A list of cases and a more detailed methodological discussion is available in Page, Shapiro, and Dempsey (1985a, b).

The dependent variable for each case is simply the level of public opinion at the time of the second survey (T2), that is, the percentage of the survey sample, excluding "don't know" and "no opinion" responses, that endorsed the most prominent (generally the first) policy alternative mentioned in the survey question. As will be seen, our method of using T2 level of opinion as the dependent variable and including first survey (T1) opinion as a predictor yields nearly identical estimates of media effects as does using a difference score—the magnitude and direction of opinion *change*—as the dependent variable.

For each of the 80 cases, we and our research assistants coded the daily television network news from one randomly selected network (in a few low-salience cases, *all* networks) each day, using the summaries found in the *Television News Index and Abstracts* of the Vanderbilt Television News Archive. These summaries, while rather brief and not intended for such purposes, were generally satisfactory in providing the fairly straightforward information we sought, especially since they were aggregated over several weeks or months. We coded all news stories that were at least minimally relevant to the wording of each opinion item, beginning two months before the T1 survey—in order to allow for lagged effects and for discrepancies or changes in media content—and continuing with every day up to T1 and through to the date of the T2 survey.

Being interested in the effects of particular actors or *sources*—particular providers of information, or Downsian "agents" of analysis and evaluation—whose rhetoric and actions are reported in the media, we distinguished among the original sources found in each news story. We used 10 exhaustive and mutually exclusive categories: the president; fellow partisans and members of his administration; members of the opposing party; interest groups and individuals not fitting clearly into any of the other categories; experts; network commentators or reporters themselves; friendly (or neutral) foreign nations or individuals; unfriendly foreign states or individuals; courts and judges; and objective conditions or events without clearly identifiable human actors (e.g., unemployment statistics, natural disasters, unattributed terrorist acts).

Our independent variables characterize *reported statements or actions by a specified source*. Each such *source story, or "message,"* constitutes a unit of analysis in measuring aggregate media content over the time interval of a particular case. For each reported statement or action by a particular source—each source story—we coded the following: 1) its degree of *relevance* to the policy question (indirectly relevant, relevant, or highly relevant); 2) its *salience* in the broadcast (its inclusion in the first story or not, its proximity to the beginning of the broadcast, its duration in seconds); 3) the pro-con *direction* of intended impact of the reported statement or action in relation to the most prominent policy alternative mentioned in the opinion item; 4) the president's popularity (measured by the standard Gallup question) as an indication of his *credibility* as news source at the time of his statement or action; and 5) some judgments—not used in this paper—concerning the quality of the information conveyed, including its logic, factuality, and degree of truth or falsehood.

The most important part of the coding effort concerned the directional thrust of reported statements and actions in relation to each opinion question. Proceeding a little differently from the method of our earlier work on newspapers (Page and Shapiro 1983b, 1984), we measured directional thrust in terms of the intentions or advocated positions of the speakers or actors themselves. We took considerable care in training and supervising coders and in checking the reliability of their work. We prepared detailed written instructions and held frequent group discussions of coding rules and the treatment of problematic cases. All pro-con coding decisions, and those on other variables central to our analysis, were validated by a second coder and also by one of the present authors, who made the final coding decisions.[1] We masked the public opinion data so that coders would not be affected in any way by knowledge of whether or how policy preferences changed; we gave them only the exact wording of each opinion item and the time periods to be examined, not the responses to the questions.

As a result of these efforts we are confident that very high quality data were produced. It proved rather easy to code reported statements and actions on a five-point directional scale with categories "clearly pro," "probably pro," "uncertain or neutral," "probably con," and "clearly con" in relation to the main policy alternative outlined in each opinion question.

For each type of news source in each opinion case, we summed and averaged all the numerical values of pro-con codes (ranging from $+2$ to -2, with 0 for neutral) in order to compute measures of total and average directional thrust of the news from each source. The sums and averages of directional codes for television news content prior to T1 and between T1 and T2—for all messages coming from all sources combined and for messages coming separately from each distinct source—constitute our main independent variables. Most of our analysis is based on measures restricted to "relevant" or "highly relevant" source stories because we found that inclusion of less relevant source stories weakened the observed relationships.

Our principal mode of analysis was ordinary least squares regression analysis, in which we estimated the impact of each news source (or all sources taken together) along with opinion levels at T1, upon the level of public opinion at T2. We analyzed all cases together and also each of our two independently selected subsets of 40 cases, as well as subsets of cases involving different kinds of issues (e.g., foreign versus domestic policies), different time periods, and different levels of source credibility (popular versus unpopular presidents).

After testing hypotheses and exploring the aggregate data, we closely examined individual cases of public opinion change, scrutinizing media-reported statements and actions and the precise sequence of events. This served two purposes. First, it helped us with causal inference, shedding light on possibilities of spuriousness or reciprocal influence. Second, it enabled us to generate some new hypotheses about effects on opinion by certain sets of actors not clearly differentiated in our aggregate data.

Findings

. . . News commentary (from the anchorperson, reporters in the field, or special commentators) between the T1 and T2 surveys is estimated to have the most dramatic impact. A single "probably pro" commentary is associated with more than four percentage points of opinion change! This is a startling finding, one that we would hesitate to believe except that something similar has now appeared in three separate sets of cases we have analyzed. It was true of editorial columns in our earlier analysis of 56 two-point opinion series using the *New York Times* as our media source (Page and Shapiro 1983b), in the first 40 TV news cases we collected (Page, Shapiro, and Dempsey 1984), and in the 40 new TV cases, which we analyzed separately before doing all 80 cases together.

We are not convinced that commentators' remarks in and of themselves have such great potency, however. They may serve as indicators of elite or public consensus (Hallin 1984; McClosky and Zaller 1984; Noelle-Neumann 1973, 1980). Or the commentaries may—if in basic agreement with official network sentiment or the attitudes of reporters (perhaps providing cues for reporters . . .) —indicate slants or biases in media coverage that are transmitted to citizens in ways that supplement the statements of the commentators. These could include the selection of news sources and quotes, the choice of visual footage, the questions asked in interviews, camera angles, and so forth.

Certain other estimated effects on opinion are probably important even though some do not reach the .05 level of statistical significance according to a conservative two-tailed test. . . . Most notably—and clearly significantly—a single "probably pro" story about experts or research studies is estimated to produce about three percentage points of opinion change, a very substantial amount. Presidents are estimated to have a more modest impact of about three-tenths of a percentage point per "probably pro" story, and stories about opposition party statements and actions may also have a positive effect.

There are indications, on the other hand, that interest groups and perhaps the courts (in recent years) actually have negative effects. That is, when their statements and actions push in one direction (e.g., when corporations demand subsidies or a federal court orders school integration through busing) public opinion tends to move in the opposite direction. We are not certain about the negative effect of courts, however, because of the instability of coefficients across data sets.

Certain kinds of news appear on the average to have no direct effect at all upon opinion, or less impact than might be expected. The president's fellow partisans, when acting independently of the president himself, do not appreciably affect opinion. Events may move public opinion indirectly, but they do not speak strongly for themselves. They presumably have their effects mainly through the interpretations and reactions of other news sources. The same applies to statements and actions from foreign countries or individuals, whether friends or foes. U.S. citizens apparently do not listen to foreigners directly but only through interpretations by U.S. opinion leaders.

The marked distinctions among types of news fits well with our idea that information from different sources has different degrees of credibility. It is quite plausible, for example, that the public tends to place considerable trust in the positions taken by network commentators and (ostensibly) nonpartisan experts. Some other sources may be considered irrelevant. Still others, like certain interest groups that presumably pursue narrowly selfish aims, may serve as negative reference points on public issues (see Schattschneider 1960, 52-53). Similarly, the federal courts may have served as negative referents in the 1970s and the early 1980s because of their unpopular actions on such issues as busing and capital punishment. In any case, it is clearly important to distinguish among sources of news. . . .

When presidents are popular, they tend (though the estimate falls short of statistical significance) to have a small positive effect on public opinion. Each "probably pro" statement or action is estimated to produce more than half a percentage point of opinion change. Part of the effect is undoubtedly temporary and part reciprocal. The impact presumably could not be multiplied indefinitely by talkative presidents because of potential saturation and overexposure of the reporters' and editors' desires for fresh topics to cover. Still, this constitutes some evidence that a popular president does indeed stand at a "bully pulpit." On an issue of great importance to him he can hammer away with repeated speeches and statements and can reasonably expect to achieve a 5 or 10 percentage point change in public opinion over the course of several months (see Page and Shapiro 1984).

Unpopular presidents, in contrast, apparently have no positive effect on opinion at all. They may try—like Glendower in *Henry IV*—to call spirits from the vasty deep, but none will come.

There are some indications that the effects of other news sources interact with presidential popularity. . . . [C]ommentaries may have their strongest effects when presidents are unpopular. Perhaps news commentators
substitute for a respected leader, challenging the one that is out of favor.
In addition, administration officials and the president's fellow partisans in
Congress and elsewhere, when acting independently of a popular president, appear to have a slightly negative impact on opinion, whereas they
may have positive effects when presidents are unpopular. The opposition
party, rather strangely, seems especially potent when presidents are popular. In short, there may be some substantial differences in the dynamics of
opinion change depending upon whether the president in office at a particular time is popular or not.

Discussion

Our examination of a number of specific cases of opinion change has
bolstered our general confidence in the aggregate findings. . . .

News Commentary

The most dramatic finding . . . is the strong estimated impact of news
commentary. Our examination of specific cases provides a number of instances in which the statements of news commentators and reporters
clearly parallel opinion change. Examples include Howard K. Smith's
praise for Nixon's policies and his criticism of calls for unilateral withdrawal from Vietnam in 1969; various newsmen's support for continued
slow withdrawal from Vietnam during 1969-70; commentary favoring conservation and increased production rather than stopping military aid to Israel in order to get cheap oil during 1974-75; Smith's and others' support
for more attention to the Arabs during 1974-75 and during 1977-78; Eric
Severeid's, David Brinkley's, and Smith's advocacy of campaign contribution limits in 1973; Brinkley's and Smith's backing of stricter wage and
price controls during 1972-73; John Chancellor's editorializing on the importance of fighting unemployment (versus inflation) in 1976; Smith's
support for federal work projects in 1976; and commentaries in the spring
of 1981 that Reagan's proposed tax cuts would benefit the wealthy.

   . . . We would not claim that individual news commentators like Howard
K. Smith—for all the esteem in which they are held—are, in themselves,
the biggest sources of opinion change (but cf. Freeman, Weeks, and
Wertheimer 1955). We do not believe that Walter Cronkite single-
handedly ended the Vietnam War with his famous soul-searching broadcast
in 1968.

   Instead, the commentary we have examined may reflect the positions of
many journalists or other elites who communicate through additional chan-

nels besides TV news or even a widespread elite consensus in the country (see McClosky and Zaller 1984). Or commentators' positions may be indicators of network biases, including subtle influences of reporters and editors upon the selection of news sources and upon the ways in which stories are filmed and reported. Or, again, commentators and other sources with whom they agree may (correctly or not) be perceived by the public as reflecting a climate of opinion or an emerging national consensus on an issue, which may weigh heavily with citizens as they form their own opinions (see Lippmann 1922; Noelle-Neumann 1973). With our present data, we cannot distinguish among these possibilities. But news commentators either constitute or stand for major influences on public opinion.

Experts

. . . [T]hose we have categorized as "experts" have quite a substantial impact on public opinion. Their credibility may be high because of their actual or portrayed experience and expertise and nonpartisan status. It is not unreasonable for members of the public to give great weight to experts' statements and positions, particularly when complex technical questions affect the merits of policy alternatives.

The existence of a reciprocal process, influence by public opinion upon experts, cannot be ruled out (particularly to the extent that the audience-seeking media decide who is an expert based on the popularity of his or her policy views), but it is probably limited in the short run because experts do not face immediate electoral pressures—that is, public attitudes may ultimately influence who are considered experts and what their basic values are, but once established, experts are less likely than presidents or other elected officials to bend quickly with the winds of opinion.

One striking example of the influence of expert opinion as reported in the media concerns the Senate vote on the SALT II arms limitation treaty. Public support for the treaty dropped 5.5% from February to March 1979 and 19% from June to November. During both periods many retired generals and arms experts spoke out or testified against the treaty, citing difficulties of verification and an allegedly unequal balance of forces favoring the Soviets.

Presidents

. . . [N]umerous cases support the inference that popular presidents' actions and statements reported in the media do affect public opinion. These include President Nixon's persistent opposition to accelerating U.S. troop withdrawals from Vietnam during 1969, 1970, and 1971; Reagan's 1981 argument for AWACS airplane sales to Saudi Arabia; Carter's 1977-78 increased attention to Arab countries; Carter's early 1980 movement (during a temporary peak in popularity) toward toughness in the Iranian hostage crisis; Reagan's 1982 bellicose posturing toward the Soviet Union; Ford's 1974-75 defense of military spending; Ford's 1976 and Carter's 1980 advocacies of cuts in domestic spending; and, perhaps, Nixon's 1972-73 support for wage and price controls.

On the other hand, as our regression results showed, unpopular presidents do not have much success at opinion leadership. In a number of cases unpopular presidents made serious efforts to advocate policies but failed to persuade the public. This was true of Ford's attempts to increase military spending in 1976 and his resistance to jobs programs and health and education spending in the same year. Jimmy Carter in early 1979, with his popularity at 43% approval and falling, failed to rally support for SALT II. Carter was also unsuccessful at gaining significant ground on gasoline rationing, the military draft, or the Equal Rights Amendment in 1979 and 1980. Even Ronald Reagan, when near a low point of popularity (44%) in mid-1982, failed to move opinion toward more approval of a school prayer amendment to the Constitution. Because this distinction between popular and unpopular presidents emerged clearly in our previous analysis of newspaper data (Page and Shapiro 1984), we are inclined to believe that it is real (though modest in magnitude) even though the popular president effect does not quite reach statistical significance. . . .

Interest Groups

Our regression analysis indicated that groups and individuals representing various special interests, taken together, tend to have a negative effect on public opinion. Our examination of the cases supports this point but also suggests that certain kinds of groups may have positive effects while others have negative impact.

We found many cases (more than 20) in which public opinion unequivocally moved *away* from positions advocated by groups and individuals representing special interests. In some cases the groups may have belatedly spoken up after public opinion had already started moving against their positions, producing a spurious negative relationship. But in many instances they seem actually to have antagonized the public and created a genuine adverse effect.

Such cases include Vietnam War protestors from 1969 to 1970, protestors against draft registration in 1980, and perhaps the nuclear freeze movement in 1982. U.S. citizens have a long history of opposition to demonstrators and protestors, even peaceful ones, and apparently tend not to accept them as credible or legitimate sources of opinion leadership. . . .

In general, the public apparently tends to be uninfluenced (or negatively influenced) by the positions of groups whose interests are perceived
to be selfish or narrow, while it responds more favorably to groups and
individuals thought to be concerned with broadly defined public interests.
The best examples of the latter in our data are environmental groups and
perhaps also general "public interest" groups like Common Cause.

From 1973 to 1974, for example, support for leasing federal land to oil
companies declined as TV news reported conservationists challenging the
positions of the profit-seeking and presumably less credible oil companies.
During the same period, support for a freeze on gasoline, heating, and
power prices increased a bit despite opposition by gas station owners and
oil companies.

Not only business corporations, but also some mass membership groups
representing blacks, women, the poor, Jews, and organized labor seem to
have been held in disrepute and to have had null or negative effects on
opinion about issues of direct concern to them, including social welfare
policies and some Middle East issues. . . .

Conclusion

We believe we have identified the main influences on short-term and
medium-term opinion change.

Our analysis does not offer a full account of certain glacial, long-term
shifts in public opinion that reflect major social, technological, and demographic changes such as rising educational levels, cohort replacement, racial
migration, or alterations in the family or the workplace. The decades-long
transformations in public attitudes about civil liberties, civil rights, abortion,
and other matters surely rest (at least in an ultimate causal sense) upon such
social changes. . . . If news reports play a part in such major opinion shifts,
they may do so mainly as transmitters of more fundamental forces.

Within the realm of short- and medium-term effects, however, we have
had striking success at finding out what moves public opinion. Our TV
news variables, together with opinion at the time of an initial survey, account for well over 90% of the variance in public opinion at the time of a
second survey. The news variables alone account for nearly half the variance in opinion change. . . .

The processes of opinion change are not simple. In order to account for
changes between two opinion surveys, for example, it is essential to examine media content before the first survey. *Discrepancies* between current
news and prior news (or prior opinion) are important. Part of the media
impact is temporary so that there is a tendency for opinion in the T1-T2
period to drift back, to move in a direction opposite to the thrust of the
media content prior to T1.

Moreover, it is important to distinguish among news *sources* rather than aggregating all media content together. The effects of news from different sources vary widely.

Among the sources we examined, the estimated impact of news commentary is strongest of all, on a per-story basis, though such messages are aired less frequently than those from other sources. The causal status of this finding, however, is uncertain. Commentary may be an indicator of broader influences, such as media bias in the selection and presentation of other news, of consensus among the U.S. media or elites generally, or of a perceived public consensus.

Experts, those perceived as having experience and technical knowledge and nonpartisan credibility, also have very sizable effects. A policy alternative that experts testify is ineffective or unworkable tends to lose public favor; an alternative hailed as efficient or necessary tends to gain favor.

We found that messages communicated through the media from or about popular presidents tend to have positive effects on opinion. Presidents respond to public desires, but they can also lead public opinion (see Page and Shapiro 1984). Active presidential effort can be expected to yield a 5- or 10-percentage point change in opinion over the course of a few months.

News commentators, experts, and popular presidents have in common a high level of credibility, which we believe is crucial to their influence on the public. Rational citizens accept information and analysis only from those they trust. In contrast, news sources with low credibility, such as unpopular presidents or groups perceived to represent narrow interests, generally have no effect, or even a negative impact, on public opinion.

Some of these findings might be thought to be limited to the recent period we studied, in which the public has relied heavily on TV and is better educated and more attentive to politics than U.S. citizens in the past. Our confidence in the generality of the findings, however, is bolstered by their consistency with our previous analysis (using newspaper stories) of opinion change from 1935 onward (see Page and Shapiro 1983b, 1984). This similarity also reinforces the observation that the national news media in the U.S. are very much of a piece. They all tend to report the same kinds of messages concerning public policy, from the same sources. This can be attributed to the norms and incentives—and the organizational and market structure—of the news industry and especially to the pervasiveness of the wire services (see Epstein 1973; Gans 1980; Roshco 1975). In this respect the contents of one medium is a good indicator of the content of many media.

In terms of our concerns about democratic theory, it is interesting to observe that relatively neutral information providers like experts and news commentators apparently have more positive effects (at least direct effects) than do self-serving interest groups. It is also interesting that popular presidents, who presumably tend to embody the values and goals of the public, are more able than unpopular ones to influence opinions about policy. These findings suggest that objective information may play a significant part in opinion formation and change and that certain of the more blatant efforts to manipulate opinion are not successful.

On the other hand, unobtrusive indirect effects by special interests—through influences on experts and commentators, for example—may be more dangerous than would be a direct clash of interests in full public view. Clearly there is much more to be learned before we can be confident about the fundamental sources of influence on public opinion. The same is true of judging the quality of information received by the public.

In order to judge to what extent the public benefits from constructive political leadership and education and to what extent it suffers from deception and manipulation, we need to examine the truth or falsehood, the logic or illogic, of the statements and actions of those who succeed at gaining the public's trust (see Bennett 1983; Edelman 1964; Miliband 1969; Wise 1973; contrast Braestrup 1983; Robinson 1976; Rothman 1979). This applies to the sources whose messages are conveyed through the media and to the media themselves. There is much to learn about whether various sources lie or mislead or tell the truth; about how accurately or inaccurately the media report what the sources say and do; and about the causes of any systematic distortions or biases in the selection and reporting of policy-related news.

Note

1. . . . Any disagreements about coding were resolved through meetings and discussion. Some reliability analysis was done, with Dempsey and Shapiro coding cases independently. Their intercoder reliability coefficients for the variables coded were in the .7 and .8 range. For the all-important pro-con codes, the two authors never disagreed by more than one unit on the 5-point scale.

References

Bennett, W. Lance. 1983. *News: The Politics of Illusion*. New York: Longman.

Braestrup, Peter. 1983. *Big Story*. New Haven, Conn.: Yale University Press.

Chaffee, Steven H. 1975. *Political Communication: Enduring Issues for Research*. Beverly Hills: Sage.

Cook, Fay Lomax, Tom R. Tyler, Edward G. Goetz, Margaret T. Gordon, David Protess, Donna R. Leff, and Harvey L. Molotch. 1983. Media and Agenda Setting: Effects on the Public, Interest Group Leaders, Policy Makers, and Policy. *Public Opinion Quarterly* 47:16-35.

Davis, James A. 1975. Communism, Conformity, Cohorts, and Categories: American Tolerance in 1954 and 1972-73. *American Journal of Sociology* 81:491-513.

Downs, Anthony. 1957. *An Economic Theory of Democracy.* New York: Harper.

Edelman, Murray. 1964. *The Symbolic Uses of Politics.* Urbana: University of Illinois Press.

Epstein, Edward J. 1973. *News from Nowhere.* New York: Random House.

Erbring, Lutz, Edie N. Goldenberg, and Arthur H. Miller. 1980. Front Page News and Real World Cues: A New Look at Agenda-Setting by the Media. *American Journal of Political Science* 24:16-49.

Freeman, Howard E., H. Ashley Weeks, and Walter J. Wertheimer. 1955. News Commentator Effect: A Study in Knowledge and Opinion Change. *Public Opinion Quarterly* 19:209-15.

Funkhauser, G. Ray. 1973. The Issues of the Sixties: An Exploratory Study in the Dynamics of Public Opinion. *Public Opinion Quarterly* 37:63-75.

Gans, Herbert J. 1980. *Deciding What's News.* New York: Vintage.

Graber, Doris A. 1984. *Mass Media and American Politics.* 2d ed. Washington, D.C.: Congressional Quarterly.

Hallin, Daniel C. 1984. The Media, the War in Vietnam, and Political Support: A Critique of the Thesis of an Oppositional Media. *Journal of Politics* 46:2-24.

Hovland, Carl I., and Walter Weiss. 1951-52. The Influence of Source Credibility on Communication Effectiveness. *Public Opinion Quarterly* 16:635-50.

Iyengar, Shanto, Mark D. Peters, and Donald R. Kinder. 1982. Experimental Demonstrations of the "Not-So-Minimal" Consequences of Television News Programs. *American Political Science Review* 76:848-58.

Jaccard, James. 1981. Toward Theories of Persuasion and Belief Change. *Journal of Personality and Social Psychology* 40:260-69.

Katz, Elihu, and Paul F. Lazarsfeld. 1965. *Personal Influence: The Part Played by People in the Flow of Communications.* Glencoe, Ill.: Free Press.

Klapper, Joseph T. 1960. *The Effects of Mass Communication.* Glencoe, Ill.: Free Press.

Kraus, Sidney, and Dennis Davis. 1976. *The Effects of Mass Communication on Political Behavior.* University Park: Pennsylvania State University Press.

Lippmann, Walter. 1922. *Public Opinion.* New York: Macmillan.

McClosky, Herbert, and John Zaller. 1984. *The American Ethos: Public Attitudes toward Capitalism and Democracy.* Cambridge, Mass.: Harvard University Press.

McCombs, Maxwell E., and Donald L. Shaw. 1972. The Agenda-Setting Function of the Mass Media. *Public Opinion Quarterly* 36:176-87.

McGuire, William J. 1985. The Myth of Mass Media Effectiveness: Savagings and Salvagings. In *Public Communication and Behavior,* ed. George Comstock.

MacKuen, Michael B. 1981. Social Communications and Mass Policy Agenda. In *More than News: Media Power in Public Affairs,* by Michael B. MacKuen and Steven L. Coombs. Beverly Hills: Sage.

MacKuen, Michael B. 1984. Exposure to Information, Belief Integration, and

Individual Responsiveness to Agenda Change. *American Political Science Review* 78:372-91.

Miliband, Ralph. 1969. *The State in Capitalist Society*. London: Quartet.

Noelle-Neumann, Elisabeth. 1973. Return to the Concept of Powerful Mass Media. In *Studies in Broadcasting*, ed. H. Eguchi and K. Sata, 67-112. Tokyo: The Nippon Hoso Kyokai.

Noelle-Neumann, Elisabeth. 1980. Mass Media and Social Change in Developed Societies. In *Mass Communication Review Yearbook*. Vol. 1, ed. G. Cleveland Wilhoit and Harold de Bock. Beverly Hills: Sage.

Noelle-Neumann, Elisabeth. 1984. *The Spiral of Silence*. Chicago: University of Chicago Press.

Page, Benjamin I., and Robert Y. Shapiro. 1982. Changes in Americans' Policy Preferences, 1935-1979. *Public Opinion Quarterly* 46:24-42.

Page, Benjamin I., and Robert Y. Shapiro. 1983a. Effects of Public Opinion on Policy. *American Political Science Review* 77:175-90.

Page, Benjamin I., and Robert Y. Shapiro. 1983b. The Mass Media and Changes in Americans' Policy Preferences: A Preliminary Analysis. Paper presented at the annual meeting of the Midwest Political Science Association, Chicago.

Page, Benjamin I., and Robert Y. Shapiro. 1984. Presidents as Opinion Leaders: Some New Evidence. *Policy Studies Journal* 12:649-61.

Page, Benjamin I., Robert Y. Shapiro, and Glenn R. Dempsey. 1984. Television News and Changes in Americans' Policy Preferences. Paper presented at the annual meeting of the Midwest Political Science Association, Chicago.

Page, Benjamin I., Robert Y. Shapiro, and Glenn R. Dempsey. 1985a. The Mass Media Do Affect Policy Preferences. Paper presented at the annual meeting of the American Association for Public Opinion Research, McAfee, N.J.

Page, Benjamin I., Robert Y. Shapiro, and Glenn R. Dempsey. 1985b. What Moves Public Opinion. Paper presented at the annual meeting of the American Political Science Association, New Orleans.

Robinson, Michael J. 1976. Public Affairs Television and the Growth of Political Malaise: The Case of "The Selling of the Pentagon." *American Political Science Review* 70:409-32.

Roshco, Bernard. 1975. *Newsmaking*. Chicago: University of Chicago Press.

Rothman, Stanley. 1979. The Mass Media in Post-Industrial Society. In *The Third Century: America as a Post-Industrial Society*, ed. Seymour Martin Lipset, 346-88. Stanford: Hoover Institution.

Schattschneider, E. E. 1960. *The Semisovereign People*. New York: Holt.

Wagner, Joseph. 1983. Media Do Make a Difference: The Differential Impact of the Mass Media in the 1976 Presidential Race. *American Journal of Political Science* 27:407-30.

Wise, David. 1973. *The Politics of Lying*. New York: Vintage.

Zaller, John. 1985. The Diffusion of Political Attitudes. Princeton University. Photocopy.

11

TELEVISION NEWS AND CITIZENS' EXPLANATIONS OF NATIONAL AFFAIRS

Shanto Iyengar

Editor's Note

Most studies of agenda setting involve content analysis of news media and interviews with media audiences to assess the extent to which they share the priorities reflected in news content. By contrast, Shanto Iyengar controls the news to which respondents in his laboratory experiments are exposed so that he can measure effects more accurately. The drawback in laboratory studies is making artificial situations totally realistic.

Iyengar's study sheds light on an important aspect of agenda setting—the power of newspeople to present news in various contexts and, in the process, to suggest various types of causes for the happenings. In turn, the causes of a situation suggest what the appropriate remedies might be. Like other agenda-setting studies, the findings reported here demonstrate that media influence varies depending on the subject matter and on extraneous political conditions.

At the time of publication, Iyengar was associate professor of political science at the State University of New York, Stony Brook. The article is part of a large research project reported in Shanto Iyengar and Donald R. Kinder, News That Matters: Television and American Opinion *(Chicago: University of Chicago Press, 1987). The selection comes from "Television News and Citizens' Explanations of National Affairs,"* American Political Science Review *81:3 (September 1987): 815-31. Several tables have been omitted.*

Explanations as Knowledge

Explanation is an essential ingredient of human knowledge. To explain events or outcomes is to understand them: to transform the "blooming, buzzing confusion" of today's world into orderly and meaningful patterns. Psychological research has demonstrated that causal relationships feature

Reprinted by permission of the author and the American Political Science Association.

prominently in individuals' perceptions of social phenomena (Nisbett and Ross 1980; Weiner 1985). In fact, causal thinking is so ingrained in the human psyche that we even invent causation where none exists, as in purely random or chance events (see Langer 1975; Wortman 1976).

Explanatory knowledge is important to political thinking for two reasons. First, answers to causal questions abound in popular culture, making the task of explanation relatively inexpensive. One need not devour the pages of the *Wall Street Journal* or study macroeconomics to "know" why there is chronic unemployment. Second and more important, explanatory knowledge is connotative knowledge. To "know" that unemployment occurs because of motivational deficiencies on the part of the unemployed is relevant to our attitudes toward the unemployed and our policy preferences regarding unemployment. In other words, explanatory knowledge is usable knowledge. Simple factual knowledge, on the other hand (e.g., the current rate of unemployment), does not so readily imply political attitudes and preferences. It is not surprising, then, that opinions, attitudes, feelings, and behaviors in a multitude of domains are organized around beliefs about causation (for illustrative research, see Schneider, Hastorf, and Ellsworth 1979, chap. 2). . . .

Framing Effects in Political Explanation

When individuals engage in causal reasoning, their thinking processes are rarely systematic or exhaustive (see, for example, Kelley 1973). Virtually all forms of human judgment are infinitely labile, with outcomes hinging on a variety of circumstantial and contextual cues (for illustrative evidence, see Kahneman, Slovic, and Tversky 1982). The term *framing effects* refers to changes in judgment engendered by subtle alterations in the definition of judgment or choice problems. Tversky and Kahneman (among others), in a number of ingenious studies, have shown that choices between risky prospects can be profoundly altered merely by altering the description of the alternatives. Framing the prospects in terms of possible losses, for example, induces risk-seeking behavior while describing the identical prospects in terms of potential gains makes people risk averse (Kahneman and Tversky 1982, 1984; for illustrations of framing effects in consumer behavior, see Thaler 1980). In short, the invoking of different reference points triggers completely different strategies of choice or judgment.

Political explanation would seem a particularly promising real-world domain for the occurrence of framing effects. Political stimuli are generally remote from everyday life, and ordinary citizens are unlikely to have developed strong commitments to particular explanations; accordingly, one would expect citizens to be highly susceptible to political framing effects.

Because citizens must depend primarily upon the media for information about the political world, there can be no better vehicle for examining political framing effects than media news presentations in general and television news presentations in particular.[1] The evidence reported here indicates that, according to the manner in which television news frames national issues, individuals' explanations of these issues are altered. Moreover, by altering explanations of national issues, the media alter attitudes toward the incumbent president.

Method

Residents of the Three Village area of Brookhaven Township, Suffolk County, New York, participated in a series of studies described to them as investigations of "selective perception" of television newscasts. Individuals responded to newspaper advertisements offering $10 as payment. This procedure yielded samples that were approximately representative of the local area. . . .

Procedure

When participants arrived at the Media Research Laboratory, they completed an informed consent form and a short pretest questionnaire probing personal and political background variables. They then watched a 20-minute videotape containing seven news stories described as a representative selection of network news stories broadcast during the past six months. On average, each viewing session had two participants. The fourth story on the tape represented the experimental manipulation and, depending on the condition to which participants were assigned (randomly), they saw different coverage of poverty, unemployment, or terrorism. With the exception of the treatment story, the videotapes were identical.

Following viewing of the videotape, participants completed a lengthy posttest (individually, in separate rooms) that included the key questions probing their explanations for the target problem as well as other questions on their issue opinions, their perceptions of President Reagan's issue positions, their assessments of the president's overall performance, his competence and integrity, and his performance in specific domains. On completing the posttest, participants were paid and debriefed.[2]

Measures

I relied entirely on unstructured questions to get at participants' causal accounts. These questions, though unwieldy and coding intensive, are relatively nonreactive. Given the paucity of research into citizens' explanations of political issues, it would have been presumptuous for the researcher to define the appropriate causal categories. The approach was to let each individual choose his or her own categories, with no prompts whatsoever.

The posttest began by asking participants "When you hear or read about ___, what kinds of things do you think about? Please list as many thoughts as you have." Responses to this "thought-listing" question ranged widely. Nevertheless, it was possible to separate explanatory statements from other categories with a high degree of reliability.[3] Statements were coded as explanatory if they made reference to antecedent causes of the target issue either specifically ("If people would try harder to find work, we would all be better off") or vaguely ("Society screws the poor; the rich get richer, the poor poorer"). Later in the questionnaire, participants were asked to identify what they considered to be "the major causes of ___." The thought-listing method was designed to provide evidence on the spontaneity of causal reasoning; the "most-important-causes" question identifies the specific content of causal beliefs.

Study 1: Poverty

We established five experimental conditions. In the first condition *(national poverty)*, participants watched a news story that documented the increase in poverty nationwide and the significant reductions in the scope of federal social-welfare programs under the Reagan administration. In the second condition *(high unemployment)*, participants watched a story that juxtaposed the national unemployment rate with the size of the federal budget deficit. The three remaining conditions all framed poverty in terms of particular instances or victims of economic hardship. The first *(the high cost of heat)* portrayed two families unable to pay their heating bills. The second *(the homeless)* focused on homeless individuals—two black teenagers living on the streets of New York City, and a white couple forced to live in their car in San Diego.[4] Finally, the third case-study condition *(unemployed worker)* described the financial difficulties facing the family of an unemployed auto worker in Ohio. These case-study stories were edited so as to be entirely descriptive; the news stories simply presented the predicament of each victim.

Results

The results of the "thought-listing" procedure revealed quite clearly that causal attributions of poverty figure prominently in participants' store of information. Participants listed a total of 322 thoughts, of which 124 (39%) represented explanatory statements. The causes people cited most often fell into five categories—inadequate motivation, poor education and inadequate skills, welfare dependence, the economy in general, and governmental actions/inactions. Even allowing for the possibility that respondents may have thought of these antecedent factors only in a loose causal sense, it is still impressive that explanatory thoughts take precedence over evaluations or feelings. Respondents were much more likely to offer reasons for poverty than affective reactions.

Turning to the "most-important-causes" question, the categories of causes parallel perfectly those that emerged from the thought-listing question. . . . Participants were far from mystified by the question—a total of 189 causes were cited, for an average of 2.2 per person. Virtually every respondent mentioned at least one cause (98%), and their responses were remarkably homogeneous in that five categories accounted for almost all the responses (183 out of 189). . . .

. . . Causal beliefs were significantly molded by the manner in which the news framed poverty. After watching accounts of specific homeless people, participants were especially drawn to poor motivation or inadequate skills as causal factors. After watching the news story that documented trends in the national poverty rate and federal spending on social programs, participants were especially drawn to economic and governmental/societal factors. If we combine the two systemic response categories *(economy* and *government)*, the proportion of systemic attributions ranges from .33 in the *homeless* condition to .81 in the *high unemployment* condition. Conversely, the proportion of dispositional attributions *(motivation, skills,* and *culture)* ranges from a low of .17 in the *high unemployment* condition to a high of .69 in the *homeless* condition.

Framing poverty in terms of individual victims did not always draw individuals to dispositional accounts of poverty. The homeless, the unemployed, and those unable to afford heat all represent people facing economic difficulties, yet they elicit very different explanations of poverty. The type of victim makes a difference. While the homeless trigger personal or dispositional attributions, people unable to pay their utility bills elicit a preponderance of economic and societal attributions, with the unemployed worker falling in between, eliciting a relatively even mix of societal and dispositional attributions.

. . . [T]hese results drive home the point that explanations of poverty depend considerably upon the particular informational context in which poverty is encountered. When poverty is framed as a societal outcome, people point to societal or governmental explanations; when poverty is framed in terms of particular victims of poverty, particularly the homeless, people point instead to dispositional explanations.

To assess whether these framing effects withstand controls for built-in or chronic differences in causal beliefs, the analysis incorporated individuals' socioeconomic status, partisanship and approval of presidential performance, issue opinions, and degree of political involvement. It computed two indexes corresponding to the number of systemic *(governmental* and *economy)* and dispositional *(motivation, skills,* and *culture)* causes mentioned and subjected them to a multiple-regression analysis. . . .

The effects of the framing manipulations emerged relatively unscathed after taking into account longstanding individual differences in causal beliefs.[5] . . .

In sum, though causal knowledge is embedded in individuals' socioeconomic circumstances and partisan attitudes, media frames affect this knowledge independently of these antecedents. When the media direct individuals' attention to national outcomes, explanations for poverty become predominantly systemic; when the media point to particular instances of poor people, explanations for poverty become predominantly dispositional.

The final analysis assesses whether explanations for poverty spill over to evaluations of the president. Specifically, the question was whether individuals who understand poverty as a societal or governmental outcome are less apt to praise President Reagan's performance. In this analysis the reverse possibility must also be considered, since supporters of President Reagan systematically discount systemic causes when asked to account for poverty. . . .

Systemic explanations of poverty exerted powerful effects on participants' ratings of Reagan's overall performance even after controlling for the effects of partisanship, ratings of his performance in the specific issue areas of arms control, the budget deficit, and unemployment, assessments of his competence and integrity, and the reverse effects of his overall performance. . . .

Study 2: Unemployment

Three conditions were established, each providing a different perspective on unemployment. Two of the conditions were taken from the first study— *high unemployment* and *unemployed worker.* The former represents a systemic frame with the focus on the national unemployment rate, while the latter is a case study of a particular victim of unemployment. In between these two extremes was a third level of coverage describing the serious economic difficulties facing the U.S. steel industry. The expectation was that this presentation would trigger *the economy* as the dominant reference point. (Note that all three conditions featured the identical "lead-in" by the newscaster, who noted the persistence of high unemployment.) In all other respects, the procedures and method were identical to those of Study 1.

Results

As was the case with poverty, causal attributions were offered spontaneously. The 40 subjects listed a total of 110 thoughts on unemployment, of which 40 took the form of causal attributions. . . . [T]he framing manipulations had no impact on the relative prominence of economic (or any other) causes. In fact, explanations of unemployment stand in marked contrast to explanations of poverty. While the former is understood uniformly as a systemic problem regardless of the news frame, the latter is seen as having a mix of both systemic and dispositional causes, the precise composition of the mix being significantly influenced by media presentations.

Even though participants' causal beliefs were unaffected by the framing manipulation, these beliefs did carry over to evaluations of President Reagan. . . .

The more dispositional the attribution, the more positive the rating of President Reagan's overall performance. This effect was uncontaminated by any feedback from the Reagan performance ratings because ratings of Reagan's overall performance had no effect on the number of either dispositional or systemic causes for unemployment. Respondents who cited more systemic attributions did tend to be less supportive of the president, but this relationship did not quite attain conventional levels of statistical significance.

Study 3: Terrorism

The target issue in this study was terrorism. The stimulus event was the June 1985 hijacking of TWA Flight 847 and the subsequent hostage drama in Beirut. Following the release of the hostages, all three networks aired detailed recapitulations of the crisis. One such story (ABC's) was edited into three very different versions. The first condition *(U.S. role)* viewed the hijacking incident as a protest against the United States. The U.S. role in the region as the principal ally of Israel was noted as was the hijackers' demands that Israel release the Shiites being held prisoners. President Reagan was shown declaring that the U.S. would never concede to terrorists. The second condition *(local politics)* shifted the focus to the internal politics of Lebanon. The report traced the history of Amal, the Shiite organization holding the hostages, and described its political ideology and its efforts to gain a power base in Beirut. The third condition *(hostages released)* showed the hostages saying goodbye to each other prior to their release. Red Cross officials were interviewed regarding the state of the hostages' health and their treatment during captivity. The hostages were then shown arriving in Damascus. Finally, unlike the earlier studies, a control condition was added in which subjects saw no story on the target issue, that is, subjects watched the identical videotape without the story on the hijacking.

Results

As usual, participants were asked to list the things they thought about when they heard or read about terrorism. The 92 participants mentioned a total of 201 thoughts. Cause and effect were prominent in the thoughts listed. Many participants explicitly raised causal *inquiries* (e.g., "Why do people do things like this?"). Causal attributions were also frequent, the most common being dispositional—terrorists as fanatics, deranged extremists, and so on. Terrorism was also traced to situational causes including local political disputes, U.S. policy toward the Middle East, and the support provided terrorist groups by radical leaders such as Colonel Qaddaffi. Causal inquiries and attributions together accounted for 31% of all thoughts. All told, the distribution of responses to the thought-listing question maintained the pattern established in the first two studies, namely, that causal attributions (and questions) are offered spontaneously when individuals think about political issues.

What did participants consider to be the prime causes of terrorism, and to what degree were their causal attributions susceptible to framing effects? Three classes of attributions dominated responses to the "most-important-causes" question. *Dispositional* attributions trace terrorism to personal traits, particularly extremism, fanaticism, and a craving for recognition. *Situational* attributions cover characteristics of the immediate situation and range from general political instability, to governmental oppression, to poverty and injustice. *Policy* attributions encompass actions of the U.S. government, including support for Israel and opposition to the Arab or Palestinian cause, Israeli dominance, and concerted efforts (primarily by "communists") to weaken the U.S. These three broad categories accounted for 175 of the 198 causes mentioned.

. . . Dispositional attributions tended to be greatest in the *U.S. role* condition, followed closely by the condition in which there was no media frame *(hostages released)*. More in keeping with expectations, situational attributions were most frequent in the *local politics* condition (which differed significantly from the *U.S. role* and *hostages released* conditions). Contrary to expectations, individuals given no news of terrorism tended to attribute terrorism to situational rather than dispositional factors. Finally, framing the hijacking as an act of protest against the U.S. did raise the proportion of policy attributions.

. . . [P]articipants were asked to indicate (on a five-point scale) the degree to which they approved or disapproved of the president's performance in dealing with terrorism (this study did not include the question on the president's overall performance).

Both policy and dispositional attributions affected ratings of the president's performance, but in opposite directions. The greater the number of policy attributions, the more critical the terrorism performance rating. This effect was substantial, despite having been purged of the reciprocal influence of participants' evaluations of the president's performance. It was also independent of partisanship, issue opinions, race, gender, and a measure of political interest. The number of dispositional attributions also affected participants' ratings of the president's performance: the more dispositional one's understanding of terrorism, the more positive the rating. This effect, however, was noticeably weaker than that exerted by policy attributions.

To sum up, attributions for terrorism are influenced by the perspectives television news presentations impose on terrorist acts. When these acts are placed in the context of a local political situation, situational attributions predominate; when terrorism is framed as a protest against the U.S., policy and dispositional attributions come to the forefront of individuals' explanations. Finally, as was true for poverty and unemployment, explanations for terrorism are relevant to evaluations of the president, in this case to ratings of the president's performance in regard to terrorism.

Conclusion

People can and do explain the issues and events they encounter in the world of public affairs. These explanations are politically consequential, for they can be and are integrated with evaluations of the incumbent president. The more individuals attribute problems to structural or systemic causes, the more critical they are of President Reagan's performance.

Individuals are quite sensitive to contextual cues when they reason about national affairs. Their explanations of issues like terrorism or poverty are critically dependent upon the particular reference points furnished in media presentations. Whether terrorists are seen as protesting U.S. actions or as attempting to strengthen their political influence has the effect of invoking very different attributions of terrorism. Similarly, whether news about poverty takes the form of particular victims or of nationwide outcomes makes a difference to viewers' attributions of poverty.

The exception to this pattern is unemployment, where attributions are heavily systemic regardless of the media frame used. It may be that the term *unemployment* is itself a sort of semantic frame or wording effect that directs individuals to think of the concept as a collective rather than individual outcome. Asking people to explain "why John Smith was laid off" or "why so many Americans are out of work" may elicit a different set of attributions. Alternatively, the sustained prominence of economic problems in the nation's political rhetoric and policy agenda during the past decade may have served to alert individuals to *the economy* as a catchall cause for unemployment.

It is important to qualify these results by noting the short time interval between the experimental manipulation and the elicitation of participants' causal beliefs. The framing effects may wear off rapidly. As yet I have no evidence bearing on the question of persistence. However, the identical experimental design yielded significant delayed effects (up to a week following exposure to the treatment) on participants' responses to an open-ended question concerning "the most important problems facing the nation" (see Iyengar and Kinder 1987, chap. 3).

All told, these results suggest that it is important to document the degree to which particular media frames are more or less dominant in news coverage of current issues. To take the case of poverty, the tendency of the U.S. public to see the causes of poverty as lying within the poor themselves may be due not only to dominant cultural values like individualism and self-reliance (as argued by Feldman 1983; Kluegel and Smith 1986), but also to news coverage of poverty in which images of poor people predominate. This is in fact the case with television news coverage of poverty, where close-up depictions of personal experience far outnumber depictions of poverty that are societal or nationwide in emphasis. I have examined every story in the *CBS Evening News* from January 1981 through December 1985 that made reference to "welfare," "social programs," "poor people," "hunger," and other such referents of poverty. Ninety-eight stories contained material relevant to poverty, of which 56 (57%) presented a particular victim. The figure is actually higher if 1981 is excluded, since that was the year of the pitched battles between the Reagan administration and the Democratic Congress on appropriations for social programs, thus resulting in an abnormally high number of government-oriented poverty stories. For the 1982-85 period, the percentage of case study stories is 68. U.S. citizens who watched *CBS Evening News* during the period would, understandably, have been drawn to dispositional accounts of poverty, whatever social and economic values they subscribed to. At this point, I can only offer the pervasiveness of case-study coverage as a plausible cause of public beliefs. I do have evidence, however, that the degree to which particular issues are seen as *national* problems is significantly lowered when issue coverage takes the form of the "particular-victim" scenario. Specifically, Kinder and I found that when network news coverage of both pollution and unemployment focused on individuals or families adversely affected by either issue, viewers were less likely to come away believing that either pollution or unemployment were important national problems (Iyengar and Kinder 1987, chap. 4).

The political implications of the "particular-victim" media frame are unmistakable. Citizens' causal attributions will fix upon dispositional rather than structural factors. This is naturally beneficial to the incumbent president—people are less likely to treat the administration and its actions as causal agents. President Reagan's concern in 1982, at the height of the recession, that the networks were providing too much coverage of people who had lost their jobs ("Is it news that some fellow out in South Succo-

tash has just been laid off and that he should be interviewed nationwide?")
seems misplaced. In light of the results reported here, the White House
should encourage such coverage, for it has the effect of shielding the president from any culpability, deserved or otherwise. . . .

Notes

1. The focus on television news is justified, for it is the most preferred source of
   public-affairs information for the great majority of the U.S. public (see Bower
   1985).
2. In any experimental procedure it is imperative that the researcher guard
   against the effects of demand characteristics—cues in the experimental
   situation that suggest to participants what is expected of them. Several such
   precautions were undertaken including a plausible cover story that disguised
   the true purpose of the study. In addition, the treatment stories were compiled
   using studio-quality editing equipment so that participants could not know
   that the stories had been altered. Finally, the aura of the research laboratory
   was minimized by inviting participants to bring a spouse, friend, or colleague
   with them. Most did so and the average session size of two means that a
   participant typically watched the videotape with someone he or she knew. The
   concern over experimental demand also dictated the choice of a posttest-only
   design. Had I asked participants for their explanations of the target issue both
   before and after exposure to the videotape, this would have provided them
   with a powerful cue as to the researcher's intent, thereby affecting the posttest
   responses.
3. Responses fell into four general categories: explanations, prescriptions/
   remedies, descriptions, and expressions of affect. Using this four-fold classification, two independent coders agreed more than 90% of the time.
4. These were initially separate conditions, as we wished to investigate the
   effects, if any, of the victim's race. In this particular study, the two conditions
   elicited responses not significantly different. For purposes of this analysis,
   therefore, they were merged.
5. In this analysis and those that follow, the remaining attributional categories are
   included in the equation as control variables. This is because the number of
   causes falling into a particular category inevitably reduces the number falling
   into other categories.

12

CHARTING THE MAINSTREAM: TELEVISION'S CONTRIBUTIONS TO POLITICAL ORIENTATIONS

George Gerbner, Larry Gross, Michael Morgan, and Nancy Signorielli

Editor's Note

The authors contend that television entertainment programs mold the perceptions of reality held by "heavy viewers" (those who watch television four or more hours a day) in socially undesirable ways. Television buffs become hard-line conservatives on civil rights issues and put their personal economic well-being ahead of the public's economic welfare.

The selection reports findings from the Cultural Indicators project conducted since 1967 at the Annenberg School for Communication at the University of Pennsylvania. Investigators associated with the project have recorded and analyzed week-long samples of network television dramas each year to establish the kind of world pictured there. They call this approach "message system analysis." Then, in their "cultivation analysis," they have questioned viewers to assess to what degree their perceptions mirror either the television world or the real world, as measured by official records.

The authors compare three demographically matched categories of viewers: light viewers (25 percent), who watch less than two hours of television daily; heavy viewers (30 percent), who watch four or more hours daily; and an intermediate group of viewers (45 percent). The differences in views among these groups constitute the "cultivation differential."

Cultivation analysis findings have been challenged on methodological and philosophical grounds. Specifically, critics have alleged that viewers have been grouped improperly, that correlates of heavy television viewing have been ignored, and that the research team has misjudged the ways in which media audiences relate the media world to the real world. Still, the major point made by cultivation analysis remains intact: media images are noticeably reflected in public thinking.

At the time of writing, the authors were members of the Cultural Indicators research team at the Annenberg School for Communication at the University of

Pennsylvania. Senior author George Gerbner was dean of the Annenberg School. The selection is from Journal of Communication *32 (1982): 100-127. Several tables have been omitted.*

. . . Television is a centralized system of storytelling. Its drama, commercials, news, and other programs bring a relatively coherent world of common images and messages into every viewing home. People are now born into the symbolic environment of television and live with its repetitive lessons throughout life. Television cultivates from the outset the very predispositions that affect future cultural selections and uses. Transcending historic barriers of literacy and mobility, television has become the primary common source of everyday culture of an otherwise heterogeneous population.

Many of those now dependent upon television have never before been part of a shared national political culture. Television provides, perhaps for the first time since preindustrial religion, a strong cultural link, a shared daily ritual of highly compelling and informative content, between the elites and all other publics. What is the role of this common experience in the general socialization and political orientation of Americans? . . .

. . . Despite the fact that nearly half of the national income goes to the top fifth of the real population, the myth of [the] middle class as the all-American norm dominates the world of television. Nearly 7 out of 10 television characters appear in the "middle-middle" of a five-way classification system. Most of them are professionals and managers. Blue-collar and service work occupies 67 percent of all Americans but only 10 percent of television characters. These features of the world of prime-time television should cultivate a middle-class or "average" income self-designation among viewers.

Men outnumber women at least three to one. Most women attend to men or home (and appliances) and are younger (but age faster) than the men they meet. Underrepresentation in the world of television suggests the cultivation of viewers' acceptance of more limited life chances, a more limited range of activities, and more rigidly stereotyped images than for the dominant and more fully represented social and dramatic types.

Young people (under 18) comprise one-third and older people (over 65) one-fifth of their true proportion in the population. Blacks on television represent three-fourths and Hispanics one-third of their share of the U.S. population, and a disproportionate number are minor rather than major characters. A single program like "Hawaii Five-O" can result in the overrepresentation of Orientals, but again mostly as minor characters. A study by Wiegel and others (11) shows that while blacks appear in many programs and commercials, they seldom appear with whites, and actually interact with whites in only about two percent of total human appearance time. The prominent and stable overrepresentation of well-to-do white males in the prime of life dominates prime time. Television's general demography bears greater resemblance to the facts of consumer spending than to the U.S. Census (5, 6). These facts and dynamics of life suggest the cultivation of a relatively restrictive view of women's and minority rights among viewers.

The state in the world of prime time acts mostly to fend off threats to law and order in a mean and dangerous world. Enforcing the law of that world takes nearly three times as many characters as the number of all blue-collar and service worker characters. The typical viewer of an average week's prime-time programs sees realistic and often intimate (but usually not true-to-life) representations of the life and work of 30 police officers, 7 lawyers, and 3 judges, but only one engineer or scientist and very few blue-collar workers. Nearly everybody appears to be comfortably managing on an "average" income or as a member of a "middle class."

But threats abound. Crime in prime time is at least 10 times as rampant as in the real world. An average of five to six acts of overt physical violence per hour involves over half of all major characters. Yet, pain, suffering, and medical help rarely follow this mayhem. Symbolic violence demonstrates power; it shows victimization, not just aggression, hurt but not therapy; it shows who can get away with what against whom. The dominant white males in the prime of life score highest on the "safety scale": they are the most likely to be the victimizers rather than the victims. Conversely, old, young, and minority women, and young boys, are the most likely to be the victims rather than the victimizers in violent conflicts. . . .

The warped demography of the television world cultivates some iniquitous concepts of the norms of social life. Except among the most traditional or biased, television viewing tends to go with stronger prejudices about women and old people (5, 6, 7, 9). Children know more about uncommon occupations frequently portrayed on television than about common jobs rarely seen on the screen (1). Viewing boosts the confidence rating given to doctors (10) but depresses that given to scientists, especially in groups that otherwise support them most (4).

Cultivation studies continue to confirm the findings that viewing tends to heighten perceptions of danger and risk and maintain an exaggerated sense of mistrust, vulnerability, and insecurity. We have also found that the prime-time power hierarchy of relative levels of victimization cultivates similar hierarchies of fears of real-world victimization among viewers. Those minority group viewers who see themselves more often on the losing end of violent encounters on television are more apprehensive of their own victimization than are the light viewers in the same groups (8). Television's mean and dangerous world can thus be expected to contribute to receptivity to repressive measures and to apparently simple, tough, hard-line posturing and "solutions." At the same time, however, the overall context of conventional values and consumer gratifications, with their requirements of happy endings and material satisfaction, may suggest a sense of entitlement to goods and services, setting up a conflict of perspectives.

Thus we can expect the cultivation of preference for "middle-of-the-road" political orientations alongside different and at times contradictory, assumptions. These assumptions are likely to include demographically skewed, socially rigid and mistrustful, and often excessively anxious or repressive notions, but expansive expectations for economic services and material progress even among those who traditionally do not share such views. . . .

. . . [T]elevision alters the social significance and political meaning of . . . conventional labels. An example of this transformation is the blurring of class lines and the self-styled "averaging" of income differences. . . . [This] shows that low socioeconomic status (SES) respondents are most likely to call themselves "working class"—but only when they are light viewers. Heavy-viewing respondents of the same low-status group are significantly less likely than their light-viewing counterparts to think of themselves as "working class" and more likely to say they are "middle class." The television experience seems to counter other circumstances in thinking of one's class. It is an especially powerful deterrent to working-class consciousness.

Middle SES viewers show the least sense of class distinction at different viewing levels. They are already "in" the mainstream. The high SES group, however, like the low SES group, exhibits a response pattern that is strongly associated with amount of television viewing. . . . Television viewing tends to blur class distinctions and make more affluent heavy viewers think of themselves as just working people of average income.

These processes show up clearly when we relate television viewing to labels of direct political relevance. We used a relatively general and presumably stable designation of political tendency, most likely to structure a range of political attitudes and positions: the self-designations "liberal," "moderate," and "conservative." We are assuming that . . . most of us locate political positions on a continuum ranging from liberal to conservative (if not farther in either direction), owing in part to the generally accepted and commonplace use of these terms in interpersonal and mass media discourse. Consequently, unlike many things respondents might be asked about, we believe that these self-designations have a prior existence and are not created in response to the interview situation.

. . . The most general relationship between television viewing and political tendency is that significantly more heavy than light viewers in all subgroups call themselves moderates and significantly fewer call themselves conservatives. The number of liberals also declines slightly among heavy viewers, except where there are fewest liberals (e.g., among Republicans). [This] illustrates the absorption of divergent tendencies and the blending of political distinctions into the "television mainstream." [1]

On the surface, mainstreaming appears to be a "centering"—even a "liberalizing"—of political and other tendencies. After all, as viewing increases, the percent of conservatives drops significantly within every group (except Democrats), and the relationships of amount of television viewing with the percent of liberals are generally weaker. However, a closer look at the actual positions taken in response to questions about political issues such as minorities, civil and personal rights, free speech, the economy, etc., shows that the mainstream does not always mean "middle of the road." . . .

. . . [A]ssociations between amount of viewing and these attitudes are sharply different for liberals, moderates, and conservatives. Liberals, who are least likely to hold segregationist views, show some dramatic (and always significant) associations between amount of viewing and the desire to keep blacks and whites separate. Among moderates and conservatives, in contrast, the relationships between viewing and these attitudes are smaller and inconsistent. . . . On busing, moderates and conservatives even show a significant negative association, indicating *less* segregationist attitudes among these heavy viewers; this is an instance of viewing bringing divergent groups closer together from both directions.

In general, these patterns vividly illustrate mainstreaming. There are, to be sure, some across-the-board relationships, but even these are markedly weaker for moderates and conservatives. Overall, these data show a convergence and homogenization of heavy viewers across political groups.

The differences between liberals and conservatives—i.e., the effects of political tendency on attitudes toward blacks—decrease among heavy viewers. Among light viewers, liberals and conservatives show an average difference of 15.4 percentage points; yet, among heavy viewers, liberals and conservatives differ by an average of only 4.6 percentage points ($t=4.54$, $p<.01$).

Figure 12-1 shows the mainstreaming pattern for three of these items. In the first, opposition to busing, we can see that heavy-viewing conservatives are more "liberal" and heavy-viewing liberals more "conservative" than their respective light-viewing counterparts. In the second instance, opposition to open housing laws, viewing is not associated with any differences in the attitudes expressed by conservatives, but among liberals we see that heavy viewing goes with a greater likelihood of such opposition. Finally, in response to a question about laws against marriages between blacks and whites, we find that heavy viewers in all groups are more likely

Figure 12-1: Television Viewing and Attitudes about Blacks, by Political
Self-Designation

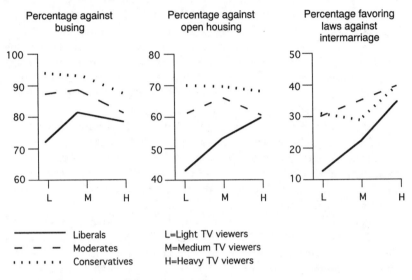

Percentage against
busing

Percentage against
open housing

Percentage favoring
laws against
intermarriage

L=Light TV viewers
M=Medium TV viewers
H=Heavy TV viewers

Liberals
Moderates
Conservatives

to favor these laws than are light viewers in the same categories, but this is significantly more pronounced for liberals.

In sum, the responses of heavy-viewing liberals are quite comparable to those of all moderates and conservatives, and there is not much difference between moderates and conservatives. The television mainstream, in terms of attitudes toward blacks, clearly runs to the right.

Many of the fiercest political battles of the past decade have been fought on the nation's "home front"—around a group of so-called moral issues which have sharply divided liberal and conservative forces. We find liberals confronting conservatives over the propriety, morality, and even legality of personal behavior. The fights involving reproductive freedom, the rights of sexual minorities, and the Equal Rights Amendment have become a focus of that confrontation.

. . . In the case of attitudes on homosexuality, abortion, and marijuana, there is considerable spread between light-viewing liberals and light-viewing conservatives (an average of 28 percentage points); the latter are always much more likely to be opposed. And, once again, the attitudes of heavy-viewing liberals and conservatives are far closer together (an average of 13 percentage points; t=16.6, p<.01), due primarily to the difference between light- and heavy-viewing liberals. . . . In all instances, the self-designated moderates are much closer to the conservatives than they are to the liberals. . . .

... [T]elevision's relationship to anti-Communist sentiments and to the tendency to restrict free speech ... shows the familiar pattern. ... Five out of ten light-viewing moderates and six out of ten light-viewing conservatives consider communism "the worst form [of government] of all." Heavy-viewing moderates and conservatives nearly unite in condemning communism as "worst" by even larger margins (64 and 67 percent, respectively). But viewing makes the biggest difference among liberals: only one-third of light-viewing but half of heavy-viewing liberals agree that communism is "the worst form" of government. ...

Responses on restricting free speech show similar patterns. Heavy viewers of all three political persuasions are more likely to agree to restrict, in various ways, the speech of "left" and "right" nonconformists than are their light-viewing counterparts. There is little difference between conservatives and moderates. But, again, the most striking difference is between light- and heavy-viewing liberals.

In general, with respect to anti-communism and restrictions on political speech of the left and right, those who call themselves conservatives are in the "television mainstream." Those who consider themselves moderates join the conservatives—or exceed them—as heavy viewers. Liberals perform their traditional role of defending political plurality and freedom of speech only when they are light viewers. Mainstreaming means not only a narrowing of political differences but also a significant tilt in the political balance.

But political drift to the right is not the full story. As we noted before, television has a business clientele which, while it may be politically conservative, also has a mission to perform that requires the cultivation of consumer values and gratifications pulling in a different direction.

A number of surveys have documented the tendency of respondents to support government services that benefit them while taking increasingly hard-line positions on taxes, equality, crime, and other issues that touch deeply felt anxieties and insecurities. The media interpreted (and election results seemed to confirm, at least in the early 1980s) these inherently contradictory positions as a "conservative trend" (2). Television may have contributed to that trend in two ways. First ..., heavy viewers have a keener sense of living in a "mean world" with greater hazards and insecurities than do comparable groups of light viewers (3, 8). Second, while television does not directly sway viewers to be conservative (in fact, heavy viewers tend to shun that label), its mainstream of apparent moderation shifts political attitudes toward conservative positions.

When positions on economic issues are examined, however, a different if perhaps complementary pattern emerges. ... We examined patterns of responses to questions about government spending on 11 programs. ...

Seven are traditional "liberal" issues: health, environment, cities, education, foreign aid, welfare, and blacks. . . .

Here, instead of heavy-viewing liberals taking positions closer to conservatives, the opposite happens: heavy-viewing conservatives, as well as moderates, converge toward the liberal position on six of the seven issues. The
more they watch, the less they say the U.S. spends "too much." On these
six issues, the average distance of 16 percentage points between liberal
and conservative light viewers is only 9 percentage points for heavy viewers, with conservatives accounting for most of the convergence ($t=8.2$,
$p<.001$). The exception is the relatively distant issue of foreign aid.

The remaining four issues are crime, drugs, defense, and space exploration. . . . Here again, with the exception of space, heavy viewers generally
want to spend more. As these are somewhat more "conservative" issues, it
is the moderates and conservatives who are in the "television mainstream," taking a position toward greater spending, and heavy-viewing liberals stand close to them. On these four issues an average liberal-conserva-
tive spread of nearly 10 percentage points for light viewers compares with
a gap of 4 percentage points among heavy viewers ($t=2.2$, $p<.12$).

To investigate further the populist streak in the otherwise restrictive
political mix of the typology of the heavy viewer, we looked for . . . respondents who oppose reductions in government spending and yet feel their
taxes are too high. . . . [H]eavy viewers are more likely to express this
contradictory position in every subgroup (although the relationship remains significant at $p<.05$ only overall and within six of these groups). . . .

As on the other economic issues, liberals and moderates are close together while heavy-viewing conservatives join the liberal-moderate mainstream; the tilt is in the liberal (if conflicted) direction. Heavy-viewing
Republicans and Independents also express attitudes closer to the Democratic position than do their light-viewing political counterparts. But all
heavy viewers are more likely to want a combination of more social spending *and* lower taxes. . . .

Our analysis shows that although television viewing brings conservatives,
moderates, and liberals closer together, it is the liberal position that is
weakest among heavy viewers. Viewing blurs traditional differences,
blends them into a more homogeneous mainstream, and bends the mainstream toward a "hard line" position on issues dealing with minorities and
personal rights. Hard-nosed commercial populism, with its mix of restrictive conservatism and pork-chop liberalism, is the paradoxical—and potentially volatile—contribution of television to political orientations.

The "television mainstream" may be the true twentieth-century melting
pot of the American people. The mix it creates is of central significance for
the theory as well as the practice of popular self-government. If our chart-

ing of the mainstream is generally valid, basic assumptions about political orientations, the media, and the democratic process need to be reviewed and revised to fit the age of television.

Note

1. . . . [T]his moderating effect seems to be a specific correlate of television viewing, and not a general media exposure phenomenon: neither radio listening nor newspaper reading are associated with similar results. . . .

References

1. DeFleur, Melvin L. and Lois B. DeFleur. "The Relative Contribution of Television as a Learning Source for Children's Occupational Knowledge." *American Sociological Review* 32, 1967, pp. 777-789.
2. Entman, Robert M. and David L. Paletz. "Media and the Conservative Myth." *Journal of Communication* 30(4), Autumn 1980, pp. 154-165.
3. Gerbner, George, Larry Gross, Michael Morgan, and Nancy Signorielli. "The 'Mainstreaming' of America: Violence Profile No. 11." *Journal of Communication* 30(3), Summer 1980, pp. 10-29.
4. Gerbner, George, Larry Gross, Michael Morgan, and Nancy Signorielli. "Scientists on the TV Screen." *Society* 18(4), May/June 1981, pp. 41-44.
5. Gerbner, George, Larry Gross, Nancy Signorielli, and Michael Morgan. "Aging with Television: Images on Television Drama and Conceptions of Social Reality." *Journal of Communication* 30(1), Winter 1980, pp. 37-47.
6. Gerbner, George and Nancy Signorielli. "Women and Minorities in Television Drama 1969-1978." The Annenberg School for Communication, University of Pennsylvania, 1979.
7. Morgan, Michael. "Longitudinal Patterns of Television Viewing and Adolescent Role Socialization." Unpublished Ph.D dissertation, University of Pennsylvania, 1980.
8. Morgan, Michael. "Symbolic Victimization and Real-World Fear." Paper presented at the Symposium on Cultural Indicators for the Comparative Study of Culture, Vienna, Austria, February 1982.
9. Signorielli, Nancy. "Television's Contribution to Sex Role Socialization." Paper presented at the Seventh Annual Telecommunications Policy Research Conference, Skytop, Pennsylvania, April 1979.
10. Volgy, Thomas J. and John E. Schwarz. "TV Entertainment Programming and Sociopolitical Attitudes." *Journalism Quarterly* 57(1), 1980, pp. 150-155.
11. Weigel, Russel H., James W. Loomis, and Matthew J. Soja. "Race Relations on Prime Time Television." *Journal of Personality and Social Psychology* 39(5), 1980, pp. 884-893.

III

INFLUENCING
ELECTION OUTCOMES

In no area of public life have practicing politicians taken media effects more seriously than in the area of elections. Ever since the old politics of strong parties and bosses gave way to the new politics of direct primaries and candidate-centered elections, political campaign organizations have spent much time, effort, and money to attract favorable media attention to candidates for major electoral offices. When their candidates lose, they frequently blame the tone of media coverage or the lack of adequate media coverage. Because vigorous, information-rich electoral contests are essential to the democratic process, scholars regularly have put the activities of involved parties, including the media, under the microscope.

The readings in Part III evaluate the images that media create for political candidates. Selections depict the difficulties campaign staffs and newspeople encounter in covering elections. They also record what types of coverage spell victory or defeat for political contenders. Dean E. Alger's essay sets the stage. It summarizes and critiques major recent research and presents an overview of the questions that scholars of media influence on campaigns have pursued.

Thomas E. Patterson describes how media present every phase of presidential campaigns as a horse-race scenario. In primary contests, in daily routines, in debates, and in public opinion polls, newspeople always designate winners and losers. Although the supporting evidence for these judgments may be flimsy, the designation nonetheless provides winners with tremendous momentum and drags losers to defeat. Martin Schram focuses on the crucial role that television has come to play in presidential campaigns. He considers it the candidates' most powerful campaign tool. If candidates excel in front of the cameras, good visuals become a teflon coat that wards off the effects of harsh verbal commentary.

There is an old saying that "there is many a slip twixt the cup and the lip." It is one thing for politicians to try to create particular images and another for these images to be conveyed to reporters and, through them, to the voting public. Can candidates control their media coverage? Larry Sabato, in partial disagreement with Martin Schram, contends that they cannot. Reporters have become more interested in producing sensational headlines about the candidates' foibles and missteps than in telling the duller stories about policies and political strategies that candidates want to disseminate. Competitive pressures force even reporters who prefer more serious coverage to join the pack. The viciousness of current campaign journalism, with its instant reach of millions of Americans, harms electoral politics. It discourages worthy new entrants, fatally wounds the political careers of many contenders, and leaves deep personal and political scars on scores more.

An interdisciplinary team of scholars—Holli A. Semetko, Jay G. Blumler, Michael Gurevitch, David H. Weaver, Steven Barkin, and G. Cleveland Wilhoit—compare the formation of campaign agendas in the United States and Britain and try to unravel the mystery of who controls what is published. The answer is that many cooks contribute to the political broth. Their relative share of influence varies depending on the political and media structures and cultures. In general, American media enjoy more control over campaign coverage than do their British counterparts.

The final selection focuses on media coverage of congressional races. Although presidential elections remain by far the chief event in election coverage, interest in congressional election coverage has been growing. Timothy E. Cook explains the significance of media publicity in the representative's district, contrasting it with the role of the national media. The effect of election coverage, Cook notes, may last far beyond election day. A legislator whose pet projects have received favorable commentary during the campaign may find it easier to win legislative battles in the postelection years.

13

THE MEDIA IN ELECTIONS: EVIDENCE ON THE ROLE AND THE IMPACT

Dean E. Alger

Editor's Note

The impact of mass media coverage on elections has received more attention from political scientists than any other media topic. In this essay Dean E. Alger reviews and critiques the major studies of election news. He reports findings about the subject matter of news stories, the manner of framing to stress conflict, and the delight with which reporters pounce on candidates' errors and slips of the tongue.

Alger also comments on the significant influence of election coverage on the parties' choice of nominees and the equally significant influence of omissions of important stories. He analyzes the distorting effects of heaping coverage on the winners of the early primaries and caucuses, and he questions the wisdom of gauging winning and losing by scales based on comparisons of expectations with actual outcomes, rather than on the outcomes alone. On the whole, Alger finds the quality of coverage wanting, leaving the public's information supply inadequate when judged by the canons of democratic government.

At the time of writing, Alger was associate professor of political science at Moorhead State University in Minnesota. He has written numerous articles analyzing the media's role in politics and has served regularly as news analyst for a network-affiliated television news station. The selection is taken from "The Media in Elections: Evidence on the Role and the Impact," in The Media and Politics *(Englewood Cliffs, N.J.: Prentice-Hall, 1989),* 201-30.

From Dean E. Alger, *The Media in Politics,* © 1989, pp. 201-230. Reprinted by permission of Prentice-Hall, Inc.

**Media Coverage of Presidential Elections
and Campaign Response**

Nature of Coverage: The Patterson Evidence

Striking patterns of media coverage of the nomination process have been found. The most comprehensive and systematic study is that reported in Thomas Patterson's *The Mass Media Election.* . . .

This study of the media in the 1976 presidential election process found two patterns of fundamental importance in media coverage: (1) the game and strategy in the process, along with candidate style and image, were heavily covered, but issues and candidate qualifications and leadership abilities received comparatively little coverage; and (2) the basic design and intent of the process (delegate selection through 50 states and a gradual weighing of comparative appeal of candidates to voters and party activists) tended to get lost in the coverage of the game. In fact, the very nature of the process has been altered and the outcomes profoundly affected by the nature of the news coverage. . . .

The Game: Issues and "Campaign Issues."   Over all the media he studied (. . . the three networks, *Time* and *Newsweek,* and two newspapers each in two areas), Patterson found that between 51 and 58% of all the news on elections was about the *game* (i.e., about who was winning or losing, strategy and logistics, appearances and hoopla). Only 28 to 32% of election news involved the substance of the election (i.e., issues and policies, candidates' leadership traits and records, and endorsements). . . .

It should be noted that the measure of news coverage of "substance" in this study, like most others, does not appear to be terribly demanding. That is (although Patterson is not as specific about this as one would like), news content that included anything more than the briefest mention of the name of an issue or policy was included in the substance column. This does not tell us how many stories involved material that was sufficiently meaningful and substantial that there was a real chance to learn something from it. Patterson did point out, however, that the figures just cited on coverage of the game compared with substance actually understate the media's emphasis on the game. Thus when we look at stories placed in the more frequently read or watched front pages of newspapers or beginning of newscasts, there is an even greater emphasis on the game, style, and image and even less attention to substance.[1]

Patterson also found interesting patterns in the news media's interest in "issues" coverage (broadly conceived of) compared with candidates' interests and efforts. He found that the media preferred to cover "clear-cut" issues, that is, issues that neatly divide the candidates (thus fulfilling the "conflict" news criterion). The candidates generally preferred that more "diffuse" issues be the center of news attention, diffuse issues being those with broad appeal to a general public, which allows a candidate to build a larger set of supporters and offend fewer segments of voters.

To the extent that the media seek candidate discussion of serious policy issues, this tension between a media preference for clear-cut issues versus candidates' preferences for diffuse issues is as it should be; it is a welcome thing for the media to try to "smoke out" the candidates on policy issues. But is that the main emphasis of the media's interest? Apparently not. The media preference is that these issues "produce disagreement and argument among the candidates; rest on principle rather than complex details or relationships; and can be stated in simple terms, usually by reference to a shorthand label such as busing or detente." [2]

Further, one main media focus in "clear-cut issue" coverage is better referred to as "*campaign* issues" than as substantive issues. Campaign issues are those that arise as a result of incidents in the campaign, typically a mistake in judgment by the candidate or his or her campaign principles. The classic example of this was Gerald Ford's misstatement in one of the 1976 debates with Jimmy Carter that Poland was not under the domination of the Soviet Union. This received a great deal of coverage (egged on, of course, by the Carter campaign); but no serious observer of politics thought this represented Ford's view of the Eastern European situation.[3] The misstatement of his law school record by Senator Joe Biden in September 1987 was an excellent example of this phenomenon early in the campaign 1988 process.

Why the absence of coverage of policy issues—and such emphasis on nonsubstantive campaign issues? Newspeople are aware of the idea of democracy. The factors in and orientations of news production, however, push journalists to see policy statements as quickly losing their "newsworthiness," whereas campaign missteps and the tangible events of the election process are "fresh occurrences." As Patterson said, "once a candidate makes known his position on an issue, further statements concerning that issue decline in news value." [4] The journalists who are principally reporting on each campaign also sit through innumerable repetitions (and some variations) of The Speech, the standard campaign speech used at most stops around the country, which normally contains various general statements about the "issues facing our nation today." Reporters, not surprisingly, begin to question the news value of a statement on issues. Does that mean that questions on the policy issues should not be pursued, however? There is a difference between the numbing drone of a standard campaign speech (after the umpteenth hearing) and a serious effort to cross-examine prospective presidents on the significant policy issues and to find out (1) whether they have adequate knowledge about such matters, and (2) whether their general proposals on such things as budget making really add up.

Coverage of Candidates and the Nomination Process.   Those are important findings. But even more striking and important is what Patterson found regarding coverage of the candidates and the nomination process itself. The principal Patterson findings have now been echoed in many other sources, even in the media themselves, in their occasional self-analyses. The findings regarding patterns of coverage of the process and the consequences of that coverage remain of central importance for understanding the media's role in elections.

The news media's criteria for news and other news production factors lead them to focus on tangible, official events, especially the earliest such events, in the election process. And following the conflict and drama criteria, it inclines the media to highlight who has "won" and who has "lost." A candidate who did not "come in first" in the voting but who did much better than the media expected can also receive prominent, positive media coverage (under the right circumstances).

In the 1976 Democratic nomination process, for example, Jimmy Carter received about 30% of the votes cast in the Iowa caucuses, the first delegate-selection event (then held in January). (Carter had spent large amounts of time in the state over the previous two years.) Various other candidates received various lower percentages, but also, reflecting the indecision among the citizenry at that early point in time, nearly 40% of the caucus participants cast votes for uncommitted delegates. The media's response to this very mixed result was to pronounce Carter the unequivocal winner and the rest losers: "He was the clear winner in this psychologically crucial test," said network correspondent Roger Mudd, for example.[5] In New Hampshire, Carter received 28% of the primary vote, while Congressman Udall received 23%, with others dividing up the balance of the vote. Of the slightly more than 80,000 people who voted in the Democratic primary, Carter received 4500 more votes than Udall. This meant that Carter received one or two more delegates than Udall in the proportional allocation.

After Iowa and New Hampshire, Carter had a projected total of about 20 delegates out of more than 3000 to be chosen. The media verdict, however, was that Carter was the clear "front runner." He received massive media coverage, while the other candidates received little or virtually none. Thus *Time* and *Newsweek* put Carter on their cover and gave him 2600 lines of coverage, whereas Udall received only 96 lines, and all the other Democratic candidates combined got only 300 lines. In short, the media treated it as if a new President of the United States of New Hampshire had been elected.[6]

... [T] he results are meaningful for the nation as a whole. But neither Iowa nor New Hampshire were or are now representative of the national Democratic populace or the population in general, since neither state had or has any large cities, much in the way of minorities, and so on. ...

[M] edia coverage usually makes it a winner-take-all system in public perceptions. Indeed, even beyond the first caucus and primary, Patterson found that throughout the entire 13 weeks of the primaries and caucuses, in the "typical week following each primary, the first-place finisher received nearly 60% of the news coverage. ..."

[T] he problem is best illustrated by the New York and Wisconsin primaries:

> In Wisconsin Udall finished second to Carter by less than 1% of the popular vote, gaining 25 delegates to Carter's 29. On the same day, Udall easily bested Carter in New York's primary, receiving 70 delegates to Carter's 35. Thus, Udall collected 95 delegates while Carter received 61, yet Carter got more news coverage and bigger headlines. Why was this? It was because Udall did not "win" either primary.[7]

... Other studies of other presidential elections have generally confirmed Patterson's findings. Michael J. Robinson and Margaret Sheehan studied news coverage of the 1980 election on CBS and the UPI wire service.

... [T] heir conclusion and key data on issues coverage were:

> For both CBS and UPI, the totals for policy issue coverage were not impressive. [W] e found that 59% of the full-fledged presidential campaign news on CBS failed to contain even one issue sentence. On UPI, 55% of the news items made not a single meaningful reference to any one of the ninety-odd policy issues we identified during the course of Campaign '80. Using our less precise measure of general issue coverage, story by story, on CBS, 20% of the news items emphasized issues. On UPI, the figure was 18%.[8]

It is interesting to note that the UPI wire carried even less issues news than CBS. What that also suggests is that readers of local (nonmajor) newspapers receive very little issue news, since those papers rely on the wire services for national news. ... [I] n another analysis, Michael Robinson found the game dominant in 1980 election news, while candidate qualifications and leadership characteristics were given short shrift: "There were four times as many explicit references to success and failure [in primaries, caucuses, debates ...] as there were to all other candidate characteristics combined." [9] These are striking omissions in coverage. ...

One other pattern reported by Robinson and Sheehan is very interesting and important to note; it can be called: "Whatever happened to the Vice-Presidency?" In the general election of 1980, Carter's vice-presidential running mate, Walter Mondale, "was the featured candidate in a grand total of one story" on the UPI wire; and Reagan's running mate, George Bush, was the subject of only two stories. On CBS Bush and independent John Anderson's running mate Patrick Lucey were the subject of one story each; "Mondale got shut out"—no stories at all. They report that other work found the same pattern in the 1968 and 1972 campaigns.

. . . As Robinson and Sheehan importantly point out, "although four of the last six vice-presidents have become president . . . , the national press consistently ignores the vice-presidential ticket-holders, once they have been selected"; in effect, we "lose" the vice-presidency in national election news.[10]

Issues and the Game in the Election of 1984. Thomas Patterson returned to the fray in 1984, with Richard Davis, and found that it continued to be the case that "election news conveys scenes of political actions, not the values represented by those scenes. . . . Election news concentrates on competition and controversy, not basic questions of policy and leadership."[11]

. . . [T]he presidential candidates, especially in the nominating stage, were not able to get through to the public with their leadership and policy themes and ideas because of the news media's fixation on the game.

. . . Patterson and Davis found that "neither candidate's themes even appeared in more than a tenth of the articles" on the nomination process in the . . . *New York Times* and the *Syracuse Post-Standard*. (The exception was Hart's "new generation of leadership" line.) "Nor were the specific issues that contributed to Hart's and Mondale's themes singled out for heavy coverage. In 114 articles about the Democratic campaign, Mondale's charge that Reagan's tax cuts benefited the rich was mentioned only four times; his 'progressive tax plan' was not mentioned once."[12] . . .

To be as complete as possible, though, we should mention some efforts made by the networks in 1984 to add a bit to the usual level of issues coverage. A few specific examples from the general election period: CBS News ran a standard-length piece in August on winners and losers resulting from Reagan administration policy; NBC, in the "Summer Sunday USA" program in early September ran a (half-hour) review of the candidates, including a fair amount of material on qualifications and issues; CBS aired a fairly long segment (by network news standards) distinguishing the "two [different] visions" of governmental policy and society held by Reagan and Mondale in late October. CBS even made three brief tries at coverage of the Reagan campaign's comprehensive, concerted staging of events and manipulation of the media. . . .

A Note on Coverage of Minor Parties. . . . In the current media age, third parties are nearly invisible, however, especially on network TV. Robinson and Sheehan found in 1980, for example, that

> minor parties had no significant access to the news. . . . Rounding to the nearest whole number, minor party candidates received 0% of the news-time . . . on CBS and UPI.
>
>   In all of 1980, there was only one complete story on CBS weekday news about a minor party presidential candidate [excepting John Anderson's "independent, non-partisan movement"]—a less-than-3-minute piece about Libertarian candidate Ed Clark. On UPI there were two stories featuring Clark, and two featuring Citizen's party candidate Barry Commoner [distinguished biochemist and author of several highly praised books on energy and environmental issues].[13]

These were parties with coherent, intelligent general political philosophies and specific policy proposals (pointed in very different directions), which amounted to intelligent challenges to the status quo of the major parties. But they were virtually invisible to the general public. In 1984, Robinson found the same pattern: "The networks gave practically no time to the minor parties." [14] . . .

The Preprimary Period. . . . [B]efore the first caucuses, candidates build organizations, seek political support and money around the nation, and seek media attention (which confers a sort of legitimacy on the candidacy and helps bring in money). And how is that media attention gained? As Richard Joslyn points out, a principal way "the press decides who should receive media coverage during the invisible primary is by relying on the support for a candidate in Gallup's or Harris' [polls] of presidential contenders"—those registering higher in the polls receive more media attention.[15] Despite the surface logic, however, there are serious problems with this approach; in fact, such preprimary polls are largely a waste of money and news space. These polls, in most cases, do not measure real support levels for candidates; it is simply too early for the vast majority of the public to be interested in these contests. The polls in this stage measure only name recognition.

   Senators John Glenn and Gary Hart in the 1984 election cycle were good illustrations of the mistaken nature of these polls and of the consequences.

   . . . Glenn was portrayed as the "leader" because he registered high in the polls, well above any of the other candidates other than Mondale in the preprimary stage. But after a few caucuses and primaries were held, where was Glenn? Gone! The "support" he registered in polls was simply a projected name recognition and a vaguely positive image (principally from his astronaut days). Gary Hart, on the other hand, with all his well-articulated issue papers and policy proposals, was generally ignored in the media until his modest, relative success in Iowa and then his "win" in New Hampshire, after which he suddenly received vast coverage and dramatic increases in expressed support, without much public knowledge of who and what he was. This is not a very sensible way to cover potential nominees. . . .

Candidates and the Nomination Process: In 1980 and 1984.   The pattern of primary and caucus coverage Patterson found in 1976 has been amply confirmed in succeeding elections.

. . . In 1984, the pattern was again repeated—and strikingly so, with a strong impact. Mondale won 45% of the Iowa caucus vote, while Hart received 15% (second best), and Glenn received 5%. This was 15% of Iowa Democrats who turned out. The result has been documented by scholar William C. Adams:

> Despite the tiny size of the electorate, the media verdict was unequivocal, and the self-fulfilling power attributed to the caucuses was monumental: "Senators Hart and Glenn traded places in Iowa. Hart moved up to number two. Glenn became an also-ran. The effect of this surprising reversal already is being felt in their campaigns."—Tom Brokaw, NBC News Feb. 21

Further, Adams found that in the week following the Iowa caucuses Mondale "actually suffered a decline in his relative share of attention on CBS and NBC newscasts"; Hart was awarded new status as prime challenger, and he received ten times the coverage on NBC and five times the coverage on CBS that he had had the week before. Further, "Hart's coverage was virtually free of any harsh criticism, unflattering issues, or cynical commentary." [16]

And then came New Hampshire. Hart "won" New Hampshire, again upsetting media expectations. The coverage was massive. It was a replay of Carter's coverage at the same stage in 1976. Hart's picture was on the cover of *Newsweek* and *U.S. News* and it shared the cover of *Time* with Mondale (each in chariots—the chariot race, rather than the horse race!). And the prose was purple indeed regarding the epic nature of Hart's victory:

> "In a single dazzling day, he had won the most electrifying upset primary victory in years—and set off a political chain reaction that transformed campaign '84."

> "Suddenly, [Mondale's] entire campaign seemed to be on the fritz."

> "Like the once formidable John Glenn, who stumbled home third in the primary, Mondale was suddenly racing for his life."

"Reaction to televised accounts of Hart's victory was strong and immediate."
[And *Newsweek*] "detected an electorate awash in a tidal wave of support for the youthful candidate...."

"No poll taken amid the white-hot heat of the Hart explosion should be viewed as conclusive. But the dramatic implosion of Mondale's support...."

All this occurred after Hart received 15% of the 15% Democratic turnout in Iowa, while Mondale received 45%, and after Hart won a sum total of under 12,000 more votes than Mondale in the unrepresentative state of New Hampshire (a number of which voters were not Democrats).[17] This was out of the tens of millions of Democrats nationwide.

In general, as Brady and Hagen document, there was some attention to policy issues in the January "flurry of attention to the impending campaign." But "by February, policy issues and all other subjects were buried under a blizzard of speculation about who was winning and who was losing the nomination campaign." [18]

This, frankly, is just senseless; and it seriously altered the nomination process. As journalist Tom Wicker remarked and lamented, the "unexpected" Iowa showing for Hart

> produced a wave of publicity that Hart astutely rode to an upset primary victory . . . among New Hampshire's iconoclastic voters. That generated an avalanche of publicity, under which Mondale was buried in Maine . . . and Vermont. . . .
> What's wrong with publicity for the candidate with momentum? The problem is that the publicity is the momentum. . . .[19]

What also resulted from such coverage is that many candidates were effectively eliminated after the few earliest primaries and caucuses and people in other states, including such states as New York, Ohio, and California, never got to indicate their preference for a full range of candidates. Effectively, we have a media-elimination tournament, with most candidates being forced to leave the "game" before the sizable majority of the party populace can vote on them. . . .

And how were the candidates themselves treated in the news? Interestingly, Robinson and Sheehan, in their effort to assess how "fairly" the candidates were treated in 1980, came to a generalization which appears to apply to other years as well (although not without some exception): incumbents and distinct "front runners" receive decidedly tougher (at times, hostile) media coverage than other candidates. Robinson concluded that the same was the case in the 1984 general election. . . . In terms of sheer amount of time in the general election, Robinson and colleagues found nearly perfect equality of network and UPI news coverage for the two major party candidates.[20]

. . . And in 1988. In the 1988 nomination process, with no incumbent involved and with "hot races" in both major parties, the temptations of horse-race journalism were at their height. . . .

. . . [M]edia organs were very interested in the Bush-Dole conflict (and any conflict they could find on the Democratic side). But in their focus on the game and conflict in the Bush-Dole contest, the media largely lost sight of what should have been a truly central policy issue in campaign '88. In the New Hampshire case, the media focused especially on the conflict over Bush's ads saying that Dole would raise taxes and Dole's angry reaction of denial. But the prime, in fact overwhelming, issue facing American government which caused the tax question to be raised in the first place got lost in the conflict obsession: the monumental budget deficits and what action each candidate would take to (realistically) solve that problem.

. . . Clearly, this issue should have been at the center of campaign coverage in 1988, with constant efforts to get answers on solutions from candidates in *both* parties. Instead, with the huge "Super Tuesday" set of primaries and caucuses throughout the South and elsewhere, and with the Democratic Party having an active contest through much of the nomination stage, most of what the public got was the game.

On the plus side, major newspapers did continue the trend in recent elections of running special series of articles on the major party candidates, including often good synopses of background, education, career, qualities as public figure and officer, and a fair amount of material on policy positions. The networks did make a more distinct effort *before* the Iowa and New Hampshire events to point out the unrepresentative nature of those states. The networks also made more effort to give the public more information on the politics and demographics of states holding primaries prior to the events—with help from their whiz-bang, computer-generated graphics capacities. . . .

Systematically establishing the impact of election communications on the public's opinions and behavior is a real challenge. That, in fact, is an understatement. As Richard Joslyn has precisely pointed out . . . "Empirical demonstration that campaign communication has a particular effect on public opinion would ideally include prior specification of the hypothesized effect, measurement of the relevant opinions both before and after the campaign communication has occurred, a comparison of the opinions of those exposed to the communication with those who were not exposed, and the elimination of all other possible reasons that those exposed to the communication might differ from those unexposed." [21]

This is indeed a challenge—and those requirements of empirical demonstration should certainly be kept in mind whenever statements are made about such effects. . . .

*Thinking and Talking about the Campaign: Media Agenda/Voters'
Agenda.* And with all the coverage of the sort we have noted, what did the
public think was important, and what did they talk about? By this point it
should come as no news flash that what the news media emphasized—the
game and the horse race—was just what the public thought was important.

. . . This public preoccupation with the game as opposed to the substance of electoral choices appears to be a product of the post-1968 resort
to primaries and open caucuses and of the mass media treatment of the
campaign. Thus Patterson notes that the premier study of the 1948 election found that "67% of voters' conversations were concerned with the
candidates' positions and qualifications," while only one-fourth of them
discussed which candidate was likely to win. But in 1976, "only 34% of
people's conversations were concerned with substance" (with a high of
only 43% even in October).[22] Is the contemporary democratic electoral
choice process being largely lost in a fog of electoral trivial pursuit?

But Patterson also found a significant variation in that pattern of seeing
the game as the election's most important feature—a variation of striking
importance. He found that the game "was at the top of the voters' lists at
every stage of the campaign but one: It fell behind the debates during the
general election," and viewing of both the televised conventions and the
debates also increased people's sense of the importance of substance in the
election: "Indeed, debate and convention viewing was more closely related
than either newspaper or evening newscast exposure to a heightened belief
in the significance of policy and leadership matters." [23]

. . . This suggests that when serious communications about the substance of electoral choice are presented to the public (in an interesting
fashion) they respond—and begin to act more like democratic citizenship
requires. Networks (and even newspapers) are you listening?!

Jimmy Who? Awareness of Candidates. The nature of the impact of media
coverage of the nomination process is perhaps most dramatically evident in
people's awareness of the candidates and the consequences for how they
vote (our ultimate concern). In the 1976 election Patterson found that most
of the public knew little about the candidates for the Democratic nomination at the beginning of the year. . . . Even in February, after the Iowa
caucuses, only 20% said they knew anything more about Carter than his
name. Media coverage following the New Hampshire primary dramatically
changed that for Carter. Patterson found that Carter was the only candidate
whose public recognition rose dramatically: 20% said they knew something
about him in February, 81% said so by June. But the public's recognition of
his Democratic opponents increased only modestly. "Recognition levels rose
by 14% for [Congressman Morris] Udall, [Governor Jerry] Brown, and

[Senator Henry] Jackson, and by only 9% for [Senator Frank] Church . . . and even declined for [Senator Birch] Bayh and [Sergeant] Shriver."[24]

And most striking of all was the impact of that awareness, from the nature of media coverage, on the vote.

. . . "Nearly all [voters] picked a candidate they knew something about. . . ." Most specifically, about a quarter of the voters knew only one of the three candidates, usually Carter; he received 90% of those votes. And about 30% knew two candidates, typically Carter and either Jackson or Udall; Carter got 60% of those votes. The nature of campaign coverage, it appears, has a profound impact on the way people vote. This is further confirmed by how people tended to view the candidates—according to who was portrayed as the "winner" and who the "losers."

"Winning Isn't Everything, It's the Only Thing."   That old line of legendary coach Vince Lombardi seems to have been taken to heart by the media, and the public response followed suit in 1976. Who had "won" a primary or caucus event and who was likely to in the future were so prominently and constantly run as news stories that the great majority of the public was certain to have gotten the message. Patterson explained the developments and the impact:

> The first impression that most Democrats had of Carter was that he was doing extremely well in places like Iowa and New Hampshire, an accomplishment that evoked some surprise and a certain amount of admiration. As they heard more about him, most of them also regarded him as an acceptable nominee. This reaction was not based on the feeling that in Carter they had discovered their ideal candidate, for they *knew very little about his politics or abilities.* But he seemed like a sensible and personable individual and, since he had won the acceptance of voters elsewhere, he must have his good points. These were persuasive perceptions [emphasis added].[25]

This impression and the public perception of winners and losers was an especially potent factor in a nomination process where there were no clearly and strongly dominant figures before the process began, as was the case in 1976 on the Democratic side (and again in 1988). In such coverage, Patterson pointed out, was the making of a bandwagon. . . .

Images (—and Print Media versus TV).   . . . Patterson . . . found that newspapers were "more instrumental in the formation of images" and that newspaper reading "particularly contributes to the fullness of people's images." [26] This, he concluded, was because voters' impressions of a candidate's primary victories, political record, and the like are principally dependent on verbal communication, which is the strong suit of newspapers.

Patterson . . . acknowledges that "when only the voters' impressions about the candidates' personalities and leadership capacities are considered, television's impact is more apparent"—indeed, in the first half of the nomination period especially, "regular viewing of the evening newscasts was strongly associated with the formation of impressions of Carter's personality." He also noted the predominance of stylistic impressions of Carter, along with the fact that "once a candidate's image has been developed, it's unlikely to be altered significantly" by subsequent news—and that the "large majority" of voters had developed an image of Carter by April.[27] Putting those elements together suggests a larger role played by TV in image building. . . .

Information. On the other hand, Patterson reports convincingly, as have others, that newspaper reading is far more responsible for people's learning of substantive information than is watching newscasts. . . . Two specific forms of TV viewing of election coverage did contribute to people's awareness of the candidates' policy positions. . . . "Heavier convention viewers became significantly better informed about 63% of Carter's positions and 25% of Ford's [the incumbent and hence already better known]," and "exposure to the televised . . . debates . . . was significantly related to higher awareness of 50% of Carter's and Ford's policies." [28] . . .

Finally, Election Night ("Tuned-In TV, Turned-Off Voters"?)

There is one final way that the TV age has notably affected elections—final in a literal sense. Election night is the final act of the election process (the final scene of the election drama). The combination of the competition between the networks and the development of survey sampling techniques (and computers to process the data) has resulted in network projections of a presidential victor well before the polls have closed in some parts of the nation. The election of 1980 was the most notorious case: One network announced its projection of the winner nearly three hours before the polls had closed in most West Coast areas—thereby telling citizens who were preparing to vote during that time, in effect, "your vote is meaningless" (at least for the premier office in the nation). Further, in 1980 a good number of West Coast elections for the House of Representatives were decided by close votes, as will always occur in some number. Correspondingly, if even 5 or 10% of the public which would have voted is discouraged from voting by such projections, the actual outcome of elections can be affected (usually, about 15 to 20% of West Coast voters cast their votes between 6:00 and 8:00 p.m.). There were indeed accounts of voters leaving the voting places after the projections were broadcast in 1980.[29]

The debate over whether this practice has a serious impact and whether such early projections should be allowed has been fairly intense. Unfortunately, systematic evidence (data as well as accompanying logic) has been mixed (what there is of it). . . .

In late 1987, the House of Representatives passed a bill to establish a uniform poll-closing time throughout the nation (7:00 p.m. Western time), and the networks would not be allowed to broadcast projections of winners until then. It is not clear why the election day schedule and the opportunity for citizens to vote must be altered simply because of network competition and lack of responsibility. I cannot resist quoting part of journalist David Sarasohn's response to this action: "Look, if this is too inconvenient for the networks, maybe the West Coast could just give up voting for president entirely."[30] . . .

Notes

1. Thomas Patterson, *The mass media election* (New York: Praeger, 1980), p. 25.
2. Ibid., Chapter 4; quote from pp. 31-32.
3. Ibid., pp. 34-37.
4. Ibid., p. 30.
5. Ibid., p. 44.
6. Ibid., pp. 44-45.
7. Ibid., pp. 45-47, quotes from pp. 45 and 46 (footnote), respectively.
8. Michael J. Robinson and Margaret Sheehan, *Over the wire and on TV: CBS and UPI in campaign '80* (New York: Russell Sage, 1983), pp. 145-146.
9. Michael J. Robinson, A statesman is a dead politician: Candidate images on network news, in Elie Abel (Ed.), *What's news* (San Francisco: Institute for Contemporary Studies, 1981), p. 161.
10. Robinson and Sheehan, *Over the wire and on TV,* p. 168.
11. Thomas Patterson and Richard Davis, The media campaign: Struggle for the agenda, in Michael Nelson (Ed.), *The elections of 1984* (Washington, D.C.: Congressional Quarterly Press, 1985), p. 113.
12. Ibid., p. 116.
13. Robinson and Sheehan, *Over the wire and on TV,* p. 73.
14. Michael Robinson, The media in campaign '84, Part II, Wingless, toothless, and hopeless, in Michael J. Robinson and Austin Ranney (Eds.), *The mass media in campaign '84* (Washington, D.C.: American Enterprise Institute, 1985), p. 35.
15. Richard Joslyn, *Mass media and elections* (Reading, Mass.: Addison-Wesley, 1984), p. 121.
16. William C. Adams, Media coverage of campaign '84: A preliminary report, *Public Opinion* (April/May 1984), pp. 10-11.
17. *Newsweek,* March 12, 1984, pp. 20-21; see also Otis Pike column (Newhouse News Service) as run in *The Forum* (Fargo, N. Dak.), March 4, 1984.
18. Henry E. Brady and Michael G. Hagen, The horse-race or the issue?: What do

voters learn from presidential primaries, Center for American Political Studies, Harvard University, Occasional Paper (1986 APSA Annual Meeting Paper), p. 8.

19. Tom Wicker, Hart's well-managed windfall, as run in *Minneapolis Star and Tribune*, March 11, 1984, p. 17A.

20. On candidate treatment in 1980, see Robinson and Sheehan, *Over the wire and on TV*, pp. 115-134. On toughness on the incumbent in 1984, see Maura Clancy and Michael Robinson, The media in campaign '84: General election coverage, part 1, in Robinson and Ranney, *The mass media in campaign '84*; on equality of news time, see Robinson and Sheehan, *Over the wire and on TV*, Chapter 5, and Robinson, The media in campaign '84, p. 35.

21. Joslyn, *Mass media and elections*, p. 159.

22. Patterson, *Mass media election*, p. 105.

23. Ibid., pp. 98 and 103.

24. Ibid., pp. 109-110.

25. Ibid, p. 126.

26. Ibid., p. 142.

27. Ibid., pp. 143 and 134-135, respectively.

28. Ibid., p. 157.

29. See the summary in Joslyn, *Mass media and elections*, pp. 150-152.

30. David Sarasohn, A poll-closing scheme designed to keep Westerners from voting, Newhouse News Service, as run in *Minneapolis Star and Tribune*, November 18, 1987, p. 17A.

14

VIEWS OF WINNERS AND LOSERS

Thomas E. Patterson

Editor's Note

In a book that became an instant classic, Thomas E. Patterson talks about creating winner and loser images, particularly during the primaries when they are most important. Early in the campaign the winner image can create a bandwagon effect. Money, volunteers, and votes are attracted to candidates who bear the winner label. In this way media prophecies about who will win and who will lose become self-fulfilling.

Patterson's study was based on a massive collection of two types of data: media content and voters' beliefs and attitudes. Media data came from content analysis of election news in television, newspaper, and news magazine sources that voters used in Erie, Pennsylvania, and Los Angeles, California, during the 1976 presidential campaign. Audience data were obtained through multiple, lengthy interviews with panels of up to 1,236 voters conducted in Erie and Los Angeles. The voters were interviewed five times during 1976 so that evolving attitudes could be chronicled.

Patterson is professor of political science at Syracuse University. His extensive research concerning mass media effects during the 1972 and 1976 presidential elections was made possible by major grants from private and public foundations. The selection is from The Mass Media Election *(New York: Praeger, 1980). Several tables have been omitted.*

The dominant theme of presidential election news coverage is one of winning and losing. The returns, projections, and delegate counts of the primaries and the frequent polling and game context of the general election make the candidates' prospects for victory a persistent subject of news coverage throughout the campaign. The outcomes of the races are of con-

From *The Mass Media Election: How Americans Choose Their President,* by Thomas Patterson (Praeger Publishers, New York, 1981), pp. 119-132. Reprinted with permission of the author.

siderable interest to the voters as well; in 1976 this was the most frequently discussed political subject during the primaries and continued to
be a large part of political conversation during the general election.

The voters' opinions about the candidates' chances are heavily dependent on information received from the news media. To decide where a
candidate stands on the issues, voters might rely on what they know of the
candidate's partisanship, but for knowledge of the candidates' competitive
positions, they must depend for the most part on news about primary outcomes, poll results, and so on. Indeed, in 1976 people's perceptions of the
candidates' chances for nomination and election followed closely what the
news coverage indicated those chances to be. When press accounts indicated uncertainty about likely winners and losers, the judgments of the
electorate mirrored that uncertainty. When the news spoke of an almost
certain winner, the voters expressed the same optimism for that candidate. . . .

Winning and Losing: Two Examples

. . . When the Ford-Reagan race changed direction midway through the
primaries, voters revised their perceptions greatly. On April 27 Ford
wrapped up his eighth first-place finish in Pennsylvania, the state of the
ninth primary. Only Reagan's win in North Carolina on March 23 prevented Ford's sweep of the early primaries. But Reagan then retaliated
with a winning streak of his own, winning in Texas on May 1 and in both
Indiana and Georgia on May 4, then winning in Nebraska but losing in
West Virginia on May 11.

The interviews conducted between April 28 and May 18 indicate that
people's estimates of the two candidates' chances were highly sensitive to
these developments. . . . People interviewed in the three days immediately
following Pennsylvania's primary regarded Ford as an almost certain nominee and saw Reagan's chances as slim. As the days passed and Reagan's
victories accumulated, however, there was a significant change in these
estimates. Reagan's prospects were thought to have improved somewhat
following his win in Texas, to have improved dramatically after his double
victory in Indiana and Georgia, and then to have leveled off after he split
Nebraska and West Virginia with Ford. Meanwhile people's estimates of
Ford's chances slipped gradually before stabilizing near the end. Over the
intervening period, voters felt that Ford's advantage over Reagan had declined by about 60 percent. In their minds Reagan still trailed Ford, but by
a much narrower margin than before.

Close attention to the news during this period sharpened people's reactions and judgments. First, those with heavier news exposure reacted more
quickly to the changing situation. In early May, for example, nearly every

voter thought that Reagan was gaining ground on Ford, but those who followed television or the newspaper regularly came to this conclusion two to three days sooner than most nonregulars. Also, the reactions of close followers of the news were stronger. Collectively, those having attended carefully believed that Reagan had closed Ford's lead by 65 percent, nonregulars felt the gap between the candidates had shrunk by 55 percent.

The impact of new information on public judgment is even more evident in a competitive situation of another kind—the presidential debates. After each debate, the news focused on analysis of its outcome. The journalistic consensus after the second debate was that Ford had lost because he had mishandled the question on Eastern Europe. Although a number of hours passed before this message reached the voters, its effect was dramatic, for while respondents who were interviewed within 12 hours of the second debate felt that Ford had won, most of those interviewed later felt Carter had won. The passing of time required for the news to reach the public brought with it a virtual reversal of opinion (see Table 14-1). The change was clearly due to news exposure, for in their evaluation of the debate only 10 percent of the people interviewed early mentioned Ford's statement on Eastern Europe. On their own, voters failed to see in his remark the significance that the press would later attach to it. Yet over 60 percent of those interviewed late discussed his Eastern Europe statement, most indicating that they, like the press, saw it as a major error causing him to lose the second debate.

In this situation close attention to the news again intensified people's reactions. About 50 percent of nonregular news users interviewed late believed that Carter had won the debate, but nearly 65 percent of news regulars interviewed felt he had won. News regulars also were a third more likely to cite Ford's statement on Eastern Europe as the reason for his defeat.

The Making of a Bandwagon

Information about the candidates' chances can result in a bandwagon—the situation where large numbers of voters choose to back the candidate who is ahead. For a bandwagon to occur, however, two conditions must be met: first, voters must be largely unfettered by other influences; second, they must be convinced that the leading candidate is almost certain to win.

A case in point is the 1976 Democratic nominating contest. When the Democratic primaries began, most rank-and-file Democrats had few constraints on their thinking. They were concerned about the nation's unemployment level and still troubled by Watergate, but this discontent was directed at the Republican party. Unlike Vietnam in 1968 and 1972, no issue dominated their thoughts about the party's primaries. Excepting

**Table 14-1   The Effect of News Exposure on the Evaluation of Debate Winner
or Loser (percent)**

Which candidate they felt won the debate	Time elapsed between interview and second debate	
	12 hours or less	12 to 48 hours
Ford	53	29
Undecided	12	13
Carter	35	58
Total	100	100

Wallace, most Democrats had no strong feelings one way or the other about their party's active candidates. . . .

Lacking any firm notion of what or whom they wanted, many Democrats were influenced by the news coverage and outcomes of the early primaries. When a voter is firmly committed to a particular candidate or viewpoint, this attitude provides a defense against change. The commitment leads voters to see events and personalities selectively, in the way they want to see them, thus resulting in the reinforcement of existing attitudes. When voters' attitudes are weak, their perceptual defenses also are weak. When this occurs, as Herbert Krugman, Muzafer Sherif, and others have noted, voters are likely to accept incoming information in a rather direct way, thus developing a conception of the situation consistent with this information. Their perspective becomes that of the communicator, a change that directs their attention toward certain ways of acting and away from other modes of behavior. Their perception of the situation may even point toward a single option, one that they find entirely satisfactory because they had no strong initial preference. They then act upon this choice and, in doing so, form attitudes consistent with their choice. Voters, in short, have been persuaded through perceptual change rather than attitude change. Their perceptions were altered first, and then appropriate attitudes were developed.[1]

This was the process of decision for many Democratic voters during the 1976 primaries. They had no strong commitments before the campaign began, but developed perceptions of the race that led them to accept Carter and reject his opponents. In their minds the central concern became the candidates' electoral success and, once the race was seen in this way, they embraced the winner and rejected the losers. Except for Udall, the candidates who were labeled as losers by the press lost favor with the voters. . . . Jackson, Bayh, Wallace, Shriver, and Harris were regarded much less favorably after they failed to run strongly in the early primaries. This cannot be explained by the fact that Democrats had come to know and dislike these candidates' politics, for they acquired very little information of this kind during the primaries. . . . The only impression that most voters gained of any of these candidates was that they were not doing well in the primaries.

. . . The first impression that most Democrats had of Carter was that he was doing extremely well in places like Iowa and New Hampshire, an accomplishment that evoked some surprise and a certain amount of admiration. As they heard more about him, most of them also regarded him as an acceptable nominee. This reaction was not based on the feeling that in Carter they had discovered their ideal candidate, for they knew very little about his politics or abilities. But he seemed like a sensible and personable individual and, since he had won the acceptance of voters elsewhere, he must have his good points. These were persuasive perceptions. The rush to Carter's side was not because large numbers of Democratic voters wanted to be in the winner's camp; that type of bandwagon effect was not operating during the early Democratic primaries. Rather, Carter's approval by other voters, his apparent command of the nominating race, and his lack of liabilities made him the natural choice of an electorate attuned to the race and devoid of strong preferences. . . .

. . . Democrats' opinions about a candidate tended to align with their perceptions of his chances. If they regarded a candidate as having a good chance, they usually had acquired more favorable feelings toward him by the time of the next interview. On the other hand, less favorable thoughts usually followed the perception that a candidate did not have much of a chance. . . .

. . . [F]rom the evidence available it is certain that most Democrats reached a conclusion about a candidate's prospects before developing a firm opinion about him. Considering the uncertainty that the Democratic respondents expressed in the interviews completed just before the first primary, and the fact that the large majority did not even know Carter at the time, it is inconceivable that great numbers of them selected Carter before hearing about his success in the opening primaries. Thus this dual change reflects mostly the pull of their judgments about the candidates' chances on their feelings toward the candidates.

Interestingly, frequent followers of the news were slightly more likely than infrequent users to judge the candidates on the basis of performance. . . . The opposite might have been predicted, since more attentive citizens generally have stronger political convictions, ones that might retard bandwagon effects. Nevertheless, heavier exposure to the newspaper and television was related to the tendency to respond favorably to winners and unfavorably to losers. Perhaps frequent users' heavier exposure to the news media's conception of the Democratic race impressed it more thoroughly on them.

An alternative explanation for why heavy media users were more responsive to winners and losers relates to the uncertainties surrounding the Democratic race—uncertainties about the identity of the candidates, about their prospects, and about their politics. Jacques Ellul posits that conditions of uncertainty make attentive citizens particularly vulnerable to mass persuasion. According to Ellul, attentive citizens feel a greater need to understand situations, and thus feel a greater compulsion to resolve uncertainty when it exists. Because the events they wish to understand are beyond their direct observation, however, they are susceptible to the media's interpretations of reality.

. . . [O]nly a very small percentage of citizens can receive information about an event and then draw unique and perceptive inferences about it. The ordinary response of the attentive citizen is to accept the communicator's definition of the situation. The inattentive citizen, in contrast, may not care or know enough to try to understand the situation, thus being somewhat less likely to adopt the media's interpretation.[2]

Obstacles to Bandwagons

Unlike Democrats, Republicans were largely unaffected by the outcomes of their party's primaries. About 75 percent of the Republican respondents had chosen between Ford and Reagan before the campaign began, some selecting their candidate because they liked or disliked Ford's handling of the presidency, others choosing one of the two men because of a conservative or moderate preference. Moreover, the large majority of these Republicans stayed with their candidate; in June 80 percent preferred the same candidate they had preferred in February. Reasonably sure about which candidate they wanted and why, their commitments shielded them from bandwagon effects. . . . Among rank-and-file Republicans, then, the candidates' successes were generally unimportant to public response. Indeed, another pattern was evident—Republicans tended to think highly of their preferred candidate's chances. There is in fact a general tendency for voters to be optimistic about the prospects for the candidate they favor. People like to think that others will develop equally high opinions of their favorite contender; consequently, they overrate his prospects. Throughout the 1976 race, each candidate's supporters rated his chances more highly than did other voters, but the degree of exaggeration varied. People were especially positive when the indicators were soft or conflicting, as they were before the first primaries, when without a solid basis for assessing how the contests would go, voters were reasonably hopeful about their candidates' chances. It is true that Ford's backers were more confident than Reagan's and Democrats backing Jackson, Carter, and Humphrey were more optimistic than those behind other candidates, but each side held on to the possibility of victory.

Carter's success in the primaries, however, quickly dampened the hopes of opposing Democrats. Halfway through the primaries, regardless of whom they favored, Democratic voters saw Carter as the likely winner. Only Brown's supporters felt their candidate still had a reasonable chance. . . . Carter's showing had simply overwhelmed the ability of opposing voters to rationalize.

Republicans were less strongly affected by developments. After Ford's victory in Pennsylvania extended his domination of the early primaries, most of Reagan's supporters believed that Ford had the advantage. They were not convinced, however, that the race was virtually over, but felt that Reagan still had time to turn things around, an optimism apparently justified by the winning streak Reagan began in early May. His wins did more than simply persuade his supporters that his chances had improved; many felt that he had edged ahead of Ford. They were less optimistic than Ford's supporters that their candidate would prevail, but they felt he could prevail. Each side continued to feel confident through the remaining primaries—an outlook made possible by the reality of a close race. Almost certainly this impeded any bandwagon effect—most Republicans already believed their side had a good chance.

All of this helps to explain why the Republican and Democratic races, despite similar appearances at the outset, took such different routes. Ford and Carter each began the primaries with a series of victories, but only Carter's success produced a bandwagon. Once he had control of the headlines, there was little to stem the flow of Democrats to his side. To be sure, some people voted against Carter because he was winning. Jackson in Pennsylvania and Brown in California gained some votes because people saw them not as their first choice, but as capable of stopping Carter, thus enabling another candidate, such as Humphrey, to gain nomination. Voters of this type, however, were easily outnumbered by those attracted to Carter because of his success.

The Republican vote was decidedly more stable. Despite the appearance from early losses that his voters were deserting him, Reagan actually retained the large majority of his supporters throughout the early primaries, and won handily when the campaign finally reached the states dominated by conservative Republicans. Had Ford maintained his streak through the early weeks of May, Reagan supporters might have given up hope and reconciled themselves to accepting Ford as their candidate (as they did after the Republican convention). Or had a national crisis occurred, Ford might have been able to rally enough of Reagan's weaker supporters to generate a bandwagon. Or had Reagan committed a major blunder, his support might have evaporated. As things were, however, the strength of his candidacy and the commitment of his followers provided them with an effective shield from persuasion by the outcome of the early primaries.

By the same process, bandwagon effects are limited in nature during a general election. Although a third of the respondents delayed or changed their preferences during the general election, they did not gravitate toward the candidate they felt was leading. Indeed, Carter, who after the summer conventions was thought by most respondents to be ahead, lost votes during the general election. If anything, the fact that Carter appeared likely to win the presidency led voters to examine his candidacy more critically than they previously had. For the most part, changes during the general election reflected people's party, issue, and leadership preferences, influences that rather easily overrode their perceptions of the candidates' chances. Regardless of what they thought about the candidates' prospects, for example, Democrats developed increasingly negative opinions of Ford, and Republicans grew increasingly critical of Carter.

In the general election, people apparently find it easier to believe that their side can win—poll results seem to have less impact on their thinking than primary outcomes and delegate counts. When Carter led by two to one in postconvention polls, Ford's supporters felt Carter was more likely to win, but they hardly conceded him the advantage that opposing Democrats had granted him halfway through the primaries. Shortly before the general election day, when the polls had Carter narrowly in the lead, Ford backers rated Ford's chances as slightly better than Carter's, while Carter backers felt the victory would be a Democratic one. Not surprisingly, then, when a voter was faced with the possibility that his preferred candidate would lose the general election, he was more likely to change his belief about the likely winner than he was to switch candidates.

Notes

1. Herbert Krugman, "The Impact of Televised Advertising," *Public Opinion Quarterly,* Fall 1965, pp. 349-65; Carolyn W. Sherif, Muzafer Sherif, and Roger E. Nebergall, *Attitude and Attitude Change* (Philadelphia: W. C. Saunders, 1965), chap. 1; Muzafer Sherif and Carl Hovland, *Social Judgment* (New Haven, Conn.: Yale University Press, 1961).
2. Jacques Ellul, *Propaganda* (New York: Vintage Books, 1965), pp. 112-16.

15

THE GREAT AMERICAN
VIDEO GAME

Martin Schram

Editor's Note

Martin Schram, a print journalist who has watched video-age presidential campaigns closely, has concluded that seeing is believing, no matter what the words may say. Ronald Reagan, who built his 1984 presidential campaign around visual images, was playing the great American video game, knowing that viewers rely more on their eyes than on contrary messages delivered through their ears or derived from logical thinking. The selection presented here tells how this lesson was driven home to veteran television reporter Lesley Stahl during the campaign.

Schram also describes how politicians devise elaborate television news strategies and carry them out and how journalists try, and often fail, to avoid manipulation by the political image makers. Thus far in the game of video politics, Schram judges the politicians to be ahead of the journalists. The politician with the best video strategies and skills, he believes, will prevail at the voting booth.

Is the public well served by video politics? Schram thinks it is, calling television news "the nation's greatest hope" because it permits the public to assess candidates "in those intangible, up-close-and-personal ways that the newspaper can never fulfill." Much remains to be done to provide empirical support for Schram's appraisals. To date, findings have been mixed.

Schram, at the time of writing, was associate editor of the Chicago Sun- Times. *He has covered every presidential campaign since 1968, writing for the* Washington Post *and other papers. Besides the book from which these excerpts were taken, Schram has written books about the 1976 and 1980 presidential campaigns. The selection comes from "The Great American Video Game," in* The

---

Great American Video Game: Presidential Politics in the Television Age
*(New York: Morrow, 1987), 23-29, 224-26, 305-10. Several footnotes have
been omitted.*

Lesley Stahl, one of television's greatest stars of network news, sat in
silence, listening to an ominous sound she feared could seal her fate at the
White House. From the speaker of a small Sony television set wedged
between plastic coffee cups and old press releases in the cramped CBS
cubicle at the White House press room, about three hundred feet from the
Oval Office, she sat listening to the sound of her own voice. She heard
herself saying things she had long thought about Ronald Reagan and his
aides, but had never dared say publicly before.

For almost four years, Reagan and his advisers had been using television
newscasts to create an image of the Reagan presidency that just did not
square with the policies of the Reagan presidency. Now Stahl was telling
America precisely that—in the most toughly worded piece she had done in
her six years of covering the White House for *The CBS Evening News.*

Night after night, Reagan had had his way with the television news. He
had succeeded in setting their agenda and framing their stories by posing
for the cameras in one beautiful and compelling setting after another.
(Reagan officiating at the handicapped Olympics; Reagan dedicating a se-
nior-citizens housing project.) And the networks had duly transmitted
those scenes to a grateful nation on the nightly news, even though the
pictures of the president conveyed impressions that were quite the opposite of the policies of the president. (Reagan actually had proposed cutting
the budget for the disabled; Reagan actually had proposed cutting federal
housing subsidies for the elderly.)

The president couldn't control what the correspondents would be saying; but, due to the unintended compliance of the networks, he could certainly control what America would be seeing while they said it.

Now, for five minutes and forty seconds—about three times longer than
most stories she got on the air—Stahl told America all about it. Her piece
had been the subject of much internal concern and even tension within
CBS. "I went over that script as intensely as any script I've ever gone
over," recalled Lane Vernardos, who was executive producer of the CBS
Evening News with Dan Rather in that era. "This was a very sensitive piece.
It certainly was a sensitive issue. . . . I thought, 'This is a tough piece. I
know I'm going to take a lot of flak for this—not CBS flak, but the phones
ring off the hook and Larry Speakes [the White House deputy press secre-
tary] will call.' Larry calls every three or four weeks to complain about
something. Larry will be on the phone with this one."

In her script, Stahl told it like it really had been:

How does Ronald Reagan use television? Brilliantly. He's been criticized as the rich man's president, but the TV pictures say it isn't so. At seventy-three, Mr. Reagan could have an age problem. But the TV pictures say it isn't so. Americans want to feel proud of their country again, and of their president. And the TV pictures say you can. The orchestration of television coverage absorbs the White House. Their goal? To emphasize the president's greatest asset, which, his aides say, is his personality. They provide pictures of him looking like a leader. Confident, with his Marlboro Man walk. A good family man. They also aim to erase the negatives. Mr. Reagan tries to counter the memory of an unpopular issue with a carefully chosen backdrop that actually contradicts the president's policy. Look at the handicapped Olympics, or the opening ceremony of an old-age home. No hint that he tried to cut the budgets for the disabled and for federally subsidized housing for the elderly. . . .

Another technique for distancing the president from bad news—have him disappear, as he did the day he pulled the marines out of Lebanon. He flew off to his California ranch, leaving others to hand out the announcement. There are few visual reminders linking the president to the tragic bombing of the marine headquarters in Beirut. But two days later, the invasion of Grenada succeeded, and the White House offered television a variety of scenes associating the president with the joy and the triumph. . . . President Reagan is accused of running a campaign in which he highlights the images and hides from the issues. But there's no evidence that the charge will hurt him because when people see the President on television, he makes them feel good, about America, about themselves, and about him.

And as she spoke, to illustrate her sharply worded points, viewers were treated to four years of Reagan videos:

The president basking in a sea of flag-waving supporters, beaming beneath red-white-and-blue balloons floating skyward, sharing concerns with farmers in a field out of Grant Woods, picnicking with Mid-Americans, pumping iron, wearing a bathing suit and tossing a football . . . more flags . . . wearing faded dungarees at the ranch, then a suit with Margaret Thatcher, getting a kiss and a cake from Nancy, getting the Olympic torch from a runner, greeting wheelchair athletes at the handicapped Olympics, greeting senior citizens at their housing project, honoring veterans who landed on Normandy, honoring youths just back from Grenada, countering a heckler, joshing with the press corps, impressing suburban schoolchildren, wooing black inner-city kids, hugging Mary Lou Retton . . . more flags . . . red, white, and blue smoke emissions from parachutists descending, red-white-and-blue balloons ascending.

Stahl turned off the Sony, and as she sat alone in the silence of that cubicle in the nearly deserted press room on the night of October 4, 1984, a certain occupational tenseness—a mix of nervousness and apprehension—began to build within her. Reporters are an internally contradictory lot; on the one hand we want to be tough, ever-vigilant as we pursue our subjects, yet we know that the reward for tough reporting is often a deep freeze. Phone calls go unreturned, scoops suddenly drop into the laps of competitors.

And so it is understandable that this concern, which can be defined as journalistic fear of freeze-out, began to well within Stahl as she thought about what she had just told the nation in this extraordinarily long piece. ("I was worried," she recalled later. "It was a tough piece—it insinuated that the campaign wasn't being totally honest about the president's record, and I did have to go back there the next day. And, you know, it's never pleasant if they're angry at you.")

The ringing of the telephone startled her. As she reached to pick it up, she knew what to expect. It was, just as she feared, one of the president's assistants. The Reagan man had wasted no time in punching up the number of the CBS phone at the White House; he couldn't wait to give Stahl a piece of his mind after having monitored with the rest of America her evening's journalism.

"Great piece," the Reagan man said.

Stahl thought she was not hearing right.

"We loved it," he continued.

"You what?" Stahl said.

"We loved it!" he said.

"What do you mean you loved it?" Stahl asked. (It should be pointed out that, for a journalist, there is perhaps one weapon a subject-victim can use to retaliate that is worse than a deep freeze—it is high praise.) "How can you say you loved it—it was tough! Don't you think it was tough?"

"We're in the middle of a campaign and you gave us four and a half minutes of great pictures of Ronald Reagan," said the Reagan assistant. "And that's all the American people see."

Stahl, a veteran on the White House beat and star moderator of CBS's Sunday news showcase *Face the Nation,* was suddenly in no mood to take yes for an answer—she went on to repeat all the tough things she had said in her piece.

The president's man listened to this off-the-cuff replay, and then replied. "They don't listen to you if you're contradicting great pictures," he said, patiently explaining a truth his White House had long held to be self-evident. "They don't hear what you are saying if the pictures are saying something different."

So it is that Ronald Reagan has been able to maintain his public support and dominate America's politics in the 1980s, even when all the public-opinion polls were showing that Americans had seemingly fundamental differences with many of their president's policies. . . . He succeeded be-

cause he was able to employ an appeal more fundamental than government policies. He skillfully mastered the ability to step through the television tubes and join Americans in their living rooms; and together they
would watch these policies of Washington's and shake their heads—and
occasionally their fists—at Washington's policymakers. Americans came to
understand that if they were happy with Reagan's policies, the president
deserved the credit; and if they were unhappy with them, the president
was right there with them, plainly disgusted too.

Reagan accomplished all that because he was able to have his way with a
television medium that is represented on the air by journalists who, in
many cases, are considered to be decidedly more liberal than he. He did it
not by catering to them or debating with them—he did it by making America's most famous television stars irrelevant. He stepped right past these
stars and took his place alongside the Americans in their living rooms, and
together they paid no great mind to what these media elites were saying. . . . Television watching has become America's true national pastime,
and Ronald Reagan has shown the nation's political strategists how it is
possible to reduce the pronouncements of the medium's news stars to
mere dugout chatter.

Reagan accomplished this in part—but only in part—because he was a
former actor who has essentially played the same aw-shucks-cum-John-
Wayne part throughout his careers in Hollywood, Sacramento, and Washington. He mainly accomplished it because of the careful strategy-making
by top advisers who made the making of the President's image their prime
political task and highest presidential calling.

A whole new generation of political advisers has now gone to school on
the teachings of Reagan and his videologists, most notably Michael K.
Deaver, who functioned for more than four years in the White House as
the creator and protector of the president's image. . . .

Ever since the television age of politics was born in the 1952 campaign
of Dwight Eisenhower versus Adlai Stevenson, the ability to use the medium has been increasingly essential to electoral success. In 1960, John F.
Kennedy's video persona in his televised debate with Richard Nixon
proved his margin of victory. In 1968, Joe McGinniss captured America's
political imagination with his book *The Selling of the President,* which unfolded from the inside the machinations of Richard Nixon's television advertising campaign. In 1976, Jimmy Carter co-opted television in the
Democratic primaries to help him create a candidacy that was larger than
life, and then failed to master that medium and went on to appear as president smaller than the office he held.

And in 1984, the Democrats in their primaries and Ronald Reagan
throughout his presidency proved that the visual medium had become the

political message. Success on the TV news has come to overshadow success with TV ads; and in the primaries, success on the local newscasts in
the primary states has come to overshadow the much shorter network evening news shows as shapers of electorate opinion.

In all the presidential primaries of that year, it was the candidate's ability to get his daily message out on the nightly television news that unquestionably was the single greatest factor in determining the winner. This was
even true in the caucus states, where traditional political punditry maintained that machine organization was key and television impact was minimal.

When people vote for president, they are most interested not in policy
specifics but in taking the measure of the candidate—what kind of leader
will he or she be? How will the candidate react in the crisis to come, which
involves issues unknown? That is the greatest service television performs
in this democracy's rites of succession. Television's greatest disservice is its
difficulty in dealing with governmental policies and their consequences
and showing that they are in fact very much a part of the candidate's real
leadership skills.

In the years of the Reagan presidency, the White House advisers have
succeeded in getting the television news shows to do their bidding whether
the electronic journalists realized it or not. They were able to do this in
part because of the nature of the medium. And they were able to do it
because there are some pols who understand TV better than the TV people themselves.

They understood early that in areas of government policy and global
complexity the nature of the medium is tedium. And so by controlling the
pictures, they could control the pacing—and the entertainment quality—
of the news shows. . . .

. . . [T]he Reagan campaign of 1984 showed that a shrewd and politically sophisticated group of strategists and a willing and communicatively
sensitive candidate can manipulate the messages of the spring and summer
so they work *for* their campaign. They showed that it is possible to use the
mix of television news and ads to in effect achieve victory—or at least lay
the groundwork for victory—before the traditional Labor Day kickoff.

This crucial public mood of patriotism and optimism was designed and
nurtured by Reagan's top strategists—James Baker, Michael Deaver, and
their associates on the White House staff—plus the group of some forty
Madison Avenue advertising-agency brainstormers who called themselves
the Tuesday Team (named for Election Day) and worked to produce commercials to sell Ronald Reagan as skillfully as they had sold Campbell's
soup, Prego spaghetti sauce, Pepsi-Cola, Gallo wine, and Yamaha motorcycles. . . .

Michael Deaver said that watching the way the Democrats conducted their televised primary-election debates convinced him of the direction the Reagan news and ad-message campaigns should take. "I thought the way the Democrats handled the primary situation was abominable," said Deaver. "It was far too scrappy and disagreeable. No one emerged as acting presidential". . . . If that is what the public was getting from the Democrats—political harangues and lectures about what was wrong with America—then the Reagan campaign would give the public just the opposite. Deaver recalled one meeting of the Reagan strategy-makers in Baker's White House office. "We decided early on that the best thing we had going were all these guys [the Democrats] screaming and scratching. . . . While all these people are fighting, we've got to go with nice old couples walking down the street eating ice cream cones, and kids waving the American flag, and people buying houses, and more people getting married, and more people believing in America again. . . .

"We felt not only because of the Olympics, but a feeling we got through [polling] research . . . that this idea of making people feel good was the way to go. As long as it worked, we ought to use it forever. . . . That's the Reagan constituency; all we were trying to do was show that visually."

The orchestral theme music, soothing and uplifting at the same time, plays in the background, and the scenes that drift through the Reagan ad are done in soft-focus photography, which complements the soft-sell messagery. First there is an ideal factory, then people working, a cowboy dusting himself off, people getting married, people building a house.

ANNOUNCER: It's morning again, in America. Today more men and women will go to work than ever before in our country's history. With interest rates at about half the record highs of 1980, nearly 2,000 families today will buy new homes, more than at any time in the past four years. This afternoon, 6,500 young men and women will be married, and with inflation at less than half what it was just four years ago they can look forward with confidence to the future. It's morning again, in America. And under the leadership of President Reagan, our country is prouder and stronger and better. Why would we ever want to return to where we were less than four short years ago? . . .

The instrument of television has taken control of the presidential-election process. It is the single greatest factor in determining who gets nominated every fourth summer and who gets elected that fall. Some politicians and strategists have shown remarkable skill at regulating and even manipulating the television news coverage. The most successful of them have also enjoyed a good bit of luck.

Television news has become the greatest force in the nation's presidential process; it also stands as the nation's greatest hope. It remains the only medium that can give the public what it wants most: the ability to take the measure of the candidates for president in those intangible, up-close-and-personal ways that the newspaper page can never fulfill.

This is of great and perhaps even overriding importance, because a vote for president is a special and rather personal thing for many people, a bit like casting a vote for father, or grandfather (or maybe, in the case of John F. Kennedy, a vote for husband). People often find it difficult to sort through the complexities of even the best-explained national issue, to decide which position they believe is right and which they believe is wrong. But they often find it easy to look at the candidates and decide which they would most like to lead the nation through the next crisis, whatever that crisis may be. The task of television-news journalists is to do their journalistic best to tell people what is really going on, to make the issues and controversies as understandable as possible, even as the camera provides the crucial, close, personal insights into the candidates. . . .

In The Great American Video Game, the goal of the politicians and image-makers is relatively simple: to design visual settings that will put the candidate and his or her policies in the best possible light, images that encourage television journalists to focus their stories around the photo opportunities provided.

The goal of the television journalists (reporters, editors and producers, and executives) is much more difficult—tougher than that of the politicians or the image-makers, and certainly tougher than that of the print journalists. It is to withstand the designs and schemes of the image-makers and to maintain journalistic control of their news product. It requires an unceasing effort to withstand the temptation to build a story around an event—such as Ronald Reagan's Fourth of July, 1984—simply because it was a day of fascinating pictures. It means they must build the story around his statements that day, relegating the pictures of stockcar racing and holiday spirit to their proper and secondary perspective.

The Great American Video Game will always produce competition verging on warfare between the pols and the television journalists. The task of the journalists is to see that their relationship with the candidates and image-makers remains healthily adversarial rather than symbiotic.

America's television news and its voters do not have to lose every time the Great American Video Game is played. . . .

Behind the examples of television news's failures to resist the enticements of campaign image-makers in 1984, there is also this central reality: There is nothing that television news correspondents or anchors or producers could have done that would likely have altered the outcome of the 1984 campaign. Reagan would likely have won reelection no matter what—even if the television networks had not catered to his made-for-television pageants and his visually compelling ways.

Reagan's campaign hummed in perfect political harmony with its blend of feel-good imagery and economic fact. Beating a president in a time of relative peace and prosperity is as unlikely as it sounds. The unenviable job of having to show the nation that the "peace" was problematic, what with those 261 marine deaths in Lebanon and the efforts to overthrow the Sandinistas in Nicaragua, was left to Mondale and his strategists. And it was left to Mondale and his strategists to convince their countrymen that the prosperity they felt and saw every time they went to the store was not real, and that a deficit they could not see, feel, or understand loomed as the economic undoing of their children or themselves.

But it is also true that Mondale and his strategists were singularly not up to the challenge of this tough assignment in message politics in 1984. Reagan and his advisers were masterful. And the television networks were often unable to cope with and unable to gain control of their own medium.

16

OPEN SEASON: HOW THE NEWS MEDIA COVER PRESIDENTIAL CAMPAIGNS IN THE AGE OF ATTACK JOURNALISM

Larry J. Sabato

Editor's Note

Modern presidential campaign coverage is often mean-spirited and ugly. It destroys candidates' political careers by magnifying their human foibles and physical infirmities. Larry J. Sabato shows how attack journalism inflicted deep political wounds on Democratic presidential candidate Michael Dukakis and Republican vice-presidential candidate Dan Quayle during the 1988 presidential campaign. The consequences of such treatment, Sabato concludes, are candidates who are increasingly secretive because they fear reporters, and reporters who cover less substantive news because they are obsessed with detecting scandals. Deprived of information needed to make sound choices, the public becomes ever more cynical and filled with disgust for politicians as well as the press.

Larry J. Sabato is Robert Kent Gooch Professor of Government and Foreign Affairs at the University of Virginia. He has been a prolific, highly respected writer on political campaigns. The selection comes from Under the Watchful Eye: Managing Presidential Campaigns in the Television Era, *ed. Mathew D. McCubbins (Washington, D.C.: CQ Press, 1992).*

. . . The issue of character has always been present in American politics—not for his policy positions was George Washington made our first president—but rarely, if ever, has character been such a pivotal concern in presidential elections, both primary and general, as it has since 1976. The 1976 Carter campaign was characterized by considerable moral posturing; Edward Kennedy's 1980 candidacy was in part destroyed by lingering character questions; Walter Mondale finally overcame Gary Hart's 1984 challenge in the Democratic primaries by using character as a battering ram; and 1988 witnessed such a forceful explosion of concern about character that several candidates were eliminated and others badly scarred by it.

Whatever the precise historical origins of the character trend in reporting, it is undergirded by certain assumptions—some valid, others dubious. First and most important of all, *the press correctly perceives that it has mainly replaced the political parties as the "screening committee" that winnows the field of candidates and filters out the weaker or more unlucky contenders.* Second, many reporters, again correctly, recognize the mistakes made under the rules of lapdog journalism and see the need to tell people about candidate foibles that affect public performance. Third, the press assumes that it is giving the public what it wants and expects, more or less. Television is the primary factor here, having served not only as handmaiden and perhaps mother to the age of personality politics but also conditioning its audience to think about the private lives of "the rich and famous."

Less convincing, however, are a number of other assumptions about elections and the character issue made by the press. Some journalists insist upon their obligation to reveal everything of significance discovered about a candidate's private habits; to do otherwise, they say, is antidemocratic and elitist.[1] Such arguments ignore the press's professional obligation to exercise reasonable judgment about what is fit to be printed or aired as well as what is most important for a busy and inattentive public to absorb. Other reporters claim that character matters so much because policy matters so little, that the issues change frequently and the pollsters and consultants determine the candidates' policy stands anyway.

Perhaps most troubling is the almost universally accepted belief that private conduct affects the course of public action. Unquestionably, private behavior can have public consequences. However, it is far from certain that private vice inevitably leads to corrupt, immoral leadership or that private virtue produces public good. Indeed, the argument can be made that many lives run on two separate tracks (one public, one private) that should be judged independently. In any event, a focus on character becomes not an attempt to construct the mosaic of qualities that make up an individual but rather a strained effort to find a sometimes manufactured pattern of errors or shortcomings that will automatically disqualify a candidate. . . .

Not surprisingly, politicians react rather badly to the treatment they receive from the modern press. Convinced that the media have but one conspiratorial goal—to hurt or destroy them—the pols respond by restricting journalists' access, except under highly controlled situations. Kept at arm's length and out of the candidate's way, reporters have the sense of being enclosed behind trick mirrors: they can see and hear the candidate, but not vice versa. Their natural, human frustrations grow throughout the grueling months on the road, augmented by many other elements, including a campaign's secrecy, deceptions, and selective leaks to rival newsmen, as well as the well-developed egos of candidates and their staffs. Despite being denied access, the press is expected to provide visibility for the candidate, to retail his or her bromides. Broadcast journalists especially seem trapped by their need for good video and punchy soundbites and with regret find themselves falling into the snares set by the campaign consultants—airing verbatim the manufactured message and photoclip of the day. The press's enforced isolation and the programmed nature of its assignments produce boredom as well as disgruntlement, yet the professionalism of the better journalists will not permit them to let their personal discontent show in the reports they file.

These conditions inevitably cause reporters to strike back at the first opportunity. Whether it is emphasizing a candidate gaffe, airing an unconfirmed rumor, or publicizing a revelation about the candidate's personal life, the press uses a frenzy to fight the stage managers, generate some excitement, and seize control of the campaign agenda. Media emotions have been so bottled and compressed that even the smallest deviation from the campaign's prepared script is trumpeted as a major development. . . .

Does press frustration, among other factors, ever result in uneven treatment of presidential candidates, a tilt to one side or the other, further helping to foster attack journalism? In other words, are the news media biased? One of the enduring questions of journalism, its answer is simple and unavoidable: of course they are. Journalists are fallible human beings who inevitably have values, preferences, and attitudes galore—some conscious and others subconscious—all reflected at one time or another in the subjects or slants selected for coverage. To revise and extend the famous comment of Iran-Contra defendant Oliver North's attorney Brendan Sullivan, reporters are not potted plants. . . .

. . . [P]ress bias of all kinds—partisan, agenda setting, and nonideological—has influenced the development of junkyard-dog journalism in covering presidents and presidential candidates. But ideological bias is not the be-all and end-all that critics on both the right and left often insist it is. Press tilt has a marginal effect, no more, no less.

Two Cases of Attack Journalism in the 1988 Presidential Election: Dukakis and Quayle

Michael Dukakis's 1988 mental-health controversy is one of the most despicable episodes in recent American politics. The corrosive rumor that the Democratic presidential nominee had undergone psychiatric treatment for severe depression began to circulate in earnest at the July 1988 national party convention. The agents of the rumormongering were "LaRouchies," adherents of the extremist cult headed by Lyndon LaRouche, who claims, among other loony absurdities, that Queen Elizabeth II is part of the international drug cartel.[2]

Shortly after the Democratic convention, the Bush campaign—with its candidate trailing substantially in the polls—began a covert operation to build on the foundation laid by the LaRouchies. As first reported by columnists Rowland Evans and Robert Novak,[3] Bush manager Lee Atwater's lieutenants asked outside Republican operatives and political consultants to call their reporter contacts about the matter. These experienced strategists knew exactly the right approach in order not to leave fingerprints, explains Steve Roberts of *U.S. News & World Report:*

> They asked us, "Gee, have you heard anything about Dukakis's treatment? Is it true?" They're spreading the rumor, but it sounds innocent enough: they're just suggesting that you look into it, and maybe giving you a valuable tip as well.[4]

Many newspapers, including the *Baltimore Sun* and the *Washington Post,* at first refused to run any mention of the Dukakis rumor since it could not be substantiated.[5] But on August 3 an incident occurred that made it impossible, in their view, not to cover the rumor. During a White House press conference a correspondent for *Executive Intelligence Review,* a LaRouche organization magazine, asked Reagan if he thought Dukakis should make his medical records public. A jovial Reagan replied, "Look, I'm not going to pick on an invalid." Reagan half apologized a few hours later ("I was just trying to be funny and it didn't work"), but his weak attempt at humor propelled into the headlines a rumor that had been only simmering on the edge of public consciousness.

Whether spontaneous or planned, there is little doubt that "Reagan and the Bush people weren't a bit sorry once it happened," as CNN's Frank Sesno asserts.[6] The Bush camp immediately tried to capitalize on and prolong the controversy by releasing a report from the White House doctor describing their nominee's health in glowing terms.[7] But this was a sideshow compared with the rumor itself. The mental-health controversy yanked the Dukakis effort off track and forced the candidate and then his doctor to hold their own press conference on the subject, attracting still more public attention to a completely phony allegation. False though it was, the charge nonetheless disturbed many Americans, raising serious doubts about a candidate who was still relatively unknown to many of them. "It burst our bubble at a critical time and cost us half our fourteen-point [poll] lead," claims the Dukakis staff's senior adviser, Kirk O'Donnell. "It was one of the election's turning points; the whole affair seemed to affect Dukakis profoundly, and he never again had the same buoyant, enthusiastic approach to the campaign." [8]

As is usually the case, the candidate unnecessarily complicated his own situation. Until events forced his hand, Dukakis stubbornly refused to release his medical records or an adequate summary of them despite advance warning that the mental-health issue might be raised. But the press can by no means be exonerated. While focusing on the relatively innocent casualty, most journalists gave light treatment to the perpetrators. In retrospect, several news people said they regretted not devoting more attention to the LaRouche role in spreading the rumor, given his followers' well-deserved reputation as "dirty tricksters." [9]

Overall, one of the most important lessons of the Dukakis mental-health episode is that caution must be exercised in reporting on presidential campaign rumors. "The media are really liable for criticism when we get stampeded by competitive instincts into publishing or airing stories that shouldn't be on the record," says National Public Radio's Nina Totenberg. "We were stampeded on the Dukakis story, and we should never have let it happen." [10]

The perils of vice-presidential candidate Dan Quayle became perhaps the most riveting and certainly the most excessive feature of 1988's general election. For nearly three weeks, coverage of the presidential campaign became mainly coverage of Quayle. Most major newspapers assigned an extraordinary number of reporters to the story (up to two dozen), and the national networks devoted from two-thirds to more than four-fifths of their total evening-news campaign minutes to Quayle. Combined with the juicy material being investigated, this bumper crop of journalists and stories produced, in the words of a top Bush/Quayle campaign official, "the most blatant example of political vivisection that I've ever seen on any individual at any time; it really surpassed a feeding frenzy and became almost a religious experience for many reporters." Balance in coverage, always in short supply, was almost absent. First one controversy and then another about Quayle's early life mesmerized the press, while little effort was made to examine the most relevant parts of his record, such as his congressional career.

It was the big-ticket items about Quayle—his National Guard service, the alleged love affair with Paula Parkinson, and his academic record—that attracted the most attention. At the convention, wild rumors flew, notably the false allegation that Quayle's family had paid fifty thousand dollars to gain him admission to the Guard. It was unquestionably legitimate for the press to raise the National Guard issue, although once the picture became clear—Quayle's family did pull strings, but not to an unconscionable degree—some journalists appeared unwilling to let it go. Far less legitimate was the press's resurrection of a counterfeit, dead-and-buried episode involving lobbyist Paula Parkinson. As soon as Quayle was selected for the vice-presidential nomination, television and print journalists began mentioning the 1980 sex-for-influence "scandal," despite the fact that Quayle had long ago been cleared of any wrongdoing and involvement

with Parkinson. "When Quayle's name came up as a vice-presidential possibility, before his selection, the word passed among reporters that Bush
couldn't choose Quayle because of his 'Paula problem,' " admitted one
television newsman. "It was the loosest kind of sloppy association . . . as if
nobody bothered to go back and refresh their memory about the facts of
the case."

Some of the rumors about Quayle engulfing the press corps stretched
even farther back into his past than did the womanizing gossip. Quayle's
academic record was particularly fertile ground for rumormongers. By his
own admission, the vice-presidential nominee had been a mediocre student, and the evidence produced during the campaign suggests that mediocre was a charitable description. At the time, however, a rumor swept
through Quayle's alma mater, DePauw University, that he had been
caught plagiarizing during his senior year. This rumor, which cited a specific teacher and class, was widely accepted as true and became part of the
Quayle legend on campus.

Within a day of Quayle's selection as the vice-presidential nominee, the
rumor had reached the New Orleans GOP convention hall. Hours after the
convention was adjourned, the *Wall Street Journal* published a lengthy article on Quayle's problems, noting unsubstantiated "rumors" of a "cheating
incident." [11] This story helped to push the plagiarism rumor high up on
the list of must-do Quayle rumors, and soon the press hunt was on—for
every DePauw academic who had ever taught Quayle, for fellow students
to whom he might have confided his sin, even for a supposedly mysterious
extant paper or bluebook in which Quayle's cheating was indelibly recorded for posterity.

As it happens, the plagiarism allegation against Quayle appears to have a
logical explanation, and it was apparently first uncovered by the painstaking research of two *Wall Street Journal* reporters, Jill Abramson and James
B. Stewart (the latter a graduate of DePauw, which fortuitously gave him a
leg up on the competition). Abramson and Stewart managed to locate almost every DePauw student who had been a member of Quayle's fraternity, Delta Kappa Epsilon, during his undergraduate years. Approximately
ten did remember a plagiarism incident from 1969 (Quayle's year of
graduation), and the guilty student was in fact a golf-playing senior who
was a political science major and a member of the fraternity—but *not*
Quayle. The similarities were striking and the mix-up understandable after the passage of nearly twenty years. What was remarkable, however, was
the fact that an undistinguished student such as Quayle would be so vividly
remembered by the faculty. Abramson and Stewart also uncovered the reason for this, and even two decades after the fact their finding makes a
political science professor blanch. Quayle was one of only two 1969 seniors

to fail the political science comprehensive exam, a requirement for graduation. (He passed it on the second try.) Abramson's conclusion was reasonable: "Jim Stewart and I believed that people had confused Quayle's failure on the comprehensive exam with his ... fraternity brother's
plagiarism, especially since both events ... occurred at the same time." [12]
Unfortunately for Quayle, however (and also for the public), this explanation did not reach print, even though it might have provided a fair antidote
to the earlier rumor-promoting article. Instead, the assumption that
Quayle must have cheated his way through college solidified and led to
other academically oriented rumors and questions, among them how a student with such a poor undergraduate record could gain admission to law
school.

An observer reviewing the academic stories about Quayle is primarily
struck by two elements. First, despite the windstorm of rumor that repeatedly swept over the press corps, there was much fine, solid reporting, with
appropriate restraint shown about publishing rumors, except for the original *Journal* article mentioning plagiarism and some pieces about Quayle's
law-school admission. Of equal note, however, was the overwhelming emphasis on his undergraduate performance. As any longtime teacher knows,
students frequently commit youthful errors and indiscretions that do not
necessarily indicate their potential or future development. Thus, once
again, the question of balance is raised. How much emphasis should have
been placed on, and precious resources devoted to, Quayle's life in his
early twenties compared with his relatively ignored senatorial career in his
thirties?

Consequences

Having examined some of the truths about feeding frenzies, we now
turn to their consequences. Attack journalism has major repercussions on
the institution that spawns it—the press—including how it operates, what
the public thinks of it, and whether it helps or hurts the development of
productive public discourse. The candidates and their campaigns are also
obviously directly affected by the ways and means of frenzy coverage, in
terms of which politicians win and lose and the manner of their running.
The voters' view of politics—optimistic or pessimistic, idealistic or cynical—is partly a by-product of what they learn about the subject from the
news media. Above all, the dozens of feeding frenzies in recent times have
had substantial and cumulative effects on the American political system,
not only determining the kinds of issues discussed in campaigns but also
influencing the types of people attracted to the electoral arena.

One of the great ironies of contemporary journalism is that the effort to
report more about candidates has resulted in the news media often learn-

ing less than ever before. Wise politicians today regard their every statement as being on the record, even if not used immediately—perhaps turning up the next time the news person writes a profile. Thus the pols are much more guarded around journalists than they used to be, much more careful to apply polish and project the proper image at all times. The dissolution of trust between the two groups has meant that "journalists are kept at an arm's length by fearful politicians, and to some degree the public's knowledge suffers because reporters have a less well-rounded view of these guys," says Jerry terHorst, Gerald Ford's first press secretary and former *Detroit News* reporter.[13] The results are easily seen in the way in which presidential elections are conducted. Ever since Richard Nixon's 1968 presidential campaign, the press's access to most candidates has been tightly controlled, with journalists kept at a distance on and off the trail.[14] And as 1988 demonstrated, the less accessible candidate (Bush) was better able to communicate his message than the more accessible one (Dukakis); the kinder and gentler rewards of victory went to the nominee who was better able to keep the pesky media at bay. . . .

Consequences for the Presidential Candidates

The two cases of attack journalism examined above provide a reliable indication of a frenzy's consequences for a politician. The rumors of Dukakis's mental impairment certainly took his campaign off its stride and probably played at least some role in his defeat. And the attack on Quayle may have permanently damaged his chance of ever being elected to the presidency. Despite somewhat more positive coverage of Quayle during the 1992 campaign, his press secretary, David Beckwith, sees little likelihood that his boss can overcome the frenzy-generated image burdens any time soon: "For the indefinite future there will be lingering questions about Quayle based on what people saw or thought they saw in the [1988] campaign, and it's going to be with him for a number of years." [15] Quayle can be certain that remnants of his past frenzy will resurface and develop in his next campaign. . . .

Consequences for Voters

To voters, what seems most galling about attack journalism in presidential election campaigns is not the indignities and unfairness inflicted on candidates, however bothersome they may be. Rather, people often appear to be irate that candidates are eliminated before the electorate speaks, that irreversible political verdicts are rendered by journalists instead of by the rightful jury of citizens at the polls. The press sometimes seems akin to the Queen of Hearts in *Alice's Adventures in Wonderland*, who declares, "Sentences first—verdicts afterwards."

The denial of electoral choice is an obvious consequence of some frenzies, yet the news media's greatest impact on voters is not in the winnow-
ing of candidates but in the encouragement of cynicism. There is no doubt
that the media, particularly television, have the power to influence people's attitudes. With the decline of political parties, news publications and
broadcasts have become the dominant means by which citizens learn about
public officials; and while news slants cannot change most individuals' basic views and orientation, they can dramatically affect *what* people think
about and *how* they approach a given subject.[16]. . .

Consequences for the Political System

The enhanced—some would say inordinate—influence of the contemporary press is pushing the American political system in certain unmistakable directions. On the positive side are the increased openness and
accountability visible in government and campaigns during the last two
decades. This is balanced by two disturbing consequences of modern press
coverage: the trivialization of political discourse and the dissuasion of
promising presidential candidacies.

As to the former, the news media have had plenty of company in impov-
erishing the debate, most notably from politicians and their television consultants. Nonetheless, journalists cannot escape some of the responsibility.
First, the press itself has aided and abetted the lowering of the evidentiary
standards held necessary to make a charge stick. In addition to the publication of rumor and the insinuation of guilt by means of innuendo, news
outlets are willing to target indiscriminately not just real ethical problems,
but possible problems and the perception of possible problems. Second,
the media often give equal treatment to venial and mortal sins, rushing to
make every garden-variety scandal another Watergate. Such behavior not
only engenders cynicism, but also cheapens and dulls the collective national sense of moral outrage that ought to be husbanded for the real thing.
Third, the press often devotes far more resources to the insignificant gaffe
than to issues of profound national and global impact. On many occasions,
peccadilloes have supplanted serious debate over policy on the front pages.

The second troubling consequence of media coverage has to do with the
recruitment of presidential candidates.[17] Simply put, the price of power
has been raised dramatically, too high for some outstanding potential officeholders.[18] An individual contemplating a run for office must now accept
the possibility of almost unlimited intrusion into his or her financial and
personal life. Every investment made, every affair conducted, every private
sin committed from college years on may one day wind up on television or
in a headline. For a reasonably sane and moderately sensitive person, this
is a daunting realization, with potentially hurtful results not just for the

candidate but for his or her immediate family and friends. American society today may well be losing the services of many exceptionally talented individuals who could make outstanding contributions to the commonweal, but who understandably will not subject themselves and their loved ones to abusive, intrusive press coverage. . . .

Fortunately, we have not yet reached the point where only the brazen enter public service, but surely the emotional costs of running for office are rising. Intensified press scrutiny of private lives and the publication of unsubstantiated rumors have become a major part of this problem. After every election cycle, reflective journalists express regret for recent excesses and promise to do better, but sadly the abuses continue. No sooner had the 1992 presidential campaign begun in earnest than Democratic front-runner Bill Clinton was sidetracked for a time by unproven allegations from an Arkansas woman, Gennifer Flowers, about an extramarital affair. The charges were initially published in a supermarket tabloid, the *Star*, and while some news outlets at first downplayed the story because of the questionable source, others ballyhooed it so extravagantly that Clinton was forced to respond, thus legitimizing full coverage by virtually all news organizations.

This classic case of lowest-common-denominator journalism guaranteed the continued preeminence of the character issue for yet another presidential campaign cycle, and in many ways the situation frustrated reporters and voters alike. Both groups can fairly be faulted for this trivialization of campaign coverage: reporters for printing and airing unproven rumors, and voters for watching and subscribing to the news outlets that were the worst offenders. But journalists and their audiences also have it within their power by means of professional judgment and consumer choice to change old habits and bad practice.[19] Hope springs eternal . . . and in the meantime, attack journalism flourishes.

Notes

1. See the journalists quoted by John B. Judis, "The Hart Affair," *Columbia Journalism Review* 25 (July/August, 1987): 21-25.
2. Dennis King, *Lyndon LaRouche and the New American Fascism* (Garden City, N.Y.: Doubleday, 1989). See especially 121-122.
3. Rowland Evans and Robert Novak, "Behind Those Dukakis Rumors," *Washington Post*, August 8, 1988, A13. Reporters from six major news organizations (all three networks, the *Washington Post*, *U.S. News & World Report*, and the *Los Angeles Times*) told us they had been contacted by Bush operatives about the rumor, and they knew of colleagues at other outlets who had also been called. See also Thomas B. Rosenstiel and Paul Houston, "Rumor Mill: The Media Try to Cope," *Los Angeles Times*, August 5, 1988, 1, 18.
4. Roberts interview.

5. See Edward Walsh, "Dukakis Acts to Kill Rumor," *Washington Post,* August 4, 1988, A1, 6.

6. Frank Sesno, interview with author, Charlottesville, Va., September 27, 1989.

7. Gerald M. Boyd, "Doctor Describes Bush as 'Active and Healthy,' " *New York Times,* August 6, 1988.

8. Kirk O'Donnell, telephone interview with author, June 29, 1990.

9. Dennis King, in *Lyndon LaRouche,* 122, commented upon "the usual [media] reluctance to cover anything relating to LaRouche."

10. Nina Totenberg, telephone interview with author, October 4, 1989.

11. Jill Abramson and James B. Stewart, "Quayle Initially Failed a Major Exam at DePauw, Former School Official Says," *Wall Street Journal,* August 23, 1988, 54.

12. Jill Abramson, interview with author, Washington, D.C., August 4, 1989.

13. Jerald terHorst, interview with author, Washington, D.C., August 4, 1990.

14. See Joseph McGinniss, *The Selling of the President 1968* (New York: Trident, 1969).

15. David Beckwith, telephone interview with author, December 27, 1989. For example, David Broder and Bob Woodward wrote an influential and generally positive series assessing Quayle's career that ran in the *Washington Post* January 5-12, 1992. The series helped to take some of the disparaging edge off Quayle's image.

16. Shanto Iyengar and Donald R. Kinder, *News That Matters: Television and American Opinion* (Chicago: University of Chicago Press, 1988); Thomas E. Patterson, *The Mass Media Election* (New York: Praeger, 1980); Charles Press and Kenneth VerBurg, *American Politicians and Journalists* (Glenview, Ill.: Scott, Foresman, 1988), 62-66; Shanto Iyengar, Mark D. Peters, and Donald Kinder, "Experimental Demonstrations of the 'Not So Minimal' Consequences of Television News Programs," *American Political Science Review* 76 (December 1982): 848-858; and Roy L. Behr and Shanto Iyengar, "Television News and Real-World Cues and Changes in the Public Agenda," *Public Opinion Quarterly* 49 (Spring 1985): 38-57.

17. On this general subject, see also Laurence I. Barrett, "Rethinking the Fair Games Rules," *Time* 130 (November 30, 1987): 76, 78; Richard Cohen, "The Vice of Virtue," *Washington Post,* March 10, 1989, A23; Charles Krauthammer, "Political Potshots," *Washington Post,* March 1, 1989; Norman Ornstein, "The *Post*'s Campaign to Wreck Congress," May 29, 1989, A25; and "Ethicsgate," *Wall Street Journal* editorial, July 15, 1983, 26.

18. Increasing intrusiveness and scrutiny are also factors in the lessened attractiveness of nonelective governmental service. See Lloyd M. Cutler, "Balancing the Ethics Code," *Washington Post,* March 13, 1989, A15; Ann Devroy, "Current Climate of Caution: Expanded FBI Checks Slow Confirmations," *Washington Post,* March 13, 1989, A1, 4-5.

19. Some remedies from the perspectives of both journalists and news consumers are proposed in Larry J. Sabato, *Feeding Frenzy: How Attack Journalism Has Transformed American Politics* (New York: The Free Press, 1991), Chapter 8.

17

THE FORMATION OF CAMPAIGN AGENDAS IN THE UNITED STATES AND BRITAIN

Holli A. Semetko, Jay G. Blumler, Michael Gurevitch,
David H. Weaver, with Steve Barkin and
G. Cleveland Wilhoit

Editor's Note

Candidates for political office and their parties struggle to control media coverage of election campaigns. The authors of this selection describe the battle fought between opposing political groups as well as between politicians and journalists. Comparisons of the battlefields in Britain and the United States show that politicians' attempts to control the media agenda are resisted more fiercely by American journalists than by their British counterparts. Hence American media are less likely than British media to publicize the politicians' pronouncements.

The study clearly demonstrates that media agendas bear the imprint of multiple political institutions and that the interaction chemistry varies in different political cultures and at different historical times. Besides providing keen insights into the reasons for contrasts in British and U.S. campaign coverage, the study counteracts the common tendency to exaggerate the scope of media power in electoral contests.

At the time of writing, this interdisciplinary team of authors and researchers represented three universities: Holli A. Semetko at the University of Michigan; Steve Barkin, Jay G. Blumler, and Michael Gurevitch at the University of Maryland; and David H. Weaver and G. Cleveland Wilhoit at Indiana University. The selection comes from The Formation of Campaign Agendas: A Comparative Analysis of Party and Media Roles in Recent American and British Elections *(Hillsdale, N.J.: Erlbaum, 1991), chap. 9.*

. . . [A]cademic researchers need to appreciate more fully a basic truth about the formation of campaign agendas, which most practitioners (politicians and journalists alike) have entirely absorbed by now—namely, that the process is a deeply political one, as is the role of the media in it.

From *The Formation of Campaign Agendas: A Comparative Analysis of Party and Media Roles in Recent American and British Elections,* © 1991. Hillsdale, NJ: Lawrence Erlbaum Associates.

Agenda-setting terminology is not well placed to alert us to this. It tends to reduce the process to a semi-mechanical practice, connoting a sedate ordering of items for sequential consideration before the real business of debate and decision taking over them begins.

In election communication, however, the reality is quite different. Once a campaign is announced (or approaches), a common element in both the United States and Britain is the unleashing in earnest of an implacably competitive struggle to control the mass media agenda, a struggle that pits, not only candidates and parties in contention for agenda domination, but also political campaign managements against news organization teams. Awareness of their involvement in such a struggle is a leitmotif of our observations of NBC and BBC journalists, expressed variously as a "tug of war," a desire not to give electioneering politicians a "free ride," and a concern to show that they were not completely in the pockets of the candidates and political parties. It is true that acknowledgment of this tussle was more open at NBC and less explicit at the BBC in 1983, when it was conditioned by "prudential" and "reactive" justifications for passing on the party message more or less as offered. Even there, however, the "conventional journalists" strove to repackage it in newsvalue terms, whereas the more analytically minded correspondents sought to reshape it for coherence and meaningful electoral choice.

Moreover, another observation exercise during the British election of 1987 found, throughout the BBC news team, an acute awareness of much discomfort over the parties' tactics for besting their opponents and mastering television in the pursuit of agenda control (Blumler, Gurevitch, & Nossiter, 1989).

The root of this process is the fact of course that (apart from advertisements and party broadcasts) journalists command the gates of access for political messages to reach the electoral audience, including powers not only of selection but also of contextualizing commentary, packaging, and event definition. To would-be wooers of increasingly volatile voters, breaking through those gates with one's preferred message as intact as possible is quite vital. Interpreting the ensuing struggle as "political" is useful in highlighting an advantage that politicians bring to it. They have no difficulty or inhibition about treating message projection as a process of exerting leverage, pressure, and manipulation. After all, they regularly play games of that kind in all their other activities. For media personnel this does present a problem, however, because it highlights their involvement in a political process, despite their claims to be outsiders and their protestations that they are merely observing and reporting campaign events through the self-denying norms of objectivity and impartiality.

Indeed, the tensions inherent in their position may be seen in the near consensual view expressed by television newspeople in the American presidential election of 1988, that campaign managers and their media mavens had "discovered" and exploited the medium's Achilles heel, namely the predictability of the journalists' news judgments, and their inability to resist "good pictures." Consequently, many of them felt that they had ended up being "the losers" in that campaign, acknowledging thereby that they are indeed involved in a struggle over the agenda. The resulting frustration probably helps to explain their readiness, when politicians seem to have put one over on them, to "disdain" the news they are presenting by drawing attention to its deliberately crafted and manipulative origins. And although such disdaining responses were more evident at NBC in 1984 than at BBC in 1983, in 1987 they were being voiced more often by British television reporters, justified at times in the language uncannily similar to what we had been told in New York (see Blumler, Gurevitch, & Nossiter, 1989; see also, Semetko, 1989).

[Another] major implication of this analysis is quite simply that future studies should not take mass media agenda setting for granted (as in much of the past literature). That is, media agendas should not be regarded as solely determined by journalists and news organizations. Nor should they be regarded as primarily determined by political parties and candidates during election campaigns. Instead there are a number of differentiating influences that affect how much discretion both journalists and politicians have in setting campaign agendas, and these influences must be considered in drawing conclusions about how much either journalists or politicians contribute to campaign agendas.

At the system level, such influences include:

1. The strength of the political party system—with a stronger party system generally associated with less discretion on the part of journalists to set the campaign agenda and more opportunity for politicians to do so.
2. Public service versus commercial media systems—with commercial systems associated with more desire by journalists to set political agendas and not merely reflect party and candidate agendas, but with less newshole space into which to squeeze their contributions.
3. Differing levels of competition for media audiences—with more competition being associated with more attention to perceived audience interests and less attention to politicians' agendas by journalists.
4. Differing degrees of professionalization of the campaign—with more professional management of political campaigns being associated with less discretion for journalists to set the agenda and with a growth of

cynicism and skepticism about the legitimacy of the election communication process generally.

5. Cultural differences—with more respect for politics being associated with a greater willingness on the part of journalists to let the political parties and candidates have more discretion in setting the campaign agenda and less emphasis on the election as a game or a horse race at the expense of substantive issues.

These system-level or macro influences are not the only ones affecting the agenda-setting process. There are also more specific, or microlevel, conditions that enhance and limit the discretionary power of journalists and politicians to set campaign agendas. Our study identified several, including:

1. The partisan or ideological leanings of specific media organizations. Even though this influence is more obvious in editorials, feature columns, and commentaries, there is some evidence that it can affect specific subject and theme agendas in news coverage.
2. The status of the candidate. An incumbent president or prime minister is usually in a better position to influence the campaign agenda than a challenger. Even in a system historically endowed with third parties, like that in Britain, their agenda-setting powers are limited.
3. Journalistic norms of balance and objectivity. These are most likely directly to affect the amount of coverage of each party and the number of sources cited from the different campaigns rather than their issue agendas, although covering candidates with balance and objectivity may have some effect on which issues are emphasized.
4. The size of the newshole. Most newspapers have far more space for news of a campaign than do television news programs, and full-size broadsheets have more space than tabloids. More space permits more issues to be covered in greater detail and has the potential to broaden the agenda.
5. Journalists' notions of what roles are most appropriate (e.g., prudential, reactive, conventionally journalistic, analytical; or neutral transmitter, interpreter, adversary) when covering a campaign. Our studies suggest that the roles of analyst or interpreter and adversary are more likely to be associated with more endeavor by journalists to shape the campaign agenda by initiating stories and raising questions that politicians might prefer not to address.

Taken together, these influences suggest that the formation of the campaign agenda is a complex process that varies from one culture and one election to another. Scholars of media agenda setting need to take these factors into account when theorizing about the process, even if their primary interest is in relationships between media and public agendas as has been the case for most research on this topic in the United States.

Whether or not the media are actively setting agendas or simply passing on the agendas of powerful news sources (to think of the extremes) very much depends on the influences just itemized. In the case of Britain it is difficult to speak of the media *setting* agendas, whereas even in the U.S. case it is clear that the major news media do not have unlimited discretion to set campaign agendas. Perhaps a more accurate term for the role of the news media in recent American campaigns might be *agenda shaping,* whereas some portion of their contribution to British campaigns might be termed *agenda amplifying.*

Indeed, future studies of the formation of media and public agendas might wish to conceive of a continuum from "agenda setting" to "agenda reflecting" with "agenda shaping" and "agenda amplifying" falling in between the two extremes. Regardless of the labels applied, future studies of media agendas need to take into account a variety of macro- and micro-level influences in analyzing how the media agenda is formed before trying to relate that agenda to public concerns. Extension of the comparative approach to other societies, beyond the two countries in which we were able to work, could bring to light yet other macro- and micro-level influences. Without taking into account the various influences on the formation of the media agenda, there is a tendency to overestimate the power of journalists and news organizations to set campaign or other agendas and thus to oversimplify the influence of journalists, however crucial, on public priorities. . . .

The Comparative Dimension

. . . To what insights, then, has this piece of comparative work helped to open our eyes? Our answer takes three forms.

First, and most generally, it strongly underlines the presence of political communication variability *within* the broad category of competitive democratic politics. Societies that are alike in their commitment to a periodic democratic choice of leaders, a public airing and discussion of alternative issue priorities and policies, and the ideals of free journalism can operate political communication systems that differ significantly from each other— for example, in the kinds of agendas placed before audiences in the media, in the levels of ease or difficulty that parties and candidates have in getting their messages into such agendas on their own terms, and in the macro-societal forces that help to determine this. . . .

Second, a higher level of media discretionary power was found in the American campaign, when compared with the behavior of the British media in reporting the British campaign. Thus, the American coverage tended to give proportionately less space to candidates' statements than did the British, to surround them with evaluative remarks more frequently, to be based more often on media-initiated rather than politician-initiated news and events, and to offer an issue agenda less closely in line with the competing politicians' agendas.

. . . [T]wo patterns in the findings were not anticipated when we designed this study. One of these differentiates the two media under examination. Although British television performed differently from American television on almost all agenda-forming indicators, for the press the Anglo-American differences were less numerous. It is true that relatively more party-initiated material appeared in the election news columns of the British newspapers compared to the American ones. The party leanings of the former were also more evident in their news coverage. But cross-national press differences were slight or nonexistent over story length, election news prominence, proportions of space devoted to comment beyond straightforward news reports, and the use of directly quoted politicians' statements.

This pattern introduces an important comparative complication: Macrosocietal system influences may bear somewhat differently on different media within their ambit. In our case, very likely the different role of the British press when compared to the U.S. press may be explained by (a) its place in a culture that accords a higher valuation to "politics as such" and (b) its ties to a stronger party system. Such sources of differences are mitigated, however, by the subordination of the commercially owned newspapers of both countries to market pressures and by a need not to stretch unduly the tolerance of less politically minded readers for campaign news.

Thus, the more comprehensive set of agenda-forming differences found for the role of television in the two societies' elections is probably best explained by the contrast between a public service system, which in Britain could afford to make all sorts of exceptional arrangements to ensure an ample and tolerably sustained and substantive campaign coverage, and a commercial television system, which in the United States tended to subordinate election news to everyday news selection values and routines and to the imperatives of intense competition for ratings and advertising income between the three national networks.

The other "departure" from our original expectations concerns the television coverage itself, where cross-national differences were predominantly found on the verbal plane and were hardly noticeable at all in the visual material. Although, for example, stories were more often media initiated in the American than the British television coverage, and American reporters offered more directional and even disdaining commentary, the parties and candidates in both countries managed to initiate the majority of the visuals presented to viewers—and most of these were positive.

This suggests that although more journalistic mediation is possible in certain political communication systems than others, such discretionary scope is greater with verbal material than for pictures. This has important implications for our assessment of the balance of forces that play on the formation of campaign agendas. In both countries, parties and candidates are clearly able to determine much of the pictorial part of the coverage. The visuals are thus a very important source of candidate input. In the United States this may be countered somewhat by critical reporter commentaries. Campaign managers, however, continue to believe firmly in the power of the visual over the verbal. Further research in this area should focus on whether visuals do have a stronger or more lasting impact on viewers' impressions than does the verbal element of television news.

Third, our comparative findings draw attention to important differences in how the choice is presented to voters through politicians' statements on television in the two national systems. Soundbites in the U.S. campaign coverage are generally shorter than in the British, and they are saying on average much less than are their British counterparts. This lends itself to an emphasis on the simplistic and snappy, whereas in Britain there is room for more extended comment and more complex dialogue. One could say that in the United States, politicians are rewarded for the provision of succinct soundbites; this is less the case in the United Kingdom.

Furthermore, there is less discussion of substantive issues in the American campaign in comparison with the British coverage. Of course, in both countries much election news is driven by the day's events on the campaign trail, which are geared in turn to the perceived needs and deadlines of television. The greater room for issue coverage in British television news stems from a different philosophy about the importance of the election and the responsibility of television news during it. More issue attention on British television also stems from the fact that politicians spend more time presenting their views on such issues, with more opportunities for this built into the structure of the campaign day. Press conferences every morning and leader speeches at party rallies most evenings are two important sources of substantive issue statements by politicians that are usually fed into the appropriate news bulletins. What is most often carried in U.S. network news is the equivalent of the British politicians' afternoon "walkabouts" which are heavy on imagery and light on substance. . . .

References

Blumler, J.G., Gurevitch, M., & Nossiter, T.J. (1989). The earnest vs. the determined: Election newsmaking at the BBC, 1987. In I. Crewe & M. Harrop (Eds.), *Political communications: The general election campaign of 1987* (pp. 157-174). Cambridge: Cambridge University Press.

Semetko, H.A. (1989). Television news and the "Third Force" in British politics: A case study of election communication. *European Journal of Communication, 4* (4), 453-479.

18

SHOW HORSES IN HOUSE ELECTIONS: THE ADVANTAGES AND DISADVANTAGES OF NATIONAL MEDIA VISIBILITY

Timothy E. Cook

Editor's Note

Timothy E. Cook discusses the increasing importance of mass media publicity for members of Congress. Work horses, who concentrate on legislative duties, are turning into show horses, who prance around seeking publicity. Media coverage is particularly crucial during elections, when name recognition boosts a member's chances of being elected. Local coverage is generally more helpful than national coverage, however. Local newspeople usually feature the representative's achievements in matters of high concern to constituents. Reporters for the national media are apt to be more negative and to write stories that may be of limited local interest.

The study combines two research approaches: content analysis of national nightly television news and the New York Times, *and interviews with press secretaries whose views about the value of media coverage were elicited in two surveys. Contrary to political folklore, frequency of coverage by the national news media did not influence vote totals, but it did have other effects. Negatively, national coverage tended to attract stronger, better-financed rivals, thereby reducing the chances of reelection. Positively, it helped representatives become national spokespersons for issues of special interest to them and created national constituencies for these issues. Being a show horse thus ultimately aids the work horse role. It may also indirectly help reelection by strengthening the representative's legislative record.*

At the time of writing, Cook was associate professor of political science at Williams College, specializing in legislative and electoral politics. In 1984-1985 he served as a congressional fellow in the office of Ohio representative Don Pease. The selection comes from "Show Horses in House Elections: The Advantages and

The unabridged version of this essay appears in *Campaigns in the News: Mass Media and Congressional Elections,* Jan Pons Vermeer, ed. (Greenwood Press, Inc., Westport, CT, 1987), pp. 161-182. Copyright © 1987 by Jan Pons Vermeer. Abridged and reprinted with permission.

Disadvantages of National Media Visibility," in Campaigns in the News:
Mass Media and Congressional Elections, *ed. Jan Pons Vermeer (New York:
Greenwood Press, 1987), 161-81. Several tables and footnotes have been
omitted.*

A familiar complaint in current assessments of Congress has been to
decry the preoccupation in both the House and the Senate with publicity.
According to numerous scholars, beginning with Mayhew's (1974a) influential essay, Congress is nowadays organized less to address constructively
public problems than to provide maximum opportunities for self-promo-
tion. The "work horse," some say, has been succeeded by the "show
horse," to the point that the mass media's effects on Congress include
exacerbating the dispersion of power, increasing the dilemmas of coalition
building in the institution, and contributing to the decline of Congress as a
national policy-making body (see especially Robinson, 1981, Ornstein,
1983, and Ranney, 1983; a journalistic account that stresses this shift is
Broder, 1986).

Evidence abounds that members of both the House and the Senate devote increasing resources to the search for publicity, not only through self-
promotional efforts like trips home and mass mailings but also through the
mass media. For example, the recent institutionalization of a designated
press secretary position in House offices attests to the importance of the
media as one focus for congressional activity. As of the Ninety-eighth Congress, in 1984, only 28 percent of House offices listed no staffers with
press responsibilities—a striking shift from the Ninety-first Congress, in
1970, in which 84 percent of House offices had no designated press aide
(Cook, 1985). Likewise, the national publicity accorded to House members has expanded during the same time period; whereas only 24 percent
of House members were covered *at all* by the network news in 1970, more
recent figures are as high as 55 percent in 1981 (Cook, 1986). Members
may then be spending more time publicizing themselves and their activities, and they may be receiving more coverage, but it is less clear why they
are doing so, how they are doing so, and with what effect.

The most common presumption has been that members of Congress
pursue publicity to ensure reelection. There can be little doubt that the
mass media play an important and growing role in congressional elections
and reelections. Recognition of the competing candidates is a central determinant of voting decisions, and is highly affected by media coverage. As
media advertising takes ever larger chunks of campaign finances, receiving
free media exposure becomes crucial (see especially Goldenberg and
Traugott, 1984). However, our knowledge approaches completeness only
on the impact of local media coverage of the incumbent on congressional

elections, where the symbiotic relationship of members and local media appears to work to the decisive benefit of the incumbent.[1] By providing newsworthy items to report, the members help the local media fill their newsholes; by reporting about the incumbents uncritically, the local media not only assure their own continued access to the newsmaking members, but also help to boost the incumbents' name recognition and favorable popular assessments of their activities.

The local media, however, make up only one part of what Robinson (1981) nicely terms the members' "media mix." We understand far less about the importance and impact of another component—national media visibility—on congressional elections, even though it is there that "show horses" often direct their attention. National media visibility has traditionally been assumed to be an advantage to members seeking reelection. For instance, Mayhew's (1974a) concept of advertising and Payne's (1980) consideration of "show horses" both suggest the national media as a key conduit of publicity with presumably beneficial effects on getting returned to Congress. Likewise, some members of Congress were initially prone to anticipate the incursion of national media into the House—especially the broadcasting of floor proceedings—as helping in reelection. In 1979 then-Representative John Anderson, a Republican from Illinois, called the nascent House television system "one more incumbent protection device at taxpayers' expense [that will] distort and prolong our proceedings by encouraging more and longer speeches for home consumption" (in Cooper, 1979, p. 252). On the other hand, there is reason to doubt that national media attention is seen to be as much of a plus for members in reelection as has been commonly assumed. Robinson (1981), for one, contends that most members of Congress see the national media as being tougher and less fair to them than the pliant local media. And insofar as news coverage of Congress does tend to be more negative than positive (see Miller et al., 1979; Robinson and Appel, 1979; Tidmarch and Pitney, 1985), members may wish to avoid any guilt by association with the disdained institution far from the home district where the incumbent's support is best nurtured and reinforced.

It is then unclear whether the national media help or hurt the incumbents' pursuit of reelection. . . . [National] media coverage could empirically influence congressional election outcomes in interrelated ways. First, there could be a direct relationship between media visibility and the percentage of votes received by the incumbent; voters could respond directly, whether favorably or unfavorably, to noticing their representative in the national news. . . .

Second, and probably more likely, given the even chances that a representative will not be mentioned in the network news in a given year

(Cook, 1986) and the general inattentiveness of the mass public to nightly network news (Comstock et al., 1977), there could be an indirect relationship mediated through the strength of the challenger as measured by the funds he or she is able to raise and spend (Jacobson, 1980). . . .

To test these suggestions, data were collected for a variety of activities engaged in by members at least in part for electoral benefit (e.g., trips home, bills co-sponsored, district staff allocations), the member's position within the House (e.g., leadership status, seniority), and electoral liabilities (e.g., estimates of policy discrepancy from the district, ethical accusations), as well as indicators of partisan strength and the incumbent's past electoral performance in previous years, in order to assess the impact of media coverage over and above those variables more commonly thought to affect congressional elections. . . .

The media visibility variables are straightforward. For visibility in the network news, a count was made of the number of times each member was mentioned on any nightly network news broadcast according to the Vanderbilt Television News Abstracts and Indices. . . . For visibility in the national print media, a similar count was taken using the *New York Times Index*. . . .

. . . [I]n neither 1978 nor 1980 did network news visibility have a significant direct effect on the vote totals; instead, the election returns were best explained by long-term and short-term partisan conditions, the challengers' expenditures and political experience, and accusations of ethical improprieties. Appearing on the network news had no independent impact on the vote totals. Similar results obtain if visibility in the *Times* is included in the equation in lieu of the media visibility variable. . . .

Interestingly, media coverage in the network news did have an effect on challengers' strength as measured either by their expenditures or their political action committee (PAC) contributions. The effect is negative in 1978 but is not significant at a .05 level. In 1980, however, network news visibility *positively* predicted challenger moneys, and similar effects were in evidence on challengers' PAC contributions (see Ragsdale and Cook, 1987). Whether or not one was covered by the nightly news apparently increased one's chances of facing a strong opponent, even over and above the effects of variables that would best predict media visibility such as leadership status and ethical accusations.[2] Moreover, at the same time that incumbents' media visibility apparently assisted challengers in their abilities to raise and spend funds, it had no similar effects for incumbents attempting to match challengers' efforts. . . . In sum, national media coverage either in print or over the air seems not to be, at best, a credible strategy for incumbents in seeking reelection, and, at worst, it may be a way to enhance the strength of one's opponent.

Members and National Media:
The Press Secretaries' Perspective

The results from the 1980 election show the perils of national media visibility. Members more visible in the national news were more likely to face credible opponents than those not covered. Receiving what "show horses" seek—coverage by the national media—not only seems not to pay dividends at the polls; it may actually hurt, indirectly but effectively, the member's chances for reelection.

Yet, despite . . . empirical indicators and Robinson's (1981) contention that members and their staffs see the national media as tough and unfair, we know that members of Congress seldom hide from national attention. Of course, it may be that the national media may be worth the reelection risks in order to attain other goals—public policy accomplishments, influence in Washington, progressive ambition, or just plain ego gratification—but could there be subtle benefits from national news attention about which members and staffers are aware?

To estimate whether and why House press operations would pay attention to the national media, I proceeded in two complementary ways. First, I conducted forty semistructured interviews with a representative sample of press secretaries in the fall directly preceding the 1984 election. All interviews were held under "not-for-attribution" conditions in which strict anonymity for member and staffer alike was guaranteed. A semistructured format was chosen in order to ask particular questions while permitting the interviewee to digress into potentially important areas. Although this format does not permit easy quantification, it provides a rich basis for conclusions. Second, through the Association of House Democratic Press Assistants, a three-page questionnaire composed by myself and Lynn Drake, then-president of the association, was sent out in November 1984, after the election, to all Ninety-eighth Congress Democratic House offices, asking the press secretary to respond to questions pertaining to their media operations and their perceptions of a number of strategies and news outlets. The response rate was a reasonably strong 46 percent (N=123), an acceptable percentage considering that numerous House offices do not have any one designated press aide. Only Democrats were studied because of the importance of being able to determine the member for which particular press secretaries worked, and because of the sensitivity of press strategies. Although each of these approaches is imperfect, our ability to triangulate between the two studies enhances the confidence with which one can make conclusions. Moreover, although these surveys cannot give the perceptions of members themselves (or, for that matter, fellow staffers) on the presumed importance of the national media to congressional operations, they do provide solid indications of the strategies preferred by those most closely working with the press and the approaches that they bring to the relationship of Congress and the media.[3]

During the semistructured interviews I asked what the major focus of the press secretaries' jobs were, what they spent the most time doing, who they dealt with, and the strategies they used to get their members' names in the news. Questions about the national media were expressly reserved until later in the interview. Frequently, at this point, the respondents had mentioned nothing about the national media—either electronic or print. Moreover, to the pursuant question, "Do the national media help in getting the job done?" press secretaries were often incredulous, some indicating that nobody in the district read the *Washington Post* or the *New York Times*. National media do not seem to help most press secretaries in their daily work, as can be seen by the results from the questionnaires of Democratic press secretaries. Table 18-1 reports the mean ratings (on a scale running from a low of 1 to a high of 10) for various outlets and strategies that help to get the press secretaries' jobs done. There was strong consensus on the positive value of local newspapers—either dailies or, to a lesser extent, weeklies—and a slightly weaker agreement on the worth of local television news. However, the national media, whether electronic or print, are rated considerably lower in their value to press secretaries. . . .

. . . [T]here were strong indications that the local media came first. One press secretary said early on, "We'd rather get in the [hometown paper] than the front page of the *New York Times* any day," and only one press secretary among the forty semistructured interviews disagreed with that statement. Getting mentioned on the front page of the *Times* is unlikely, and similar results obtain with a more realistic choice, as found in the questionnaire: only 15 percent disagreed with the statement "I'd rather get on the front page of my hometown daily than in the *New York Times* or the *Washington Post* any day," as reported in Table 18-2.

The national media are then not central to the aims of the vast majority of press secretaries, who generally see their task as getting the member's name and accomplishments publicized back home. The national media are not viewed as less fair to their bosses. Few emphasized that their member discouraged, explicitly or implicitly, national media attention in general. In the survey of Democratic press secretaries, asked to agree or disagree with the statement "The local media are fairer to my boss than the national media," the bulk (59 percent) neither agreed nor disagreed; only 26 percent agreed. Likewise, in Dewhirst's (1983) survey of sixty-two press secretaries in 1981-1982, thirteen rated the national media as fairer, fifteen rated the district media as fairer, and the remainder reported no difference (p. 142). The national media are thus less important

Table 18-1   Democratic Press Secretaries' Evaluation of Media Outlets and Strategies

	Mean	Standard deviation
Local dailies	9.0	1.5
Local weeklies	8.2	2.0
Press releases	8.1	1.8
Newsletters	7.8	2.0
Local television news	7.4	2.6
Targeted mail	6.7	2.7
Radio actualities	5.6	3.3
Recording studio	4.9	2.9
Weekly columns	4.8	3.2
Washington Post	4.7	3.1
Network television news	4.4	3.2
New York Times	4.3	3.1
Televised floor proceedings	3.8	2.7

Source: Calculated by the author from Democratic press secretary questionnaire, November-December 1984.

Note: The question was: "Please rate how valuable each is in getting your job done (on a scale of 1 to 10 with 1 being very low and 10 being very high)." $N \geq 120$.

to House press operations than local media, but they are not shunned as being unfair or negative. . . .

. . . [D]espite . . . potential advantages of using the national media for reelection, not to mention other goals like internal influence and policy accomplishments, virtually all press operations in the House primarily focus on the local media.[4] However, the possible liabilities of national visibility that were apparent in 1980 do not seem to weigh heavily on press secretaries' minds. Instead, several other factors propel press operations to favor local over national media in the pursuit of reelection.

First, the local media are the main customers for their product. Not only do press secretaries find local outlets more valuable, but local reporters are generally in much closer contact, sometimes on a daily basis, than national reporters. Local media, after all, come to depend on individual members to regularly make news for them. In the words of the press secretary to a four-term midwestern Republican from a rural district, "journalists are glad to talk to a member of Congress. It's an easy story, it's good copy 'cause anything he says is news. It makes the day easier to fill twenty column-inches or thirty seconds that way instead of a leaves-turning-color story." Not only may representatives provide stories of grants being awarded or

Table 18-2   Democratic Press Secretaries' Attitudes on Local Versus National Media

Attitude	"I would rather get in the front page of my home-town daily any day than the New York Times or the Washington Post."	"The local media are fairer to my boss than the national media."
Agree strongly	45% (56)	7% (9)
Agree somewhat	26% (32)	19% (23)
Neither agree nor disagree	10% (13)	59% (73)
Disagree somewhat	12% (15)	9% (11)
Disagree strongly	3% (4)	6% (7)
No answer	3% (4)	1% (1)
Total	99% (124)	101% (124)

Source: Calculated by the author from Democratic press secretary questionnaire, November-December 1984.
Note: Columns do not add to 100% due to rounding.

local heroes being recognized, their reactions can provide a local angle to a national story, making the event more saleable to editors and (presumably) audiences. Most interactions are then with local newspersons; Dewhirst found his sample of sixty-two press secretaries estimating on the average that 76 percent of their time was spent dealing with district media, as compared with 18 percent with national media and 11 percent with statewide media, even though the press releases sent out were approximated to be just about evenly divided between national and local issues (1983, p. 142). It is then difficult to establish rapport with national media, who have numerous reporters covering Congress, sometimes by issues rather than by beat, and with whom contact is sporadic. Keeping regular customers happy and willing to come back to buy a product again is something every enterprise aims for; congressional enterprises are no exception.

Second, even if the member is newsworthy to both local and national media, the latter has different needs, which places an angle on the story that deemphasizes the member's personal role in favor of the issue or controversy concerned. The national media cannot be expected to find 1 out of 435 newsworthy in the same way that the local outlets find the lone representative important. Unlike in the local media, obtaining almost any member's reactions to some national event would not be considered nationally newsworthy unless that member had a base of legitimation as an "authoritative source." The distinction is then not only between local media attending to members versus national media ignoring, but also in what each level considers important, especially since what is newsworthy to the national media can often get covered without covering the member pushing it. . . .

. . . [A]s a result of these two factors, any national coverage on one's own terms requires much more expenditure of resources than it would cost to obtain an equivalent or greater amount of local coverage. This is especially true of network television news, the national medium most likely to directly reach the voters but where the vagaries of the twenty-two minute constraints are unpredictable and where the preparation involved is daunting. As the press secretary to a southern Democratic committee chair concluded, "to do an interview here, it takes up thirty or forty minutes just to get set up and then some more to do it. And then he gets seven seconds of time. Sure seems like a lot of trouble for not very much meat.". . . Given that serving the needs of the local media could easily become a full-time job in any media market, devoting resources to enticing the national media with only uncertain prospects for beneficial results is not an efficient way to ensure that the member almost continually makes news.

Thus dealing with the national media is seldom pursued for reelection purposes. Why, then, do members have any interest in national media visibility? . . . In the questionnaire of the Democratic press secretaries, the respondents were asked to rate the importance of five long-term goals in their work; these variables were then correlated with an index of the value of national media in general. . . .

As reported in Table 18-3, the index of the value of national media was highly correlated with two goals: national spokespersonship and creating national constituencies for an issue. By contrast, the correlations were insignificant with the two constituent-oriented goals and only marginally significant with the goal of progressive ambition.

. . . The national media, it seems, are largely important for national goals. Even considering a run for a more salient office only somewhat impels House press operations to find national media more useful, and they are seldom perceived as an effective way to gain the local benefits, which, more often, are, at best, a useful by-product.

Table 18-3   Correlates of Democratic Press Secretaries' Perceived Value of National Media

Importance of long-term goals	Pearson's r with index of value of national media
Building name recognition of member in district	.06
Creating national constituency for issue	.51[a]
Enabling member to run for higher office	.19[b]
Serving as liaison to different constituent groups	.05
Making member national spokesperson on an issue	.52[a]

Source: Calculated by the author from Democratic press secretary questionnaire, November–December 1984.

[a] $p < .001$.
[b] $p < .05$; all other coefficients not statistically significant at $p < .05$.

Conclusion

Members of Congress have sought publicity throughout history. The show horse—work horse distinction is far from new to students or members of the national legislature. What is new are the allegations that the incentives and rewards for being a show horse now outstrip those for being a work horse. Yet the results here suggest that if being a show horse is primarily oriented toward national media visibility, the main incentives do not include winning reelection, the usual "proximate goal" (Mayhew, 1974a) of members of Congress. Aggregate analyses of election outcomes in 1978 and 1980 show that the aim of show horses, national media visibility, does not seem to help in reelection; the only significant effect was to bolster the campaign moneys and PAC contributions of challengers in 1980. Nor do the interviews with and questionnaires from House press secretaries in 1984 display any dependence on national media attention for getting reelected. Local media are seen as more reliable and predictable outlets, more eager not only to cover the member's activities, but also to stress the member's role itself as the most newsworthy aspect of a story. The national media, it appears, are seldom spurned, but they are not openly pursued in most House offices for reelection. Despite the frequently perceived advantages of the publicity that "trickles down" from national to local coverage, it is simply too costly to spend limited resources getting in the national news when other, less expensive means of publicity exist for the folks back home.

It may well be that more and more members of the House are courting national publicity in a manner once reserved for senators (see, e.g.,

Ornstein, 1981). However, it seems that national media visibility is sought for national goals that cannot be achieved through the local press—especially influence in Washington and attainment of public policy goals. In that sense, members' attentiveness to national media is much more an element exclusively of their Washington styles, not their home styles, to recall Fenno's (1978) crucial distinction. Particularly with the ascendancy of a president, much of whose power rests on the ability to control the agenda through the media (see, e.g., Sinclair, 1985), and with an exceedingly complex Congress in which consensus is difficult to achieve by the old rules of bargaining, members can find that strategies to work with and through the national media are central ways to attain goals inside the institution through such an outside strategy. If there are some slight advantages for reelection as a by-product, so much the better; if there are risks involved, as the aggregate findings from 1980 suggest there may be, most members do not apparently conclude that such risks rule out the importance and value of dealing with the national media.

"Show horses" in Congress are not, then, primarily receiving a boost for reelection, nor are they primarily getting ego gratification from their names in the national headlines and their faces on the nightly news. Even if they do not exploit such strategies much for reelection, being a show horse is rationally goal-oriented more than it is an effect of personality dynamics alone—oriented toward goals that make being a show horse and being a work horse more compatible than mutually exclusive. If members were interested only in reelection, we might not see them paying any attention to the national media. That the national media are not ignored is then testimony to two crucial arguments: members of Congress have important multiple goals beyond reelection and, just as important, media effects must be presumed to go beyond electoral politics in a way whereby the audience usually studied, the mass public, is not directly involved. Whether legislative styles geared toward and dependent on national media are effective ways to get things done in Congress cannot be answered here; all we can conclude is that such styles are not efficient tools for reelection. National media visibility is indeed a resource much more accessible to incumbents than to challengers. But, unlike its local counterpart, its effects as a key perquisite of office are mixed.

Notes

1. . . . Book-length treatments that underscore this point include Clarke and Evans (1983) and Goldenberg and Traugott (1984).
2. It has been suggested that 1979 might have been a year of unusually bad news. Yet, despite the well-known tribulations of the Carter administration, 1979 was, in most ways, a typical news year for Congress. . . .

3. The two samples are fairly representative of the larger populations. In the sample of House press secretaries who were selected from semistructured interviews, Southerners are slightly underrepresented, whereas Northeastern-ers are slightly overrepresented; fortunately the biases were reversed in the questionnaire of Democratic press secretaries. The questionnaire also over-represents press secretaries to freshmen representatives, although this bias will help us to distinguish more clearly the differences between those engaging in the "new apprenticeship" of the first term and those who have gotten past their first reelection.

4. Even in the Senate, long known for being a publicity chamber and president incubator, a recent study concludes that most senators' press operations are largely focused on the home state media (Hess, 1986).

Bibliography

Broder, David. (1986). "Who Took the Fun Out of Congress?" *Washington Post Weekly Edition.* (February 17): 9-10.

Clarke, Peter and Susan H. Evans. (1983). *Covering Campaigns: Journalism in Congressional Elections.* Stanford, California: Stanford University Press.

Comstock, George et al. (1977). *Television and Human Behavior.* New York: Columbia University Press.

Cook, Timothy E. (1985). "Marketing the Members: The Ascent of the Congres-sional Press Secretary." Paper presented at the annual meeting of the Midwest Political Science Association, Chicago, Illinois.

———. (1986). "House Members as Newsmakers: The Effects of Televising Congress." *Legislative Studies Quarterly.* 11:203-26.

Cooper, Ann. (1979). "Curtain Rising on House TV Amid Aid-to-Incumbent Fears." *Congressional Quarterly Weekly Report.* (February 10): 252-54.

Dewhirst, Robert E. (1983). "Patterns of Interaction Between Members of the U.S. House of Representatives and Their Home District News Media." Ph.D. dissertation, University of Nebraska-Lincoln.

Fenno, Richard F., Jr. (1978). *Home Style: House Members in Their Districts.* Boston: Little, Brown.

Goldenberg, Edie N. and Michael W. Traugott. (1984). *Campaigning for Congress.* Washington, D.C.: CQ Press.

Hess, Stephen. (1986). *The Ultimate Insiders: The Senate and the National Press.* Washington, D.C.: The Brookings Institution.

Jacobson, Gary C. (1980). *Money in Congressional Elections.* New Haven, Connecti-cut: Yale University Press.

Mayhew, David R. (1974a). *Congress: The Electoral Connection.* New Haven, Connecticut: Yale University Press.

Miller, Arthur H., Edie N. Goldenberg, and Lutz Erbring. (1979). "Type-set Politics: The Impact of Newspapers on Public Confidence." *American Political Science Review.* 73:67-84.

Ornstein, Norman J. (1981). "The House and the Senate in the New Congress." In Thomas Mann and Norman Ornstein, eds., *The New Congress.* Washington,

D.C.: American Enterprise Institute, pp. 363-83.

————. (1983). "The Open Congress Meets the President." In Anthony King, ed., *Both Ends of the Avenue*. Washington, D.C.: American Enterprise Institute, pp. 185-211.

Payne, James L. (1980). "Show Horses and Work Horses in the United States House of Representatives." *Polity*. 12:428-56.

Ragsdale, Lyn and Timothy E. Cook. (1987). "Representatives' Actions and Challengers' Reactions: Limits to Candidate Connections in the House." *American Journal of Political Science*. 31:45-81.

Ranney, Austin. (1983). *Channels of Power: The Impact of Television on American Politics*. New York: Basic Books.

Robinson, Michael J. (1981). "Three Faces of Congressional Media." In Thomas E. Mann and Norman J. Ornstein, eds., *The New Congress*. Washington, D.C.: American Enterprise Institute, pp. 55-96.

Robinson, Michael J. and Kevin R. Appel. (1979). "Network News Coverage of Congress." *Political Science Quarterly*. 94:407-13.

Sinclair, Barbara. (1985). "Agenda Control and Policy Success: Ronald Reagan and the 97th House." *Legislative Studies Quarterly*. 10:407-13.

Tidmarch, Charles and John Pitney. (1985). "Covering Congress." *Polity*. 17:446-83.

IV

CONTROLLING MEDIA POWER: POLITICAL ACTORS VERSUS THE PRESS

Political actors try to control how journalists portray them and their causes in the mass media. The outcome of this perennial struggle is uncertain because journalists receive conflicting demands, and they also want to use their own insights. Part IV begins with a look at normal coverage patterns for the presidency, the office most in the media limelight. It then turns to routine coverage of Congress and its members. The contrast between media impact on senators and representatives and media impact on the president puts the distinctions between these political actors into sharper focus. An example of news coverage when the presidency is in crisis follows. It points out how all parties to a major conflict use the media to compete for favorable public opinion. Part IV concludes with two selections that show how media coverage affects politically disadvantaged interest groups: ordinary people at the fringes of the power structure and ordinary people who defy the mores of the established culture.

The first selection offers a systematic analysis of media coverage of presidents over a sixteen-year period. Fred T. Smoller delineates how impressions about presidents are created by the media. He explains why these impressions are so politically potent and contends that, on balance, they have diminished the stature and power of the presidency. Bruce J. Evensen continues in a similar vein. His essay documents a successful attempt by the *New York Times* to torpedo the foreign policy of the Truman administration. While both writers are undoubtedly correct in their assessment that presidential control over the media is bounded, the reverse side of the power coin cannot be ignored. By virtue of the preeminence of their office, presidents have become the prime sources of political news in the world. The press must listen and cater to them and their surrogates to get the ample news that it wants.

Michael J. Robinson's essay explains variations in media treatment of Congress. Stories differ in nature and impact depending on whether they appear in the national or local press or in publications issued by the legislator's office or campaign. Robinson points out that publicity that may hurt a political institution may, at the same time, help its office holders, and vice versa. His comparison of media treatment of Congress and the presidency puts the congressional analysis into illuminating perspective.

Stephen Hess speculates about Congress members' motivations for seeking media attention. If, as Hess argues, efforts to attract press coverage have relatively few political pay-offs for most legislators, why undertake them? The answer is vanity—a human quality that abounds in politicians who know that modesty is no asset in their line of work.

What happens when a president is under serious attack? Do newspeople close in for the kill like a wolf pack stalking wounded prey? Gladys Engel Lang and Kurt Lang reach surprising conclusions after examining the role played by the mass media in the resolution of the Watergate scandal. Their study also sheds light on the media's function in defining public opinion for policy makers.

From people in formal positions of power, the discussion turns to citizens who band together to seek governmental remedies for shared problems or who strive to gain favorable public attention for their chosen causes. Gadi Wolfsfeld describes how groups of students, industrialists, and Palestinians tried different techniques, matched to their resources, to attract media attention to support their causes. Their efforts met with mixed success, and their benefits from coverage varied widely. In the final selection Douglas M. McLeod and James K. Hertog use a content analysis of media coverage of anarchist protest groups to demonstrate how easy it is to denigrate such unpopular movements. A favorite tactic, used effectively by the mainstream press, is to suggest that public opinion opposes the movement and that the group's behavior violates accepted social norms. By contrast, anti-establishment media support the group's goals by picturing the protest as an epic battle in which the targets are evil and the protesters are moral heroes.

19

THE SIX O'CLOCK PRESIDENCY: PATTERNS OF NETWORK NEWS COVERAGE OF THE PRESIDENT

Fred T. Smoller

Editor's Note

Does television enhance the power of the presidency, particularly in relation to Congress, and increase presidents' ability to mobilize public support for their programs? Unlike many scholars, Fred T. Smoller answers this question in the negative. In his view the emergence of television as a primary news source about presidents has contributed to the decline of the presidency. His theory is based upon analysis of CBS news coverage of the presidency from 1968 to 1985.

Smoller contends that news practices designed to keep tales about the presidency exciting on a daily basis undermine the dignity and efficiency of the office. Exceptional rather than normal occurrences are featured and conflicts are exaggerated. The need for pictures makes reporters focus on the superficial. Good news becomes better and bad news becomes worse than the situation warrants. When Washington insiders are asked to comment about the president, reporters usually call on the president's antagonists because their comments make a racier story. To twist a familiar saying, when it comes to covering the presidency, "good news is no news." In the presidencies from Nixon to Reagan, negativism tended to increase as time progressed. Smoller credits Reagan with partially surmounting this trend through his skilled use of the media opportunities under his control.

At the time of writing, Smoller was assistant professor of political science at Chapman College in California. His research has focused on the impact of electronic media on the presidency. The selection comes from "The Six O'Clock Presidency: Patterns of Network News Coverage of the President," Presidential Studies Quarterly *16:1 (Winter 1986): 31-49. Several tables, figures, and footnotes have been omitted.*

Permission to reprint granted by the Center for the Study of the Presidency, publisher of *Presidential Studies Quarterly*.

Introduction

The Constitution makes no provision for television networks, nor does any act of Congress mandate their existence. Nevertheless, the three networks (ABC, CBS, and NBC) and their nightly news programs are major actors in American politics. They are the primary source from which the public gains its information both about the state of the nation and the conduct of the nation's public officials in promoting its general welfare. This pivotal role gives them immense power to shape the direction of American politics. This power is particularly evident in the area of presidential politics, since the president is the nation's single most important political official and therefore the special object of attention by the nightly news programs.

The great power of the network news programs, and their special attention to the presidency, enable them to play a major role in determining the fate of modern presidents, as well as the fate of the institution itself. This essay will argue, in fact, that the networks, seeking to realize their own goals, set in motion a dynamic pattern that can unravel the career of individual presidents and the public's support for the Office of the Presidency. Thus, the era of televised news coverage has produced a tendency for the modern presidency to be defined by, and systematically destroyed by, the image of presidential performance presented on the evening news. I call this phenomenon the Six O'Clock Presidency because its origins are the needs of the commercial networks rather than the values implicit in the Constitution.

The purpose of this essay is to explore the existence of the Six O'Clock Presidency through two strategies. First, it will present the argument that suggests how and why networks may systematically, if inadvertently, pursue organizational interests that can undermine the presidency. This argument is bolstered by interviews with television news executives, correspondents and technicians, primarily from CBS News, and observations made as a participant-observer in the White House press room during the spring of 1982. Second, it will then look at the actual pattern of news coverage of one network, CBS, from January, 1969 to January, 1985, seeking to document the nature of the negative coverage. . . .

Decisions concerning news coverage and the implementation of network policies are made in the Washington bureau. This is where presidential news stories are "built," and where the limitations imposed by the nature of the medium are accommodated. Three factors in particular—format constraints, the need for pictures, and assumptions about the nature of the viewing audience—systematically influence television news coverage of the president.

Format of the Evening News

The fixed time limit of the evening news program (22 minutes, without commercials) coupled with the belief that the audience will be bored with pieces that run for more than a few minutes, mean that news reports must be short (usually no more than two minutes in duration, frequently less), and therefore uncomplicated, producing, in Walter Cronkite's words, "inadvertent and perhaps inevitable distortion." [1] This means that complexity of the presidency is rarely captured in news reports. Dan Rather put it this way:

> [T]here is no way that I, or any other White House correspondent . . . can come out there in a minute and 15 seconds and give the viewer even the essence, never mind the details or the substance [of a president's policies]. . . . One of the great difficulties of television is that it has a great deal of trouble dealing with any subject in depth. [2]

The Need for Pictures

Television news uses its technology ("pictures") to compete with other news media. The need for pictures affects news coverage of the president in three ways. First, it makes the reporting of complicated stories that focus on complex issues more difficult. Second, it highlights those aspects of the Office that are amenable to pictures and ignores those that are not. Finally, the need for "interesting" pictures reinforces journalism's penchant for the novel and the unusual (e.g., presidential faux pas).

The need for pictures contributes to the distortion of the presidency because pictures capture, condense, simplify and exaggerate complex political phenomena. Pictures often portray politics in "black" and "white," "good" or "evil" terms. The "grays," the qualifications, the nuances, are often lost. News pictures, like political cartoons, are effective devices for symbolic communication (which is why television is ideally suited to political campaigning). Thus, when presidents or candidates control media access, they have a formidable political tool at their disposal. But because pictures present complex political phenomena in symbolic terms reality is often exaggerated. This is how a producer for ABC's "World News Tonight," who was formerly a deputy White House press secretary during the Carter Administration, explained it to me:

> Basically, when things aren't going well at the White House, the evening news' portrayal is worse than in fact the reality is. And then when things are going well for an Administration the stories suggest that things are far better than they are. There is a tendency to extremes because television is so dependent on pictures.
>
> The Camp David peace agreement between Israel and Egypt is a good example. Those pictures of Carter and Begin and Sadat embracing are just

wonderful visuals. The impression they leave is that what occurred was 100 percent positive. A newspaper reporter, however, might go on for two-thirds of his story about what a great achievement it was. But might for the last third talk about the history of the problem and certainly how insurmountable it has been up to this point. He might also add that this achievement hasn't been as great as it may appear.

A negative example would be hecklers at an event who threw tomatoes at the president. This is so visually compelling that the resulting story will be a one minute spot that says, yes, the president spoke, but he was heckled throughout, and following his speech the crowd threw three tomatoes. The visuals of the tomatoes splattering on the secret service agent would be the lasting impression that you would come away with. It would have to be arguably ten times more dramatic to come across in print. So in print you would talk about what was said in the speech and so forth, that he was heckled throughout, and then three tomatoes were thrown.[3]

The need for pictures also biases news coverage toward those aspects of the presidency that are amenable to visual portrayal. Many times this is due to White House restrictions. There are aspects of the Office, however, that simply cannot be photographed. For example, President Carter's efforts to get the hostages released could not be shown in pictures. Instead descriptions of the president's actions had to compete with visually and emotionally engrossing pictures of angry Iranian students burning the American flag. Presidential actions such as the ordering of troops on a mission to free the hostages will receive more coverage than stories concerning the evolution of that policy decision, or, more important, the constraints which inhibit the exercise of presidential power. Because actions (e.g., ceremonies, bill signing, a presidential tour of a disabled nuclear power plant) receive more attention and have greater impact than "processes" (such as the development of policy options, negotiations, the evolution of ideas, the structure and functioning of the office, or the constraints on presidential power), the power, purpose, and functioning of the Office is systematically exaggerated and distorted. This is a direct consequence of the environmental constraints affecting television coverage of the president.

Finally, the need for interesting pictures reinforces journalism's penchant for the unusual, the departure from the norm. Thus, network news coverage of presidential faux pas and clumsiness (e.g., presidents falling down stairs, dropping their election ballot, being attacked by a "killer rabbit," bumping their head on a helicopter door) and visually compelling but often gratuitous, trivial, and unrepresentative stories containing compelling visuals receive more coverage than they might otherwise merit solely because of their value in pictures. In addition, the need for pictures encourages coverage of conflict and controversy and other melodramatic events rather than the plain, routine functioning of government, which is not amenable to interesting pictures. As one producer for the CBS Evening News explained to me:

> There is a real big mandate for pieces to not be boring; no standup, no bland looking stuff. [CBS News] wants it to be more visually enticing. So you try to be more creative. People are not going to watch if it is just a standup. And Que polls show that they like what we are doing, which is pepping up the news. I covered President Reagan when he went to Pittsburgh. There were the angriest demonstrators in the two years that I have been travelling with him. However, if I just had the two crews that was the normal standard on the road I couldn't have gotten good pictures of those demonstrators. I had another crew sent in from New York just to cover them, and that became the main focus of the story.[4]

Audience Assumptions

News coverage of the president is also greatly influenced by network policies which stem from their understanding of the nature of the viewing audience. Specifically, that viewers have a very limited attention span. The first assumption is that "reports are more likely to hold a viewer's attention if cast in the form of the fictive story, with narrative closure."[5] Producers attempt to keep their reports light and entertaining by accentuating conflict and drama and by telling their stories based on a "narrative form."

The narrative form reinforces television's simplistic, abbreviated, and truncated portrayal of the president. In particular, it accentuates reporting of conflict within the administration, and between the administration and other political actors, notably the congress. I am not suggesting that this conflict does not exist; only that the format of the television news story leads itself to its being highlighted. Of course when a president is successful (when his programs are being passed by the congress, and critics have not yet emerged) during the initial months of a new Administration this works in the president's favor. Later, however, when the president is more moderately successful, or simply less successful, the tendency to report the extreme increases the negative portrayal of the president.

The White House and Media Coverage

The White House has a virtual monopoly over information about the president through its control over news gathering. Nevertheless, reporters do not rely solely on the White House for news stories because over-reliance on the White House is frowned on by the producers of the Evening News and because a unitary executive cannot generate enough news to meet the network's demand.[6] To get "airtime," which is necessary for professional advancement, White House reporters must produce stories that meet the needs of the bureau: the stories must be short, uncomplicated, visually interesting when possible, and contain, when possible, elements of conflict, drama, and balance, stressing analysis and criticism over description.[7] Given the factors which constrain and influence correspondent's news judgment (e.g., deadline pressure, rapid turnover, competition, journalistic norms) White House reporters frequently turn to interviews with Washington-based elites for stories about the president. Interviews provide original ideas for new stories and new angles on old ideas. Interviews generally require a minimum of effort on the reporter's part: they can be obtained quickly (often over the phone), are beyond the White House's control, do not require in-depth, time consuming research or specific expertise in a policy area, and can provide the elements of conflict and drama favored by the narrative form.

News stories based on interviews with Washington based elites, however, often contribute to a negative portrayal of the president. If a source is from an interest group, he or she is prone to evaluate the president along narrow or self-interested lines. If the source is a Member of Congress, he or she has partisan and institutional interests to protect. And if the source is a permanent member of the Washington Community, he or she may have reasons for disliking the president which have little or no bearing on the performance of the president's official duties—such as the president's and his staff's ability to conform to the norms and mores of Washington Society (e.g., Carter's "Georgia" mafia, Nancy Reagan's redecorating the White House). Most important, because "president judging" is such a major topic of conversation, it is arguably the case that Washingtonians tend to judge the president sooner and more harshly, and perhaps with a different set of standards, than those who live outside the nation's capital.

The Growth of Negative News Coverage of Presidents and the Presidency

I have argued so far that the networks have reason to give the president extensive coverage and for the bulk of this coverage to be negative in character. But the Six O'Clock Presidency involves more than extensive-negative coverage. It involves: 1) a tendency toward a growth in negative coverage during a president's term of Office, 2) a growth in negative coverage across presidencies, and 3) an erosion of public support for the Office. Here I will present data that support these expectations.

To document these suggested patterns of coverage, I read and coded the transcripts to the CBS Evening News from January 1968 to January of 1985.[8] Approximately 5500 news stories concerning the president, the White House family, the president's staff, and the president's foreign and

Table 19-1   Story Tone by Administration

Administration	Positive	Neutral	Negative	Net tone
All Administrations	18	55	27	−9
Nixon (first)	28	51	20	+8
Nixon (second)	10	50	39	−29
Ford	20	59	21	1
Carter	17	55	28	−11
Reagan	13	57	30	−17

domestic policies are included in the sample. . . . Unfortunately, a full set of transcripts prior to January 1969 is not available. Therefore only three of the presidents in the sample (Nixon, Carter, and Reagan) completed a full four year term. Nevertheless, I believe that this sample of presidents is a diverse one and that it will support a sufficient exploration of the thesis.[9] The president's examined differ in personality, party affiliation, and ideology. Most important, they achieved different levels of success while in Office. . . .

The results of this study show that the tone of the 55% of the 16 years of presidential news considered was neutral (Table 19-1). This finding is not completely surprising, however, because so much presidential news is the routine coverage of the institution. (Notice in Table 19-1 the consistency of the neutral coverage across the presidents.) Stories concerning presidential appointments and nominations and White House statements tend to have no evaluative dimension, yet they make up a great deal of White House coverage. Moreover, the conventions of modern journalism, which are strictly adhered to by CBS News, require news reports to be balanced, fair, and free from personal bias. Stories with a balance of positive and negative comments were coded neutral. Nevertheless, despite these conventions 27% of the coverage of the president was negative, compared to 18% positive. That is, 60% of the directional press was negative. This invites further investigation.

The measure "net tone" is used to pursue this investigation. It captures the net evaluative portrayal of the president. An example illustrates how this measure was computed: Suppose the evening news one night contained three stories about the president, and the first one was positive and was 100 transcript lines long, and the second was neutral and 80 lines long, and the third story was negative and 60 lines long. The total amount of presidential coverage in transcript lines for that show would be 240. Forty two percent (100/240) of this coverage was positive, 33% (80/240) was neutral, and 25% (60/240) was negative. The "net tone" as measured in lines of coverage was 17 (42%−25%=17). The net presentation of the president that

Figure 19-1: Net Tone Score Broken Down by Year

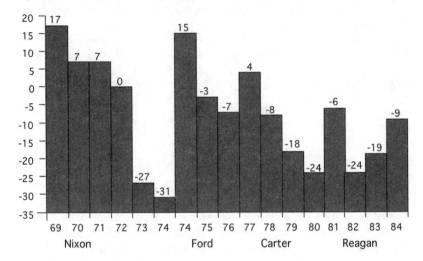

evening therefore was positive. Similarly, if the first story was negative and the third story was positive, the "net tone" as measured in lines of coverage would be −17, and the net presentation of the president that evening would have been negative. This measure assumes that neutral stories have no evaluative impact on public opinion. It also assumes that positive news stories and negative new stories in effect "cancel" one another. This measure allows us to capture the "net image" of the president portrayed on the evening news for a given period of time. For example, the "net tone" for the entire sample was −9. This means that the net evaluative portrayal of the presidency during the years considered was negative.

Main Patterns of Coverage

Figure 19-1 shows net tone scores broken down by year and contains the study's first finding: the net-portrayal of modern presidents on the evening news becomes more negative as their terms progress. This pattern holds for the Nixon, Ford, Carter and the first two years of the Reagan Administration. In only 5 of the 17 years studied (1974 is partitioned between Nixon and Ford) did the incumbent receive a net positive portrayal: 11 of the years were negative, with the bulk of the positive scores occurring in Nixon's first term. Nixon received a negative net portrayal on the evening news for one and a half of his five and a half year tenure. Net tone scores for two of Ford's approximately three year presidency were negative, while Carter received a negative score for three of his four years in Office. Sure prisingly, in his first term Reagan received negative scores each of his four years as president.

My second major finding is that news coverage of the Office of the presidency has grown increasingly negative. Each of the full term presidents (i.e., Nixon—first term, Carter, Reagan) studied received more negative coverage than his predecessor. Nixon's net tone score for his first year in Office was 17; Ford, 15; Carter, 4; and Reagan, −6. ... "[H]oneymoons" are also becoming much less enjoyable. Nixon's net tone score during his "honeymoon" (defined here as approximately the first 100 days in Office) was 30; Ford, 15; Carter, 28 and Reagan, 20. Moreover, honeymoons, at least with the electronic media, are ending more abruptly and more decisively. Nixon's first term net tone score following his first three months in Office drops 18 points (30−12), Ford, 15; Carter, 39 and Reagan, 38. Finally, the average post-honeymoon net tone score for Nixon was 5, for Ford −5; Carter −16 and Reagan, −17. Note that no president since Richard Nixon (first term) has received a net positive portrayal on the evening news after his first three months in Office. Negative coverage on the evening news appears to be the norm for the televised presidency.

The study's third expectation was that negative coverage has undercut public support for the president. Public approval influences the reception a President's proposals receive in Congress, his clout with foreign and domestic elites, and the boundaries of a President's Constitutional power. A president's approval rating, as measured by Gallup, has been shown to be a good predictor of the vote share received by incumbents running for re-election and of the success members of the president's party encounter in midterm elections.[10] Because the presidents need public support to govern effectively, political analysts are disturbed by the tendency for presidents to lose support as their terms progress. ...

Citizens, it is assumed, monitor various performance dimensions of the presidency through the media, which disseminates information concerning the president and his policies.... [T]he strong positive correlation ... between net tone scores and Gallup support ratings (averaged for corresponding periods), suggest that the president's portrayal on the evening news is one, albeit of several, determinates of public support.[11] The correlation coefficients for net tone score with Gallup approval ratings for each presidency were as follows: Nixon, .89; Ford, .54; Carter, .83 and Reagan, .72.

Ronald Reagan: The Great Communicator?

Contrary to his popular image as a "great communicator," his acting skills, his landslide defeat of Carter, the assassination attempt on his life; and despite his string of legislative victories, Ronald Reagan received more negative coverage than any of the presidents considered (See Table 19-1). Nevertheless, he has been able to transcend the consequences of this negative portrayal: he's maintained popular support; won the endorsement of his party and an overwhelming victory against Walter Mondale. Instead of contradicting the Six O'Clock presidency thesis, however, I believe the Reagan Administration may help confirm it.

To understand the Reagan presidency it is necessary to distinguish two forms of the electronic media, "controlled" and "uncontrolled." Controlled media is the form of electronic media over which the White House has the most influence. The tone of such coverage is generally positive, but this can vary depending on the personal attributes of the president and the skills of his staff. Examples of controlled media include presidential addresses and political advertisements. Toward the other end of the continuum is "uncontrolled" media, principally the evening news. The White House can exert some influence over the coverage the president receives on the evening news through its control over the president's schedule, access to the president and his aides, and the release of information. However, the White House cannot significantly influence the tone of the coverage the president receives on the evening news over an extended period of time.[12] Arrayed along the continuum lie the other forms of coverage, their position based on the level of control the White House has over the president's portrayal.

The Reagan Administration has been able to maintain public support despite its negative portrayal on the evening news by effectively using the controlled electronic media. Where once presidents used the press to "go over the heads of Congressmen," the Reagan Administration has used controlled electronic media (e.g., weekly radio broadcasts, political advertisements prior to the electoral season, and recently, the setting up of the White House News Service which will distribute the Reagan Administration's version of the news to radio stations and small newspapers) to transcend the pattern of network news coverage I have described. This unexcelled use of controlled television coupled with the public relations skills of the president's top aides has, for Reagan's first term, allowed Reagan to transcend the negative coverage he has received and has buttressed his political popularity.

Notes

1. Walter Cronkite, as quoted in Marvin Barrett, *Rich News, Poor News* (New York: Crowell, 1978): 10.
2. Dan Rather, as quoted in Hoyt Purvis, editor, *The Presidency and the Press* (Austin, Texas: The University of Texas Press, 1976), proceedings of a symposium on the presidency and the press, sponsored by the Lyndon B.

Johnson School of Public Affairs. Also see, Ron Nessen, "The Washington You Can't See on Television," *TV Guide* (September 20, 1980): 9-12.

3. Interview with Rex Granum, ABC News.

4. Interview with Susan Zirinski, CBS Evening News producer.

5. As quoted in Edward J. Epstein, "The Selection of Reality," *The New Yorker* (March 3, 1973): 41.

6. Interview with Susan Zirinski, producer for CBS Evening News. Also, see "Fairness: Network Fear of Flacking" in Michael J. Robinson and Margaret A. Sheehan, *Over the Wire and on TV: CBS and UPI in Campaign '80* (New York: Russell Sage Foundation, 1980): 91-139.

7. Robinson and Sheehan: 139. Also, James Fallows argues that reporters' lack of knowledge of history results in an insensitivity to the constraints which inhibit the exercise of presidential power[.] . . . Fallows believes that White House reporters feel confident in reporting five types of news stories: scandals or criminal activity, internal rivalries among administration aides, presidential politics, presidential gaffes, and fifth, the "business of winning elections and gaining points in the polls." See James Fallows, "The President and the Press," *The Washington Monthly* (October, 1979): 9-17.

8. . . . [T]he study's results are generalizable to ABC and NBC because the norms which guide the gathering and editing of news, and the constraints under which reporters and technicians work are fairly consistent across the three networks. See Epstein, 1973: xvi.

9. On average . . . the evening news was examined on pre-determined weekdays, two days each week for each of the 832 weeks in the study. The sample was also stratified by day of the week to insure that variations in number and percentage of weekdays (that is, "Mondays," "Tuesdays," etc.) were kept to a minimum. . . .

All stories which referred directly to the president, the presidency, the president's family, friends, staff or references to the president's policies; the secretary of state and the vice president would be included in the analysis. Excluded were stories concerning Executive Branch departments (Office of Management and Budget, for example) which did not refer specifically to the president or the Administration; stories about a remote "presidential task force" or commission which have only a tangential relationship to the president and which are not discussed directly in terms of the president's policies; and network announcements of news coverage of the president or related programming, e.g., "CBS will present a special on President Reagan's first year in Office tonight at 10 pm." The unit of analysis is the news story. . . .

Positive Tone: Legislative success, public or private approval for the president's policies; reports which portray the president in a favorable light. Words used by anchors or correspondents to characterize president's behavior or policies—"bold adventure," "statesmanlike," "restrained during crisis"— that represent values which are associated with effective presidential performance. Stories which show the president endorsing values which are integral to American society, the so-called "motherhood" issues, were also coded positive. Finally, stories which show that the president's policies are working (troop withdrawals from Vietnam, positive economic reports) were coded positive.

Neutral Tone: balance of positive and negative coverage, or no evaluative tone whatsoever. For example, stories concerning the introduction of legislation, presidential appointments and nominations, were generally coded neutral.

Negative Tone: legislative setbacks or defeats, bad policy or personal evaluations (when they are the main emphasis of the story); disparaging remarks about the president or the president's policies (e.g., policies are unfair, vague, ineffective). Also coded negative were stories which show that the president's policies aren't effective or which portray the president in an unfavorable light.

10. See George C. Edwards, *Presidential Influence in Congress* (San Francisco: W. H. Freeman, 1980); Richard E. Neustadt, *Presidential Power* (New York: John Wiley, 1980); Louis Fisher, *The Constitution Between Friends* (New York: St. Martin's Press, 1978); Edward Tufte, "Determinants of the Outcomes of Midterm Congressional Elections," *American Political Science Review* 69 (September, 1975): 812-826.

11. Gallup support score averages were derived from the *The Gallup Opinion Index,* report No. 182, October-November, 1980 (Princeton, New Jersey: The Gallup Poll, 1980).

12. These results are particularly surprising given reports of the Reagan Administration's success at staging events, limiting access to the president, and otherwise managing the news so as to get a favorable portrayal. See Steven R. Weisman, "The President and the Press: the art of controlled access," *The New York Times Magazine* (October 14, 1984): 34-83.

20

SURROGATE STATE DEPARTMENT? *TIMES* COVERAGE OF PALESTINE, 1948

Bruce J. Evensen

Editor's Note

When news stories are told from a particular perspective, is the choice purposely designed to achieve political ends? "Yes," says Bruce Evensen in the case of Palestine in 1948. His painstaking search of relevant documents and memoirs has unearthed evidence that New York Times *stories were deliberately used by the paper's staff to guide U.S. Middle East policies in directions contrary to President Truman's choices. The effort by the* Times, *which was supported by other news media, succeeded.*

The actions by the Times *raise important ethical and political questions. Should journalists attempt to influence policy so that it conforms to their judgments, or does their professional code of ethics demand neutrality? Should journalists seek to shape public opinion? Is it a patriotic obligation of the press to support a president in matters of foreign policy? It has been frequently claimed that the press, including the* New York Times, *routinely supports presidential foreign policies, even though it often criticizes domestic policies. The Palestine case runs counter to these claims. Does it record an undesirable deviation or a desirable model, and does it represent a common pattern or a rare occurrence?*

At the time of writing, Professor Evensen taught in the Department of Communication at Chicago's DePaul University. Previously, he covered the Middle East as a reporter. He is the author of Truman, Palestine, and the Press: Shaping Conventional Wisdom at the Beginning of the Cold War *(New York: Greenwood Press, 1992). The selection comes from* Journalism Quarterly *67:2 (Summer 1990): 391-400. Several footnotes have been omitted.*

. . . This study analyzes coverage by the New York *Times* of East-West relations during the winter of 1947-1948 and how this coverage influenced

Reproduced from *Journalism Quarterly,* vol. 67, no. 2, summer 1990, pp. 391-400, with permission of the Association for Education in Journalism and Mass Communication.

its reporting of developments in the Middle East. The withdrawal of British forces from the Eastern Mediterranean had jolted the *Times'* editorial board into the sudden realization that the United States stood alone in its crucial competition with the Soviet Union in shaping the course of the post-war world. This was particularly true in Palestine, where U.N. support for a Jewish state, in the eyes of the *Times,* tested American willingness to serve as moral leader to the Western world.

At issue in this study is not only the interpretative role of the press in the Cold War period, but how this interpretative framework creates a realm of the politically possible within which policy-makers act. This research relied on three kinds of evidence in arguing that the press, led by the New York *Times,* joined by aroused public opinion, helped to constrain Truman administration policy initiatives on Palestine at the coming of the Cold War. This conclusion is suggested by documents drawn from the Truman Library in Independence, Mo., as well as from poll data collected during the winter of 1947-1948, and a content analysis of the New York *Times* in the 168 days separating the U.N. decision to partition Palestine and the establishment of a Jewish state on May 14, 1948. Also analyzed were collateral writings of *Times'* editors. They ran nearly 1,200 stories on Palestine in the 24 weeks leading to Israeli independence, an average of seven a day, with the story appearing on the front page nine days out of ten. The emphasis here is not on the magnitude of *Times'* coverage, but the interpretative framework of that coverage and its relation to Cold War policy-making.[1]

The *Times,* joined by much of the nation's press, read administration intentions in Palestine in terms of widespread fears the Great Power Cold War would soon become a shooting war. This proved to be of considerable significance when in March 1948 Communists unexpectedly seized control of Czechoslovakia and President Truman went before a joint session of the U.S. Congress urging a return to the military draft. The press interpreted Truman's decision to scrap his support for the partitioning of Palestine in favor of a U.N. trusteeship over the area as a sign the President was afraid to stand up to Soviet designs on the oil rich region. The Truman administration attempted to defeat this interpretation, failed, and was forced to quietly adapt its policy to the pressure of a deeply disturbed and highly attentive public. . . .

Truman and the *Times*

. . . Truman's perceived waffling on Palestine was fed by the fear of many on the *Times'* editorial board that Truman was not up to the challenges of leading the nation through the perils of the post-war world. The paper's suspicions were widely shared by several veteran reporters who

covered the Truman White House and by senior officials within the administration who had served with Franklin Roosevelt.[2] C. L. Sulzberger, the
nephew of the paper's publisher and its chief foreign correspondent, left a
private Oval Office audience with the President convinced Truman was
both "naive and simple-minded" with "a rather rural knowledge of the
world." [3] The paper's chief diplomatic correspondent, James Reston, was
disturbed by the President's inability to forge consensus within his own
administration on the outlines of a post-war foreign policy.[4] The *Times'*
Washington correspondent, Arthur Krock, thought the President's problem
was one of public relations. Franklin Roosevelt worked to get a good press,
Krock thought, but Truman failed to use his press conference as a means
of giving the American people the broad outlines of his policies.[5]. . .

The *Times* as Surrogate State Department

The editorial board of the New York *Times* considered the newspaper as
uniquely qualified to influence the course of American foreign policy at
the coming of the Cold War. The paper's publisher saw the *Times* as an
American institution now called upon to preserve the country's basic freedoms through vigorous editorial crusading. Through the leadership of
Charles Merz, the *Times'* editorial page chief, the paper saw its mission as
"stirring the American people and the Congress to their responsibilities." [6]
Markel castigated fellow editors who were part of the "fourth estate" for
their failure to "educate public opinion at home" to the "unceasing and
unscrupulous appeals of Communist propagandists." [7]

The *Times'* editorial policy was rooted in the conviction of its publisher
and editors that the paper was more than the mere purveyor of the government's foreign policy initiatives, but a molder of those opinions in its role
as communicator of the informed judgments of its readers.[8] Arthur Hays
Sulzberger saw these readers as "intelligent Americans who desire information rather than entertainment" and who recognized "in this critical
period of our nation's history the need for responsible journalism" rooted
in the time-tested values of Americanism.[9]

Both Markel and Reston saw the *Times* as an important link in the construction of America's post-war foreign policy. They saw the *Times* organizing public opinion through the paper's interpretation of foreign policy initiatives. These interpretations were not to be saved for the editorial page.
Markel wanted interpretative reporting throughout the paper to produce
"the kind of public opinion we need." [10] Central to that interpretation, in
Reston's mind, was helping large numbers of people to see "the changes
and convulsions in the world in which America must operate." [11]

The *Times* had no illusions that in matters of foreign policy the president
was at the center of the stage. Initiative rested with him. He alone would

be held responsible for the results of that policy.[12] Insofar as it was able, it would support those initiatives and mold the opinion of that fraction of the American public most interested in the nation's foreign policy. During war-scare month, March 1948, that constituted a large fraction of the American people. And the actions of their president and his State Department had the *Times* greatly worried.

Secrecy and the State Department

The Truman administration's switch on Palestine brought lingering doubts into focus within the *Times'* brain trust that the President and the public were being well-served by the advice from the State Department. In Krock's view, the challenges of the cold war fundamentally changed the department's ability to manage foreign policy without significant participation by the Congress and the American people.[13] Markel was convinced the department's leadership failed to recognize this.[14]. . .

. . . When the Arab League announced on February 16 that it would fight any United Nations police force sent to Palestine, the *Times* editorially urged the administration to tell Arab leaders "they are challenging the authority, the prestige and the very right to exist of the United Nations." [15] When the American Ambassador to the United Nations, Warren Austin, failed to clarify the administration's position one week later, the nation's radio commentators joined in the attack. The administration was mute, the commentators claimed, on the one issue that would determine the future of the United Nations and ultimate control of the West's most strategic outpost.[16] The press office at the U.S. mission at Flushing Meadow was of little help. It was operating under orders to "respond to reporters' questions without seeking them out." [17]

Inside the Truman administration a heated battle was waged over its position on partition. The State Department's point man on Palestine, Loy Henderson, and Defense Secretary James Forrestal wanted to bring the nation's influential editors and commentators in to convince them partitioning Palestine would lead to Soviet gains in the Eastern Mediterranean.[18] The President's Chief Counsel, Clark Clifford, his Special Assistant on Minority Affairs, David K. Niles, and Truman's press aides argued against this advice. Clifford wondered how the United States could stand up to the Russians if it was perceived in the press to be appeasing the Arabs.[19]

Truman set himself up for a public relations fiasco on Palestine. As he dangled between two positions, the press rushed in to fill the information vacuum. Reston predicted if the administration failed to act decisively, partition would never be enforced.[20] The Washington *Star* excoriated the President for "his lack of clarity and candor." [21] When the President and

Secretary of State George Marshall failed to unequivocally indicate the administration position in subsequent news conferences, press criticism soared. The *Times* cited U.N. sources in concluding the administration appeared to lack the will to back up the United Nations.[22] Daniel Bishop in an editorial cartoon appearing in the St. Louis *Star-Times* showed a nervous Uncle Sam in a rudderless rowboat about to go over a falls marked "World War III." [23] A Boston paper spoke for many in the press when it said that what Truman now needed "was a good dose of moral guts!" [24]

The Power of Interpretation

. . . The perception in the press and public that the Truman administration had betrayed the United Nations over Palestine blunted administration efforts to argue otherwise. The *Times,* joined by other elite papers and radio commentators, portrayed an administration in disarray.[25] The *Times'* U.N. correspondent, Thomas Hamilton, claimed the organization's morale had sagged badly as a result of the American switch on Palestine.[26] The *Times'* principal problem with Truman was his alleged failure to lead. It had resulted in a Palestine policy "as bungled, as confused, and as inconsistent as any policy could be." [27] Krock thought it proved Truman incapable of facing up to the challenges of the Cold War. Washington was coming to realize that "Truman cannot succeed himself, whether or not he remains in the field," Krock wrote.[28] The Washington *Post* demanded an explanation for what seemed a "non-sensical" policy.[29] Syndicated columnist Marquis Childs attacked Truman for his "lack of candor." [30] Mutual Radio's Cecil Brown saw in the decision "the mortal wounding of the United Nations" and "the abandoning of our moral position as the champion of democracy." [31] One Congressman saw it as "the worst sellout of the common people since Munich." [32] Said another of Truman, "Just as the Republicans were getting set to kill him off next November, up comes Truman and commits suicide on them." [33]

Presidential aide Eben Ayers reported telegrams began pouring into the White House in record numbers. The President seemed "shocked and depressed." [34] Truman wrote in his diary, "I've never felt so low in my life." [35] Ayers noted, "the political effect may be terrifically bad." [36] Hasty efforts at damage control made matters worse. When Marshall told reporters they were mistaken in interpreting support for trusteeship as a switch in administration policy, the press rejected his argument.[37] When Truman attempted to put the same spin on events two days later he was charged "with a comic opera performance." [38] The administration could not shake the impression it had failed a critical test of Cold War leadership.[39] Within days of the debacle, Marshall conceded to Bohlen the department's handling of the affair had subjected the President to what he was attempting most to avoid—"a political blast from the press." [40]. . .

Conclusion

The vigor and near unanimity of public and press reaction to the Truman administration switch on Palestine aborted the trusteeship plan. The administration had failed to calculate how the press' reading of the situation was tied to deepening public fears over the possibility of war. Truman complained that "striped pants conspirators" in the State Department "cut my throat." [41] But Truman's silence on Palestine had given reporters the knife they needed. . . . The *Times* claimed credit for its role in reversing a policy not in the best interest of the nation.[42] Markel observed that "opinion which is the sine qua non of a sound public opinion is, in large part, the assignment of the mass media," and his paper stood guard to assure that opinion remained sound and that politicians were reminded to listen to it.[43]

Controversy over the Truman administration's handling of its Palestine policy emerged as the Cold War debate over press self-definition deepened. Some old-timers, like Edward Folliard, who had begun his work on the Washington *Post* in 1923, believed the essence of a good reporter was to be objective, "to give the readers the facts and assume the reader could make his own judgments." [44] But the Commission on Freedom of the Press, composed of leading academics, claimed in 1947 "it is no longer enough to report the fact truthfully. It is now necessary to report the truth about the fact" in a context which gives facts meaning.[45] This way of defining the press' responsibility emphasized interpretation as a key contribution to the formation of an informed public opinion. As the *Times* saw it, the Cold War required a press dedicated to molding public opinion consistent with its perception of the national interest. The controversy over Palestine created conditions in which the national interest was vigorously debated, and a policy undertaken, within the context of an interpretative framework both the press and the public opinion had a major hand in fashioning.

Notes

1. Diplomatic historians have questioned the degree to which a mobilized public shaped President Truman's Cold War policy and the extent to which that opinion was shaped by him and members of his administration through the nation's press. See John L. Gaddis, *The United States and the Origins of the Cold War* (New York: Columbia University Press, 1972), p. 360. Also, John L. Gaddis, "The Emerging Post-War Synthesis on the Origins of the Cold War," *Diplomatic History* 7: 177-180 (Summer 1983); Charles S. Maier, "Revision-

ism and the Interpretation of Cold War Origins," *Perspectives in American History* 4: 313-347 (1970); J. L. Richardson, "Cold War Revisionism: A Critique," *World Politics* 24: 579-612 (1972); Richard A. Melanson, "Revisionism Subdued? Robert James Maddox and the Origins of the Cold War," *Political Science Reviewer* 7: 229-271 (1977).

2. Oral History Interview: Jack Bell, p. 47. Harry S. Truman Library, Independence, Missouri. Oral History Interview: Robert G. Nixon, pp. 445-696. Truman Library. Oral History Interview: Robert L. Strout, pp. 1-2, Truman Library. Oral History Interview: Robert L. Riggs, pp. 13-15, Truman Library. Oral History Interview: Raymond P. Brandt, p. 25, Truman Library. Oral History Interview: Carleton Kent, Truman Library. See also, Alonzo L. Hamby, "The Accidental Presidency: Truman vs. Dewey, The 1948 Election," *Wilson Quarterly* (Spring 1988), 49.

3. Cyrus L. Sulzberger, *A Long Row of Candles* (New York: Macmillan, 1969), pp. 362-363.

4. James Reston, "The Number One Voice," in Lester Markel, *Public Opinion and Foreign Policy* (New York: Harper and Row, 1949), p. 75. Also, James Reston, *The Artillery of the Press* (New York: Harper and Row, 1967), pp. 75-76.

5. Arthur Krock, *Memoirs: Sixty Years on the Firing Line* (New York: Funk and Wagnalls, 1968), 181-182. For background see Louis Liebovich, "Failed White House Press Relations in the Early Months of the Truman Administration," p. 17, a paper delivered at the Midwestern Journalism Historians Conference at the University of Illinois, on April 11, 1987.

6. Meyer Berger, *The Story of the New York Times, 1851-1951* (New York: Simon and Schuster, 1951).

7. Markel, *Public Opinion*, pp. 34-35. In this statement, Markel associates himself with the report of the Committee on Foreign Relations, No. 855, 5. R. 161, Eightieth Congress, 2nd Session, 1948, pp. 3 and 4.

8. *Ibid.*, p. 45. Also, Reston, *Artillery*, Introduction.

9. Berger, pp. 473-475.

10. Markel, *Public Opinion*, p. 33.

11. Reston, *Artillery*, Introduction.

12. *Ibid.*, p. 76. Also Thomas G. Paterson, "Presidential Foreign Policy, Public Opinion and Congress: The Truman Years," *Diplomatic History* 3: 1-16 (Winter 1979); and Manfred Landecker, *The President and the Public Opinion* (Washington, D.C.: Public Affairs Press, 1968), preface and pp. 63-72, where Landecker observes that even Presidents determined to lead public opinion realize the eventual success of their policies are dependent on winning that opinion.

13. New York *Times*, December 6, 1944, p. 26 and December 10, 1944, p. 12.

14. Markel, *Public Opinion*, pp. 6-7. Editorially, the *Times* had been particularly critical of the State Department's command structure, its failure to appoint a permanent undersecretary and Secretary of State George Marshall's lack of diplomatic experience. See New York *Times*, December 30, 1946, p. 18 and

January 8, 1947, p. 22.

15. New York *Times*, February 17, 1948, p. 24 and February 22, 1948, Section E, p. 5.

16. Cecil Brown Radio Scripts. February 16, 1948. Cecil Brown Papers. Box 15, Folder 3, State Historical Society of Wisconsin, Madison, Wisconsin. Also, Clifton Utley Radio Scripts. February 22, 1948. Clifton Utley Papers. Box 50, Folder 2, State Historical Society of Wisconsin.

17. *Foreign Relations of the United States,* 1948, V, pp. 626-627.

18. Walter Millis (ed.), *The Forrestal Diaries* (New York: Viking Press, 1951), pp. 371-372. Forrestal's diary entry of February 12, 1948. Also, Memo by Loy Henderson. Not dated. U.S. State Department Files, 501.BB Pal/3-24-48. Box 2148, National Archives, Washington, D.C.

19. Ayers diary entry of February 17, 1948. Papers of Eben A. Ayers. Box 16, Folder 4. Truman Library. Also, Harry S. Truman, *Memoirs: Years of Trial and Hope* (Garden City: Doubleday, 1956), p. 159. And, *FRUS,* 1948, V, pp. 632-633. Also, Memo by Loy Henderson, March 26, 1948. U.S. State Department Files. 867N.01/3-2648. National Archives, Washington, D.C.

20. New York *Times*, February 25, 1948, p. 1.

21. Washington *Star*, February 25, 1948, p. 1.

22. An analysis of *Times'* reporting on this issue can be found in *FRUS,* 1948, V, p. 701.

23. St. Louis *Star-Times*, March 12, 1948, p. 18. The Chicago *Daily News* of February 20, 1948, ran an editorial cartoon showing Palestine as a land mine drifting dangerously at sea.

24. *The Jewish Advocate* (Boston), March 11, 1948, p. 2.

25. See Foreign Relations: Palestine. The Papers of George Elsey. Box 60, Truman Library. It contains an annotated copy of the New York *Times*, p. 1 criticism of the administration on March 21, 1948. See also, Joseph Harsch Radio Scripts, March 21, 1948. Joseph Harsch Papers. Box 12, Folder 2, State Historical Society of Wisconsin. And, Clifton Utley Radio Scripts, March 21, 1948. Utley Papers, State Historical Society of Wisconsin.

26. New York *Times*, March 28, 1948, Section E, p. 4.

27. New York *Times*, March 26, 1948, p. 20.

28. New York *Times*, March 28, 1948, Section E, p. 3.

29. Washington *Post*, March 22, 1948, pp. 1 and 22.

30. See copy of Childs' column in Foreign Relations: Palestine. Elsey Papers, Box 60, Truman Library.

31. Cecil Brown Radio Scripts. March 22 and March 30, 1948. Cecil Brown Papers. Box 16, Folder 1. State Historical Society of Wisconsin.

32. The remark of New York Representative Emanuel Cellar appears on p. 1 of the March 20, 1948 edition of the New York *Times* and also appears in Box 60 of the Elsey Papers, along with eight other *Times* articles which appeared on that date.

33. Israel File. Papers of David K. Niles. Box 30, Folder 3. Truman Library. The comment is by North Carolina's Robert "Muley" Doughton.

34. Ayers diary, March 20, 1948 entry. Ayers Papers. Box 16, Folder 5. Truman Library.
35. Margaret Truman, *Harry S. Truman* (New York: William Morrow, 1973), p. 387.
36. Ayers diary, March 20, 1948 entry. Ayers Papers. Box 16, Folder 5. Truman Library.
37. *FRUS*, 1948, V, p. 749. New York *Times*, March 21, 1948, p. 1. Cecil Brown Radio Scripts, March 22 and March 30, 1948. Cecil Brown Papers. Box 16, Folder 1. State Historical Society of Wisconsin.
38. The account in *Time* appears in Foreign Relations: Palestine. Elsey Papers, Box 60. Daily summaries of the Elsey file were made available to Truman. For Truman's attention to those summaries and how his administration was being perceived in the press see Oral History Interview: George Elsey, vol. 1, pp. 34 and 77, and vol. 2, p. 249.
39. New York *Times*, March 26, 1948, p. 20 and March 28, 1948, Section E, p. 3.
40. *FRUS*, 1948, V, p. 750.
41. M. Truman, *Harry S. Truman*, 387.
42. New York *Times*, March 26, 1948, p. 20.
43. Markel, "The Real Sins of the Press," *Harper's*, December 1962, pp. 85-94.
44. Oral History Interview: Edward T. Folliard, 73-74. Truman Library.
45. The Commission on Freedom of the Press, *A Free and Responsible Press* (Chicago: University of Chicago Press, 1947), pp. 20-27.

21

THREE FACES OF
CONGRESSIONAL MEDIA

Michael J. Robinson

Editor's Note

Michael J. Robinson spotlights the changes that modern media coverage have brought about in Congress. He provides fascinating details about the manner in which Congress is covered by a variety of media. Each medium differs in impact from the others, and the impact of the same medium even varies at different times. Accurate assessments of the overall effects of all media singly or in combination remain elusive because there are no adequate weighting criteria.

Robinson outlines the major effects of media coverage. It produces telegenic candidates, safe House incumbents, vulnerable senators, and a Congress that lacks the public's confidence. By contrast, respect for the presidency as an institution remains high in the wake of deferential news treatment. Incumbent presidents, however, generally receive rougher media treatment than do incumbent members of Congress. If Robinson is correct in his assessments, the media have indeed altered the face of U.S. politics.

Robinson, a political scientist trained at the University of Michigan, has devoted much of his career to the study of the media's influence on U.S. politics. At the time of writing, he was teaching at Catholic University and was directing the Media Analysis Project at The George Washington University. The selection is from Thomas E. Mann and Norman J. Ornstein, eds., The New Congress (Washington, D.C.: American Enterprise Institute, 1981), 55-96. Several tables have been omitted.

Ask anybody on Capitol Hill about the most basic change in the relationship between Congress and the media since 1960 and the response is practically catechistic—the media have become harder, tougher, more cynical. Committee chairmen, senior Republicans, press secretaries, aides in the press galleries and media studios at the Capitol, and members of the Washington press corps express what amounts to a consensus: the biggest change in the relationship between Congress and the media is that the press has grown more hostile to Congress.

Having conducted almost fifty personal interviews and collected some sixty questionnaires from representatives, staff, and reporters between 1977 and 1980, I found that only one person in fifteen thought this toughening was not the major development.[1] One official in the House of Representatives, who has worked personally with congressional correspondents for almost thirty years, put it this way: "The biggest change has been readily discernible—the greater emphasis on the investigative approach. Years ago there was an occasional exposé, but the last six to eight years there has been a shift toward the Watergate approach."

Press secretaries seem particularly sensitive to the change in attitudes. One former reporter, who has now served almost twenty years as press secretary to a senior House Democrat, expressed his frustration with the "new journalism" he sees in and around the Capitol. The press, he says, has become "bloodthirsty." It has "developed a sickly preoccupation with the negative aspects of governmental operations, the presidency, the Congress, the administrative agencies." The media "think we're all crooks and it only remains for them to prove it." This man speaks for many of the staff who work directly with the press corps in Congress. . . .

Despite the prevailing view, this essay argues: that the mass media, in toto, have *not* hurt the membership electorally, especially in the House; that even the news media have *not* been of a piece in their relationship with Congress; that many of the major changes brought by the media to Congress have been brought *not* by a "new journalism" but by the campaign media or by practices associated with "old journalism"; that change has *not* been fundamental and continuity has *not* disappeared.

Combining these points with what I shall present later, . . . I offer these conclusions concerning the changing relationship between the in-house, campaign, and news media and the Congress over the last twenty years:

1. The in-house media in Congress have changed as fully as the news media since 1960, and they have tended to negate much of the effect that the new, hardened Washington press corps has had on incumbents.
2. The campaign media around Congress have grown at least as fast as the news media in Congress, and under most circumstances they still tend to benefit incumbents, especially in the House.
3. The new toughness of the national press corps is not much in evidence in the local press. In some respects, the local media may have actually become "softer" than they were in 1960.

4. The discrepancy between the "soft" local press and the "tough" national news media has grown wider since 1960, and this widening gap goes a long way toward explaining why people hate Congress but love their congressman.

5. The "media-mix" that has developed in Congress since 1960 helps explain both the increase in safety of House incumbents and the concomitant decline in the safety of incumbents in the Senate.

6. The greatest effect of the new media-mix on Congress as an institution has been to attract a new kind of congressman.

7. The new media-mix has continued the evolutionary process, begun with radio, through which the executive branch grows increasingly more important than Congress as a policy-making institution.

8. *The media, taken together, have not done much to damage the members of Congress* but have damaged the institution of Congress—at least a little.

This last point may be the most important of all. In fact, I believe that the membership has learned to cope very effectively with the modern congressional media—even if the institution and the leadership have not. So, while it may be true that the mass media have proved somewhat detrimental to the institution, their three faces have not looked unkindly on the members per se. The overall pattern is one of change much in keeping with David Mayhew's notions about Congress. One finds, as Mayhew might have guessed, resourceful members who have restricted the impact of the media and adapted beautifully to their new forms, but a disunified institution far less able to restrict or adapt to those very same forms.

To understand all of this, however, one must remember that the congressional media are a mixture of the national, local, and regional press, an in-house press, and an ever-growing campaign media. Any analysis that stresses only the so-called new journalism oversimplifies the changing relationship between Congress and the mass media. One must emphasize the pluralism of congressional media if one takes into account all the major dimensions of modern, mass, political communication.

"In-House" Media—Unambiguous Advantages

. . . The ability to communicate more often with more constituents directly through the mail has been one of the most important changes in the in-house media. In fact, much of the technology adorning the new congressional office either produces mail or can be used to facilitate mail. Mail—in its volume alone, which has increased over 300 percent—represents a revolutionary change in in-house communications over the last two decades.[2] Currently, the average American receives two pieces of mail every year from Congress.

The increase in congressional mail can be explained in part by population growth, in part by an increasing national politicization. But the major explanation is the coming of modern computer technology to Congress. In 1960 nobody had a computerized mail system. As of 1979 almost every Senate office and, according to *Congressional Quarterly,* 300 House offices have computerized mailing facilities.[3] Younger members increasingly consider computerized mail a political necessity. The House itself found in a study conducted in 1977 that the freshman class was almost twice as likely to employ computerized correspondence as senior members.[4] One can expect "managed mail" to increase rapidly as the seniors leave.

But the new in-house correspondence systems mean more than a greater quantity of mail, and more than efficient mail. The new system can also mean "targeted" mail. Most mail from members is computerized, and most of it is sent in direct response to a constituent inquiry or problem. But more and more "personalized" mail is unsolicited and is sent to types of individuals who might be pleased by what it says: this is "targeted" mail, one of the big new phenomena on Capitol Hill.

. . . If the member wants to send letters to all Blackfoot Indians who have written to him on ERA and who live on a particular street or block, he can do it without much effort. . . .

. . . As early as 1956 the Senate and House began operating separate in-house recording studios for members and leaders. The studios in both houses have always been used for the same purposes—to provide members with convenient, cheap, and sympathetic programming that can be mailed home to broadcasters and used on local channels as news or public affairs presentations. . . . My interviews . . . indicate that members are using the studios more and more, especially the younger members. . . .

. . . The radio and TV studios are only part of the congressional in-house press. For over 120 years the House and Senate have maintained a network of auxiliary offices which aid the press as it covers the membership day to day. It all began in 1857 when the Senate and then the House opened their own Press Galleries. Following the establishment of the first two Press Galleries in the nineteenth century, Congress responded with five more in the twentieth—a Radio and Television Gallery and a Periodical Gallery for each house and a Photographers' Gallery for both, all of which existed by 1960. The staffs in all seven galleries work in a rather strange environment, servants of the media as well as of the Congress. While the correspondents are paid by their respective news organizations, the gallery employees are paid by the House or Senate. The galleries are there to help both the press and the Congress. . . .

Thus, in terms of in-house media, *Congress has expanded and adapted most in the areas that help members directly. It has done less in the areas that are general and institutional in emphasis.* Congress has adjusted to developments in the media . . . selectively, and "personally," with special concern for the electoral life of its individual members.

There is one final dimension, perhaps more important than the rest, which suggests how much the in-house media have grown in the last twenty years. . . . [P]ress secretaries labeled as such were few in number in the Senate and practically nonexistent in the House when Congress entered the 1960s. Because definitions change and press secretaries are often called something other than "press secretary," it is almost impossible to quantify precisely the growth of the congressional press secretariat, but the information that does exist indicates that that growth has been striking. . . .

The growth in the congressional press secretariat suggests again that the media-mix in Congress has not been so bad for the members. They hire press people, after all, to praise them, not to harm them. It is not possible to say which side started the escalation in personnel, the press or the Congress. But in either case the growth of the new journalism has probably been countered, or its effects at least diluted, by the growth in the press secretariat. . . .

. . . Nothing stands more visibly for change in the relationship between Congress and the media than the national televising of House floor proceedings. But along with change has been a commitment to continuity—House TV is another case study in how Congress has adapted to the media by looking out for number one, the membership. . . .

. . . [A]ll equipment and all personnel in the system are part of the House of Representatives. Control of the system is in the hands of the Speaker, who exercises that control through a Speaker's advisory Committee on Broadcasting and an advisory team working in the House Recording Studio.

In keeping with the tradition of adapting the media to their own needs, the members and the leadership have provided for themselves quite well. H. Res. 866 provides for in-house technicians with stationary cameras (nobody can be pictured falling asleep or inadvertently acting uncongressional under this system), blackened screens during roll-call votes (members cannot be caught changing their votes at the last moment, or even voting at all for that matter), and ready access to videotape files (members can, if they wish, send "news" clips to the stations back home at very low cost). Added to all that is continuous live coverage of all proceedings, broadcast by over 850 cable TV systems across the nation on C-SPAN (Cable Satellite Public Affairs Network).[5] . . .

Two factors confounding attempts to evaluate the impact on the public have been the lack of information on the size of the audience watching House proceedings on television and the lack of network (or station) utilization of the tapes themselves. The major audience for television would, of course, be the network audience—now estimated to be above 55 million viewers nightly. But the networks have tended not to use the tapes of floor proceedings, in part because they objected to the House's decision to keep control of the cameras and in part because the networks still regard the House as less newsworthy than the Senate.

The only other news audience comes through C-SPAN, the 850 cable systems which tie directly into the Capitol telecasts. The potential audience for C-SPAN is, at present, 18 million viewers, but nobody knows who watches, or how often. The fact that the networks and C-SPAN only provide for a limited coverage or a small audience is a major reason for assuming that House TV has caused little public response. . . .

The Campaign Media: Potential Problems for Incumbents

Campaign media are those that candidates use to get elected. The major difference between campaign media and in-house media is who pays: Congress pays for in-house media out of general office accounts; candidates pay for campaign media out of private campaign funds. Since 1960 three basic changes have occurred in the relationship between Congress and its campaign media: (1) candidates now use the media more, (2) they use them more effectively, and (3) challengers find in the campaign media a new opportunity, but one still qualified by the old reality of incumbent advantage. . . .

While comparable and detailed figures on media expenditures are not available for the last twenty years, we know from the work of Edie Goldenberg and Michael Traugott that by 1978 congressional candidates were spending well over half (56 percent) of their total campaign budgets on all the mass media combined.[6] These authors estimate that in the six years between 1972 and 1978 the amount spent on broadcasting alone in House elections tripled.[7]. . .

. . . By spending so much more than ever before, congressional candidates have both created and understood a new electoral environment. The increasing use of the media is both cause and reflection of the growing impact of campaign dollars on electoral returns. . . .

. . . [A]s voters continue to grow less loyal to party and candidates continue to spend more money to attract votes, the campaign media become more influential. . . .

. . . [T]he campaign media remain for most members of Congress a *potential* threat. A serious attack that relies on campaign media *can* fatally damage an incumbent. But most often no such challenge materializes. For one thing, most challengers cannot compete in dollars and cents. . . . At least in the House, a case can be made for arguing: that the campaign media have not much redefined congressional electoral politics; that television advertising is still too expensive and too inefficient for most House campaigns, where TV dollars are largely wasted reaching people who live outside the district; that incumbents still make more use of the media than their challengers; and that, at best, the campaign media have made House campaigns a wee bit less certain than before. . . .

The News Media: Cynicism and Symbiosis in the Two Worlds of [the] Press

The news media are what most of us think of as *the* media. But even the news media are less than monolithic in their relations with Congress. Television news differs from print, print differs from radio, radio differs from TV; and in each medium, local coverage differs from national. In terms of impact these differences are crucial.

. . . The intuition that the news media are increasingly hostile to Congress fits best the reality of the *national* press. The evidence abounds. . . .

My own content analysis of network news coverage of Congress leads me to believe that this approach is not confined to the national print media. Back in 1976, after the Supreme Court in *Buckley* v. *Valeo* gave Congress thirty days to reconstitute the Federal Elections Commission or witness its demise, David Brinkley commented to an audience of 15 million, "It is widely believed in Washington that it would take Congress thirty days to make instant coffee." [8] The complete results of my analysis of network coverage of Congress suggest much the same thing—the national press is fairly tough on Congress. ABC, CBS, and NBC ran 263 "Congress stories" in January and February of 1976, according to my analysis, and among them I found not a single item that placed Congress or its members in a positive light. I did find 36 stories (14 percent) that tended to present Congress or its members in a negative light.[9] The fact that Congress received no good press on the evening news for a period spanning five weeks in 1976 suggests that the national press do not find much about Congress to their liking. . . .

. . . In December 1969, Senator Daniel Brewster (Democrat, Maryland) was indicted in federal court on charges that included illegally accepting money for what amounted to legislative favors—bribery. Nine years later, Congressman Daniel Flood (Democrat, Pennsylvania) was indicted on federal charges of much the same sort. Though the two cases are not identical, it seems reasonable to compare the coverage given them in the press and to take that coverage as evidence of how the behavior of the press had changed.

Using the Vanderbilt *Television News Index and Abstracts,* I counted the stories that network television broadcast on the Brewster and Flood cases, including all network stories heard on the evening news in the year of the indictment or the year following—1969 and 1970 for Brewster, 1978 and 1979 for Flood.

... According to the *Index*, Flood was referred to in fifty-nine different news stories, while Brewster was mentioned in eight. More incredible, Flood was the principal news focus or a secondary news focus for 4,320 seconds of network time, while stories about Brewster amounted to only 170 seconds. Flood-related stories received twenty-five times as much network news attention as did Brewster-related items, even though Brewster was a senator and Flood "only" a representative.

Some of this difference is accounted for by the fact that Brewster stood alone in his scandal, while Flood had the misfortune of being implicated in a much broader scandal—along with then Congressman Joshua Eilberg and then U.S. Attorney David Marston. Marston in particular increased the newsworthiness of the Flood case because Marston was a Republican in a Democratic administration and was eventually fired by President Carter for reasons having more to do with "old politics" than incompetence. But these extraneous factors cannot easily account for all of the difference. The Flood coverage, so much more extensive than anything even dreamed of in the Brewster case, serves to corroborate the idea that the national press had changed during the 1970s—had become more "cannibal" in its congressional reporting.

... History, logic, and the evidence all indicate that the local media have not really been overcome by the Watergate syndrome, so conspicuous in the national media. ... At least as late as 1974, critics of the press were still complaining about what one might best call a *symbiotic* relationship between the local media and incumbents in Congress—symbiotic not only because each "partner" profited from the continued relationship, but also because each clearly understood the other's mission and needs. ...

What may be the best evidence for believing that the local press is not Woodstein—let alone Evans and Novak—comes from the Center for Political Studies (CPS) at the University of Michigan. ... Using a sample of 216 newspapers, CPS found that in the last phase of the 1978 congressional campaign the average congressman received a score of 1.9 for his coverage in the local press, on a scale ranging from 1.0 (totally positive) through 3.0 (totally negative).[10] Incumbents fare well, getting positive attention, and lots of it. Incumbents receive twice the coverage their challengers get and ... more positive coverage than challengers or Congress as an institution or the government generally.[11] The differences are small, but they always favor incumbents. ...

... One of the less conspicuous changes affecting press coverage of Congress has been the steady increase in the size of the Capitol Hill press corps. . . . Without doubt the greatest growth has come in radio . . . an increase of 175 percent in the number of both radio and TV correspondents admitted to the congressional press corps in a sixteen-year period. During the period, the number of print journalists increased by "only" 37 percent. The rate of increase for electronic news people has been precisely five times greater than for print, and the overwhelming majority of the new media people are in radio.

Radio and electronic news coverage of Congress has rendered the Capitol Hill press corps more regional—hence, more local—in its behavior. This localizing of news through "regional" coverage of Congress has probably meant that the news about members comes out much "softer" than would have been the case without the explosion in radio. For two reasons, regional radio has probably worked to dilute the impact of the new journalism in Congress. First, regional electronic news people are, by definition, more local in outlook than the national press and, therefore, more dependent on access to members. Regional radio and local television people bring their local concerns with them to Congress, and they need to establish good relations with the new members who share those concerns. Second, the electronic media *generally* treat Congress "better" than the print media. . . .

. . . The local and national press are two separate worlds, and since 1960 they have grown more distinct. Why is this so, and what are the implications?

First, a qualification. The differences between the national and local press should not be exaggerated. The nationals do not often go out of their way to be tough when toughness is unwarranted; our analysis of congressional news in 1976 showed that eight out of ten stories on network news were *not* negative.[12] . . .

Moreover, locals can be tough when they have to be. Milton Hollstein describes, for example, the treatment Congressman Allan Howe received at the hands of the Salt Lake City media. The press, he said, served as "pillory" when Howe was caught with a decoy prostitute, and its "excessive," "gratuitous," "knee-jerk," and "questionable" coverage of the incident "made it impossible for [Howe] to be reelected" to Congress, even before the reported facts had been corroborated.[13]

Nonetheless, the basic differences in local and national coverage need some explanation. Most of those who have offered explanations have emphasized the variations between the local and national press in size and beat. A few others have dwelled on the economic self-interest of the local press; the theory holds that publishers urge editors to persuade journalists to treat the local congressman kindly in the hope that he may, at some point, vote for or amend legislation that will profit the newspaper. Another form of economic determinism has been used to explain the pleasant relationship between local broadcasters and congressmen. The theory here is that a contented congressman might go to bat for an FCC-licensed broadcaster if there were a licensing challenge. Both of these economic theories hinge on the owners' seeking to maximize their economic self-interest. The journalists are secondary.

But social psychology probably has as much to do with the relationship between the media and Congress as economics does, and the correspondents' behavior probably matters more than the interests of their capitalist publishers. At least half a dozen studies all make it clear that symbiosis emerges from a network of friendships and "mutual dependencies" between journalists and newsmakers. . . . But the representatives of local media are drawn in closer to the sources than the national press; mutual dependency is a larger ingredient in their friendships with the newsmakers. . . .

. . . [S]ize—especially the size of the networks—gives the national press a real advantage in dealing with members. The local media are still imprisoned by their smallness and weakness. . . . Nationals for the most part focus on the institution, not on individual members. . . . Focusing on institutions makes it easier to be tough. One does not have any particular pair of eyes to avoid when one attacks Congress. This is one reason why, as we have seen, Congress received more negative coverage than positive in 1978 but congressional *candidates* got more positive coverage than negative.

Add to all this the very real tendency for the national media to recruit the tougher journalists coming out of the local press and you get a fairly complete explanation for the hardness of the Washington press corps and the softness of the local news. The nationals look hard at the institution. The locals exchange glances with their representatives. This pattern holds unless the local member gets into trouble: then all the press—national, regional, local—glares. Such is the nature of the press in Congress.

Consequences

Now that we have considered the changes in the in-house, campaign, and news media as each relates to Congress, we must ask, So what? What has the new media-mix done to or for Congress? Let us consider this question along three dimensions: attitudinal, electoral, and institutional.

. . . Because the national news media have grown apart from the local media, and because the local media have probably been expanding more rapidly than the rest, the news media help explain a most interesting paradox in American public opinion—nationwide contempt for Congress and district-wide esteem for its members. The two types of media covering it coincide with the two sides of Congress's image. . . .

Of course, there are other interpretations of the paradox of opinion in Congress. Some authorities on Congress contend that members actually do a good job as representatives but that the institution actually fails to do its job as a legislature. Others . . . contend that members work the bureaucracy so effectively in the interests of their constituents that constituents learn to respect them but not the institution. Both of these interpretations seem ultimately too literal. Constituents simply do not deal enough with their congressmen to produce the paradox of congressional public image. Only the media are broad enough in reach and scope to account for the bulk of opinion toward Congress or its members. CPS congressional election studies in the 1970s indicate that 52 percent of all citizens read about their member in the newspapers; 14 percent had met the member personally. Fewer than one person in six ever deals with a member directly, even using a very loose definition of "direct" contact.[14]

Knowing what we do about local coverage, we may plausibly assume that the local press accounts for much of the favorable image that members enjoy. . . . [D]istricts with more negative press about Congress, the institution, hold more negative news of Congress—districts with more positive press go significantly in the other direction. The national media, which reach everyone with their critical coverage of the institution, and the local media, which reach constituents and accommodate members, *together* serve as the single best explanation for the paradox of public opinion toward Congress.

. . . The fact that the nationals relinquish to the locals the job of covering individual congressmen has direct implications for the members' safety at election time. Locals keep their readers relatively happy with their representatives by giving incumbents lots of coverage, most of it favorable. The result is safer incumbency. And when one factors in the growth of the in-house media, which inevitably serve to protect incumbents, the result is ever greater safety for those holding office—precisely the pattern that has prevailed among House membership since 1960. . . .

. . . House members control much of their own press—much more than presidents, governors, or senators. Members control their press because they (1) make greater and more sophisticated use of in-house media, (2) attract, by and large, more money than challengers in ad campaigns, (3) maintain a closer relationship with the local press than senators, and (4) attract much less coverage from the nationals so long as they stay unindicted. House members have grown increasingly safe electorally as they have gained greater control of all the media at their disposal. . . .

The Senate media-mix is very different. Senators' relationships with the local media are less intimate because senators deal with whole states, not with one or two papers as House members do. If propinquity explains cordiality, senators lose out because they simply cannot be as close to their press—or their constituents—as members of the House. The senator also attracts better financed challengers, who can buy TV time and who can use their resources more efficiently than practically any House member. The campaign media can hurt senators more because their challengers are more likely to be able to afford them. But most important, senators attract national coverage—a must for any potential presidential contender, but a potential disaster for an incumbent who comes out looking bad on the evening news. . . . Somewhat ironically, powerful senators are less able to control their images than "invisible" House members. In the Senate campaign of 1980, thirteen of twenty-nine incumbents went down to defeat, which approaches a 50 percent attrition rate. In 1980, as in the recent past, the House incumbents were four times safer than the Senate incumbents.

. . . Obviously, not everything has changed. Some of the most important aspects of the relationship between the mass media in Congress continue much as they were in 1960. One of these is the news media's preoccupation with the presidency. Although the data are inconclusive, it seems that Congress as an institution is still very subordinate to the executive in news attention and news manipulation.[15] The print media have been inching back toward a more equitable balance between presidency and Congress, but television has stayed with the executive. . . .

The presidential hegemony that is still felt in the press means a public that "thinks presidential" and relies on presidents to get us through, make things happen, control public policy. This is not simply a quantitative advantage that the presidency enjoys. The media have consistently treated the executive less negatively than the Congress. For reasons that follow rather closely those which explain the easier coverage given the membership than Congress per se, the executive generally gets better press than the legislative branch. Even in 1974—the year of Nixon's resignation— the press treated Congress more negatively. . . . [A]ccording to the Center for Political Studies at Michigan, the president received coverage that was 39 percent negative, but the Congress was saddled with negative press amounting to 42 percent of the total.[16]

The results of this continued assault on Congress have proven to be substantial. Whether the explanation is "reality" or "the media," Congress has not had a better public image than the president since 1960, except in some of the Watergate years. In fact, even in September 1979, when Jimmy Carter's public approval rating on the Associated Press/NBC poll plunged to 19 percent—the lowest level of public approval assigned to his or *any* presidency, ever—the Congress still did worse: the Congress stood at 13 percent—six points, or 30 percent, below Carter. Both the quality and quantity of national press coverage of Congress has hurt Congress in its competitive relations with the presidency. After Watergate, after Vietnam, after all of it, the media still help render us a "presidential nation"—while making us less "congressional."

There is perhaps a major lesson in all this concerning the media, our political institutions, and their respective roles. *The media,* by focusing so fully on the office of president and then inevitably on the inadequacies of any person holding the job, *may be producing an office that is more powerful but at the same time may be weakening the political power of each individual president.* On the other hand, *the media,* by treating Congress poorly but its incumbents relatively well, *may be strengthening incumbents but weakening their institution. . . .*

. . . [T]he most important institutional change to have occurred as a result of the new media-mix in Congress has been with the membership. The new media-mix, in and out of Congress, has manufactured a new kind of candidate, a new kind of nominee, and a new kind of incumbent. This is not simply a matter of looks or hair style, although clearly they are part of the change. It comes down to a question of style or legislative personality—what James David Barber might call "legislative character."

We have already seen evidence of how different the new generation in Congress is in its attitude toward the media. Compared with the class of 1958, the class of 1978 was three times more likely to make heavy use of the congressional recording studio, three times more likely to regard the House TV system as "very useful," three times more likely to have relied "a lot" on TV in the last election. Over 60 percent of the class of 1978 said "yes" when asked if they had used paid media consultants in their first successful campaign for Congress. Nobody in the class of 1958 answering my survey had used a media consultant to get elected the first time. Almost beyond doubt the media culture of the membership has changed.

Although these figures pertain to campaign style more than legislative character, one may infer that the increasingly greater reliance on the media for nomination, election, status in the Congress, and reelection is one sign of a new congressional character—one more dynamic, egocentric, immoderate, and, perhaps, intemperate. The evidence here is speculative and thin. But interviews and recent studies indicate that the media, intentionally or unintentionally, have recruited, maintained, and promoted a new legislative temperament.

One media consultant . . . believes that the media (plus the decision in *Buckley* v. *Valeo,* the case outlawing limits on a congressional candidate's spending) have changed the type of congressional candidate and officeholder.

You look through . . . and you get the guys with the blow-dried hair who read the
script well. That's not the kind of guy who'd been elected to Congress or Senate
ten years ago. You've got a guy who is not concerned about issues; who isn't
concerned about the mechanics of government; who doesn't attend committee
meetings; who avoids taking positions at any opportunity and who yet is a master
at getting his face in the newspapers and on television and all that. You get the
modern media candidate which is, in a lot of ways, Senator [name], who has no
objective right to be elected to public office.

The same consultant sees a new style of legislator:

You get a lot of young guys particularly who do two things, sort of the typical
young congressman these days. He gets elected, he hires a bunch of pros to run
his office, sets up a sophisticated constituent contact operation through the
mails and through other things and an actuality service and all that kind of
thing. Then he goes out and showboats to get more press so that he gets
reelected and is considered for higher office. Those become of much more
importance to him than the functioning as a national legislator or part of a
branch of government. . . .

. . . In the final analysis the changes in congressional media over the last
twenty years have produced mixed blessings and not just a few ironies—
for Congress, for its members, and for us.

For the House membership the changes have meant greater safety but,
at the same time, greater anxiety about getting reelected. . . .

For the senators, changes in the media-mix have meant less safety but,
at the same time, greater opportunity for achieving national prominence.
Network news coverage of the Senate can make an investigating senator a
household word in a matter of days. Some senators have become nationally
prominent through television almost overnight.

On both sides of the Capitol the changes in the media have given younger members and maverick members more political visibility—and consequently greater power—than ever before. But at the same time, modern
news media have also meant that all the members of Congress work in an
institution that has ever increasing image problems. In a final irony the
modern media in Congress mean that although more policy information is
directly available to members than ever before, the members themselves
spend no more time with that information than they ever did. Public relations, after all, has become more and more demanding on the members'
time. Policy can be more efficiently handled by staff or subcommittee.

The media generally benefit public people, not public institutions. For
the most part the new media-mix has rendered Congress no less safe, but a
little less serviceable—the members no less important, but the Congress a
little less viable. The major impact of the modern media on Congress has

not been the result of post-Watergate journalism but the inevitable consequence of focusing more public attention on elected officials, all of whom owe their jobs to local constituents. The media have made congressmen somewhat more anxious, somewhat more adept at media manipulation, and somewhat more responsive to local interests. But this merely shows us that Congress and its membership have a highly democratic base. What the news media have done to Congress is what one would expect when the level of information concerning an essentially democratic institution increases—greater responsiveness to the locals and greater concern about saving oneself. In all that, there is obviously good news, and bad.

Notes

1. Unless otherwise noted, the quotations in this chapter are from these interviews.
2. Figures supplied by the Senate Appropriations Committee.
3. Irwin B. Arieff, "Computers and Direct Mail Are Being Married on the Hill to Keep Incumbents in Office," *Congressional Quarterly Weekly Report,* July 21, 1979, p. 1451.
4. Dianne O'Shetski, "Analysis of Survey on Computer Support Provided to Member Offices, As of April 1977," House Administration Committee Report, August 1977, p. 10.
5. For a thorough discussion of the history and politics of House TV, see Donald Hirsch, "Televising the Chamber of the House of Representatives: The Politics of Mass Communication in a Democratic Institution," thesis, Oxford University, 1979.
6. Edie Goldenberg and Michael Traugott, "Resource Allocation and Broadcast Expenditures in Congressional Campaigns" (paper presented at the annual meeting of the American Political Science Association, Washington, D.C., September 1979), p. 7.
7. Ibid., p. 6.
8. David Brinkley, NBC "Nightly News," February 3, 1976.
9. Michael J. Robinson and Kevin R. Appel, "Network News Coverage of Congress," *Political Science Quarterly* (Fall 1979), p. 412.
10. Arthur Miller, "The Institutional Focus of Political Distrust" (paper prepared for the American Political Science Association, Washington, D.C., September 1979), p. 39. . . .
11. Miller, "Institutional Focus," p. 39.
12. Robinson and Appel, "Network News."
13. Milton Hollstein, "Congressman Howe in the Salt Lake City Media: A Case Study of the Press as Pillory," *Journalism Quarterly,* vol. 54, no. 3 (Autumn 1977), p. 454.
14. Miller, "Institutional Focus," p. 37.
15. My own research shows practically no change in the level of presidential news on network evening news (all networks) between 1969 and 1977. . . . Susan

Miller, using 1974—the year when impeachment proceedings were instituted against Nixon—reached very different results, with Congress getting slightly more print coverage than the president. See "News Coverage of Congress: The Search for the Ultimate Spokesman," *Journalism Quarterly*, vol. 54, no. 3 (Autumn 1977), p. 461.

16. Arthur Miller, Edie Goldenberg, and Lutz Erbring, "Type-Set Politics: The Impact of Newspapers on Public Confidence," *American Political Science Review*, vol. 73 (June 1979), p. 71.

22

I AM ON TV THEREFORE I AM

Stephen Hess

Editor's Note

Michael J. Robinson in "The Three Faces of Congressional Media" (Selection 21) and Timothy E. Cook in "Show Horses in House Elections" (Selection 18) argue that media coverage of Congress and its individual members has significant political consequences. Stephen Hess is not so sure. In his study of Congress and the media, which focuses primarily on local media coverage, he contends that Congress members receive so little publicity, especially on television, that the political consequences are minimal. Nonetheless, senators and representatives crave media attention and make concerted efforts to get it. The main reason, Hess thinks, is the pleasure that comes from viewing oneself as a media star. Moreover, most Congress members seem to believe that the presence of reporters in their surroundings means that their activities will be publicized. Such wishful thinking is comforting because Congress members cherish the myth that harnessing media power is an essential ingredient for political success.

Stephen Hess is a senior fellow in the governmental studies program at the Brookings Institution in Washington, D.C. The essay comes from his book Live from Capitol Hill: Studies of Congress and the Media *(Washington, D.C.: The Brookings Institution, 1991), 102-109. The book is the fourth study in Hess's acclaimed 'Newswork' series in which he dissects the relationship between government institutions and the media from a Washington perspective.*

. . . The press is important to presidents, and hence to the presidency.[1] Even if most Americans—and most news organizations—did not believe that the president is more important than Congress, the oneness of the presidency would give its coverage a unitary character. The nature of White House reporting is to act as a concave reflector, narrowing and maximizing attention. But Congress is 535 individuals with a jumble of interests, and reporting from Capitol Hill has the effect of atomizing the institution, separating particles of information to fit the diverse needs of legislators and news organizations. One reporter writes of legislation to regulate commodity markets, another on funding for repaving a highway through Altoona, others on other subjects.

Congress, of course, demands a fair share of media attention. Borrowing from a theory of political scientist James Q. Wilson—"organizations come to resemble the organizations they are in conflict with"—Senator Daniel Patrick Moynihan invented the Iron Law of Emulation: "Whenever any branch of the government acquires a new technique which enhances its power in relations to the other branches, that technique will soon be adopted by those other branches as well." [2] At least since Franklin D. Roosevelt invented the fireside chat, presidents have attempted to exploit technical advances provided by the news media. Which helps explain why legislators have hired press secretaries, allowed television cameras into committee rooms, supported the creation of C-SPAN, and expanded House and Senate recording studios. A great deal of information gets transmitted by means of these innovations. But in the end, partly because of the principle that dissemination is also dispersion, legislators can rarely concentrate enough video time or command enough newspaper space to make a difference in promoting a policy or even getting themselves reelected.

Still, not all legislators are equal. From the vantage point of the press, the House Speaker and the Senate majority leader can be handy institutional counterweights to the president. During Ronald Reagan's first term, with the Republicans in control of the Senate, Thomas P. "Tip" O'Neill suddenly became "the most televised Speaker in history." [3] His visibility was further enhanced by his imposing physical stature, by skillful public relations help, and by Republican attempts to turn him into a campaign issue—a confluence of circumstances not likely to occur very often. Yet he appeared on less than 7 percent of the network evening news programs—whereas a president almost always gets at least one story a day (97 percent of the time, by one count) and usually two or three. [4] And such differences in coverage are not simply quantitative. Presidents can be certain that everything they want reported will be reported. This allows them to use the media to semaphore political friends and foes. Legislators, even the leaders, have no guarantees that the press will play this game.

Nor, in terms of press coverage, are all issues equal. An investigation of a Watergate or Iran-contra scandal, a debate on a Panama Canal Treaty or a resolution to go to war in the Persian Gulf, a confirmation fight over a pivotal Supreme Court appointment—all can galvanize and focus the attentions of correspondents covering Congress, although the issue is usually framed as "Will the President Win or Lose?" [5] There are, of course, exceptions. A modest issue such as the members of Congress voting themselves a pay raise can have "talk radio" resonance. And sometimes there are rare legislators, a Phil Gramm or Newt Gingrich, without seniority or previous celebrity status or even the physical attributes that are supposed to attract television cameras, who have been able to exploit the media to advance themselves and their causes. "No camera, microphone, or notebook could be too inconveniently located for Phil Gramm," recalled National Public Radio's Cokie Roberts of the Texas senator, who was ninety-ninth in seniority when he brought into being the deficit reduction law that bears his name.[6] And Gingrich, then a junior Republican House member in an overwhelmingly Democratic body, is supposed to have said, "We are engaged in reshaping a whole nation through the news media." [7] So far, his campaign has contributed significantly to the unseating of House Speaker Jim Wright and to his own election as minority whip.

That Congress does not get all the television attention it might want partly results from the nature of legislative activity: it represents the quintessential talking-heads story. The president can take the cameras to China as he walks along the Great Wall or to the beaches of Normandy for the fortieth anniversary of D-Day. Even a presidential candidate can make his point from a boat in a polluted harbor. But the best a legislator can usually offer the cameras is a finger pointed at a recalcitrant committee witness. This lack of visual drama has meant that even the regional television bureaus in Washington, once exclusively moored on Capitol Hill, are more and more focusing their attention away from Congress as new technology has given them greater flexibility.[8] But perhaps a deeper reason for the lack of attention is that Congress moves too slowly for the dailiness of American journalism or, for that matter, for the action-now psyches of most reporters. This is the pace I recorded in my Senate diary of October 5, 1984:

> Floor debate on deficit reduction plans continues. . . . Clearly everyone has already said everything, yet it drones on. It is obvious that the reporters have become bored, and, more important, that they do not have front page stories until something passes. So the impression lingers that the Senate isn't doing much. Yet it's a question of time frame. Is several weeks really too much time for cutting the budget by $149 billion over three years?

Since the studies of Joe S. Foote early in the 1980s, it has been confirmed that most legislators are seldom seen on network news. As I showed in *The Ultimate Insiders,* for example, during 1983 one-third of the members of the Senate appeared only one time or not at all on the ABC, CBS, or NBC evening news programs.[9] According to Timothy E. Cook in *Making Laws and Making News*, 53 percent of the members of the House of Representatives were never mentioned on these programs during 1986.[10] But at the same time, virtually every journalist's and scholar's account of Congress-media relations has asserted that the situation is otherwise on local television news, where legislators have been turned into "media stars in [their] home towns."[11] So I looked at who appears on local television news, a strangely ignored area of inquiry, and discovered that most members of Congress also rarely get seen on these programs. Congress remains largely a print story, and as newspapers lose out to television as the news purveyor of choice for Americans, Congress loses out to the president.[12]

The conundrum, then, is why television appears to be so important to the life of Congress. As researchers are finally figuring out how to measure the place of television in the political process, television's importance for Congress is best measured by the degree to which [the] House and Senate are not covered.[13] But members of Congress and congressional reporters do not seem to have noticed. Quite the contrary, in fact: they tend to overestimate the extent of television coverage and hence its importance in the legislative and electoral processes.[14] Partly this stems from the journalist's habit of ignoring the average, the typical, and the routine. When Hedrick Smith in *The Power Game: How Washington Works* made the case for media politics as a staple of the House of Representatives by citing the activities of Stephen Solarz, Les Aspin, Richard Gephardt, and Newt Gingrich, it was as if he had chosen Larry Bird, Patrick Ewing, Michael Jordan, and Magic Johnson as representative players in the National Basketball Association.[15] But a more important explanation is the solipsistic view of the world that permeates Capitol Hill. Reality to reporters is what they can see, to politicians what they can touch. And Capitol Hill is always crammed with cameras, lights, sound equipment, tape recorders, news conferences, handouts, stakeouts. This is their reality. This also contributes to the myth of television's power as they react to its presence rather than to its output.

The output, as I have demonstrated, is often small. Timothy Cook has told the affecting story of Don J. Pease, a staid and hardworking backbench congressman, who wanted to extend a program of unemployment benefits that was about to expire in 1985. His staff convinced him that a visual aid was just what he needed to get himself on television:

When his turn came up [at a rally], Pease vigorously deplored official Washington's callousness toward unemployed workers: "If you want to know the truth, the Reagan administration acts as if you don't exist." Then raising the spatula in his right hand, he shouted, "Do you know what this is? *This* is a burger flipper. *This* is the Reagan administration's answer to unemployment. And *you* can flip burgers all day, and *your spouse* can flip burgers all day, and you *still* won't get above the poverty line!"

The results of this exercise, according to Cook, were that the "network evening news programs ignored the story . . . and the next morning neither the *New York Times* nor the *Washington Post* mentioned it. The staff's one consolation was a color photograph in the *Baltimore Sun,* although the caption neglected to explain why Pease was waving the spatula." The legislation did not get out of committee.[16]

Nevertheless, Congress and its members are spending more each year trying to influence news media coverage.[17] But the interest is not as pervasive as I had expected after reading some accounts of Capitol Hill activities. . . . Electronic news releases, for instance, are far more rare than is suggested by the newspaper and magazine stories that focus on legislators who produce the tapes and ignore those who do not. Press secretaries by my calculations rank a lowly fifth in the pecking order of both House and Senate offices; in the House they also spend a fair amount of time on activities that have nothing to do with the media. And perhaps one House member in five feels virtually no need to seek publicity. Jamie Whitten, chairman of the House Appropriations Committee, in nearly a half-century of being a member of Congress, is said never to have held a press conference: "You do your job best when you do it quietly," he summarized.[18]

Indeed, legislators should know that sound bites on the evening news will not get them reelected. Other avenues of publicity in which they can target the audience and control the message are infinitely more effective and involve less risk of losing voters. The odds of being able to move a policy debate by using television news are very long for the average member of Congress. Why then do they devote such energy to this pursuit?

One answer could be that legislators do not know of television's limited impact because it does not appear limited from their vantage point. It is limited only if the question is framed: How many impressions of me, for how long, how positively, is a voter likely to get from my effort? Rather, staff and friends collect and comment upon their appearances, thus magnifying them. (It is similar to what I witnessed a few years ago when I watched a cabinet officer reading his daily press clippings. His senses told him that an awful lot was being written about him. It was harder for him to recall that he was the only one reading all of it.) Under this closed system, even an obscure cable program at an obscene hour can produce a reenforcing feedback.

Another answer could be that legislators are cockeyed optimists. Is there not some of this quality in everyone who seeks elective office? Senator William S. Cohen believed that the politicians' common denominator is ambition. "Whether it is noble or ignoble," he wrote, "it is an all consuming passion which refuses to acknowledge the folly of its relentless pursuit." [19] In pursuit of the elusive sound bite, surely each member of Congress thinks he is as energetic, articulate, and intelligent as Phil Gramm and Newt Gingrich. Moreover, sound-bite journalism protects legislators from themselves. Although television and newspapers work off the same definition of news, their needs differ—TV needs nine seconds, and thus must edit out redundancy and even the awkward pauses of conversational speech. This will not necessarily make legislators look good, but it keeps them from looking bad.

Add to Senator Cohen's definition of political ambition Joseph A. Schlesinger's theory of progressive ambition: "The politician aspires to attain an office more important than the one he now seeks or is holding." [20] More than a third of the Senate once served in the House. How many senators would rather be president? On December 30, 1971, Jim Wright wrote in his diary, "In two days, a New Year will begin. It is my 50th, will be my 18th in Congress. . . . Maybe just in the past year have I really acknowledged that I won't ever be president." [21] For some legislators, perhaps, being on television has less to do with the next election than with some future election that may only be a dream.

So, as the members of Congress supposedly rush to recording studios to tape instant reactions to the president's State of the Union message, the political pluses outweigh the minuses. Getting on the air is an advantage, even if an exaggerated one. The costs are small, both in time and money, and the money is provided by taxpayers or campaign contributors anyway. Also, because most legislators sincerely wish to be noticed, there is no longer a stigma—the "show horse" label—attached to those who are exceedingly good at getting themselves on television.[22]

Yet there is still something else. It is August 1, 1984, and I am sitting next to Senator Alan Dixon in a screening room in the basement of the Capitol. This is part of the Senate's television complex, a railroad flat of a place carved out of long and narrow space that had once been the path of the capitol subway. There are two television studios with a control room between them, two radio studios with a control room between them, and two TV editing rooms in addition to the room where we are now watching a tape of the town meeting that the senator has recently broadcast from a cable station in Peoria. A question put to him requires a delicate answer. Dixon listens to his response. He smiles, then issues a laugh that comes from deep inside him. "I got out of that pretty good," he says. Watching a man so thoroughly enjoy watching himself is an exquisite experience. Few senators—only Moynihan and Cohen come to mind—get the same satisfaction from the printed word.

For the legislators of Capitol Hill, television is not primarily about politics at all, I realize. Or rather, without elections to be won and legislation to be passed, there would still be the rush to television. For television is about being a celebrity. Television appearances are analogues of the decor of their offices, which are filled with cartoonists' impressions of them and photographs of them taken with famous people at important events. *"The celebrity is a person who is known for his well-knownness,"* said Daniel J. Boorstin. In his brilliant essay, *The Image,* he concluded, "The hero created himself; the celebrity is created by the media." [23] I am on TV therefore I am.

Notes

1. See Elmer E. Cornwell, Jr., *Presidential Leadership of Public Opinion* (Indiana University Press, 1965); Michael Baruch Grossman and Martha Joynt Kumar, *Portraying the President: The White House and the News Media* (Johns Hopkins University Press, 1981); and Richard L. Rubin, *Press, Party, and Presidency* (Norton, 1981).

2. Daniel Patrick Moynihan, *Counting Our Blessings: Reflections on the Future of America* (Little, Brown, 1980), pp. 117-18.

3. Joe S. Foote, *Television Access and Political Power: The Networks, the Presidency, and the "Loyal Opposition"* (Praeger, 1990), p. 129.

4. Speaker O'Neill was seen on the network evening news programs 184 times in 1981, 146 times in 1982, 159 times in 1983, and 168 times in 1984. See Timothy E. Cook, *Making Laws and Making News: Media Strategies in the U.S. House of Representatives* (Brookings, 1989), pp. 196-97. For presidential appearances, see Fred Smoller, "The Six O'Clock Presidency: Patterns of Network News Coverage of the President," *Presidential Studies Quarterly,* vol. 16 (Winter 1986), p. 46. Doris A. Graber, *Mass Media and American Politics,* 3d ed. (Washington: CQ Press, 1989), who charted all network evening news broadcasts from July 1986 to June 1987, found that "the president received roughly seven and one-half hours of television news coverage each month from the networks, compared with slightly over one hour for Congress" (pp. 236-37).

5. See Denis Steven Rutkus, *Newspaper and Television Network News Coverage of Congress during the Summers of 1979 and 1989: A Content Analysis* (Congressional Research Service, 1991), pp. 35-40.

6. Cokie Roberts, "Leadership and the Media in the 101st Congress," in John J. Kornacki, ed., *Leading Congress: New Styles, New Strategies* (Washington: CQ Press, 1990), p. 91.

7. Quoted in John M. Barry, *The Ambition and the Power* (Viking, 1989), p. 166.

8. See Larry Makinson, *Dateline: Capitol Hill* (Washington: Center for Responsive Politics, 1990), p. 62.

9. Stephen Hess, *The Ultimate Insiders: U.S. Senators in the National Media* (Brookings, 1986), p. 16.

10. Cook, *Making Laws and Making News*, p. 60.

11. See Roger H. Davidson and Walter J. Oleszek, *Congress and Its Members*, 3d ed. (Washington: CQ Press, 1990), p. 147.

12. For the case that more coverage does not lead to more power, see Stephanie Greco Larson, "The President and Congress in the Media," *Annal*, vol. 499 (September 1988), pp. 64-74.

13. For some studies that have measured television's political effect, see Thomas E. Patterson, *The Mass Media Election: How Americans Choose Their President* (Praeger, 1980); George Gerbner and others, "Charting the Mainstream: Television's Contributions to Political Orientations," *Journal of Communication*, vol. 32 (Spring 1982), pp. 100-27; Larry M. Bartels, "Expectations and Preferences in Presidential Nominating Campaigns," *American Political Science Review*, vol. 79 (September 1985), pp. 804-15; Benjamin I. Page, Robert Y. Shapiro, and Glenn R. Dempsey, "What Moves Public Opinion?" *American Political Science Review*, vol. 81 (March 1987), pp. 23-43; and Shanto Iyengar and Donald R. Kinder, *News That Matters* (University of Chicago Press, 1987).

14. See, for example, Michael D. Wormser, ed., *Guide to Congress*, 3d ed. (Washington: CQ Press, 1982), p. 744. Scholars, however, have been less likely to fall into the journalists' trap. A number of studies have noted the modest television coverage of congressional campaigns. See, for example, Mark C. Westlye, *Senate Elections and Campaign Intensity* (Johns Hopkins University Press, 1991), pp. 39, 41. John W. Kingdon, *Agendas, Alternatives, and Public Policies* (Little, Brown, 1984), pp. 61-64, also describes a more limited role for the media in setting congressional agendas.

15. See Hedrick Smith, *The Power Game: How Washington Works* (Random House, 1988), pp. 139-46.

16. See Cook, *Making Laws and Making News*, pp. 132-46. Cook's point, however, is that Pease's media campaign, of which the spatula incident was a part, is what allowed his bill to get within two votes of passage. My interpretation of his case study is that the bill did as well as it did because Pease convinced Speaker O'Neill to support him.

17. See Walter Pincus, "TV Staff for House May Grow," *Washington Post*, April 25, 1990, p. A26, and "House TV Expansion Deferred," *Washington Post*, April 26, 1990, p. A21.

18. Quoted in Peter Osterlund, "Media-Savvy Congress Turns to TV," *Christian Science Monitor*, June 3, 1988, p. 3.

19. William S. Cohen, *Roll Call: One Year in the United States Senate* (Simon and Schuster, 1981), p. 165.

20. Joseph A. Schlesinger, *Ambition and Politics* (Rand McNally, 1966), p. 10. Articles relating ambition theory to Congress include Michael L. Mezey, "Ambition Theory and the Office of Congressman," *Journal of Politics*, vol. 32 (August 1970), pp. 563-79; Jeff Fishel, "Ambition and the Political Vocation: Congressional Challengers in American Politics," *Journal of Politics*, vol. 33 (February 1971), pp. 25-56; David W. Rohde, "Risk-Bearing and Progressive Ambition: The Case of Members of the United States House of Represen-

tatives," *American Journal of Political Science*, vol. 23 (February 1979), pp. 1-26; Paul Brace, "Progressive Ambition in the House: A Probabilistic Approach," *Journal of Politics*, vol. 46 (May 1984), pp. 556-71; and Paul R. Abramson, John H. Aldrich, and David W. Rohde, "Progressive Ambition among United States Senators: 1972-1988," *Journal of Politics*, vol. 49 (February 1987), pp. 3-35.

21. David J. Montgomery, "Jim Wright, The Speaker of the House for the 100th Congress," *Fort Worth Star-Telegram*, December 9, 1986, p. 1.

22. See John R. Hibbing and Sue Thomas, "The Modern United States Senate: What Is Accorded Respect," *Journal of Politics*, vol. 52 (February 1990), pp. 126-45.

23. Daniel J. Boorstin, *The Image: or What Happened to the American Dream* (Atheneum, 1962), pp. 57, 61.

23

THE MEDIA AND WATERGATE

Gladys Engel Lang and Kurt Lang

Editor's Note

This selection further illustrates how and why political leaders vie for media coverage during power struggles. Gladys Engel Lang and Kurt Lang assess the extent to which news stories affected the course of political events during the Watergate scandal that led to President Richard Nixon's resignation. They conclude that despite voluminous news stories, media influence was only peripheral to the outcome. Their analysis is important because it indicates the limitations, as well as the potency, of media coverage. Even peripheral media involvement, however, can be crucial. Would the Watergate affair have grown to major proportions without news coverage?

The selection also highlights how the media are used as a battleground in the fight to win public opinion support. The Langs call attention to the major role played by news stories in forming public opinion and in gauging and interpreting what the public thinks. These interpretations influence the conduct of politics because decision makers usually accept the media's assessment.

The authors have collaborated in numerous path-breaking studies of mass media images and their effects on public opinion. At the time of writing, both were professors of sociology at the State University of New York at Stony Brook. The selection is from The Battle for Public Opinion: The President, the Press, and the Polls During Watergate *(New York: Columbia University Press, 1983).*

. . . What was the effect of the media on the creation, the course, and the resolution of Watergate? The answer is not as obvious as it may appear. Despite the heroic efforts of some journalists, Watergate had no visible effect on the 1972 presidential election. Yet six months later, even before the televised Senate Watergate hearings, the nation's attention had become riveted on the issue, and for more than a year thereafter, until Richard Nixon's dramatic exit, Watergate dominated the headlines and the network news. . . .

Richard Nixon himself believed that public opinion was the critical factor in what he called the "overriding of my landslide mandate." For him, the struggle to stay in office, especially after the firing of Special Watergate Prosecutor Archibald Cox, when impeachment first became a real possibility, was a "race for public support." He called it his "last campaign," only this time it was not for political office but for his political life.[1]

As the President saw it, the main danger of being impeached resided in the public's becoming conditioned to the idea that he was going to be impeached. This was a good enough reason for Nixon's strategists to keep a close watch on all indicators of public sentiment—letters, telegrams, telephone calls, editorials, television commentaries, press reports, and, especially, what the polls showed. At the same time, the President developed a media strategy specifically and directly aimed at winning the battle of the polls. The media were the principal battlefields on which the major confrontations took place. Television, because of how it was used by all sides, played a most active role in the conflict.

Many observers of Watergate agree that it was Nixon's defeat in the battle for public opinion that forced him to retreat at crucial points when he failed to rally support for his stand to limit the scope of any probe into the Watergate break-in. Ultimately, it left him no alternative but to bow out. In this view, the way public opinion made itself felt exemplified "democracy at work," a favorite cliché of the news media. Ford lent it official sanction in his inaugural address when he told the nation, "Here the people rule." The view in the Nixon camp was less benign. Public opinion was seen as an ever-present danger. Stirred up by the media, deliberately manipulated by his enemies, and tracked by pollsters, public opinion was to become the hostile force that ultimately *drove* Nixon from office.

Not everyone believing that public opinion influenced the resolution of Watergate agrees that it hastened the end. In fact, an argument can be made that public opinion had exactly the opposite effect, that it slowed the process and prolonged the crisis. Some members of Congress, reluctant to move against the President unless assured that they had a majority solidly behind them, felt restrained by public opinion. Polls that continued to show most people opposed to Nixon's removal from office failed to provide this reassurance, though these same polls also showed large majorities believing that the President was somehow involved in a "serious" scandal and not just caught up in the usual politics. Critics of opinion research have gone so far as to argue, some most vociferously, that during most of

Watergate the major polls, whether by inadvertence or design, exaggerated the extent of opposition to impeachment. Consequently, the media were slow to register the groundswell for impeachment.

A third group of political analysts regards this emphasis on public opinion as totally misplaced and the Nixon strategy as misdirected. To them the battle for public opinion was only a sideshow. The media, in treating the issue as a political struggle for public support, diverted attention from the one crucial element in the downfall of Richard Nixon: the accumulation of incriminating evidence. If Watergate was a political contest, as it obviously was, the stakes consisted of information. Those pressing the case on legal grounds had to be mindful of public reaction but only insofar as people had to have confidence in the fairness and objectivity of the process by which the President was being judged.

Clearly the nation had experienced a dramatic shift in public opinion during the more than two years of controversy, which began with a break-in and ended with Nixon's resignation. What could account for such a reversal? The first place to look for an explanation is in the behavior of the media. TV, radio, and print are essential to the formation of public opinion in the modern nation in two ways. They disseminate information that allows members of the public to form opinions and, just as important, they convey to politicians and to others an image of what public opinion is, thus giving it a force it would not otherwise have. . . .

Watergate had broken into public consciousness only after the coverage had created a sense of crisis. This is not to say that the Watergate issue was something that the electronic and print media had created out of whole cloth. The coverage, which had stirred interest in Watergate, was dictated by events but the media themselves had become part of the field of action. Political figures with a stake in the outcome were using whatever publicity they could attract to advance their own goals and interests, thereby providing grist for the media and adding to the number of Watergate-relevant events there to be covered. As a result, the coverage reached saturation levels with Watergate on the front page and on the evening news day after day after day as well as on early morning, late evening, and Sunday public affairs programs. But the headlines alone would not have sufficed to make a serious issue out of a problem so removed from most people's daily concerns. Continuity was necessary to rivet attention to new facts as they emerged. The process is circular. Media exposure and public attention generate responses at the elite level that produce still more news in a cycle of mutual reinforcement that continues until politicians and public tire of an issue or another issue moves into the center of the political stage.

. . . On matters of concern to people, because they fall within their direct experience, as is the case with various bread-and-butter, sickness-and-health, life-and-death issues, the media clearly lack power to suppress concern. But they can do more than stimulate interest. By directing attention to these concerns, they provide a context that influences *how* people will think about these matters—where they believe the fault lies and whether anything (and what) should be done. Publicity given to essentially private concerns transforms them into public concerns. Whether or not it increases the problem for those affected, it does increase morale and legitimates the will to protest.

With regard to high-threshold issues like Watergate, the media play an even more essential role. Had it not been for the news reports about Watergate, hardly anyone would have known about campaign finance violations, "dirty tricks," illegal surveillance by persons connected with the White House, and the lot. Media attention was necessary before Watergate could be considered a problem. Yet, in publicizing a high-threshold issue like Watergate, the media do more than direct attention to a problem; they influence how people will think about it. They supply the context that, by making the problem politically relevant, gives people reasons for taking sides and converts the problem into a serious political issue. In this sense the public agenda is not so much set by the media as built up through a cycle of media activity that transforms an elite issue into a public controversy.

None of this should be read to mean that the media, all on their own, dictate the public agenda. They cannot "teach" the public what the issues are. They certainly do not operate in total autonomy from the political system. The gradual saturation of news content with Watergate depended on political developments in which the press itself was only one of several movers. Agenda building—a more apt term than agenda setting—is a collective process in which media, government, and the citizenry reciprocally influence one another in at least some respects.

Let us ... sketch out how the news media affect this agenda-building process.

First, they highlight some events or activities. They make them stand out from among the myriads of other contemporaneous events and activities that could equally have been selected out for publicity. Making something the center of interest affects how much people will think and talk about it. This much is only common sense.

But, second, being in the news is not enough to guarantee attention to an issue. The amount and kind of coverage required varies from issue to issue. Different kinds of issues require different amounts and kinds of coverage to gain attention. Where news focuses on a familiar concern likely to affect almost everyone, this almost guarantees instant attention. In the case of a high-threshold issue like Watergate, which also surfaced at the wrong time, it takes saturation coverage to achieve this result. Specifically, recognition by the "cosmopolitan" media was not enough. Only after the more locally oriented press had become saturated with news of Watergate developments did it emerge as an issue that would remain on the political and public agenda for nearly 16 months.

Third, the events and activities in the focus of attention still have to be framed, to be given a field of meanings within which they can be understood. They must come to stand for something, identify some problem, link up with some concern. The first exposé of the political fund used to finance the unit responsible for the break-in was publicized during a Presidential campaign. It was reported and interpreted within the context of that continuing contest. The Democrats' effort to change this context by interpreting Watergate as a symptom of widespread political corruption within the Administration was not very successful. Watergate remained, at least for a while, a partisan issue. The context had first to be changed.

Fourth, the language the media use to track events also affects the meaning imputed to them. Metaphors such as "Watergate caper" and "bugging incident," which belittled the issue, disappeared that spring under an avalanche of signs of a high-level political scandal. The press, along with politicians, adopted less deprecatory codewords. "Watergate" or "Watergate scandal" came to denote the various questionable activities now being disclosed. The words stood for nothing specific, yet for anything that could possibly happen.

Fifth, the media link the activities or events that have become the focus of attention to secondary symbols whose location on the political landscape is easily recognized. They also weave discrete events into a continuing political story, so that the lines of division on the issue as it develops tend to coincide with the cleavage between the organized political parties or between other sharply defined groups. . . . When Watergate first surfaced during the 1972 campaign, it was defined primarily as a partisan clash between Democrats and Republicans. By Spring 1973 opinion still divided along political lines, but a realignment was under way as the issue changed and sides began to shape up around the "need to get the facts out," over the public "right to know" vs. "executive privilege," and on the question of confidence in the integrity of the government.

Finally, there are the prestige and standing of the spokesmen who articulate these concerns and demands. Their effectiveness stems in good part from their ability to command media attention. Democratic politicians like Larry O'Brien and George McGovern had been lonely voices . . . when, during the campaign, they pressed for a full investigation. Their demands, though publicized, were neither much heard nor much heeded. They were known as people with an axe to grind. But as the controversy escalated, the

publicity given Judge Sirica's admonishment that the full truth had not
been told led prestigious Republicans to call for explanations, and their
various attempts to get at the facts put pressure on the White House. The
bystander public was being wooed. . . .

. . . Based on the evidence, we reject the paranoid version of Watergate
propagated by the White House that the crisis was manufactured by a hostile press which finally drove Nixon from office. But we also reject the
populist view that Nixon was forced to resign because he lost his battle for
public opinion. The moving force behind the effort to get to the bottom of
Watergate came neither from the media nor public opinion but from political insiders. The conflict pitted the White House against those who, for
whatever reason, wanted full disclosure of the facts behind the illegal attempt to plant wiretaps in the national headquarters of the Democratic
Party. . . .

The press was prime mover in the controversy only in its early phase,
when the Woodward and Bernstein tandem first linked the Watergate bur-
glars to the Nixon campaign committee and, during the campaign, uncovered other stories that hinted at the politically explosive potential of the
"bugging" incident. But with Nixon's decisive electoral victory, the press
came close to abandoning Watergate. Then, as the issue revived and conflict over the scope of the investigation intensified, the press mainly lived
off information insiders were happy to furnish it. . . .

Had the news media, by their coverage of Watergate, directly persuaded
the public of the seriousness of White House misdeeds, of Nixon's com-
plicity, of a threat to basic values, and that impeachment might be war-
ranted? Not directly, but by their reporting and their comments, by the
way they highlighted some events, by the context within which they
framed these events, by the language they used to track developments, by
linking news they reported to symbols familiar to the audience, and by the
persons they singled out (or who offered themselves) as spokesmen in the
controversy, the media certainly influenced the way the public—and politicians as well—thought about and defined the underlying issue.

. . . [I]t is difficult to demonstrate, in the narrowly scientific way that
has become the researcher's norm, that watching or listening to a particular
Watergate speech, press conference, or televised testimony was what directly changed people's opinion. Many media effects remain elusive and
can be understood only as the outcome of a cumulative process. Thus we
have pointed to evidence that minor, incremental, and sometimes subtle
changes sooner or later contributed to major shifts. For example, the most
important effect of the televised Senate Watergate hearings was a
"sleeper," not immediately noticeable. By subtly changing the issue, the
televised hearings prepared the ground for the outburst that so instanta-

neously followed the firing of the Special Watergate Prosecutor. Similarly, it was the high regard in which the major spokesmen against impeachment were held as the result of the televised Judiciary Committee proceedings that made their subsequent defection so persuasive.

The charge that the Watergate coverage was unfair or somehow "distorted" remains basically unsubstantiated. Nixon was hardly at the mercy of the media. The same publicity that was effectively utilized by his opponents was available to Nixon whenever he chose to make use of it. And Watergate did yield the headlines to other news on several occasions—not only during the Middle East crisis in October 1973 but later when, shortly before the impeachment debate, Nixon traveled abroad in what he called his "search for peace." As President, it was easy for Nixon to command attention; as leader of his party, he was apt to be treated gingerly by Republican editors until his intransigence overtried their loyalties. There is no question that the media thrive on scandal, and they did thrive during Watergate; but by the yardstick of reporting during the impeachment and trial of Andrew Johnson or during the Dreyfus case, they more than adhered to the norms of journalistic objectivity.

The main contribution of the media to moving opinion along was their extensive and full coverage of critical events. The visibility of the controversy helped more than anything to legitimate the process by which Nixon was ousted. . . . Because the deliberations of the House Judiciary Committee were televised, they were cast into the mold of an adversary proceeding, with most arguments couched in legal rather than political language. The decision was depicted as compelled by the evidence, with members— regardless of personal conviction—accepting the majority decision. They saw themselves, as they had told the nation, as representatives of the impersonal authority embodied in the Constitution, the highest law of the land. . . .

Still another question is how much the public was reacting to the substance of the Watergate disclosures or to Nixon himself. After all, other Presidents had been guilty of acts whose constitutionality was questionable or of behavior that fell short of the expected high standards of personal or political propriety. Yet these others somehow managed to avoid Nixon's fate. They somehow managed to keep up appearances either by sacrificing subordinates, who took the blame, or making sure that nothing beyond unsubstantiated rumor ever got out. Why should Nixon have failed with a similar strategy, one that he had previously employed with striking success? For one thing Nixon by his behavior throughout his political career had made enemies within the working press. As President, however, he commanded deference and respect and was treated with caution. Yet, once insiders put him on the defensive, these reporters were astounded at how far Nixon had evidently been willing to go to assure his reelection and to punish his "enemies." Thereafter they were ready to resurrect the image of the "old Nixon" and were less willing to declare sensitive areas out-of-bounds. Nixon was to harm himself further with the press by a pretense of openness. When pressed on Watergate, he repeatedly assured his questioners that he would cooperate to clear up the scandal, yet always with a proviso that allowed him to renege at a later date. As a result, Nixon was to appear less and less ingenuous even to his own followers. It was not the abuse of power, revealed in the Senate hearings, as much [as] his obstruction of the legal process that in the last analysis cost him the most support. The constituency that in the early months backed him on Watergate became increasingly impatient to have the issue resolved. This included many people who were still confident that the evidence would show that Nixon had done nothing worse than had other Presidents.

In this climate the opposition to Nixon gradually gained strength. It became difficult to defend Nixon on any but the narrowly legal grounds staked out by Republicans on the Judiciary Committee. . . .

Be all this as it may, there could have been no real public opinion on Watergate without the media. They alone could have called into being the mass audience of "bystanders" whose opinion had to be taken into account. It was likewise the media which, by reporting and even sponsoring polls, presented the cast of political actors in Watergate with a measure of public response to their every move. . . . The impression of public support made it easier to move against Nixon simply because the bystander public withheld the vote of confidence the President had so eagerly sought in order to defeat impeachment politically. Only in this sense, and this sense alone, was Nixon "driven" from office by his loss of public support.

Note

1. Richard M. Nixon, *RN: The Memoirs of Richard Nixon* (New York: Grosset and Dunlap, 1978), pp. 971, 972.

24

MEDIA, PROTEST, AND POLITICAL VIOLENCE: A TRANSACTIONAL ANALYSIS

Gadi Wolfsfeld

Editor's Note

In their quest for attention from the government and the public, interest groups are increasingly adopting media strategies. This is especially true of poor and powerless groups that cannot afford expensive legal or lobbying strategies. But mere attention is not enough. The struggle to gain publicity becomes a battle over the framing of news accounts. Each side in the conflict tries to have its version adopted by the media.

Using several case studies from Israel as examples, Gadi Wolfsfeld describes how powerless and powerful interest groups employed media strategies to protest government actions. Favorable media coverage turned out to be most crucial for powerless groups. From his field studies Wolfsfeld deduces seven media strategy rules for protest groups. His research, grounded in transactional theories, constitutes an important step in understanding the interactive roles of journalists and nongovernmental political actors.

At the time of writing, Wolfsfeld held a joint appointment in the Communications Institute and the Department of Political Science at Hebrew University in Jerusalem. The selection is from Journalism Monograph *127 (June 1991). Footnotes have been omitted.*

A Transactional Analysis

The role of the mass media in political protests is determined by the interaction between the antagonists (e.g., protest group(s) and the political authorities) and the mass media. The research question can best be formulated by asking: "Which political actors interact with which types of media coverage to produce what types of outcomes?" A transactional ap-

Reproduced from *Journalism Monographs,* 127, June 1991, pp. 1-61, with permission of the Association for Education in Journalism and Mass Communication.

proach to this issue views the process as a two-way flow of influence in which it is just as important to study the influence of the antagonists on the mass media as it is to look at the more conspicuous influence of the mass media on political actors. . . .

The basic relationship between the antagonists and the mass media can be thought of as a "competitive symbiosis" (Wolfsfeld, 1984) in which each side is dependent on the other for needed services but each tries to obtain those services on its own terms. These two sets of interests can lead to both cooperation and conflict (Blumler and Gurevitch, 1981). . . . The relationship between the antagonists and the mass media is also defined by a set of cultural transactions in which each side presents its own ideological interpretations of reality. . . . The relationship between political actors and the press is much more than a straightforward business deal: it is a form of social interaction in which the behaviors of each side are regulated by elaborate, independent sets of ideologies which go far beyond simple calculations of cost and benefit.

The most useful way for researchers to deal with this aspect of the relationship is to focus on the interpretive frames which are put forth by the mass media and the antagonists (Gamson, 1989; Gamson and Modigliani, 1989; Linsky, 1986; Bennett, 1983; Gitlin, 1980). In the present essay we shall adopt the definition of frames which has been proposed by Gamson: "A central organizing idea for making sense of relevant events and suggesting what is at issue" (1989, 35). A great many political conflicts center on disputes over frames as each of the antagonists attempts to market his or her own package of ideas to the mass media and the public. It is important to examine the level of correspondence between the frames adopted by the media and those offered by each of the political antagonists in order to better understand the process of reciprocal influence. A transactional analysis enables us to deal with both the quantitative and qualitative aspects of the media-antagonist relationship. . . .

Three very different conflicts were chosen in order to examine the utility of the model. The first case is a protest by Israeli students over the government's plans to raise tuition. The second was one of the largest industrial conflicts in Israel in which the Israel Aircraft Industry attempted to thwart government plans to scrap the building of the Lavi aircraft. The final case was the Palestinian *intifada* (uprising) in which the Palestinians living in the West Bank and Gaza carried out massive, violent protests against Israeli occupation. The protests over student tuition and the Lavi were passing conflicts while the Palestinian uprising continues at the time of this writing.

The major method used in the study combined direct observations of the conflicts with in-depth interviews with group leaders, journalists, and

Table 24-1   The Quantity of News Coverage in One Month

Group	Number of articles	Size of articles (cm²)	Page 1 stories	Multiple articles
Students	31	6,846	7	9
The Lavi	146	43,592	26	24
Palestinians	224	99,181	27	27

Note: Newspapers do not appear on Saturday, so there are usually 26 or 27 newspapers issued in a month.

political authorities. The direct observations were carried out by accompanying reporters to the scenes of conflicts (demonstrations, strikes, and riots) in order to get first-hand information about the interactions between reporters and protesters.

The interviews focused on perceptions about these interactions and asked about media strategies and media effects. All of the interviews were flexible but all discussions revolved around the same issues: the specific and general influence of media presence and coverage on the antagonists, strategies for manipulating or accommodating the news media, the centrality of the media in group planning, the ways in which the role of the media changed during the course of the conflict, the nature of the relationship between the actors and journalists, attempts at punishment and rewards of actors and reporters, how "fair" and "representative" was the coverage the groups were given, and what lessons they have learned about the media from their own experience. The interviews were carried out in Hebrew, apart from those with members of the foreign press. These sessions generally lasted about an hour and were taped and then transcribed.

There was also a modest content analysis of newspaper articles written about the conflicts in the major Israeli newspaper (*Yidiot Achronot*). The major purpose of this analysis was to examine the quantity of material written about each conflict and to collect some impressions about the dominant media frames for each confrontation. The amount of space given to each conflict in the first month of each protest is presented in Table 24-1. While all three protests were national events, the relative importance of the three stories is clear: the students received the least amount of coverage followed by the Lavi while the Palestinian *intifada* understandably received the most coverage.

The Students

. . . Attempts to raise tuition have traditionally been the one issue which has provoked the students to collective action. The conflict which is de-

scribed below took place between the end of February and the middle of
June 1987. The government was planning to raise tuition dramatically in
order to alleviate the precarious financial position of the universities. The
student union reacted with partial and general strikes which were accompanied by large and often violent demonstrations. . . .

The mass media played a central part in students' protest strategy from
the beginning of the conflict. Based on previous experience, the student
leaders were not confident about their ability to bring out a large number
of students to their demonstrations. A strategy of staged "gimmicks" was
planned for getting into the news in order to raise the level of consciousness among both students and the general public. Small groups of protesters would lie down in front of the Prime Minister's office or would block
streets in order to attract media attention.

These gimmicks were successful and the resulting publicity was invalu-
able in bringing out students to demonstrations. The rise in media status
also had a significant impact on the relations between the students and the
mass media. The head of the student union described the stages:

> In the beginning, of course, we were running after the reporters: the gimmick
> stage, the gambling stage. Disturbances in front of the Knesset [the Israeli
> parliament] and the like. What happened was the press became warmer and
> warmer towards us. I remember how one of the reporters told us that after the
> third or fourth demonstration the editors were realizing that the story was an
> important one.

. . . One of the reporters described the student struggle in terms of a
curve:

> There is a curve, really a hyperbole. They were weak in the beginning and
> they had a lot of trouble getting the media out. I covered them because I was
> convinced that there would be a story there. Then they proved that there were
> a lot of people behind them by bringing out thousands. It was somewhat
> different than a normal curve, they really took off. . . . They decided in
> advance that they would get arrested and they'd be willing to have tear gas and
> the whole bit. The level of media attention went way up because they [the
> media] saw there was real violence and ministers were coming to talk to the
> students and then they [the students] reached their peak. The students used
> extremism to break into the news and were then able to switch to more
> conventional media strategies.

It is important to point out that what the reporter calls "extremism" is
better labeled staging. The violence was not completely genuine—it was
designed primarily for media consumption. This is a clear example of media influence as the students adapted their behavior to suit the needs of
the press.

... The change in the behavior of the reporters was very dramatic. They were calling the students at all hours in the night, and every student planning meeting became a public event. Some students attempted to use this new power to their own advantage. . . .

One of the reporters was punished by the students when a relatively minor story about a student having AIDS was being distributed by the student leaders. The reporter was not given this story and the leaders claim that this sanction had a definite effect on subsequent coverage by that particular newspaper.

Nevertheless, the relationship with the press was, for the most part, a close one. Many of the reporters were young, had been students themselves and, as often happens in such ongoing protests, found themselves identifying with the students' cause. One of the reporters who was interviewed talked about her changing relationship with the student leaders:

> The relations are basically those of interested parties. I have an interest in getting from them all of the information and they have an interest in giving me as much one-sided information as possible. But what happened was that because the events were very intensive, and they were in contact daily, or even several times a day, I began to identify with them. . . . I gave them advice about when to have a demonstration and when not to have one . . . even though I tried not to be too biased in my writing, I was definitely on their side.

This growing sense of closeness between reporters and protest leaders is not at all unusual (Wolfsfeld, 1984). There are a number of reasons for this closeness between the students and the press. The symbiosis between the students and the reporters was enhanced by the fact that the themes being promoted by the students fit easily into traditional media frames. The protesters and the press were both interested in stressing the risk and danger of the protests, and the theme of "social equality" (i.e., poor people should also go to university) is one which also receives a great deal of sympathy in the mass media.

One should not, however, exaggerate the extent of media control by the students. They still had to accommodate the media, and they were especially attentive to the needs of radio and television. They arranged as many demonstrations as possible for Jerusalem because the television station was based there. They also made a point of only calling the television station to come to a demonstration when they felt that they had the numbers to justify such a summons; television coverage is expensive. . . .

The massive amounts of publicity had dramatic outcomes for all of those involved in the conflict. One of the leaders described the effects of their growing stature:

Publicity is power, tremendous power. The fact that you are known makes you super-influential. Why? Because there is a relationship between publicity and electoral ability, and whoever works in the political system understands that very quickly.

In order to illustrate the point, he told of an incident in which the office of the Mayor of Jerusalem called and tried to coordinate having a photo taken with the students to show his support.

The media coverage also had an influence on both the student body and on the leaders. The morale of the students rose and there is no doubt that many saw the publicity as a sign of success. The leaders also became public figures, and many planning sessions began with a discussion of the previous day's coverage. As aspiring politicians, each of the leaders was carefully monitoring the media to make sure that the credit was being distributed fairly.

The mass media were definitely one of the reasons behind the use of violence by the students. The arrival of cameras had a clear effect on the level of disorder, because a great deal of the violence was being staged for the media. Violence was especially likely to occur during small demonstrations in order to insure that the events would still get coverage. . . .

The issue of whether or not to use violence was, however, a controversial one and there was a great deal of debate about whether such violence would prove counterproductive. While the major leaders felt that such violence was critical to the campaign, some of the other representatives opposed breaking the law. Those who favored violence claimed that it was the only way to get real coverage. One of these leaders pointed out during one of these meeting that even when he called the Minister of Finance a liar, he barely received two minutes on the evening news. . . .

As suggested earlier, the students were fairly successful at controlling the media frames for their protest. One example, a variation on the risk and danger theme, was the *militancy* frame. Stories in the media which stressed this frame focused on threats of escalation and violence by the students. One illustration of this theme is a picture of an angry student making a fist with the caption "War Room in the Dormitories." Another picture has students wearing gas masks with the caption "We Won't Stop the Demonstrations." The importance of this frame to the students is illustrated by the photograph in one of their own newspapers which shows students (including a crying woman) being taken into custody by police with the caption "Till the End."

The students did not only initiate media frames; they also reacted to unfavorable publicity in order to improve their image. One demonstration had gone somewhat out of control producing more violence than the students had planned. The resulting media frame was far less sympathetic to the students and the next demonstration included a media stunt of handing out flowers to the police. This is probably the only example where the mass media served as a moderating force in this conflict.

A second traditional frame which emerged was that the students were *victims of police brutality*. One cartoon which was published at the time was entitled "Lessons in Astronomy." It portrayed a policeman on horseback after hitting a student who sees stars. . . . The sympathy for the students was displayed in a picture of several police with sticks (one on horseback) converging onto one student. The caption read "Police Batons and Water Cannons Fall on Students' Heads."

The police were able to get their point across in at least one case. The headline read "The Police: 'The Students Wanted to Conquer the Treasury [Ministry], We Had to Disperse Them by Force.' " The subtitle read: "They Were Blood Thirsty." In this case, the accompanying picture was very different: many students standing on a wall above one lone policeman.

Two additional frames which were promoted by the students were the *social inequality* theme and the *end of higher education*. The former theme was advanced with headlines such as: "Students to Peres—We Don't Have a Rich Father" and "Knesset Member Ali: 'We Won't Let the University Be Closed to the Children of the Poor.' " The end of education theme was suggested by the now traditional tactic of carrying a suitably marked coffin at the head of a demonstration and a second gimmick in which students tied chains around their neck. As expected, these props served as the focus for news photographs which were accompanied by the appropriate captions. . . .

The interaction between an antagonist and the press ends when it is no longer profitable for one or both of the sides. In cases of protest, it is usually the mass media which lose interest as newer stories push older ones to the side. The curve which was described above also has a down side which all protest groups must eventually face.

One of the reporters was asked whether the students' ability to attract media attention declined as the protests continued:

> Yes. . . . You really see it. They're not mentioned on television anymore and in the newspapers they are moving from the first page to the last. Reporters get sick of it. Every evening you get an announcement that there will be another strike. . . . The drop is very steep and very sharp.

The students were also aware of this change and turned their attention to the political channels of communication which had been opened by their surge in the media. For a time they were able to use their fame in the media to their advantage. The decision which was finally passed by the government left the level of tuition almost unchanged. . . .

The Lavi

. . . The Lavi was designed to be the Israeli jet fighter for the 1990s. The Israeli government had invested billions of dollars in the project in an attempt to develop a jet which would equal or surpass the most sophisticated planes in the world. As often occurs with such projects, the costs of developing the plane far exceeded the initial estimates, and the government had to decide whether or not to abandon the venture. In the spring of 1987, after a number of special cabinet meetings, the government of Israel decided to end the development of the Lavi.

The conflict over the Lavi was one of the largest industrial conflicts in the history of Israel. The Israel Aircraft Industry (IAI) is an extremely powerful organization in Israel and employs over 20,000 workers around the country. The Lavi had become the major project of this industry, and its abandonment meant the loss of enormous amounts of money and thousands of jobs. The executive committee and the workers council fought bitterly to convince the government to continue the project.

The massive amounts of news coverage given to the conflict can be related, among other things, to the symbolic significance of the government's decision. The Lavi project had been seen as a source of national pride, and the political debate involved honor as much as money. The political and media status of the major actors in this drama ensured a very wide audience. In an unusual precedent, the Israeli army also became publicly involved in the conflict, when the chief of staff and the head of the air force proclaimed their opposition to the Lavi. . . .

Despite the thousands of articles written about the conflict, and the hundreds of hours broadcast about the plane, the evidence collected suggests that the role of the mass media was a limited one. This conclusion may be considered tentative due to the breadth of the conflict and the resulting difficulty in isolating media influence. Nevertheless, the struggle over the Lavi was essentially a political struggle between powerful institutions in which the press was much more of an observer than a participant. . . .

IAI is . . . less dependent on the press than most other "protest groups" because it had direct access to the government. A great deal of effort was put into lobbying Knesset members and government ministers, and the media campaign was seen as an additional source of pressure. The ability to combine direct political influence with media pressure demands a great deal of organization, resources, and political prestige. Such political contacts also increase the dependency of the press on the antagonist, because information about such efforts is also newsworthy.

One of the factors which weakened the bargaining position of the aircraft industry was the breadth of the conflict. The aircraft industry found it much more difficult than usual to control press coverage during this confrontation because there were so many other institutions sending information to the media. . . . Each of the reporters who were covering the conflict tended to reflect the perspective of his or her beat. The economic reporters stressed the enormous cost of the aircraft while the labor reporters talked about the dangers of unemployment. The industry's problem was exacerbated by the fact that the majority of alternative sources were coordinating the efforts to defeat the Lavi. . . .

The power of the aircraft industry over the press was certainly equalled by the government forces. The Defence Ministry, the army, and the Ministry of the Treasury all joined forces in the battle against the Lavi. The Minister of the Treasury offered briefings on the "costs" of the Lavi, which suggested that continuing the Lavi would bring about economic disaster, and that there would be no more money for health, education, or welfare. . . .

. . . [M]ost media frames about the Lavi were set by the antagonists themselves. Each had its own in-house reporters assigned to it; their quotes and press releases appeared almost verbatim in the press. There was no need for media stunts or gimmicks; the conflict itself was inherently newsworthy and thus the press simply reflected the perspective being promoted by each of these powerful antagonists. The competition among actors prevented any one source from dominating all of the coverage, but the antagonists were able to ensure that their own message would be heard verbatim. . . .

In this type of confrontation, the media can best be thought of as a conflict arena, in which two or more gladiators fight for political supremacy. The public reads and watches as each of the participants throws accusations, innuendoes, and insults at each other, and the final decision is left to a small set of judges known as the government.

The mass media offers a convenient meeting place for all of these parties, and its traditions certainly have some influence on how the battle is fought. The fact that so many important parties want to get involved in the contest increases the political and social status of the media arena. The arena itself, however, has very little influence on either the course of the confrontation or its conclusion. In part this is because the battle is also being fought in a number of other arenas in which the combatants and the judges all have direct contact with one another. The final outcome of the conflict ultimately depends on which side has more political power.

The Palestinian *Intifada*

. . . The Palestinian *intifada* (the uprising) began in December of 1987. The role of the news media in this conflict quickly became a major controversy both in Israel and abroad. At the beginning of the *intifada* many Israelis felt that the presence of the media was the major cause of violence and called for banning the press from the territories. A great of deal of the initial debate within the Israeli government centered on what should be "done" about the media (Schiff and Ya'ari, 1990).

The overall conclusion of this research can be summed up by suggesting that the news media did indeed have an important impact on the course of the Palestinian *intifada*, due to the nature of the antagonist goals and the particular context of that conflict. The conflict with the Palestinians in the territories was, as much as anything else, a battle for public opinion. The Palestinians were depending on the news media to mobilize world opinion and Israel was forced to respond in public. Ironically, it was the Palestinians who were in the best position to control the events and the resulting media frames, while the Israeli army could only concern itself with "damage control." The case of the *intifada* offers an important illustration of the ways in which political context can have an effect on the relative power of the antagonists and the centrality of the media in such conflicts. . . .

. . . The best way to describe the influence of the mass media on protest in the territories is to consider them a catalyst for violence. The impact of a catalyst depends on the condition of the substances and their environment as much as the catalyst itself. As an analogy, it is useful to remember that wind can either rapidly spread a fire or, in the case of a match, extinguish it.

The mass media certainly do not cause the protest: the protests come from a genuine sense of anger and frustration. The willingness of Palestinians to use violence was not staged for the media; few would be willing to risk their lives merely for publicity. The mass media can, however, create or inflame protests because people change their behavior in keeping with the message they want to send. . . .

It is critical to keep in mind, however, that the presence of the media has exactly the opposite influence on soldiers and Jewish settlers in the area. Soldiers tend to be much more restrained in front of the TV cameras, more reluctant to use violence; this is the message the army wants to send to the world. The Jewish settlers sometimes carry out retaliatory raids on Arab villages (Weisburd, 1989) and it is noteworthy that the press is never invited to these events. Indeed, the settlement leaders are often embarrassed when the results of such raids are publicized. . . .

. . . [T]he relationship of the Israeli army and the press during the Palestinian *intifada* offers an almost textbook example of the limits of power.

While Israel is always considered newsworthy, her ability to control media frames of the *intifada* was severely limited by two major factors. The first was the nature of the events themselves. The *intifada* was inherently embarrassing for Israel and it fit neatly into a well-known media frame of *David and Goliath*. The second limiting factor was the inability of the Israeli government to control either the events themselves or information about them. While the Israeli army is normally in the business of initiating news, in this case it was forced to react to events which were thrust upon it.

. . . [T]he role of the mass media in the Palestinian *intifada* was probably more central than in the other two conflicts. The news media became an important participant in this conflict for three major reasons: 1) the major goal of the *intifada* was to mobilize world opinion and the news media were the central means of achieving that goal. 2) The Israeli-Palestinian conflict had a high level of media status around the world and the world media allocated a great deal of resources to covering this confrontation. 3) Israel is also very dependent on world opinion and is in no position to either ignore negative coverage or to close itself off from the news media.

The importance of the mass media to this conflict is reflected in the ways each of the antagonists dealt with the press. The presence and coverage of the news media had a very clear influence on the behavior and morale of the Palestinians. The mass media were seen as the only channel for redress and the protesters were very conscious of the presence of the cameras and the opportunities they represented. The Palestinians were sending two messages to the world: one of victimization and the other of defiance. While both of the messages are extremely expensive to transmit they clearly fall into the definition of news. Nevertheless, it is important to remember that many of the outcomes of the interaction between the Palestinians and the news media are initiated by the Palestinians themselves. It is much more appropriate to ask what the Palestinians do with the news media than what the news media do to them.

The *intifada* also shows how difficult it can be for even the most powerful actors to control media frames. The Israeli army was unable to control either the events or the "story." They found themselves constantly reacting with too little information which was delivered too late. It is less clear how much the news media actually had an independent effect on the army's behavior in the territories. It is clear, however, that the role of the news media was a constant concern for the Israeli political leaders, the army, and the soldiers themselves.

Ultimately, then, the mass media played a central role in the Palestinian conflict because the Palestinians wanted it that way. In contrast to the conflict over the Lavi, the mass media became, at least for a time, the central arena of conflict. The Palestinians had no hope of militarily defeating the Israeli army and they depended on the news media to mobilize third parties to their cause. The violence in the territories was also designed to send a more direct message to the Israeli people: that there is a price to be paid for occupation. This message is also taken home by the Israeli soldiers who serve there. The news media, however, represent a much more efficacious channel of communication and the Palestinians are well aware of that fact.

Conclusion

It is valuable to conclude with . . . seven rules of transaction and some of the empirical evidence which was brought in support of these postulates.

Rule Number 1: The centrality of the news media to any conflict hinges on the extent to which either or both of the sides is dependent on the services of the media for mobilizing third parties into the conflict.

The news media were much more central to the student protests and the Palestinian protests because of each group's dependence on the media for mobilizing allies. Despite the enormous differences between the two conflicts, the role of the media was in many ways familiar. In each case the press was used as battering ram to break down the walls of political indifference. The institutional channels of redress began to open and the political authorities were forced to respond. The exploitation of the press by the students was, albeit, more premeditated, but the Palestinians were quickly socialized in the importance of mobilizing the media.

The role of the news media in the dispute over the Lavi, it was argued, was less central. The Defence Ministry and the Israeli Aircraft Industry were fighting a political battle in which the news media served more as an observer than a participant. The importance of the media was reduced by the inherent power of the two antagonists and the availability of alternative modes of political influence.

Rule Number 2: The lower the level of the antagonist's (social, political, and media) status, organization, and resources, the greater the level of media influence on the antagonist.

The students and the Palestinians were much more focused on the media because of their dependence on the press. This was especially obvious in the student protests in which almost all of their activities were staged specifically for the news media. The Palestinian violence was authentic, but the Palestinians were also vulnerable to press influence due to their high level of dependence. This dependence was reflected in the way they responded to the needs of the press and the extent to which they apparently looked to the press as a barometer of success.

The antagonists involved in the Lavi conflict tended to be less affected by the news media. The level of status and resource of the Israel Aircraft Industry not only made them more inherently newsworthy, it also lowered their need for the services offered by the news media. In addition, having a sophisticated department of public relations not only insures more influence over the news media, it also insulates powerful antagonists from media effects. Professional media people are more likely to plan and execute a long-range strategy of public relations, and less likely to overreact to each day's coverage.

Rule Number 3:   The higher the antagonist's level of (social, political, and media) status, organization, resources, and/or newsworthy behavior, the greater the level of antagonist influence on the media.

This rule was best illustrated by the Lavi conflict which saw a number of very powerful political actors virtually dictating the content of news stories. The army, the treasury department, and the Israel Aircraft Industry were all able to use the Israeli media as a personal bulletin board for carrying their message to each other and to the public at large. These actors had all of the advantages which institutional wealth has to offer: public status, a well-developed public relations staff, and "in-house" reporters competing for the information they had to offer.

The Palestinians were able to substitute newsworthy behavior for other resources and this brought them higher levels of political and media status. The students were much weaker in this respect and had to rely on staged gimmicks to demand attention. Both of these strategies offer a rather effective substitute for more concrete resources but the ability of such groups to stay in the news is sorely limited. Those who come through the back door of the news media not only have to come in costume, they are also quickly asked to leave.

Rule Number 4:   The higher the level of the news medium's social and political status, organization and resources, and/or distributional capacity, the greater the level of media influence on the antagonists.

Political antagonists are very aware of the relative importance of various news media and they adapt their behavior accordingly. The students, the Palestinians, and the army were all more likely to adapt themselves to the needs of television because they believed that it was the most powerful medium. It is quite clear that political actors must pay more to obtain television coverage, in part due to the limited amount of space offered by that medium. This is especially true in Israel where there is essentially only one television station with one national news department.

Political authorities are also more willing to accommodate the more powerful media. The army spokesperson's office is understandably much more willing to grant exclusive interviews where they will do the most good. They also tend to monitor major news organs (e.g., *The New York Times,* the *Washington Post,* the *London Times*) and are more sensitive to the editorial line of these media.

Rule Number 5: Influence on the news media depends on the antagonists' level of relative newsworthiness at the time of the transaction.

The relationship between the mass media and antagonists changes over time. Those competing for public attention must continually prove themselves worthy: all news stories are doomed to end. This rise and fall of celebrity for the students and the Palestinians is the rule for successful protests; unsuccessful protests never rise at all. When these groups are at their peak, they find themselves surrounded by reporters pleading for more information, but as the conflict continues it is the protesters who are running after the journalists.

Certain actors, especially political authorities, are defined as more inherently newsworthy and others can often store their media status in the bank of public recognition for future use. In general, however, the definition of news make it almost impossible for most political actors to remain in the public eye.

As stated, this process often makes it difficult for protest groups to achieve success. Novice political activists are often swept off their feet by their meteoric rise in the press and are unaware of the drop which awaits them. The more experienced political authorities are much better equipped to wait out any momentary storm; their story will continue. The wiser protest group will know how and when to turn media success into political access.

Rule Number 6: The nature of the antagonist's influence on the news media depends on the antagonist's level of event and information control at the time of the transaction.

This rule is meant to offer some initial direction for those who attempt to understand the limits of power. It is useful to think of a continuum of control. As was previously discussed, the IDF spokesperson's office ordinarily has a great deal of control over media frames because it normally has a monopoly on military information. The army was also quite successful in controlling the press in the case of the Lavi, although due to the breadth of the conflict, it had to share the stage with others. The opposite end of the continuum is offered by the case of the *intifada.* As stated, the army had very little control over either the events themselves or information about those events.

The level of informational control then tends to vary among both antagonists and contexts. It is perhaps surprising that a relatively weak group such as the students could achieve such success in this area. As stated, the reason for this anomaly is that they found themselves playing mostly on an empty field. They were thus quite capable of sending the messages they chose.

Rule Number 7: The nature of media influence on the antagonists depends on the antagonists' political goals at the time of the transaction.

The picture which emerges from these case studies is one in which media influence is an outcome which is best attributed to conscious attempts by political actors to respond to the media in the most effective way possible. The response of each is determined more by collective goals than by any media hypnosis.

The differential reactions of soldiers, settlers, and Palestinians to the presence of the news media graphically illustrates this point. The level of violence carried out by the students was also carefully planned to insure the greatest coverage with the least risk. Political authorities must also constantly weigh the costs and benefits of various reactions to media coverage. It is the actors who make these decisions and for the most part they do so in a very conscious, calculating manner. . . .

References

Benett, W. L. (1983). *News: The politics of illusion.* New York: Longman.

Blumler, J., & Gurevitch, M. (1981). Politicians and the press: An essay in role relationships. In D. P. Nimmo & K. Sanders (Eds.), *Handbook of Political Communication* (pp. 467-469).

Gamson, W. A., & Modigliani, A. (1989). Media discourse and public opinion on nuclear power: A constructionist approach. *American Journal of Sociology, 95*: 1-37.

Gamson, W. A. (1989). News as framing. *American Behavioral Scientist, 33*: 157-161.

Gitlin, T. (1980). *The whole world is watching.* Berkeley: University of California Press.

Linsky, M. (1986). *Impact: How the press affects federal policymaking.* New York: W. W. Norton.

Schiff, Z., & Ya'ari, E. (1990). *Intifada: The Palestinian uprising—Israel's third front.* New York: Simon and Schuster.

Weisburd, D. (1989). *Jewish settler violence—Deviance as social reaction.* University Park, PA: The Pennsylvania State University Press.

Wolfsfeld, G. (1984). The symbiosis of press and protest: An exchange analysis. *Journalism Quarterly, 61*: 550-556.

25

THE MANUFACTURE OF 'PUBLIC OPINION' BY REPORTERS: INFORMAL CUES FOR PUBLIC PERCEPTIONS OF PROTEST GROUPS

Douglas M. McLeod and James K. Hertog

Editor's Note

When journalists lack sympathy for their cause, protest groups must work hard to win favorable media coverage. If protest groups fail to win media approval, they are likely to be savaged by a hostile press. This selection also shows that catering to the media becomes far less important when journalists are already favorably inclined. Accordingly, coverage of anarchist groups by the anti-establishment press is usually supportive.

The mainstream press professes to be governed by a code of neutrality; therefore it rarely attacks unpopular targets directly. Instead, journalists prefer to quote hostile sources. One of these sources is "public opinion"; negative reactions by the public are either proclaimed outright or implied by the press. Given the high regard of average Americans for public opinion, people and events that seem to engender public disapproval lose their political legitimacy. Conversely, people and events that ostensibly bask in public approval become politically legitimate and worthy of praise and support.

The authors report ways in which the specter of public opinion can be evoked to help or harm groups. They speculate about the impact of such tactics but provide no evidence regarding their successes or failures. In addition to explaining how suggestions by the press about public opinion reactions can influence public demonstrations, the article clarifies the different socio-political roles played by mainstream and alternative media.

At the time of writing, Douglas M. McLeod was a member of the Department of Communication at the University of Delaware, and James K. Hertog taught in the School of Journalism at the University of Kentucky. The article comes from Discourse and Society *3:3 (1992): 259-75.*

From *Discourse and Society 3:3*, pp. 259-275. Copyright © 1992 by Sage Publications, Inc. Reprinted with permission of Sage Publications, Inc.

It has been effectively argued that mass media coverage of social protest groups tends to 'marginalize' groups which challenge the prevailing power structure (Gitlin, 1981; Shoemaker, 1984; Donohue et al., 1987). Media depictions of public opinion about the protest groups may be particularly powerful marginalizing symbols. Research has demonstrated that an individual's perceptions of public opinion influence such attitudes as: acceptance of discriminatory behavior (O'Gorman, 1975; O'Gorman and Garry, 1976-7); willingness to publicly advocate a political stand (Noelle-Neumann, 1974, 1984); and even basic perceptual judgments (Asch, 1956). These studies underscore the potential power of public opinion and consequently motivate inquiry into how conceptions of public opinion are communicated in news-coverage of protest groups. . . .

Public opinion is embedded in news-coverage at two levels: characterizations of public opinion at the micro-descriptive level and general conceptions of public opinion at the macro-conceptual level. This investigation of mainstream and alternative media coverage of three anarchist marches examines the use of four types of micro-descriptive level characterizations of public opinion: (1) statements about public opinion, (2) depictions of violations of social norms and of (3) community laws, and (4) portrayals of bystanders as symbols for public opinion. The analysis then proceeds to the macro-conceptual level in order to extract general underlying conceptions of public opinion inherent in mainstream and alternative media coverage of the anarchist protests.

The Journalistic Paradigm for Social Protest

One of the keys to whether a protest group is 'isolated' or 'accepted' by the larger society is the mass media's treatment of the protesters. This treatment is to a great degree shaped by a routinized journalistic paradigm for covering social protest. Journalists are socialized to focus on the actions, conflict and especially violence of protests. Often, the emphasis on overt action obscures the issues raised by the protesters.

Journalists' tendency to seek out the 'unusual' is very much in evidence in protest coverage. Coverage gravitates toward individuals exhibiting the most extreme appearance and behaviors. In the process, protesters are often characterized as being more 'deviant' from the mainstream than they really are.

Journalists are also trained to seek out the views of 'official' institutional spokespersons (Sigal, 1973). As a result, protest coverage adopts 'official' definitions of the protest situation by focusing on questions of the 'legality of actions' as opposed to the 'morality of issues'. In the process, coverage legitimizes official authority and marginalizes radical protest groups.

Media characterizations of public opinion are a product of this journalistic protest paradigm and as such are likely to contribute to authority support. As Edelman (1977: 55) asserts: 'Rather than curbing a regime, "public opinion" as a symbol enlarges official discretion by immobilizing potential opposition.' In essence, media characterizations of public opinion toward the protest groups, their views and actions, are potentially influential guidelines which can constrain the growth of radical movements both by questioning the legitimacy of the protest group and by contributing to fear of isolation for group members and potential converts.

Public Opinion at the Micro-Descriptive Level

At the micro-descriptive level, the concept of public opinion is constantly woven into news stories. In its most obvious form, public opinion is demonstrated by the ever-increasing number of public opinion poll results in the news. . . . However, opinion polls are rarely used in the coverage of social protest. Depictions of public opinion appear more frequently in protest coverage through informal representations of public opinion.

Informal characterizations of public opinion take a number of forms. First, in seeming violation of the canons of objectivity, reporters often make general statements describing the social consensus. This is exemplified by the use of such phrases as 'the national mood', 'public sentiment' or 'most people feel'.

A second form of characterization is the invocation of social norms. News stories often contain comments on the extent to which ideas, actions or appearances conform to or violate social norms, thus indicating the boundaries of mainstream public opinion. The application of social norms has been shown to be important to the identification of deviance (McKirnan, 1980).

Third, to the extent that laws represent a codified consensus, media depictions of actions upholding or violating community laws represent applications of public opinion. The distinction of legal violations, particularly in cases of civil disobedience, is often a matter of interpretation provided by journalists and their sources.

Finally, news stories often use bystanders to comment on protests. The way bystanders are typically used serves as a metaphor for public opinion similar to the 'chorus' of Greek drama described by Back (1988).

To some extent, these four types of depictions of public opinion may influence audience reactions to the issues and actions of the protest by indicating what is considered mainstream and what is considered deviant.

Public Opinion at the Macro-Conceptual Level

. . . Hennessy (1985) and Herbst (1991) discuss three alternative conceptions of public opinion: (1) public opinion as aggregated individual opinion much like it is measured by public opinion polls; (2) public opinion as the active attempts of groups and individuals to influence public policy; and (3) the 'general will' or 'zeitgeist' which acts as an expression of the consensus beliefs and moral values of some social group.

Historically, the most common conceptualization of public opinion in mass communication research has been the first of the three views. The prominence of opinion polls results and considerable growth of survey research methods and technology since the 1930s contribute to a 'one person, one vote' orientation toward public opinion (Herbst, 1991). In its most simplistic form, this view ignores individual differences in opinion-holding and the impact of group affiliation.

The second view of public opinion, rooted in a pluralist political orientation, envisions public opinion as the clashing of interest groups in the political arena. Unlike the first view, this conception, outlined by Blumer (1948), does not treat every individual's opinion equally. Interest groups marshall resources to represent common interests thereby increasing group members' influence over public policy. Ultimately, this view of public opinion is concerned with the impact of such aggregations on issues of social concern.

The third view treats public opinion as a set of shared norms, values and beliefs in society. The social consensus, which is commensurate with mainstream public opinion, comprises a system of social control which serves to maintain the social order. This system has built-in incentives and sanctions which encourage conformity to social norms. In sum, this view conceives of public opinion as a set of social norms and values enforced by a system of social control. . . .

Using the perspective of public opinion as social consensus, representations of public opinion may be seen as mechanisms of social control. Reports of public opinion reinforce the boundary between the acceptable and unacceptable in society. . . .

The public visibility of social protest may make protesters more susceptible to the fear of isolation. When the protest group represents a small minority, critical of the mainstream and on the periphery of the political spectrum, the pressure of social control may inhibit participation by potential converts to the protest group by stimulating fear of isolation.

Methods

This investigation of the use of micro-descriptive and macro-conceptual forms of public opinion analyzes news-coverage of three anarchist marches in the US city of Minneapolis, Minnesota. The first two marches, which took place on 16 October 1986 and 22 June 1987, were very similar in nature. These marches, which the anarchists labeled 'War Chest Tours', consisted of a connected series of symbolic demonstrations in front of downtown Minneapolis government and business establishments. The symbolic gestures were designed to highlight the criticisms that the anarchists were leveling against the existing power structure. For example, dollar bills were burned outside a local bank to underscore the anarchists' criticisms of corporate capitalism. The anarchists distributed pamphlets which explained the symbolic significance of each of the gestures, which included smashing a television set and burning the US, Soviet and McDonald's flags. Each march included some property damage, confrontations with the Minneapolis police and a number of arrests.

The third protest, on 3 June 1988 in Minneapolis's uptown area, was labeled 'Bash the Rich'. The demonstrators were protesting the displacement of minorities and the poor by the gentrification of the area. Again, various symbolic actions were used to highlight the protest. There were several altercations with police which resulted in 12 arrests.

All accessible coverage from these protests was analyzed including news stories from two metropolitan daily newspapers (*The Minneapolis Star Tribune* and the *St. Paul Pioneer Press-Dispatch*), one college newspaper (*The Minnesota Daily* from the University of Minnesota), one regional daily newspaper (*The Fargo Forum,* which directly printed the Associated Press state newswire), three alternative newspapers (*Overthrow* and *The Guardian* from New York, and *Fifth Estate* from Detroit) and three local television stations (WCCO—CBS affiliate, KSTP—ABC affiliate, and KMSP—an independent). The coverage consisted of 13 stories in mainstream newspapers, 4 stories in the alternative newspapers and 9 stories in the television coverage.

The analysis begins by isolating the use of micro-descriptive representations of public opinion in mainstream and then alternative media. These micro-descriptive representations provide cues for subsequent interpretations of macro-conceptual orientations toward public opinion. . . .

Micro-Descriptive Representations in Mainstream Media Coverage

No public opinion polls were taken to present the spectrum of public reaction to the anarchist protesters; consequently, representations of public opinion were the product of interpretation by reporters, editors and their sources.

Statements about Public Opinion

In a few cases, reporters directly characterized public reaction to the protesters. One example from the *Minnesota Daily* (1987) stresses that the anarchists are very different from the general public: 'Conflict and controversy were as prevalent among the participants as they are between anarchists and society at large'.

Statements about public opinion were more commonly found in material attributed to sources than in direct statements by the reporter. For example, both the *Star Tribune* (1986) and the *Fargo Forum* (1986) quoted a Minneapolis police officer who emphasized the minority status of anarchists by characterizing them as 'a bunch of punk-rockers from the Hennipin-Lake area, led by a *small* number, and I mean a small number of people'.

Embedded within another *Star Tribune* story (1987) is the assumption that if the public truly understands the anarchists, the public would support police actions to 'control' the protests. The story reports Deputy Police Chief Robert Lutz's statement that: 'If anybody has any questions about how the police performed, they should look up in the dictionary the definition of "anarchist"'.

Anarchist statements concerning public opinion were also found in the coverage. As a whole, the view presented characterizes the public as duped by the powers that be into 'militarism, capitalism, racism and sexism'. During the 1986 KSTP coverage, a protester spoke to the screen after a shot showing the US flag in the foreground burning, along with a hammer-and-sickle flag and a third barely seen at the edge of the screen:

> We want to put an end to all nationalism. We also burned a Soviet flag and a McDonald's flag. We consider these three of the major institutions that have the undeserved allegiance of millions of people.

Several anarchists' statements imply that the general public is lethargic and apathetic. In a *Pioneer Press-Dispatch* (1987) story, one anarchist explained the need for tactics involving property damage by saying: 'It doesn't seem like other tactics work to wake people up'. Another protester stated that: 'I support people trying to raise others' consciousness' (*Star Tribune* 1986). A characterization of the public as apathetic is implied in an organizer's explanation of the protest rationale (WCCO 1988):

> Maybe people will open their eyes and understand the situation in the world. And hopefully they'll realize that things have to change.

Social Norms

Social norms were a far more common use of public opinion in mainstream newspaper coverage of the three demonstrations. Several references to the 'abusive' behavior, 'obscene' language and 'eccentric' appearance of the protesters clearly indicated violations of social norms. For example, the lead paragraph of a *Pioneer Press-Dispatch* reads:

> It was anarchy in downtown Minneapolis on Monday—women bared their breasts, pin-striped businessmen were spat upon, art and buildings were defaced

with spray paint, glass bottles were smashed, and people were pushed and shoved. (1987)

Another example from the *Minnesota Daily* highlighted the anarchists' 'obscene' and 'abusive' language:

Throughout the rally, protesters referred to police as 'pigs' and 'the boys in blue'. At one point, the group of more than 80 protesters chanted 'fuck you' and pointed their middle fingers at the Federal Building in Minneapolis. (1986)

Coverage often cast protesters as violating social norms of propriety in terms of appearance. Television coverage often singled out protesters with the most unusual appearances for close-ups. Similarly, newspaper coverage also drew attention to 'eccentric' protesters:

The protesters drew a great deal of attention as they moved through down-town with their pounding drums, waving flags and eccentric appearance, which included purple Mohawk hairdos, black lipstick, flowing beards, pantaloons, jackets with leaves torn out and a turban or two. (*Star Tribune* 1986)

Coverage of the marchers often mixed the forms of norm-breaking together in a way that said essentially, 'this is a deviant group'. For example, one television story began:

Just their dress alone would have gotten this group of 150 attention in downtown Minneapolis. But the group marched through downtown shouting obscenities and defacing buildings with graffiti. . . . They said Minneapolis is revolting, but most observers were revolted by the language and actions of the group. (KSTP 1986)

Another example of the use of norm-violating behaviors was television coverage's juxtaposition of the two most prominent features of the 'Bash the Rich' demonstration—rocks thrown at an expensive sports car and the apparent macing of a McDonald's customer who tried to intervene in a flag-burning. Portrayals of these events superceded any discussion of issues raised by the demonstrators.

Flag-burning, framed as an anti-social activity, was a prominent focus of coverage of the 1986 march as well. The burning of the US flag during the 1986 protest received considerable attention relative to the concurrent burning of Soviet and McDonald's Corporation flags. In television coverage, the US flag was center-screen while the others were barely identifiable. The *Star Tribune* story mentioned that the three flags were burned, but the accompanying three-column picture showed only the US flag. . . .

Mainstream coverage devoted small amounts of coverage to the anarchists' claim that police actions violated social norms. One article did note an anarchist's charge of police brutality:

Damaging property is not the same thing as being violent. Nobody did anything to instigate the kind of reaction we got from police. We have a lot of people from out of the town and they're very surprised about the repression we have in this city. The only people I saw getting pushed and shoved were the demonstrators. (*Pioneer Press-Dispatch* 1987)

Legal Conduct

The anarchists were repeatedly referred to as a group intent on violating the law. The opening lines of one television story sarcastically question the demonstrators' self-designated label and beliefs, but openly proclaim their criminal status:

These demonstrators call themselves anarchists. They claim they're opposed to any and all forms of government. Their demonstration began quietly. Then some of the anarchists became vandals, defacing some downtown buildings. (KSTP 1987)

Journalists attributed most comment on law-breaking behavior to police officers. Most newspaper and television stories contained an obligatory comment from a police official depicting the protesters as criminals. The *Star Tribune* quoted Deputy Police Chief Lutz's statement that anarchists were 'people that have no intention of obeying the laws of our community' (ST 1987:2B). Sometimes, these quotes serve the dual function of invoking criminality and legitimizing police actions. For example, the same officer was shown in KSTP's coverage making the statement: 'If any of them break the law, they'll have to suffer the consequences' (1987). A similar clip appeared in 1988:

Anybody we see on the street breaking the law is going to jail, anarchist or not. We're not checking their religion. We're just taking them to jail. (WCCO 1988)

The use of quotes from official sources to comment on the events of the protest (as opposed to direct comment by the reporter) seems to be an observance of the journalistic norm of objectivity, even though the overall tone of these mainstream newspaper articles condemned the anarchist protesters.

There is a close relationship between legal and normative critiques of the anarchists. Of course, obeying the law is a strong social norm; violations are considered permissible only in situations governed by a higher moral purpose. Mainstream coverage never addressed the anarchists' claim to a higher moral purpose. Although some of the crimes catalogued in mainstream media—conducting a parade without a permit, failure to use established routes or to coordinate their activities with police, and sundry property damage—may not be expected to upset people greatly, the idea that anarchists are law-breakers may have an impact on audience impressions. The essence of the legalistic frame of mainstream coverage is captured by one additional statement by the Deputy Police Chief (WCCO 1987): 'This is clearly whether or not citizens of this city can break the law with impunity, and the answer is NO!'

Bystander Portrayals

Perhaps the most interesting way in which public opinion was depicted in news-coverage was the use of bystanders as symbols for the reaction of the general public. There were numerous instances where newspaper coverage described the reactions of bystanders to the demonstrations. The reactions ranged from puzzlement to anger.

A reporter from the *Star Tribune* described one conversation between two onlookers: ' "What are they protesting?" one woman asked. "It's hard to tell," the other woman answered, "but I think they're protesting everything" ' (1986). Another bystander was quoted in the *Minnesota Daily* calling the anarchists: 'A pretty seedy-looking group' (1987).

The use of bystanders was much more common and more dramatic in the television coverage of the demonstrations. This distinction is illustrated by the contrast in the use of bystanders to describe flag-burning at the first protest. The *Star Tribune* article commented: 'Another woman ran from the sight of a U.S. flag being burned' (1986). The event as much more dramatic in KSTP's (1986) coverage. The video, a close-up of a sobbing woman answering a reporter's questions, was accompanied by the reporter's statement: 'The burning of the American flag was just too much for one woman who was just a bystander watching'. The reporter then asks the sobbing woman if the flag-burning bothered her. 'Yes, yes. People died for the freedom that they have. They don't seem to understand that' (KSTP 1986). . . .

In the conclusion of KSTP's coverage of the first march, the portrayal of bystander reaction clearly indicates public hostility to the anarchist movement:

> We didn't see anyone along this demonstration through the city who actually showed this group any support. And most of the people were actually disgusted with it. And one woman said, 'It's easy for them to be against everything because they themselves are not involved in anything'. (1986)

Bemusement was another commonly depicted bystander reaction. In several stories, reporters stated that onlookers were uncertain what to make of the group. In one case, reporters' comments were backed by an emotion-evincing shot of two uncertain young girls. In other cases, bystanders were shown to pay little attention to the protesters. After outlining the police-anarchist confrontations, one story continued: 'In the midst of the melee, life in Uptown continued—drinks at a cafe, a walk with the baby' (KSTP 1988).

The depiction of public opinion in the coverage of protest seems to be brought in to anchor the story as the reporter tries to provide meaning to this series of events. Bystanders are often used as a thermometer to demonstrate public reaction. The use of bystanders by reporters might be seen as the rough equivalent of taking a haphazard survey of public opinion using a very small sample. While the viewer of the news story may realize that the by-stander represents only one person's opinion, there is evidence to show that this opinion may have a disproportionately large impact on the viewer's as-sessment of public opinion (Tversky and Kahneman 1971, 1974). . . .

Whether the use of bystanders hostile to the protest group is a conscious choice by the reporter is unclear, but the bottom line seems to be that coverage serves as a social control reinforcing the social order.

Micro-Descriptive Representations in Alternative Media Coverage

Articles covering the 1986 anarchist protests were found in *The Guardian* and *Overthrow* alternative newspapers. Two issues of *Fifth Estate* in-cluded extensive articles along with several letters written to the publica-tion concerning the 1987 demonstration/conference.

Statements about Public Opinion

Explicit references to public opinion were rare in these publications. A couple of examples were found in letters printed in *Fifth Estate*. In contrast to mainstream newspaper coverage, public receptivity to the anarchists was portrayed by this Detroit-based alternative newspaper as being very high:

> There is a socialist-populist working class culture that has created, among other things, a lot of co-ops and co-op restaurants, and local restaurants and pizzerias even placed coupons in our conference brochure welcoming the anarchists to town. (1987)

The theme of community acceptance was echoed in another letter which noted that public receptivity to anarchist ideas is increasing in society as a whole.

> A generalized anti-authoritarian orientation is playing a role in the wider radicalization that has begun to sweep this country since 1980, particularly though not exclusively among young people. (1987)

Social Norms

Mainstream and alternative media had different moral interpretations of the same events. For instance, several male and female demonstrators re-moved their shirts during the 1987 march. Mainstream media labeled this as 'licentious' behavior. By contrast, the alternative press coverage treated this as a symbolic political act against pornography. . . .

The object of moral criticism in the alternative press was not the protesters, but the objects of the protest—government and business institutions. Specific charges of the protesters were much more explicit. For example, *Overthrow* (1986) included a list of specific oppressors:

> The victims included WCCO-TV, who ignore the aerial war in El Salvador and slant the news towards sensationalism; Pillsbury, whose ownership of Burger King and other fast food enterprises contributes to the destruction of the world's largest remaining rain forests in Central and South America; the Minneapolis Star and Tribune, whose board of directors interlocks with Hormel, and who constantly misrepresented the P-9 strike in Austin; Sen. Durenburger's office, whose vote on Contra aid switched when he realized it would pass without him, as a face saving gesture to the groups that repeatedly occupied his office.

Legal Conduct

Law-breaking was not considered nearly as newsworthy in the alternative press as it was in mainstream media. *The Guardian* (1986) briefly mentioned that: 'Eight people were arrested for various actions along the tour.' The article concluded with the statement: 'The tour ended with a lively dance in the streets and one last arrest after everyone had dispersed.'

When issues of legal violations were addressed more thoroughly, the alternative press framed them quite differently than mainstream media. *Fifth Estate* (1987) approached the law-breaking issue in the context of discussing the tactics of protest, how to avoid arrest and how to make bail quickly. Rather than criticizing the law violations, the alternative media questioned law enforcement. Police brutality was framed as being symbolic of state oppression. A photo accompanying the *Fifth Estate* article showed a marcher grimacing in pain as police force his arms behind his back. The caption reads: ' "Liberal" Minneapolis cops torturing an arrested demonstrator during the War Chest Tour on the final day of the 1987 Anarchist Gathering.' It should be noted that reference to the police was not so harsh elsewhere in the article:

> Thursday night there was a welcoming party at the Back Room Books, an anarchist bookstore and the sponsors of the gathering, which after some drinking and noise got flushed out by some zealous, and obnoxious, cops. Given the mild nature of the town, there was none of the brutality one would have expected, say, from Los Angeles, New York, or Chicago cops. A couple of people were arrested and later released. (*Fifth Estate* 1987) . . .

Bystander Portrayals

Reactions of bystanders were rare in alternative press coverage. The only direct discussion, found in the *Overthrow* (1986) coverage of the first march, said: 'Another participant mentioned that although the Tour started out with 85 people, by the end it had nearly doubled with people joining in out of curiosity and interest.' The tour was said to be a 'revelation' for both participants and onlookers. Most of the reactions described in the alternative press were those of participants.

Macro-Conceptual Orientations of Media Coverage

There are aspects of each of the three macro-conceptual public opinion orientations found within mainstream media coverage of the anarchist protests. The text of mainstream accounts of the protests reveals that the journalists themselves may conceive of public opinion in a manner consistent with the first two views. First, a conception of public opinion as 'aggregated individual opinion' is implied by references to the small size of the anarchist group relative to the larger population. Second, the view of public opinion as 'organized attempts of groups to influence public policy' is demonstrated by depictions of the goals and outcomes of the protests. The goals, depicted as the overthrow of government and corporate power, are never realized. Thus, the media characterize the protests as failures.

While journalists may conceptualize public opinion as 'aggregated individual opinion' or as 'attempts by groups to influence public policy', the vast majority of micro-descriptive depictions of public opinion in mainstream media contribute to a dominant news frame consistent with the third view, 'public opinion as social control'. These micro-descriptive depictions demonstrate the anarchists' deviance from social norms. In the process, mainstream coverage may marginalize and stigmatize anarchist protesters.

It is clear that the differences between mainstream and alternative media coverage go beyond different approaches to objectivity and also beyond the simple ideological differences between their respective reporters. Mainstream newspapers and the alternative press seem to serve entirely different functions. For mainstream media, dynamic protests clearly rank high on many newsworthiness criteria. While newspaper and television coverage of such routine news events may at one level impart knowledge about happenings within the social system, at another level that coverage tends to provide support and legitimation of the major institutions in society. Providing cues to public opinion about this event is part of the process by which the newspaper coverage serves this social control function.

Alternative media coverage, on the other hand, seemed to work very differently. On the basis of the analysis of micro-descriptive representations of public opinion, it seems that alternative media are aimed at providing a 'haven from fear of isolation' for the anarchists. The articles share the common theme of 'we are not alone'.

The creation of a sense of shared unpopular opinion, the expression of which might cause one to fear isolation in the general population, might actually be a binding force in a subpopulation such as the anarchists. Based on the logic of Coser's (1956) assertion that conflict with an external group leads to internal solidarity, a conflictual stance might increase solidarity among the anarchists. Thus, like hairstyles and clothing which confront social norms, shared opinions which run counter to the assumed consensus of mainstream society may help to integrate subgroup members. This might be true provided that there are some outlets which publicize group activities and issues, legitimate anarchist organizations and coordinate group members, thereby reducing the fear of isolation. This function may be provided by alternative media. In addition, the alternative media may reinforce the anarchists' willingness to express their views and, by providing discussion of anarchist issues and positions, may better equip members to articulate these positions themselves.

The alternative media coverage may reduce the fear of isolation not only by creating a sense of community and by increasing the body of knowledge shared by the anarchist group, but also by linking anarchist and other 'radical' movements nationally and internationally. It also provides 'mobilizing information' about future anarchist events.

In sum, the alternative press coverage contains elements of both the second and third type of conception of public opinion. It tends to be oriented toward building the anarchist movement as a viable power group in accordance with the second conception of public opinion. It does so by recognizing the social control function of mainstream public opinion and tries to provide a haven from its influence by establishing a distinct subgroup with its own set of norms.

Conclusion

Micro-descriptive representations of public opinion are important ideological indicators in media coverage of social protest. They may provide potentially influential cues for audience interpretations as well. This analysis revealed marked differences between mainstream and alternative media coverage for each of the four types of micro-descriptive representations. In the mainstream media, statements about public opinion were normally expressed through quotes from police officials and anarchists. Official statements emphasized the deviance of the protesters, whereas the anarchists contrasted themselves with an apathetic society. Statements about public opinion were relatively infrequent in the alternative press, appearing only in letters-to-the-editor. Violations of social norms of appearance and behavior by protesters were commonly discussed in the mainstream press. The alternative press, on the other hand, pointed accusations of norm violations at government and business agencies. Mainstream media made legal violations by protesters a prominent topic of most stories; the alternative press focused instead on issues of police brutality. Finally, the reactions of bystanders were often described in mainstream coverage, but virtually ignored by the alternative press.

Differences in micro-descriptive applications of public opinion by mainstream and alternative media were linked to differences at the macro-descriptive level. Analysis of the mainstream coverage indicates that journalists tended to view protests as attempts by anarchist groups to influence public policy. The fact that the protests did not lead to fundamental policy changes was treated by mainstream media as evidence of failure. In other words, the anarchists' failure was taken as further evidence of their deviance from mainstream public opinion. In the process, mainstream media's use of micro-descriptive representations of public opinion may ultimately contribute to social control by communicating that deviance. . . .

A different pattern emerged from the alternative press coverage. First of all, the protests were not strictly seen as attempts to change public policy. Instead, they were framed as being successful by providing opportunities for group members to express their opinions and emotions. The demonstrations were viewed as expressive activities, not necessarily dependent upon the conversion of bystanders for success. This is supported by the fact that, unlike the mainstream accounts, alternative press reports virtually ignored bystander reactions. In essence, the alternative media did not adopt mainstream media's conception of public opinion as organized attempts to influence public policy. Instead, public opinion was recognized as a form of social control. Much of the alternative press coverage represents attempts to provide a haven from isolation by celebrating the participation, comradeship and unity of the anarchists. In the process, alternative press coverage may help support the emergence of the anarchists as a mobilized power group.

Mainstream media's rather consistent use of informal representations of public opinion to marginalize the anarchists may have powerful effects. In the process, the protesters are isolated from the 'general public' even though they may share some views and concerns with significant portions of the population. In essence, the media coverage may discourage interest and participation in such protest activities and thereby inhibit the growth of critical social movements. . . .

Bibliography

Asch, S. (1956) 'Studies of Independence and Conformity: I. A Minority of One Against an Unanimous Majority', *Psychological Monographs* 70(9): 1-70.

Back, K. (1988) 'Metaphors for Public Opinion in Literature', *Public Opinion Quarterly* 52: 278-88.

Blumer, H. (1948) 'Public Opinion and Public Opinion Polling', *American Sociological Review* 13: 542-54.

Coser, L. (1956) *The Functions of Social Conflict*. New York: Free Press.

Donohue, G., Olien, C. and Tichenor, P. (1987) 'A Guard Dog Conception of the Mass Media', paper delivered to the Association for Education in Journalism and Mass Communication, San Antonio, TX, August.

Edelman, M. (1977) *Political Language: Words that Succeed and Policies that Fail*. New York: Academic Press.

Gitlin, T. (1981) *The Whole World is Watching: Mass Media and the Making and Unmaking of the New Left*. Berkeley: University of California Press.

Hennessy, B. (1985) *Public Opinion* (5th edn). Monterey, CA: Brooks/Cole.

Herbst, S. (1991) 'Classical Democracy, Polls and Public Opinion: Theoretical Frameworks for Studying the Development of Public Sentiment', *Communication Theory* 1(3): 225-38.

McKirnan, D. (1980) 'The Identification of Deviance: A Conceptualization and Initial Test of a Model of Social Norms', *European Journal of Social Psychology* 10: 75-93.

Noelle-Neumann, E. (1974) 'The Spiral of Silence: A Theory of Public Opinion', *Journal of Communication* 24(1): 43-51.

Noelle-Neumann, E. (1984) *The Spiral of Silence: Public Opinion—Our Social Skin*. Chicago: University of Chicago Press.

O'Gorman, H. (1975) 'Pluralistic Ignorance and White Estimates of White Support for Racial Segregation', *Public Opinion Quarterly* 39(3): 313-30.

O'Gorman, H. and Garry, S. (1976-7) 'Pluralistic Ignorance—A Replication and Extension', *Public Opinion Quarterly* 40(4): 449-58.

Shoemaker, P. (1984) 'Media Treatment of Deviant Political Groups', *Journalism Quarterly* 61(1): 66-75, 82.

Sigal, L. (1973) *Reporters and Officials*. Lexington, MA: D. C. Heath.

Tversky, A. and Kahneman, D. (1971) 'Belief in the Law of Small Numbers', *Psychological Bulletin* 76(2): 105-10.

Tversky, A. and Kahneman, D. (1974) 'Judgment Under Uncertainty: Heuristics and Biases', *Science* 185: 1124-31.

V

GUIDING PUBLIC POLICIES

The media affect public policies in a variety of ways. Publicity may narrow the policy choices available to public officials. It may engender governmental action when no action might have taken place otherwise. Alternatively, by mobilizing hostile public or interest group opinions, the media may force a halt to ongoing or projected policies. This section contains examples of policy impact studies involving all of these contingencies in both domestic and foreign policy domains.

The opening selection shows how media coverage may affect the decisions of public officials in the judicial branch. David Pritchard demonstrates that the decision to allow a serious criminal case to be settled through plea-bargaining, without a full trial, is strongly related to the amount of pretrial publicity given to that case. Investigations of media influence on judicial officials remain rare, but the impact of media images on foreign policy makers has been a relatively common topic of research. Thus Patrick O'Heffernan is able to make a number of general statements about media coverage in foreign policy decision making. For example, media attention to foreign policy issues may force these issues on the public policy agenda when they might otherwise have remained obscure. More blatantly, journalists may bypass diplomatic channels and serve as conduits for their own policy proposals or for proposals initiated by official partisans of various causes.

After the two opening selections point to the power that media can often wield over the actions of public officials, William A. Hachten's essay sounds a much-needed note of caution. In time of war, when foreign policy stakes often are extraordinarily high, governments usually manage to keep the media at bay. Control of news stories during the 1991 Gulf War is a perfect example. With some notable exceptions, government manipulations managed to turn the American press overall into a public relations tool that stressed military successes and failed to show the ugly costs of battle.

American journalists usually disclaim any motivation to influence public policies through their news stories. Except for the editorial pages, their credo calls for objective, neutral reporting. Investigative stories are the only major exception to this rule. They are designed to probe important social and political problems and engender remedial action. Are these goals achieved? If they are, what is the sequence of events? David L. Protess and his colleagues provide surprising answers based on unique studies of television investigative reports.

Political folklore pictures the media as adversaries of officialdom who alert Americans to governmental misdeeds or failures. In reality, there are many situations when officials and journalists work together to bring about needed action. Robert Miraldi tells a fascinating tale of one such collaboration. A crusading reporter who enlisted the suport of an enterprising state official was able to bring about major reforms, including new regulatory legislation, in New York's nursing home industry. Collaboration was crucial to the success of the venture.

The final selection deals with the impact negative publicity has had on the American nuclear energy industry. Stanley Rothman and S. Robert Lichter examine the nature of the coverage, the reasons for the negative approach, and public opinion and public policy responses over a span of several decades. They conclude that the images held and projected by media elites have greater influence on public perceptions and governmental policies than the images held by specialists in the nuclear energy field.

26

HOMICIDE AND BARGAINED JUSTICE: THE AGENDA-SETTING EFFECT OF CRIME NEWS ON PROSECUTORS

David Pritchard

Editor's Note

There has been a great deal of debate about the effect of pretrial publicity on juries. By contrast, the effect of pretrial publicity on other participants in the judicial process has been examined only rarely. David Pritchard focuses attention on the impact of pretrial publicity on the decision of prosecutors to let a case go to trial or to settle it through bargaining between the prosecution and the defense. The latter process, known as "plea-bargaining," avoids the expense of a full trial. Not surprisingly, Pritchard's findings indicate that pretrial publicity does affect prosecutors' willingness to plea bargain in criminal cases. When the amount of publicity differs in otherwise similar cases, the less well-publicized case is more likely to be settled without a full-fledged trial.

How do news stories covering the activities of other publicity-sensitive public officials affect their behavior? A great deal more research is needed to answer that question precisely. But the few studies done thus far, many of them cited by Pritchard, show that this important area of media impact warrants further exploration. It is a particularly promising area of research because it is based on pre-existing records of the activities of public officials rather than on their possibly fallible recollections about media influence, a distinction that makes the findings more credible.

At the time of writing, Pritchard was assistant professor at the Indiana School of Journalism, Bloomington, Indiana. He has investigated the types of crimes that attract media attention, and the charge that newspapers routinely downplay homicides involving minority suspects. The selection comes from "Homicide and Bargained Justice: The Agenda-Setting Effect of Crime News on Prosecutors," Public Opinion Quarterly *50 (1986): 143-59.*

From *Public Opinion Quarterly* 50 (1986): 143-159. Reprinted by permission of The University of Chicago Press.

The effect of publicity upon the adversary system of criminal justice has received an enormous amount of attention in recent years. The Supreme Court of the United States has addressed the fair trial/free press issue several times, and many social scientists have studied the effect of publicity on potential jurors (for reviews of the empirical research see Bush, 1970; Connors, 1975; Simon, 1977; Buddenbaum et al., 1981).

Generally overlooked in the fair trial/free press debate, however, is the fact that as many as 90 percent of all criminal convictions in the United States are the result of plea bargaining rather than full-blown adversary trials (Heumann, 1978; Brosi, 1979). The defendant admits guilt in return for some implicit or explicit concession from the prosecution. Because there is no jury, there is no chance that press coverage will prejudice the jury.

Nonetheless, it is possible that press coverage will taint the *process*. This study addresses that issue by examining the relationship between newspaper coverage of individual cases and whether prosecutors engage in plea bargaining in those cases.

It is an important issue to consider, because the results of the consensual process epitomized by plea bargaining are quite different from those of the adversarial process epitomized by jury trials. For example, defendants found guilty by a jury are more likely to be sentenced to a period of incarceration, and can expect to receive substantially longer sentences than those whose cases are plea bargained, everything else being equal (Uhlman and Walker, 1980; Shane-DuBow et al., 1981; Brereton and Casper, 1982; Pruitt and Wilson, 1983).

Previous Work

Prosecutors are avid readers of newspaper stories about their cases, and most say that the news media are good indicators of the public image of the criminal justice system (Drechsel, 1983). So it is not entirely surprising that some prosecutors acknowledge that they take press coverage of a case into consideration in deciding whether to engage in plea negotiations.

For example, a study of plea bargaining in two California jurisdictions found that prosecutors and defense lawyers were less likely to agree in negotiations if a case had received news coverage (Utz, 1976). Surveys of prosecutors and public defenders in Cook County, Illinois, also suggested that a substantial number of prosecutors would not plea bargain in cases that had received news coverage (Jones, 1978). . . .

Why might publicity make a prosecutor unwilling to plea bargain a case? Alschuler (1968) studied prosecutors in a dozen large American cities, and found that they were motivated more by what they perceived to be their self-interest than by considerations of justice or fairness for the defendant. . . .

In other words, prosecution is a political process, and prosecutors have a political stake in how their actions are perceived. Maintaining a public image as a crime-fighter is important to the prosecutor, perhaps to the extent of stressing adversary dispositions in publicized cases, regardless of the strength of evidence against the defendant. That way, if something "good" (like a conviction) happens, the prosecutor can take the credit. If something "bad" (like an acquittal or dismissal of charges) happens, the prosecutor can implicitly or explicitly shift the responsibility to the judge or to the jury. The result is that the blame is transferred (Newman, 1966; Galanter, 1983). Prosecutors may be especially likely to act this way in homicide cases (Alschuler, 1968).

In some cases, however, prosecutorial self-interest can lead to negotiations. This is most likely to happen when the prosecutor feels a need to get a conviction—any kind of conviction—despite weak evidence against the defendant. Alschuler writes: "Political considerations may, on occasion, make it important for a prosecutor to secure a conviction for a particular crime, and plea negotiations may provide the only practical means of achieving this objective"(Alschuler, 1968: 109).

However, prosecutors' most common reaction to publicity, the existing research makes clear, is a desire to avoid being perceived as soft on criminals.

The notion that the press may influence prosecutorial decision making has clear parallels with the familiar agenda-setting hypothesis, which suggests that the relative prominence of an issue in the news media will influence how salient that issue is to members of the audience (McCombs and Shaw, 1972; McLeod et al., 1974; Becker et al., 1975; Shaw and McCombs, 1977).

Most agenda-setting research has focused on possible effects on ordinary citizens. Only a few studies have explicitly tested the hypothesis that the press may help set the agendas of public officials. Gormley (1975) found mixed evidence for an agenda-setting effect of newspapers on state legislators. Lambeth (1978) concluded that the press helped set energy policy makers' agendas. In a study notable for the fact that it used a direct, rather than a self-reported measure of public-official behavior, Gilberg et al. (1980) found that press content set the agenda for Jimmy Carter's 1978 State of the Union speech. Swank et al. (1982) suggested, but did not test, the hypothesis that newspapers contribute to the salience of crime on local political agendas. Cook et al. (1983) found that a televised investigative report changed the agenda not only of citizens but also of elected officials.

On the other hand, Walker (1977) concluded that for three safety-related issues, the agenda of the U.S. Senate set the agenda for the *New York Times*. And Protess et al. (1985) found that the only agenda affected by a newspaper investigative series was future press coverage of the subject of the series.

In addition to the agenda-setting literature, research into reporter-source interactions contains considerable speculation (and some anecdotal evidence) suggesting that journalists' decisions about which stories to play up can influence the behavior of public officials (see, e.g., Matthews, 1960; Cohen, 1963; Dunn, 1969; Sigal, 1973; Weiss, 1974; Miller, 1978; and Peters, 1980)....

The Context of the Study

This study focuses on prosecutors in the district attorney's office in Milwaukee County, Wisconsin. The basic business of prosecutorial organizations is prosecuting criminal cases. In Milwaukee, as elsewhere in the United States, such cases are processed primarily by plea bargaining, which serves the cause of conserving relatively scarce organizational resources (Brosi, 1979). At the same time, however, it is not a popular way of settling cases (Hearst Corporation, 1983). In Milwaukee, for example, less than a quarter of the population favors plea bargaining (Metropolitan Milwaukee Criminal Justice Council, 1980). In addition, one of the city's newspapers flatly opposes the practice (Wills, 1977), while the other is merely skeptical (Milwaukee Journal, 1981).

Although in theory defendants decide whether to plead guilty or to exercise their constitutional right to a jury trial, in practice the prosecutor generally controls whether a case is plea bargained (Blumberg, 1967; Alschuler, 1968; Casper, 1972; Alschuler, 1975; Heumann, 1978; Gifford, 1981; Gifford, 1983)....

 This study hypothesizes that newspaper coverage of a criminal case influences whether prosecutors engage in plea bargaining in a given case, and that the more extensive the newspaper coverage of a case, the less likely the district attorney's office is to negotiate in the case.

Data

Data to test this study's hypothesis were extracted from police and court records and from news stories. Information was obtained on every nonvehicular homicide case presented to the district attorney's office for possible prosecution during the 18-month period between January 1, 1981 and June 30, 1982. The study focuses on homicides because lesser crimes seldom receive press coverage in a major metropolitan community like Milwaukee. Three homicides that had not been disposed of by May 31, 1983 were eliminated from the analysis. Prosecutors filed homicide charges against every suspect arrested for homicide during the study period. In all, the cases of 90 homicide defendants were included in this study.

To find out how the cases were processed, every publicly available document on each case was scrutinized. Included were the inmate registration log at the Milwaukee County Jail; case files at the office of the Milwaukee County Clerk of Courts, Felony Division, which contained copies of criminal complaints, autopsy reports and other pieces of documentary evidence, summaries (and sometimes transcripts) of hearings, and memos from the prosecution and defense; and all news items about the cases published by Milwaukee's daily newspapers, both owned by the Journal Company, which granted full access to its files of clippings. The editions of the morning *Sentinel* and the evening and Sunday *Journal* that circulate in Milwaukee County carried 744 staff-written items—news stories, editorials, and columns of staff opinion—about the homicides in this study.

Measures

The independent variable in this study is the level of newspaper interest in the defendant's case. The dependent variable is the behavior of the prosecutor's office with respect to the case.

Level of Newspaper Interest in a Case

. . . The amount of space a newspaper devotes to a case can be measured in a straightforward manner. The number of news items about a case is an interval-level variable. So is the number of paragraphs written about a case. This study divides total number of paragraphs by total number of stories to come up with a measure of the level of newspaper interest in the case: the average length of news items about the case, excluding editorials (which tend to be quite short) and excluding stories published after the prosecutor's discretionary period.

That discretionary period is defined as lasting from the date of the homicide until the mode of disposition was known, generally at the beginning of a trial or the acceptance of a guilty plea by a judge. Ending the discretionary period any earlier would skew the results of the analysis, because plea agreements can be—and in several cases were—made or unmade at the last minute. . . .

Average story length, rather than total number of stories or paragraphs, is used because average story length in theory is not a function of how long a case lingers in the felony disposition process. The total number of stories or paragraphs the press devotes to a case, on the other hand, can be more a function of how many pretrial hearings take place than of how interested the press is in the case.

Number of paragraphs, rather than number of column inches, is used to measure story length because varying column sizes in both newspapers made computing standardized column inches very difficult. Standardized column inches and number of paragraphs are highly correlated, however (Budd, 1964).

Both Milwaukee newspapers covered homicides similarly (Pritchard, 1985). For that reason, this study combines the newspapers' coverage to form a single variable: the average length of the stories the Milwaukee newspapers published about a defendant's case. Separate analyses were conducted for each newspaper's coverage, with results virtually identical to the result produced by the combined coverage variable.

The newspapers published no stories at all about 5 of the 90 homicide prosecutions in this study. Those cases are coded as having an average story length of 0.

The amount of newspaper staff effort devoted to a given case was measured by analyzing newspaper content. The typical piece of crime news comes directly from routine law enforcement or judicial sources, often documentary sources such as police blotters, jail logs, and criminal complaints (Stanga, 1971; Cohen, 1975; Sherizen, 1978; Drechsel et al., 1980). Reporters who cover police and court beats can gather such news with relatively little effort.

On some cases, however, reporters do more. The may use nonroutine sources such as witnesses to the crime, friends and relatives of the suspect and/or victim, or not-for-attribution comments from law enforcement officials. Editorials and staff-written columns of opinion also represent nonroutine kinds of coverage.

Accordingly, stories about homicide cases can be categorized either as "routine" (if only routine sources were used) or "nonroutine" (if at least one nonroutine source was used). Of the 744 news items in this study, 13.4 percent were nonroutine by this definition.[1] . . .

Prosecutor's Plea Bargaining Behavior

Plea bargaining in this study is measured not by whether a case was settled consensually, but by whether the prosecutor actually engaged in plea negotiations. This "negotiated/did-not-negotiate" variable measures the prosecutor's actual behavior, not whether that behavior led to a consensual outcome. . . .

Court records and/or news items contained explicit evidence that prosecutors engaged in negotiations in 45 of the 90 cases in this study. In 35 of the cases in which prosecutors negotiated, the result was a consensual settlement, in which the prosecutor and the defense agreed on the appropriate disposition of the case. In the remaining 10 cases, defendants refused plea bargains offered by prosecutors. Those cases either went to jury trial or were dismissed over the objection of the prosecution.

Control Variables

One of the most challenging tasks in a study of this nature is to hold constant factors that may affect both the independent and the dependent variables. In an attempt to achieve that goal, this study uses an extensive set of control variables. Much of the variation in crime seriousness, a factor that could influence both newspaper interest and prosecutors' plea bargaining behavior, is implicitly controlled by this study's exclusive focus on homicides.

Homicides themselves can vary in a number of ways, however, so additional control variables are used. They include personal attributes (race, age, and sex) of the homicide suspect and victim; whether the suspect and the victim knew each other; the suspect's prior record; the initial charge against the defendant (first-degree murder or a lesser homicide charge, such as manslaughter); whether the defendant was charged with crimes beyond the first homicide count; and the number of suspects alleged to have been involved in the homicide.

Some factors, such as the prominence of the homicide suspect and victim or the bizarreness of the incident, are difficult to quantify. In most cases, however, court records and news stories contain enough details of the incident and of the people involved in it to permit a qualitative evaluation of such aspects of the case.

Results

Discriminant analysis (Cohen and Cohen, 1975; Klecka, 1975) was used to test the hypothesis concerning the influence of newspaper coverage on plea bargaining behavior. The analysis supported the hypothesis: press behavior—specifically, the average length of stories about a case—was the strongest predictor of whether prosecutors engaged in negotiations. The proportion of stories about a case that relied partly or entirely on nonroutine sources, however, was not a significant predictor of negotiations.

Table 26-1 shows the results of the analysis. Of all the variables, five proved to be statistically significant (at p=.05) predictors; average story length (the shorter the average story, the more likely the prosecutor would negotiate); whether the defendant and the victim knew each other (negotiations were more likely if the defendant and victim had been acquainted); the defendant's prior record (negotiations were more likely if the defendant had no prior record); the seriousness of the initial charge (negotiations were more likely when charges were less serious); and whether the defendant faced multiple charges stemming from the incident (negotiations were more likely when there was only one charge).

**Table 26-1   Results of Discriminant Analysis, with Whether the Prosecution
Negotiated as the Dependent Variable**

Canonical correlation squared	.238
Improvement in ability to predict	53.3%
Relative contribution of significant discriminating variables:	
Average story length	34.8%
Suspect knew victim	26.9%
Prior record	19.5%
Initial charge	12.4%
Multiple charges	6.5%

... [The discriminating] variables ... account for 23.8 percent of the total variance in whether the prosecution engaged in plea negotiations. Average story length is the strongest predictor of prosecutorial behavior, contributing more than a third of the variance accounted for by the [discriminant analysis], 34.8 percent, which is 8.3 percent of the entire variance.

Easier to understand, perhaps, is the fact that the discriminant function correctly predicts the prosecutor's negotiating behavior in 69 of the 90 cases (76.7 percent). Without the information contributed by the variables in the function, successful predictions could be made only half of the time. In other words, knowing the values of the variables in the function provides a 53.3 percent improvement in predictive ability over chance guessing. The function is statistically significant at the .0003 level.

Discussion

This study's findings suggest that newspapers help set the plea bargaining agendas of Milwaukee prosecutors, at least in homicide cases. The amount of space newspapers were willing to devote to the typical story about a case was a stronger predictor than any other variable in this study of whether the prosecutor would negotiate.

... Most other research in this area has relied on public officials' own estimations of whether they have been influenced by the media (Gormley, 1975; Lambeth, 1978; Cook et al., 1983; Protess et al., 1985). Virtually all the measures of prosecutorial behavior used in this study, however, came directly from court records. The data came from cases that were already completed, ensuring that the participants were not aware that their behavior would become part of a research project. In addition, the data were recorded by court employees as part of the normal routine of the criminal courts, with no hint that the data would provide the raw material for an academic study. Unless the raw data contain a systematic bias that is not immediately apparent, they are unobtrusive measures (Webb et al., 1966), unlike the self-reported data used as dependent measures in much of the research into the possibility that the news media may set the agenda for public officials.

That said, it must be acknowledged that documentary records are far from perfect. The facts of certain cases ... strongly imply that the prosecution offered a deal that was turned down, despite the fact that court records and newspaper coverage contain no explicit evidence of negotiations.

Similarly ... the strength of evidence against a defendant (or a defendant's accomplice) could influence whether the prosecution negotiated a case. Evidence strength was not included as a quantitative variable in this study because it is extremely difficult to measure in any systematic way (Eisenstein and Jacob, 1977:182-183). In addition, evidence strength may well be a socially defined construct greatly dependent upon attributes of the relationships between the prosecutor and the defense lawyer, and between the defense lawyer and the defendant.

Finally, it is difficult to predict what effect a strength-of-evidence variable would have on plea bargaining. If evidence is weak, the prosecutor has an incentive not only to negotiate but to offer a good deal. If the evidence is strong, however, the defendant has an incentive to plead guilty even if not offered a good deal to avoid the so-called trial penalty (Uhlman and Walker, 1980; Shane-DuBow et al., 1981; Brereton and Casper, 1982; Pruitt and Wilson, 1983). Guilty pleas in cases where there is no evidence of negotiations often are implicit plea bargains (Heumann, 1978).

Related to the issue of evidence strength are questions involving the content of negotiations. . . .

This study did not have access to information about the offers and counter-offers that are a normal part of negotiations, but researchers should attempt to gain access to such information (see, e.g., Maynard, 1984).

Future research should also examine in detail the extent to which prosecutors (or other law-enforcement personnel) influence newspapers' decisions about which cases to cover and how to cover them (see, e.g., Drechsel, 1983). This study found no evidence of such an influence, but then court records and news coverage are not the best places to look for such an effect. Researchers need to get into newsrooms, prosecutors' offices, courthouse hallways, and courtrooms to find the answers to such questions. . . .

Note

1. All coding was done by the author. To test intercoder reliability, a colleague coded a 10 percent sample of the 744 news items. There was agreement on 96 percent of the items, resulting in a reliability coefficient (Scott's pi) of .85 (Scott, 1955).

References

Alschuler, A. 1968. "The prosecutor's role in plea bargaining." *University of Chicago Law Review* 36:50-112.

———.1975. "The defense attorney's role in plea bargaining." *Yale Law Journal* 84:1179-1314.

Becker, L. B., M. E. McCombs, and J. M. McLeod. 1975. "The development of political cognitions." In S. H. Chaffee, ed., *Political Communication: Issues and Strategies for Research*. Beverly Hills, Calif.: Sage Publications.

Blumberg, A. 1967. *Criminal Justice*. Chicago: Quadrangle Books.

Brereton, D. and J. D. Casper. 1982. "Does it pay to plead guilty? Differential sentencing and the functioning of criminal courts." *Law and Society Review* 16:45-70.

Brosi, K. B. 1979. *A Cross-City Comparison of Felony Case Processing*. Washington, D.C.: U.S. Department of Justice.

Budd, R. 1964. "Attention score: a device for measuring news 'play'." *Journalism Quarterly* 41:259-262.

Buddenbaum, J. M., D. H. Weaver, R. L. Holsinger, and C. J. Brown. 1981. *Pretrial Publicity and Juries: A Review of Research*. Bloomington, Ind.: Indiana University School of Journalism.

Bush, C. R. 1970. *Free Press and Fair Trial: Some Dimensions of the Problem*. Athens, Ga.: University of Georgia Press.

Casper J. 1972. *American Criminal Justice: The Defendant's Perspective*. Englewood Cliffs, N.J.: Prentice-Hall.

Cohen, B. C. 1963. *The Press and Foreign Policy*. Princeton, N.J.: Princeton University Press.

Cohen, J., and P. Cohen. 1975. *Applied Multiple Regression/Correlation Analysis for the Behavioral Sciences*. New York: John Wiley & Sons.

Cohen, S. 1975. "A comparison of crime coverage in Detroit and Atlanta newspapers." *Journalism Quarterly* 52:726-730.

Connors, M. M. 1975. "Prejudicial publicity: an assessment." *Journalism Monographs* 41.

Cook, F. L., et al. 1983. "Media and agenda setting: effects on the public, interest group leaders, policy makers, and policy." *Public Opinion Quarterly* 47:16-35.

Drechsel, R. E. 1983. *News Making in the Trial Courts*. New York: Longman.

Drechsel, R. E., K. Netteburg, and B. Aborisade. 1980. "Community size and newspaper reporting of local courts." *Journalism Quarterly* 57:71-78.

Dunn, D. 1969. *Public Officials and the Press*. Reading, Mass.: Addison-Wesley.

Eisenstein, J., and H. Jacob. 1977. *Felony Justice: An Organizational Analysis of Criminal Courts*. Boston: Little, Brown and Co.

Galanter, M. 1983. "Reading the landscape of disputes: what we know and don't know (and think we know) about our allegedly contentious and litigious society." *UCLA Law Review* 31:4-71.

Gifford, D. G. 1981. "Equal protection and the prosecutor's charging decision: enforcing an ideal." *George Washington Law Review* 49:659-719.

———. 1983. "Meaningful reform of plea bargaining: control of prosecutorial discretion." *University of Illinois Law Review* 1983:37-98.

Gilberg, S., C. Eyal, M. McCombs, and D. Nicholas. 1980. "The State of the Union Address and the press agenda." *Journalism Quarterly* 57:584-588.

Gormley, W. T., Jr. 1975. "Newspaper agendas and political elites." *Journalism Quarterly* 52:304-308.

Hearst Corporation. 1983. *The American Public, the Media & the Judicial System: A National Survey on Public Awareness and Personal Experience.* New York: The Hearst Corporation.

Heumann, M. 1978. *Plea Bargaining: The Experiences of Prosecutors, Judges, and Defense Attorneys.* Chicago: University of Chicago Press.

Jones, J. B. 1978. "Prosecutors and the disposition of criminal cases: an analysis of plea bargaining rates." *Journal of Criminal Law & Criminology* 69:402-412.

Klecka, W. R. 1975. "Discriminant analysis." In Nie, N., et al. *Statistical Package for the Social Sciences,* second ed. New York: McGraw-Hill.

Lambeth, E. B. 1978. "Perceived influence of the press on energy policy making." *Journalism Quarterly* 55:11-18, 72.

Matthews, D. R. 1960. *U.S. Senators and Their World.* Chapel Hill: University of North Carolina Press.

Maynard, D. W. 1984. "The structure of discourse in misdemeanor plea bargaining." *Law & Society Review* 18:75-104.

McCombs, M., and D. L. Shaw. 1972. "The agenda-setting function of mass media." *Public Opinion Quarterly* 36:176-187.

McLeod, J. M., L. B. Becker, and J. E. Byrnes. 1974. "Another look at the agenda-setting function of the press." *Communication Research* 1:131-166.

Metropolitan Milwaukee Criminal Justice Council. 1980. Public Opinion Survey 600.

Miller, S. 1978. "Reporters and congressmen: living in symbiosis." *Journalism Monographs* 53.

Milwaukee Journal. 1981. "A deeper look at plea bargains." Editorial, January 11.

Newman, D. J. 1966. *Conviction: The Determination of Guilt or Innocence Without Trial.* Boston: Little, Brown and Co.

Peters, C. 1980. *How Washington Really Works.* Reading, Mass.: Addison-Wesley.

Pritchard, D. 1985. "Race, homicide and newspapers." *Journalism Quarterly* 62:500-7.

Protess, D. L., D. R. Leff, S. C. Brooks, and M. T. Gordon. 1985. "Uncovering rape: the watchdog press and the limits of agenda setting." *Public Opinion Quarterly* 49:19-37.

Pruitt, C. R., and J. Q. Wilson. 1983. " A longitudinal study of the effect of race on sentencing." *Law & Society Review* 17:613-635.

Shane-DuBow, S., et al. 1981. *Wisconsin Felony Sentencing Guidelines: Phase 1 of Research and Development.* Madison: Wisconsin Center for Public Policy.

Shaw, D. L., and M. E. McCombs. 1977. *The Emergence of American Political Issues: The Agenda-Setting Function of the Press.* St. Paul: West Publishing.

Sherizen, S. 1978. "Social creation of crime news: all the news fitted to print." In C. Winick, ed., *Deviance and Mass Media.* Beverly Hills, Calif.: Sage Publications.

Sigal, L. V. 1973. *Reporters and Officials: The Organization and Politics of Newsmaking.* Lexington, Mass.: D.C. Heath.

Simon, R. 1977. "Does the court's decision in Nebraska Press Association fit the research evidence on the impact on jurors of news coverage?" *Stanford Law Review* 29:515-528.

Stanga, J. E. 1971. "The press and the criminal defendant: newsmen and criminal justice in three Wisconsin cities." Unpublished Ph.D. dissertation, University of Wisconsin.

Swank, D. H., H. Jacob, and J. Moran. 1982. " Newspaper attentiveness to crime." In H. Jacob and R. L. Lineberry, eds., *Governmental Responses to Crime: Crime on Urban Agendas.* Washington, D.C.: National Institute of Justice.

Uhlman, T. M., and N. D. Walker. 1980. "'He takes some of my time, I take some of his': an analysis of sentencing patterns in jury cases." *Law & Society Review* 14:323-341.

Utz, P. J. 1976. *Settling the Facts: Discretion and Negotiation in Criminal Court.* Lexington, Mass.: Lexington Books.

Walker, J. 1977. "Setting the agenda in the U.S. Senate: a theory of problem selection." *British Journal of Political Science* 7:423-445.

Webb, E. J., D. T. Campbell, R. D. Schwartz, and L. Sechrest. 1966. *Unobtrusive Measures: Nonreactive Research in the Social Sciences.* Chicago: Rand McNally & Co.

Weiss, C. H. 1974. "What America's leaders read." *Public Opinion Quarterly* 38:1-22.

Wills, R. H. 1977. Milwaukee *Sentinel* Editorial Policy.

27

MASS MEDIA ROLES
IN FOREIGN POLICY

Patrick O'Heffernan

Editor's Note

What roles do the mass media play in making American foreign policy? Political scientist Patrick O'Heffernan sought answers by questioning senior policy makers serving the federal government between November 1977 and March 1988. The data were collected through 25 in-depth interviews conducted by the author and secondary analysis of 8 interview transcripts and survey data collected from a sample of 483 high-level federal officials. The interview transcripts and survey data were gathered by a team of scholars headed by Martin Linsky for a study described more fully in Part VI, Selection 34.

The interview responses, along with three case studies of foreign policy making during the study period, indicate that mass media play a variety of potentially important roles. However, the significance of these roles varies from case to case, and foreign policy officials disagree whether, on balance, mass media influence is a boon or a bane.

At the time of writing, O'Heffernan taught at Georgia Institute of Technology in Atlanta. The selection comes from Mass Media and American Foreign Policy: Insider Perspectives on Global Journalism and the Foreign Policy Process *(Norwood, NJ: Ablex Publishing Corp., 1991), chap. 5. Several footnotes and sub-headings have been omitted.*

The mass media today play distinct roles in the shaping and reality of American foreign policy. They function as:

- a rapid source of information useful for policy decisions
- an agenda setter which influences the agendas of the U.S. and other nations

Reprinted from *Mass Media and American Foreign Policy: Insider Perspectives on Global Journalism and the Foreign Policy Process,* with permission from Ablex Publishing Corporation.

- a proxy for diplomats
- a diplomatic signaling system with policy influence
- a tool used by terrorists and nongovernmental organizations.

Television also plays distinct diplomatic roles through space bridges and on-air negotiations, sometimes called "television diplomacy." [1]

A Rapid Information Source

The mass media tell us about wars, disasters, highjackings, and elections around the world, often within hours of the event. In providing this near-instant notification of what is going on globally, the mass media serve four distinct roles as rapid information sources for policy makers: (a) policy officials use the media for immediate useful information, (b) policy makers use the mass media in the early stages of an issue to make decisions, (c) media are often the only source of policy information in crisis situations, and (d) the media's information is often seen as critical for policy making, sometimes more critical than official data. . . .

There was almost no question in the minds of policy makers interviewed that mass media are the fastest source of information on politically important events around the world. There was some divergence of opinion on how useful this information is for substantive decisions. Some policy officials interviewed indicated that the immediate media information's usefulness was limited, while others attested to both the media's speed of information delivery and its importance in their work. . . .

Daniel Kurtzer, Chief of the Middle Eastern Affairs Staff of the Policy and Planning Division of the State Department, argued that the media provided information unavailable from the official sources, even when officials were on the scene:

> . . . The embassy had its people talking to participants. I know, however, that the media's access to the participants was better than ours. So we were watching the media reporting more carefully in some respects than we were watching our own embassy's reporting.[2]

. . . Dennis Harter, Director of Press Operations at the Department of State, differentiated among the types of data delivered by the media and by other sources, and their usefulness:

> I agree [that the media is frequently the fastest source of information] for raw data, but not for analytical information. But raw information is also very important just to get a policy maker started on the right issue.[3]

. . . Eighty-seven percent of the interview respondents could recall cases when the media were the only source of information available for decision making, and 65 percent agreed that the media were frequently the fastest source of information for policy making. A small number of respondents, 8.7 percent, added that the media were the fastest information source only in crisis situations. . . .

A second aspect of the role of media as a rapid information source is the degree to which it is used at the earliest stage of the policy cycle, the Problem Identification Stage. Seventy-four percent of the foreign policy respondents to Linsky's survey indicated that mass media have some impact at this stage, compared to 28 percent who indicated no effect. Forty percent indicated that this effect was "large" or "dominant."

As shown in Table 27-1, 53 percent of the foreign policy officials who responded to Linsky's survey who perceive that the media have a large impact on policy at this stage rely on the media very much and 81 percent rely on it very much or somewhat, compared to 20 percent who perceive the media as having no impact on policy.[4]

Foreign policy personnel often rely on mass media — delivered information during crises. A majority of . . . the policy personnel interviewed indicated that media were frequently the most rapid source of information in crises situations. . . . Virtually all of those interviewed offered an anecdote or observation on the utility of the media in a crisis from their personal involvement. For example, former NSC staffer Robert Pastor pointed out that during a crisis, it is often members of the media who can make contact with key parties when official sources cannot:

> The news media is tremendously effective, more effective than anything else in following a fast-breaking violent crisis because the media can go to places that are under siege that the CIA can't go.[5] . . .

. . . In cases of fast-breaking crisis situations, most foreign policy officials interviewed reported that the media can and often does provide highly crucial information. Former Assistant Secretary of State Langhorn Motley noted that during highjackings, CNN not only got information out before the other networks, but before official sources could get geared up to let Washington know what was happening and who the players were. Eighty-seven percent of those interviewed agreed . . . and could recall situations wherein the media were the only source of information for policy making in fast-breaking crises or terrorist incidents.

Media Role: Terrorist Tool

Much has been made in the academic and popular press of "terror-vision"—the successful use of the media by terrorists to influence U.S. foreign policy—such as described in the TWA 847 highjacking case. But is terrorvision successful? Do all such media-terrorist relationships lead to

Table 27-1   Media Impact at Earliest Stage of Policy Cycle Compared with Officials' Reliance on Media for Information (percent)

Media impact	Reliance on media for information		
	Very little	Some	Very much
None	52.0	28.0	20.0
Some	21.8	40.6	37.5
Large	18.4	28.9	52.6

χ square = 12.39 @ 6 D.F., Sig = .5, R = .29, N = 95

changes in U.S. foreign policy? The policy officials interviewed for this research did not think so. They agreed that terrorists were often highly skilled and effective in using the media to provoke government responses to their actions, but they also felt that this did not necessarily result in significant policy changes in any more than a handful of cases. . . .

Eighty-three percent of the foreign policy officials surveyed by Linksy responded that the media magnify the influence of outside organizations, and 64 percent said that the use of media by outside organizations would gain attention from higher levels of government (less than 11 percent saw no effect). However, this increase in influence is not necessarily seen as changing policy outputs. Table 27-2 shows that there is no relation between policy officials' perception of the increase in a group's visibility due to media, and its effect on policy outputs.[6]

Most of those interviewed agreed that terrorists who obtained coverage in the media and used it well were treated differently than those who did not, that is, while overall policy may not necessarily be impacted by terrorist use of the media, tactical response certainly is. Ninety-one percent of the policy makers questioned agreed that the media increase the visibility of terrorists and their power to invoke governmental responses, and 74 percent said the media increase terrorists' power.[7] . . .

The ability of terrorists to use the media to force changes in U.S. foreign policy is as much or more a function of the vulnerability of the administration to publicized terrorists' tactics as to the skill of media use, and is by no means common. Poor use of media by terrorists, such as occurred in the *Achille Lauro* case, has little likelihood of impacting policy; skillful use of media, as in the TWA case, has a higher likelihood of impacting policy, but is not the sole or always the most important determinant of lasting policy change. Other factors include the domestic political situation in the U.S., the skill of the U.S. administration in using the media, the emergence of domestic lobbies and their use of the media, and ongoing relations and

Table 27-2   Perception of Media Ability to Magnify Outside Influence and Impact on Foreign Policy Outputs (percent)

	Effect on policy outputs		
			Percentage
Group's influence raised	Low	High	of total
Yes	66.6	83.5	82.9
No	33.3	16.5	17.1

R = .00867 Sig = .1977
N = 94; χ square = 5.77 @ 4 D.F., Sig = .2168

discussions with other governments who may be involved in the incident and who are impacted by the policy.

Media's Agenda-Setting Role

. . . The agenda-setting question asked of policy officials in the interviews was: "Does the media set the agenda of U.S. foreign policy officials either by globalizing local and regional events and elevating their salience, or by any other mechanism?". . .

As noted above, a high percentage of those who responded to the survey perceived that individuals or outside groups who obtained media coverage were able to magnify their influence and gain the attention of higher levels of the foreign policy community. However, the interview transcripts revealed a variance in opinion among the officials on this question. Carter administration National Security Advisor Brzezinski saw the agenda setting going from the White House to the media, not the other way around.

> I think in an administration, if it's activist—and ours was in the area of foreign policy—it tends to determine agenda for the press. Not exclusively, and certainly many events transpire over which you have no control. But by and large we set the agenda.[8]

President Carter saw a definite media role in setting agendas when it globalized regions or countries, and told of an incident when the media's globalization of a regional event that was not even news almost derailed a major policy initiative:

> . . . when reports of Soviet troops in Cuba were broadcast. This was a very disturbing thing to us and interfered with the ratification of the SALT II treaty, and caused us two-three weeks of research and the ultimate result was that it

**Table 27-3   Perceived Effect of Media Coverage on Foreign Policy Agenda
                    (percent)**

Positive coverage affects agenda	15.5
Negative coverage affects agenda	33.0
Positive and negative coverage affects agenda	27.8
Total	77.3

N = 89

was not news but some candidate (Frank Church) made it a campaign issue with the help of the media.[9]

. . . The results from survey questions that asked to what degree negative or positive media coverage affected the importance of an issue in the foreign policy bureaucracy, shown in Table 27-3, indicate that a strong majority, 77 percent, of all foreign policy officials who responded to Linsky's survey perceived that positive or negative mass media coverage can increase the importance of an issue to the bureaucracy (the remaining 23 percent perceived no effect).[10]

This result was confirmed in the interview questions: A total of 82 percent of those interviewed for this study perceived that mass media attention to a regional event can put the region or the event on the nation's foreign policy agenda. A majority attributed this capability to media-stimulated domestic political forces, although some qualified this answer by saying this was the case only part of the time.

Additionally, the results of the "action" responses (those survey responses that specify that action was likely as a result of media coverage) provided an important qualification. They indicated that, while the media are perceived to be able to establish the importance of issues and often to move an item to a more senior person, it will rarely lead to a reassessment of a policy position on an issue already on the agenda. . . .

Policy officials often noted that it is . . . "global issues," such as environment, hunger, or amnesty, that are most susceptible to agenda setting by the mass media. They also noted that important events or issues not covered by the mass media can suffer in their ranking on the foreign policy agenda.

Most of those who responded positively to an interview question regarding the agenda-setting influence of the media attributed this influence to mass media's ability to stimulate or maintain domestic political forces. A few noted that the mechanism is one of the media *creating a positive policy environment for policy initiatives to be brought forward*. Often, interviewees said that policies put on the agenda by media were under study but could not be moved for priority or political reasons. Media stories provided the positive environment necessary for them to be moved. Roman Papaduick, Assistant Press Secretary for International Affairs in the Reagan White House, used the drought in Ethiopia as an example of this:

> What television did was bring the image home to the American public, but the policy had always been there. What happens is TV finds the problem, then finds the policy and marries the two. Therefore, [it] makes it look like the policy evolved to meet the problem.[11]

Dennis Harter of the State Department pointed to other areas "discovered" by the mass media after the policy officials had spent some time working on them, such as the international drug trade. But the media's ability to do so is seen by policy officials as circumscribed by three conditions:

1. Media influence varies with the nature of the issue, with global, multilateral issues being more susceptible to media influence then bilateral or military issues.
2. Media influence derives to some extent from the media's ability to stimulate domestic political forces to support or object to a policy initiative.
3. Media influence varies with the prevailing political environment, although it can influence or create that environment.

Media Role: Diplomatic Proxy

The mass media have been often criticized for meddling in foreign policy. But policy makers see media involvement as an infrequent occurrence, although one that can have very serious consequences. The TWA hijacking case provided several examples of media intervention in a negotiation situation, both as an instrument used by all sides, and as an independent entity pursuing its own objectives. The degree of this involvement can be seen from the extreme level of complaints about it during and after the fact: Television was smugly criticized by print media for usurping diplomatic roles;[12] President Reagan criticized the media in general and television in particular for interference in the negotiation process;[13] and television criticized itself for its mostly inadvertent involvement in affairs of state.[14] Even the TWA hostages complained that the television networks were using them to boost ratings and, in doing so, may have complicated efforts to free them.[15]

Whatever the actual involvement in foreign policy was during the TWA highjacking, it signals a basic change in the mass media—foreign policy community relationship. How much of a change can be seen by comparing John Scali's role as a backchannel interlocutor between Kennedy and Soviet officials during the Cuban missile crisis with the activities and criticism of television during the TWA 847 highjacking? Scali's role was kept relatively quiet, and when it did become widely known in the press and policy communities, it was generally seen as a positive, patriotic activity.[16] In the TWA case, television was virtually charged by government, other media, and even by itself with frustrating national policy. . . .

What are the perceptions of foreign policy officials about the involvement of the media in negotiations and diplomacy, either institutionally, or on an individual basis? Do they feel it is a widespread practice and if so, what is the impact on policy outputs? Does it lead to better or worse policies?

I found that policy officials interviewed for this study were generally aware of journalistic involvement in diplomacy: 74 percent of those personally interviewed knew of such cases or had heard of them. However, they rejected the media role as a positive one: 78 percent answered an unqualified "bad" when asked about the effect of this on U.S. policy outputs, and those that did not describe involvement as negative gave a qualified answer indicating that it was justified only under special circumstances.

While the majority of policy officials indicated that they personally knew of such a case, a review of the interview transcripts reveals that most had heard of cases secondhand, rather than firsthand. Most of those interviewed also mentioned the same cases, that is, John Scali in the Cuban missile crisis and Walter Cronkite behind the scenes on the Sadat visit. The interview transcripts show that while policy officials are aware of the incidents, their perception is that journalistic involvement is an infrequent occurrence and not a significant part of the flow of diplomacy. The 78 percent negative response cited above was strongly categorical, that is, journalistic involvement in international relations was seen as bad for policy in all cases, as described by Hodding Carter [a former State Department spokesman], "There is no place in diplomacy for journalists or anyone not authorized by the government." . . .

President Carter's experience gave him a broader point of view when asked about situations involving journalists and diplomacy. While recounting instances of mass media involvement in diplomacy that had very serious negative effects, Carter recognized a valuable role for the mass media in certain circumstances:

> those efforts by journalists can either be very beneficial or damaging. In some cases the journalists have access to terrorists' spokesmen and can receive proposals that might lead to a solution of a kidnapping or a hijacking of a plane

when it is almost impossible for government policy to permit contact with criminals of that kind. Obviously, when the news is made known that the terrorists will accept these actions and the hostages will be released or the plane returned, then the government can decide whether it wants to accept terms of that kind without dealing directly with the hostage takers or hijackers.

But he added that the media can damage negotiations and put American lives and policies in danger:

> There are other times when pressures from journalists have resulted in very very serious damage to the well-being of hostages and other citizens of our country. The most notable example of that is when Mike Wallace and other reporters went to Iran and interrogated Ayatollah Khomeni very forcefully and publicly on *60 Minutes* and news broadcasts, asking "will you release the hostages, will you direct the students to leave the embassy grounds?" and the inevitable response of Khomeni to the world public was "no, not unless the Shah is brought back."
>
> Well, once the news reporters forced Khomeni, possibly against his will, to make a public commitment of that kind, it was impossible for him to meet with or talk to any intermediaries that we would want to send to explore the opportunities at least for the hostages.

... Policy officials differed about the emergence of Ted Koppel—style "television diplomacy" in which national representatives are brought together on the air for discussions of the issues that divide them. Paralleling Koppel, networks and independent producers have begun to broadcast "space bridges" which link policy officials and citizens of different countries together by television to discuss issues that divide them.

What are the ramifications of this new use of television medium? Do televised interactions between U.S. and foreign leaders impact foreign policy, and if so, is the influence positive or negative? Television diplomacy was examined extensively in the interviews, both in specific questions and in the unstructured discussions.

Interview respondents were mixed in their view of TV diplomacy's effect on policy, but the weight was toward a negative perception: Only 26 percent said it helped sound policy, 35 percent said it both helped and hindered, 17 percent said it hurt, and 22 percent thought it was irrelevant. . . .

Media Role: Diplomatic Signal

... Those interviewed agreed that the most utilized and most effective technique of media use by foreign policy officials is for signaling American preferences to other nations. . . .

President Carter also pointed out the usefulness of the media to a head of state attempting to influence other governments.

Table 27-4   Policy Maker Influence of Media (percent)

Placed 10% or more of stories on agency	72.4
Sought to influence media coverage	85.7
Felt appropriate to leak to media	50.0
Leaks ok to consolidate support	66.7
Leak ok to force action on issue	41.7

$N = 94$

> I used international media broadcast in several cases, we had nationwide
> broadcast to Poland and to Germany, including East Germany, and to Japan,
> where I would respond to questions from a fairly large audience in a town
> meeting forum. And with arrangements, even Communist governments [al-
> lowed] that the telecasts would be live and nationwide.

Diplomatic aspects of this transformation were frequently mentioned in
the interviews, ranging from the use of the media as a communications
device to negotiate with governments who cannot be contacted in other
ways, to sending influential signals to the people and the agencies of other
governments and receiving signals back from them. Examples of this use of
the media include Presidential satellite addresses to foreign audiences, ex-
changing messages with foreign leaders through press conferences and
news programs, and satellite conferences with embassy personnel in several countries simultaneously. . . .

Table 27-4 presents the results from analysis of foreign policy officials'
response to Linsky's survey regarding government influence on media for
policy purposes. The results clearly show a willingness on the part of foreign policy officials who responded to Linsky's questionnaire to obtain
press coverage and to use the press for policy purposes: 86 percent of the
survey respondents sought to influence media coverage of their agencies,
and 72 percent indicated they or their staff were responsible for at least 10
percent of the actual coverage.

Table 27-5 presents results from the interview questions concerning
the use of the media to influence foreign governments. These results
essentially confirmed the survey findings that the use of the mass media
is widespread among the policy officials interviewed: 78 percent reported
using the media, many responding that the practice is constant. Table
27-5 also echoes the indications from the transcripts that print is
the medium most often used to influence foreign governments (numbers
indicate the percentages of respondents who answered positively in each
category).

Table 27-5   Policy Maker Perception of Media Use to Influence Other Nations (percent)

	Used to influence other governments	Used to influence other peoples
Print	44	33
TV	22	56
Wires	22	0
All media	33	11
Radio in Third World	11	44
Depends on nation	11	22

Note: Numbers are the percentage of *N. N* = 23. Totals add to more than 100% due to multiple answers.

Seventy-eight percent of those interviewed agreed that mass media communication with other nations' peoples is a useful policy tool. Several volunteered that media communication with other nations' peoples has become a fact of life in the foreign policy process. A few also referred to President Reagan's use of WorldNet to broadcast to European audiences, and to the Christmas message broadcast exchange between the U.S. and the Soviet Union, as well as media events and televised speeches by U.S. officials on tour overseas.

. . . Print is the . . . medium of choice when using media to influence other government's heads. The wire services and a mix of all media are employed significantly to reach governments, but not significantly in reaching people directly. And finally, radio is seen as . . . important as television in reaching mass audiences in the Third World. . . .

The evidence is also overwhelming that U.S. policy makers perceive that foreign governments try to use American mass media to manipulate American foreign policy. Ninety-two percent of the interview respondents reported that they could recall or had heard of cases of foreign government use of media to influence U.S. policy. The perception was strong in all agencies and in all government rankings. Many of the policy officials interviewed noted that other national leaders have been increasingly turning the media tables on the U.S., using American media to influence American public opinion and policy. Hodding Carter stated it bluntly:

> Certainly foreign governments used the media to influence the U.S. Government. Officials would constantly bring reporters in to get a message across. Sometimes overtly. I know very few sophisticated governments that didn't do it.

I have known of reporters that have been used as carriers of messages. The media used the most is print.

... Harold Saunders' quote ... describing the use of mass media as a fact of life in foreign policy sums up mass media's roles in foreign policy:

international relations today is a continual process of policy making and policy influencing communities on both sides of the relationship, and television is a significant part of that interaction, and so are other forms of communication.

Notes

1. All quotes in this chapter are from my interviews with policy makers unless indicated otherwise.
2. Personal interview, Summer 1987, Department of State.
3. Personal interview, Summer 1987, Department of State.
4. Linsky's survey asked, "In your experience how significant was the impact of the press at this [the identification of the problem] stage of policy making?" and "To what degree did you rely on the [mass media] organizations for information about your policy areas?"
5. Personal interview, Carter Center, Atlanta, GA, Fall 1987.
6. Linsky survey questions cross-tabulated: #II.-10, "Overall, how great do you believe the effect of the media is on [foreign] policy?" and III.-3, "In your experience, did the ability of an individual or outside group to gain attention in the media magnify the group's influence?"
7. Interview questions #1, 2, and #13: $N = 23$.
8. Unpublished transcripts of Martin Linsky's interviews.
9. Personal interview, Fall 1987, Carter Center.
10. Question II.3a, "When an issue in your office or agency received what you saw as positive or negative coverage in the mass media, did that coverage increase the importance of the issue within the bureaucracy?"
11. Personal interview, Summer 1987, Washington D.C.
12. *Washington Post,* June 20, 1985.
13. *Washington Post,* June 21, 1985.
14. CBS News, 6/21/85; ABC, CBS specials, 6/26/85; CBS, 6/28/85, with Ken Stein accusing network correspondents of engaging in diplomacy instead of journalism.
15. CBS News, 6/28/85.
16. For more information on Scali and opinions about his role, see *New York Times,* Jan. 13-16, 1989, for stories on meetings between Soviet, Cuban, and American officials involved in the crisis.

28

REPORTING THE GULF WAR

William Hachten with the collaboration
of Marva Hachten

Editor's Note

Bloody images of war, projected on television screens, arouse antiwar sentiment in America; an emotionally stirred public will stop bellicose leaders who dare not defy public opinion. This has been the folk wisdom until recently. But the Gulf War of 1991, between Iraq and an alliance of United Nations members, proved that the antiwar scenario does not necessarily occur. Even when war images are broadcast live by an uncensored press, they can be manipulated by governments to hide the horrors of war. The military can supply attractive battlefield pictures and stories that journalists find difficult to refuse. The military also can bar press access to potentially embarrassing scenes and persuade the public that national security requires such restraints. Reporters' complaints go unheeded until after the war when it is too late to undo the harm done by controlled coverage.

The outcome, in the Gulf conflict, was a picture-book war that glorified the battlefield skills of military leaders and largely concealed the pain and suffering inflicted through air and ground combat. The public cheered. While the authorities' short-range political and military aims were well served, questions were raised about the long-term damage that flows from distortion and concealment of information. Thanks to Cable News Network (CNN), the war had a global audience. Yet, contrary to Marshall McLuhan's predictions, this common experience did not turn the world into a global village of shared perceptions. Seen through diverse national prisms, the Gulf War turned out instead to be a Tower of Babel of discordant views.

William A. Hachten is professor emeritus of journalism and mass communication at the University of Wisconsin, and Marva Hachten is a journalist. The

© 1992, Iowa State University Press, from *The World News Prism: Changing Media of International Communication.*

selection is from The World News Prism: Changing Media of International Communication, *3d ed. (Ames: Iowa State University Press, 1992), chap. 9.*

The first casualty when war comes is truth.

Senator Hiram Johnson

The Gulf War—the short but violent conflict between Iraq and the coalition forces led by the United States—lasted only 42 days, but it changed the way that future wars will be reported. Television, and especially Cable News Network, turned much of the world into a global community intently watching as the war unfolded. Because of the involvement of Western powers, particularly the United States and Britain, the Gulf War was the biggest running news story in years, and the telling of it utilized the full resources of the international news system. Eventually, over 1,600 print and broadcast journalists and technicians were in Saudi Arabia alone, with many others in nearby Amman, Baghdad, Tel Aviv, Nicosia, and, of course, Washington and London, two major news hubs.

This avalanche of live global coverage necessarily passed through the prism of deep cultural differences between the West and Islam. Each viewed the war through quite different lenses. When Iraq's Scud missiles fell on Israeli civilians, for example, Westerners were appalled, while Palestinians and Jordanians were elated. To the West and some Arabs, Saddam Hussein was a dangerous, reckless tyrant; to millions of other Arabs and Moslems, he was a hero who stood up to the West—a modern day Saladin.

But for both sides, CNN and other television broadcasters made it a "real-time" war. After hostilities began early on January 17, 1991 (Baghdad time), reporters described antiaircraft tracers in the night sky of Baghdad and flashes of bomb explosions on the horizon. On succeeding nights, viewers were provided with live video reports from Tel Aviv and Riyadh of Scud missiles, some intercepted by Patriot missiles, exploding against the night sky and television reporters donning gas masks on camera.

The press talked of the "CNN effect"—millions anchored hour after hour to their television sets lest they miss the latest dramatic development. Restaurants, movies, hotels, and gaming establishments all suffered business losses. "People are intensely interested in the first real-time war in history and they are just planting themselves in front of their television sets," one expert said. Ratings for CNN soared 5 to 10 times their prewar levels.[1]

The Gulf War was a worldwide media event of astonishing proportions. Global television never had a larger or more interested audience for such a sustained period of time. Television became the first and principal source of news for most people as well as a major source of military and political intelligence for both sides. CNN telecasts, including military briefings, were viewed in Baghdad as they were being received in Riyadh or Washington, D.C.

Because this was a war, the combatants, particularly the governments of Iraq and the United States, tried to control and manipulate the media with subtle and not-so-subtle propaganda and misinformation messages. Western journalists chafed at the restraints on news coverage of the war itself and complained there was much news they were not permitted to report. Most coalition news came from military briefings and from carefully controlled and escorted "pools" of reporters. And some official news given at the briefings was actually disinformation intended to mislead the enemy, not inform the public. For example, viewers were led to believe that Patriot missiles were invariably successful in neutralizing Scud missiles; such was not the case.

Information on the war was tightly controlled on television; one observer called it "the illusion of news." For their own valid security reasons, the military often held back or distorted the news they did release. In the opening days of the war, much was made of the "smart bombs" which hit their targets with about 90 percent accuracy. After the war, the U.S. Air Force admitted that smart bombs made up only 7 percent of all U.S. explosives dropped on Iraq and Kuwait. Television scenes of precision guided bombs going down chimneys or in the doors of targets notwithstanding, the air force said 70 percent of the 88,500 tons of bombs dropped on Kuwait and Iraq missed their targets.[2]

Peter Jennings of ABC News reminded viewers that much of what was revealed in the opening days of war was speculation, mixed with some hard facts and some rumors in the rushing river of information.[3] But whether they were getting hard news or not, many millions of viewers stayed by their television sets if only to find out what would happen next. Public opinion polls showed that the overwhelming majority of Americans supported both the war and the military's efforts to control the news; further, some thought there should be more controls on press reporting. A *Los Angeles Times Mirror* poll found that half of the respondents considered themselves obsessed with war news, but nearly 80 percent felt the military was "telling as much as it can." About the same proportion thought that military censorship may be "a good idea."

But after the war, many in the press felt that the traditional right of the American press to accompany their combat forces and report back news of war had been severely circumscribed. Michael Getler of the *Washington Post* wrote: "The Pentagon and U.S. Army Central Command conducted what is probably the most thorough and consistent wartime control of

American reporters in modern times—a set of restrictions that in its total-
ity and mindset seems to go beyond World War II, Korea and Vietnam." [4]

President George Bush and the Pentagon followed a deliberate policy of
blocking negative and unflattering news from reaching the U.S. public lest
it weaken support for the war. American casualties were reported, but
there were few pictures of dead and wounded. Details of tactical failures
and mishaps in the bombing campaign were not released. The older generation of military leaders felt strongly, despite evidence to the contrary,
that unrestricted and critical press coverage in Vietnam had contributed to
the U.S. defeat there. They were determined it would not happen again.
Some journalists blamed their own top editors and news executives for
agreeing ahead of time to the field censorship and pool arrangements instead of vigorously opposing them.

Coverage Before the War

Every war is different, and the peculiar conditions of the Gulf War affected the ways the war was reported and perceived by the public. Most
Americans saw it as a "good war" with a quick, decisive victory with amazingly few U.S. and allied casualties, so press concerns over restrictions on
war coverage had little public impact and never became an important issue. Nor did antiwar protests have time to develop.

For over five months, from August 2, 1990, when Iraqi troops first in-
vaded Kuwait, to January 17, 1991, when the bombing of Iraq started,
television played a central role in reporting all aspects of the major international crisis involving the United Nations and so many Arab and Western
nations. The press covered the rapid buildup of coalition forces in Saudi
Arabia with television pictures of armed troops arriving with heavy armor
and taking up positions in the desert. This enthusiastic coverage contributed to some Pentagon-inspired misinformation by exaggerating the ability
of U.S. troops to repel an invasion. Later, the 101st Airborne troops, first
to arrive, admitted that during those first weeks they would have been
mere road bumps for invading Iraqi forces.

Television played a clear diplomatic role as well by reporting the fate of
the thousands of hostages held by Iraq and the international efforts to obtain their freedom. More importantly, the continuing diplomatic efforts by
the United Nations and various foreign governments to resolve the conflict
were fully aired and analyzed on television. Such international television
reports, instantly available in dozens of world capitals, accelerated the often cumbersome process of diplomacy. . . .

This time, television was better equipped than ever before to report a
war. Television crews had the newest technology of small, lightweight
cameras and portable up-links that could transmit their video stories home

via satellite. Print and radio reporters could call in stories to their newsrooms with suitcase-sized satellite telephones out in the field.

Probably never before have television viewers been exposed to such an endless array of experts—diplomatic, military, political, journalistic—to analyze in excruciating detail each new phase of the unfolding drama. Journalist Elizabeth Drew commented, "Probably in no other prelude to a possible war has the media played such a prominent role as transmission belt—for feelers, for threats, for war scenarios designed to intimidate, and for military information perhaps designed to mislead." [5]

Another impressive facet of network television coverage was its ability to *interconnect* with a variety of news sources thousands of miles apart. When, say, a new peace proposal was announced in Moscow, Peter Jennings on his ABC news program immediately obtained reactions and comments for ABC reporters and their news sources located at the White House, State Department, Pentagon, London, Tel Aviv, Amman, and Paris.

Reporting the War

All this was a prelude to the shooting war, which began just as the evening news programs were beginning at 6:30 p.m. Eastern Standard Time (January 16 in the United States, January 17 in the Middle East). The networks and CNN interrupted their prepared news shows to report that aerial bombing had apparently begun in Baghdad. Then followed one of the most memorable nights in television history: the opening phases of a major conflict reported in "real time" by reporters in Iraq, Saudi Arabia, and Washington.

CNN stole the show that night as three CNN correspondents, John Holliman, Peter Arnett, and Bernard Shaw, gave vivid eyewitness descriptions of the U.S. air attack from the windows of their Baghdad hotel room. As in old-time radio, reporters relied on words, not video, that first night. Other networks reported the fireworks, but CNN with its previously arranged leased lines stayed on the longest after the lines were cut for the other networks. The next day, General Colin Powell jokingly said the Pentagon was relying on CNN for military information.

The second night of the war gave prime-time viewers another long, exciting evening as CNN and NBC reporters in Tel Aviv reported live Scud missiles landed. Reporters, often with gas masks on, put out raw and unevaluated information. At one point, NBC reported dramatically that nerve gas had been detected in one Scud attack. Tom Brokaw decried the situation for some minutes, but after the report proved false, NBC apologized. For the first three days of the war, people everywhere stayed glued to television and radio sets, including shortwave receivers. Networks expanded to near 24-hour coverage for the first 36 hours, and even the daytime soap operas were preempted briefly for war coverage. There was not that much to report at that point, and the same facts, theories, and speculations were repeated again and again. Nevertheless, the mesmerized public stayed tuned.

During this early bombing phase of the war, the Pentagon held back detailed military information, and the media sought out news elsewhere in Israel, Jordan, and, when it could, Baghdad. Within Saudi Arabia, the U.S. military had tight regulations in place. Information was withheld about the extent of the bombing and destruction within Iraq, and restrictions were placed on interviews with troops and returning pilots. Reporters could cover military activities only in designated "pools," groups of reporters accompanied by an escort officer. (One reporter likened a press pool to a group of senior citizens on a conducted tour.) All interviews with soldiers were on the record, and all reports were subject to censorship before they could be released.

Most information was available in the daily briefings held by the military in both Riyadh and the Pentagon in Washington, but much of this was rather general, vague, and lacking in detail. The military had coherent arguments for its restrictive policies. Destroying Iraq's military command and communications capability was a high priority of the bombing strategy, and it was important not to convey any useful information, via the media, that would reveal troop movements and the intentions of coalition forces. Keeping Iraq's forces off balance and without reliable information was a key part of U.S. strategy. After the ground attack began, it became apparent how important surprise was in General Norman Schwarzkopf's battle plan. . . .

However, some news executives and critics said the press restrictions went well beyond security concerns and appeared aimed at both preventing politically damaging disclosures by soldiers and shielding the American public from seeing the brutal aspects of war. Even before the fighting started, the Defense Department had barred the press from Dover Air Force Base, Delaware, where U.S. war dead are returned. The ban, which was upheld by a U.S. court, was justified by authorities as a protection of the privacy of the troops' families. A suit filed by the press charged the Pentagon's real motive was to prevent television pictures of flag-draped coffins arriving at Dover, as was done in previous wars.

If the war had gone badly, the press would have had difficulty reporting the negative aspects. With over 1,600 reporters in the theater, only about 100 could be accommodated by the pools to report the 500,000 American force. As the ground war neared, the large press corps became increasingly restive and frustrated at this lack of access.

The response of some reporters was to "free-lance"—to avoid the pools and go off on their own. Malcolm Browne reported, "Some reporters were hiding out in American Marine or Army field units, given G.I. uniforms and gear to look inconspicuous, enjoying the affection (and protection of the units) they're trying to cover—concealed by the officers and troops from the handful of press-hating commanders who strive to keep the battle field free of wandering journalists." [6] Browne noted that nearly all reporters who tried to reach front line U.S. troops were arrested at one time or another and sometimes held in field jails for up to 12 hours, facing the threat of revocation of their press credentials. Reporters for the *New York Times, Washington Post,* Associated Press, and Cox papers were arrested at one time or another. . . .

Psychological Warfare and Propaganda

Intertwined with the flow of war news was the propaganda war between Iraq and the United States, the principal power in the UN-supported coalition. Each side used information and its own, as well as international, news media to seek advantages in world and regional opinion and to undermine enemy morale. Saudi Arabia and Kuwait, both lacking effective media voices, hired prestigious U.S. public relations firms, such as Hill and Knowlton, to get their views across to Western media and publics.

Saddam Hussein's propaganda was considered crude but effective in a region where rumor and fact are often blurred and conspiracies are easily believed. Iraq's most persistent strategy was to blame the gulf crisis on an Israeli-American plot to station foreign forces in the region and seize control of Middle Eastern oil. One disinformation campaign claimed Israeli planes were painted like American planes and that Israeli soldiers had mastered American English.

Saddam's propaganda portrayed the American soldier as a foreign invader who is "drinking alcohol, eating pork and practicing prostitution," according to a broadcast on Holy Mecca Radio, a clandestine station beamed from Iraq into Saudi territory.[7] Iraqi television reported that 40 percent of American servicemen had AIDS. An Indian newspaper with ties to Iraq reported that the Pentagon had sent 5,000 Egyptian women to Saudi Arabia to serve as prostitutes for the American troops. A U.S. Information Agency official commented, "Even though a story can be incredibly preposterous to the Western mind, it can resonate deeply in other parts of the world. The key is the predisposition to believe, not the crudity of the charge." [8] Before the bombing destroyed many of its radio transmitters, Iraq had a greater power than the West to broadcast in the area, including clandestine radio stations for Egyptian and Saudi Arabian listeners. Even though the Voice of America increased its Arabic broadcasts from 7½ to 13 hours a day, Iraq was largely successful in jamming those and BBC Arabic broadcasts during the first weeks of the crisis. . . .

The main U.S. "psychwar" emphasis was on a psychological campaign designed to shake Iraq's confidence and undermine the morale of its armed forces. The campaign included broadcasts of antigovernment propaganda into Iraq and the circulation of audio- and videocassette tapes depicting U.S. forces as militarily strong and Saddam Hussein's government as corrupt. There was also a plan to smuggle thousands of small radios into Iraq to receive American broadcasts. Allied aircraft dropped 1 million leaflets into Kuwait urging the Iraqi infantry to surrender. Many who later did give up came in clutching these air-dropped "safe conduct" leaflets. . . .

The effectiveness of such psychological warfare efforts is always difficult to evaluate. In any case, the propaganda of words always gives way to the propaganda of events, and since Saddam Hussein's forces were so soundly defeated, his propaganda of words was also overwhelmed. . . .

Lessons for the Press

Wars between nations are by definition major international news stories and should be reported by the press as completely and thoroughly as conditions permit. Yet governments at war, even the most democratic, will try to control and manipulate war news to their own strategic and tactical advantage. The Gulf War provided ample reminders of this generalization. Censorship and propaganda, the twin arms of political warfare, are integral components of modern warfare. So, often the press is denied by both sides the opportunity to report objectively what has occurred. In numerous modern wars—Uganda versus Tanzania, the Sudan civil war, Ethiopia's war against Eritrean rebels and Somalia, the Soviet Union's incursion into Afghanistan—both sides either barred foreign correspondents or discouraged any coverage. The long and bloody Iran-Iraq war, precursor of the Gulf War, was severely underreported.

In the Gulf War, over 1,500 journalists were permitted into the war theater but were allowed little freedom to cover the actual fighting. On the Iraqi side, the few foreign reporters in Baghdad were severely restricted.

From all indications, the U.S. military as well as the Bush administration were pleased with the results of their policy and would do the same thing next time. But among the press, especially American and British journalists, there was a general conclusion that the press had been unduly and even illegally denied access to information about the war.

After the war, in July 1991, a report calling military restrictions in the Gulf War "real censorship" that confirmed "the worst fears of reporters in a democracy" was delivered to Defense Secretary Dick Cheney. It was signed by 17 news executives representing the four networks, AP and UPI, and major newspapers and news magazines. The news executives bitterly complained that the restrictions placed on reporters by the Pentagon were intended to promote a sanitized view of the war. The war was called the first in this century to restrict all official coverage to pools. "By controlling what reporters saw and when they saw it, the military exerted great power to shape and manage the news," the report said. Also criticized were the use of military escorts and "unwarranted delays by the military in transmitting copy." [9] The journalists sought a meeting with Cheney in hopes of changing the use of pools in future wars.

Consequently, despite all the wonders of communication technology (and perhaps in part because of them), the Western news media can be severely restricted by their own democratic governments in wartime.

Notes

1. "Tourism Shaken by 'CNN Effect'," *New York Times,* January 28, 1991, p. 8.
2. Tom Wicker, "An Unknown Casualty," *New York Times,* March 20, 1991, p. A15.
3. Alex S. Jones, "Feast of Viewing but Little Nourishment," *New York Times,* January 19, 1991, p. 8.
4. Michael Getler, "The Gulf War, 'Good News' Policy Is a Dangerous Precedent," *Washington Post National Weekly Edition,* March 25-31, 1991, p. 24.
5. Elizabeth Drew, "Letter from Washington," *New Yorker,* December 31, 1990, p. 92.
6. Malcolm W. Browne, "The Military vs. the Press," *New York Times Magazine,* March 3, 1991, p. 45.
7. Elaine Sciolino, "Iraq's Propaganda May Seem Crude but It's Effective," *New York Times,* September 15, 1990, p. E3.
8. Ibid.
9. Jason DeParle, "17 News Executives Criticize U.S. for 'Censorship' of Gulf Coverage," *New York Times,* July 3, 1991, p. A4.

29

THE IMPACT OF INVESTIGATIVE REPORTING ON PUBLIC OPINION AND POLICY MAKING: TARGETING TOXIC WASTE

David L. Protess, Fay Lomax Cook, Thomas R. Curtin, Margaret T. Gordon, Donna R. Leff, Maxwell E. McCombs, and Peter Miller

Editor's Note

The case presented here is part of a series of studies that analyzes the impact of investigative news stories on public policy, policy makers, and the general public. Through close ties with the media, the authors knew when investigative stories would be published. This enabled them to measure audience attitudes before as well as after the stories appeared. Some case studies revealed that the investigative stories had substantial influence on public policies; others did not. Comparison of the types of effects that were produced, as well as those that did not materialize, permits the authors to theorize about the conditions under which investigative stories influence public opinion and policy agendas.

Although many aspects of the cause and effect sequence remain to be clarified, one thing is certain: it is not true, as traditionally believed, that investigative journalism works primarily by mobilizing public opinion, which then pressures public officials to act. Instead, effects were produced most consistently when reporters and policy makers collaborated to produce policy changes. Unambiguous reports about new issues, which surfaced for a limited time only, were most likely to produce policy responses.

At the time of writing, Maxwell E. McCombs was professor and chairman of the Department of Journalism at the University of Texas at Austin. All other authors were affiliated with Northwestern University's Center for Urban Affairs and Policy Research, then directed by Professor Margaret T. Gordon. David L. Protess and Donna R. Leff were also associate professors of journalism in the Medill School of Journalism; Fay Lomax Cook was associate professor in the School of Education, Peter Miller was associate professor in the School of Speech, and Thomas R. Curtin was a doctoral student in the School of Education. The

From *Public Opinion Quarterly* 51 (1987) : 166-185. Reprinted by permission of The University of Chicago Press.

selection comes from "The Impact of Investigative Reporting on Public Opinion and Policymaking: Targeting Toxic Waste," Public Opinion Quarterly 51 (1987): 166-85. Several tables have been omitted.

This article reports the fourth in a series of field experiments that test the agenda-setting hypothesis (McCombs and Shaw, 1972) for news media investigative reports. Our goal is to treat these field experiments as case studies from which we can develop empirically grounded theory that specifies the conditions under which investigative reports influence public agendas and policy-making priorities. Unique to studies of agenda-setting is our use of pretest-posttest research designs, made possible by journalists' disclosure of forthcoming investigative stories to the research team with adequate time for pre- and postpublication survey interviewing. A further distinctive feature is our concern with detailed tracing of the life course of a media report from an examination of the initial investigation by journalists, to the publication of the report, the effects on the general public and policymakers, and eventual policy outcomes.

The first of these studies (Cook et al., 1983) found that a nationally televised investigative news report on fraud and abuse in the federally funded home health care program had significant effects on the agendas of both the public and policymakers. The study found that home health care-related issues (and not unrelated issues) became significantly more important to citizens and policymakers exposed to the televised report than to nonviewers. Yet, actual policy changes after the report's publication resulted more from direct pressure for change by the journalists themselves than from demands by the general public or political constituencies.

The second study (Protess et al., 1985) measured the impact of a *Chicago Sun-Times* investigative series disclosing government improprieties in the reporting and handling of rape against Chicago area women. The effects of the newspaper series were considerably more limited than in the first study, in part because the pretest disclosed an already high level of awareness and concern about the problem. The most striking result was a sharp increase in the number, length, and prominence of stories about rape in the *Sun-Times*—that is, the largest measurable effect was on the medium itself rather than on its audience. However, as in the home health care study, policymaking effects included legislative hearings and related "symbolic" political actions (Edelman, 1964).[1]

The effects of the third investigative report, a five-part local television series about repeatedly brutal Chicago police officers, provided an "in-between" case (Leff, Protess, and Brooks, 1986). The series had significant effects on viewer attitudes about police brutality but not on their assessment of the priority or salience of the problem in comparison with other social concerns. Nonetheless, the series resulted in major policy changes within the Chicago Police Department, in part because its publication coincided with a hotly contested Chicago mayoral election in which mayoral challenger Harold Washington used the series to help make the Department an issue.

Why is it that some investigative reports "catch on" and affect the views of members of the public and policy elites, while others do not? Why is it that all three investigative reports had some form of policy impact, despite the fact that they did not all have effects on the public and policymakers? In answer to the first question, several explanations have tentatively been suggested in our earlier work: the nature of the medium of presentation (print versus television); the style of presentation (unambiguous, with clear villains and heroes, versus ambiguous, where fault is not clear and where solutions seem difficult to find); the "age" of the issue on the media's agenda (a new issue that has infrequently been presented in the past and about which the public has little knowledge versus an old issue that has recurred over time on the media's agenda and about which the public is aware).

None of these explanations provides a possible answer to the second question concerning the investigative reports' impact on policy. Regardless of the above factors, some form of policy impact occurred in all the cases we have examined to date. In the home health care and rape cases, the impact was symbolic with legislative hearings and proposals for policy changes. In the police brutality case, the impact was substantive with actual, major policy changes occurring. Clearly, more case studies are needed before we can develop an empirically grounded theory that specifies under what conditions and with what kinds of issues media investigations influence public agendas and policymaking processes.

The current study examines the public opinion and policymaking impact of a local television investigative series concerning the toxic waste disposal practices of a major Chicago university. In this case, the publication format was virtually identical to the earlier police brutality study; a multipart television report, aired during a "ratings sweeps" period, by the same correspondent on the same local television station. Further, one of the primary "targets" of the series was also a city regulatory agency, the Chicago Fire Department, which was accused of failing to enforce its environmental safety regulations. However, here we examine a different kind of issue—i.e., toxic waste disposal—at a different point in the city's political history—i.e., a year into Mayor Harold Washington's first term, when he was locked in a struggle with the City Council over control of Chicago's city government.

This article first will discuss the attitudinal impact of the toxic waste series on the general public and policy elites. Next, we trace the effects of the series on public policymaking in Chicago, focusing on the Fire Department's response to disclosures about its shortcomings. Finally, we analyze the findings of the four studies and try to identify and explain emerging patterns.

Research Design

The pretest, posttest experimental design is highly appropriate, but not traditionally utilized, in research involving nonlaboratory studies of media effects (Cook and Campbell, 1979). More typical in such research endeavors is the use of cross-sectional (McCombs and Shaw, 1972; McLeod, Becker, and Byrnes, 1974; Erbring, Goldenberg, and Miller, 1980) or panel study designs (Tipton, Haney, and Baseheart, 1975; Shaw and McCombs, 1977; MacKuen, 1981). In this study, however, two factors made field experimentation practicable: the reporters' cooperation with researchers and the lengthy preparation time of the report, which made advance planning by the researchers possible. Thus, researchers were able to obtain prepublication measurements of public and policymaker attitudes about the precise subject matter of the forthcoming television series. Survey questions about unrelated matters were used to obtain control data.

The resulting television series, "Wasted Time," was broadcast on three successive nights beginning 13 May 1984 on WMAQ-TV, Channel 5, a Chicago-based station owned and operated by the National Broadcasting Company (NBC). The reporter was Peter Karl, a well-known local investigative journalist who also served as correspondent on the police brutality series that was the subject of our third study. The series was promoted heavily by the television station, since it was broadcast in the middle of a highly important ratings period.

The series disclosed that the University of Chicago was storing potentially hazardous toxic chemical and radioactive wastes beneath several of its buildings, including some classrooms. Stories alleged that the storage violated Chicago Fire Department regulations, as well as the environmental standards of several state and federal agencies, including the U.S. Environmental Protection Agency (EPA), the U.S. Occupational Safety and Health Administration (OSHA), and the U.S. Department of Energy. Each night, the broadcast described an assortment of delays by the University in constructing relatively inexpensive facilities to ameliorate the waste disposal problem, thus giving the investigative report its title "Wasted Time." At no time did the series state that anyone at the University was in immediate danger, but the use of pictures of chemical explosions and fires that had occurred on the campus a decade earlier suggested the potential harm involved. One implication of the series was that the violations would not have persisted over time if certain federal, state, and local agencies were doing their jobs properly (i.e., the EPA, OSHA, the U.S. Department of Energy and the Chicago Fire Department).

General Public

Through random-digit dialing techniques, 395 respondents from the Chicago Metropolitan area were contacted two weeks before the television series aired. . . .

The telephone sample was then stratified by the respondents' self-reported television viewing habits into regular watchers of Channel 5 news (N = 208), and watchers of other evening newscasts or nonwatchers of any television news (N = 186). We expected that Channel 5 newswatchers were likely to be exposed to the investigative series, while others would constitute a quasi-experimental comparison group. One week after the broadcast of the series, researchers recontacted the entire sample. . . . 235 persons agreed to be reinterviewed, comprising the general public sample in this study. The respondents in this sample, though proportionately more female than the pretest respondents, did not differ significantly in educational level, age, or ethnic or racial background from the individuals who refused to be reinterviewed or who could not be recontacted after the pretest.

Since general viewing habits are not perfect predictors of the public's actual *exposure* to a specific television series, respondents were asked at the conclusion of the posttest interview whether they had "seen, read, or heard anything about recent news media investigative stories about toxic waste disposal problems at the University of Chicago." Follow-up questions were then asked about the source and extent of the exposure. Those responding "yes" to the question were considered "series-aware" group members, while those responding "no" were defined as a comparison group. Respondents in these two groups did not differ significantly in gender, educational level, age, or ethnic or racial background. . . .

To avoid sensitizing respondents to the subject of the investigative series, researchers embedded questions related to toxic waste disposal and other environmental problems among questions about crime, unemployment, police brutality, child abuse, and governmental corruption. Of the forty separate items in the questionnaire, twelve were related to general environmental issues and six to chemical or radioactive waste disposal problems. We hypothesized that change would occur among the Channel 5 viewers on questions about the environment and toxic waste, while responses to other questions would remain constant from pre- to posttest. We expected the comparison groups' responses to remain constant on all questions. . . .

Policymakers and Policymaking

A purposive sample of forty policy elites was selected for their interest and potential influence on environmental policymaking. Those surveyed included public administrators from Illinois and federal environmental protection agencies, state legislators, members of the Chicago City Council, University officials, and lobbyists from public interest groups and private waste disposal companies. Persons who were considered likely to know about the investigative series prior to pretest interviewing were excluded from the sample. Interviews were conducted by telephone; 31 of the 40 respondents were reinterviewed after the television broadcast.

As in our previous studies, we made no attempt to establish a group of nonexposed elite respondents. We expected that persons with significant interest in the subject of an investigative report would almost certainly hear about it, even if they failed to view the particular stories. Indeed, 23 of the 31 respondents indicated in posttest interviews that they "saw, read, or heard" something about the series. Statistical analyses were performed on the self-defined "exposed" and "unexposed" groups.

The policymakers were asked a series of questions that were identical to those in the survey of the general public. The questions included items both related and unrelated to the subject of the investigative series. In addition, the elite respondents were asked about their past, present, and anticipated future policymaking activities related to toxic waste disposal problems.

After the series, researchers tracked policy developments that might be attributable to the Channel 5 investigation by interviewing an expanded sample of policymakers and conducting analyses of related budgets, legislation, and regulatory and administrative initiatives. Content analyses of local media coverage of environmental issues were also performed both as an additional indicator of the level of governmental response to the series and as a measure of its impact on the news media's agendas.

Impact of the Investigative Report
on the General Public

In examining public attitudes before and after the broadcast of the Channel 5 investigation, we wanted to determine whether changes occurred on questionnaire items related to the subject of the series. To test whether the changes between the pretest and posttest were different for the exposed group from the nonexposed group, we used analysis of covariance (ANCOVA), employing the pretest score as the covariate. . . .

The data show no effects of the series, as measured by the ANCOVA analysis. Some items bordered on significant change, however, giving slight indications of change in perception due to the series. In particular, compared to those unaware of the series, those exposed to the reports were slightly more likely to say that environmental news stories cause confusion. Both series-aware and unaware respondents reported worrying somewhat less about improper storage and disposal of chemical waste at the posttest. Both groups of respondents tended to decrease their evaluation of the Chicago Fire Department, which suggests that other stimuli produced a small judgmental change. Evaluation of environmental agencies other than the Fire Department remained constant, as did measures of respondent's behavior concerning environmental problems.

In short, the agenda-setting hypothesis was not supported by the findings. Responses to questions about the importance of toxic waste disposal in relation to other issues did not change significantly. In comparison with other problems, toxic chemical and radioactive waste disposal was consistently at or near the bottom of their reported agendas.

Impact of the Investigative Report on Policymakers and Policymaking

. . . [T]he mean responses of policymakers to the surveys before and after the investigative report . . . indicate stronger support for the hypotheses than do the survey results for the general public.

Policy elites were asked to evaluate the performance of eleven government agencies. We expected that the investigative report would result in policy elites' lowering their assessments of the jobs done by four agencies—the Chicago Fire Department, the U.S. Department of Energy, the EPA, and OSHA. The changes were statistically significant ($p < .05$) for the performance evaluations of three of the four government agencies targeted by Channel 5 as bearing responsibility for the problems disclosed. Change in the evaluation of the fourth agency, the Chicago Fire Department, was in the expected downward direction ($p < .10$). Change was also significant for one of the seven unrelated agencies added as controls—the U.S. Social Security Commission—but this appears to be a chance change by the unexposed policy elites whose evaluations increased to more positive ones while the series-exposed elites' evaluations did not change.

Marked changes also occurred on one of the questions designed to measure the behavior of policymakers. When asked, "In the coming months, how much of your time do you think *will* be spent on toxic waste disposal problems?" the group exposed to the series changed significantly in the direction of "more" time. This finding is consistent with our analysis of the actual policymaking consequences of the investigative series. Since the series aired, each of the governmental agencies named by Channel 5 initiated actions to monitor the University's compliance with toxic waste disposal regulations.

Perhaps the most dramatic of these enforcement efforts was made by the Chicago Fire Department. On the morning after the first broadcast, a team of high-ranking Department officials inspected the buildings where chemical wastes were stored, and cited the University for failing to comply with 20 of the City's safety regulations. The Department gave the University 30 days to comply with its standards and threatened publicly to initiate criminal proceedings if it failed to do so.

Media coverage of the Fire Department's initiative was swift. A *Chicago Tribune* headline in newspaper's next edition read: "City Faults U of C on Fire Safety," and the *Sun-Times* reported that the "U of C Is Cited as Fire Violator." The *Hyde Park Herald*, a weekly newspaper serving the community surrounding the University, headlined: "UC Responds to Hazard Charge" and called editorially for a study of the problem. All three newspapers credited the Channel 5 investigation as the catalyst for the governmental actions.

Channel 5 itself reported the "Fire Department crackdown" on its evening newscast later the same day. (The station's television competitors ignored the story, however.) Pictures of the Department's inspections were shown, and the story was repeated in the remaining two segments of the investigative series. The television station claimed that the action was taken "in response to our series on hazardous waste disposal problems at the University." In fact, however, Channel 5 correspondent Peter Karl had discussed the possibility of an inspection in several telephone conversations with Fire Department officials two days *before* the first part of the series was aired. The officials had agreed both that the inspection would occur and that it would not take place until the morning *after* the airing of the initial broadcast. Channel 5, in turn, covered the inspection as if it occurred at the initiative of the Fire Department, i.e., without direct prodding by its investigative reporter.

This form of journalist-policymaker collaboration has been described in our earlier studies (Cook et al., 1983; Molotch, Protess, and Gordon, 1987). What is significant here is that general public and policymaker respondents were exposed to news media stories about governmental "reforms" before the allegations in Channel 5's three-part series had been completely aired. Thus, the public's perceptions of the series may have been colored somewhat by media reports that included the presentation of both a problem and its "solution."

Interviews by researchers with Fire Department officials at the end of the 30-day compliance period indicated that the University had, in fact, corrected the fire hazard aspect of its waste disposal problem. The University also was implementing plans for the much-delayed facility to provide a more permanent solution to its environmental difficulties. However, content analyses of Channel 5 and other media revealed that the media did not cover these *post*series developments. Unlike our study of the *Sun-Times* rape series, the issues of toxic waste disposal at the University of Chicago or elsewhere did not rise on the news media's agenda of concerns. Content analysis of the *Chicago Tribune* for 3-month periods both before and after the publication of the Channel 5 series showed a slight *decline* in column inches of news stories and editorials on toxic waste disposal problems. A review of the assignment log at Channel 5 for the same periods showed only a minor increase in the frequency of such stories.

... Similarly, policymakers' assessments of the importance of toxic waste disposal as an issue did not change significantly after the broadcast of the series. Perhaps this was because by the end of the series and the time of the posttest interview, the problems were being eliminated. There is no indication that the series produced any substantive initiatives (i.e., legislative, regulative, or budgetary) to deal with larger questions of toxic waste disposal, either on college campuses or elsewhere in the U.S. society. Thus, we call its policy impact "individualistic" because it was specific only to the particular problem documented at the University of Chicago.

Discussion of Findings

With the completion of this fourth study, we are somewhat better able to compare the varying impacts of the different investigative reports. Table 29-1 summarizes the results of the four case studies. Both the home health care broadcast and the police brutality television series were found to have greater *public* impact than either the toxic waste or the rape series. Nonetheless, like the police brutality series, the toxic waste investigation resulted in significant changes in the attitudes and actions of *policymakers*. The policymaking impact of the current case is the most focused. It appears to be attributable more to journalistic lobbying with Fire Department officials than to published investigative reports themselves. This is similar to the developments that occurred in the home health care investigation, where we found that it was not the members of the public who were so aroused by the report that they pressured their representatives to act. Rather, it was the active collaboration between journalists and policymakers during the prepublication phase of investigation that generated the policy outcome. In the two other cases that we studied, no such collaboration occurred, but policy changes nonetheless resulted.

What factors account for these similarities and differences? This question probably has a different answer depending on the target of impact that one wishes to understand—on the public, on elites, or on policy itself. For

Table 29-1   Summary of Four Case Study Findings of the Impact of Investigative Reports on the Public, Policy Elites, and Policy

Subject of case study	Medium	Format	Journalists' involvement with policymakers	General public impact	Elite impact	Policymaking impact
1. Home health care fraud and abuse ("The Home Health Hustle")	Network television	Single report	Extensive	Yes	Yes	Yes (symbolic)
2. Assaults against women ("Rape: Every Woman's Nightmare")	Local newspaper	5-part series	Minimal	No	No	Yes (symbolic)
3. Police brutality ("Beating Justice")	Local television	5-part series	Minimal	Yes	No	Yes (substantive)
4. Toxic waste disposal ("Wasted Time")	Local television	3-part series	Extensive	No	Yes	Yes (individualistic)

public attitudes to change, two factors seem to be important—the nature of the media portrayal and the frequency of attention by the media to the issue in the past. When the media portray an issue in an unambiguous way with dramatic, convincing, and clear evidence, public attitudes are more likely to change (see also Tyler and Cook, 1984:706). For example, the police brutality series documented the seriousness of the problem thoroughly, including a statistical analysis of brutality cases against the police and a 5-year review of all lawsuits filed against police in federal courts in Chicago. Its interviews with brutalized victims and action shots of identified "villains" made for powerful drama. In all these respects, the series was most similar to the home health care television report. Both investigations had significant impacts on the public.

On the other hand, like the *Sun-Times* rape series, Channel 5's "Wasted Time" investigation was stylistically ambiguous. Villains and victims were not well-defined. Rather, the television station attributed the problem to "bureaucratic delays," not venal conduct. The harm alleged was more *potential* than actual, and the presentation of the findings contained frequent exceptions and caveats. For example, the second part of the series began with the statement by correspondent Karl that "this is not a scare story of radioactive contamination on the campus of the University of Chicago."

Moreover, the edge of the toxic waste series' potential impact may have been dulled by the simultaneous presentation of problems and their solution, which created the impression that the danger was under control. The repeated mention that a permanent solution would result from the University's construction of an inexpensive facility (which had already been planned) further circumscribed the scope of the problem.

The equivocal nature of the presentation may help to explain why there was a tendency for posttest anxiety about the problem to be reduced. It may also help to explain why respondents in the exposed groups were somewhat more likely to be " 'confused' [about] news stories about environmental problems, like chemical or toxic wastes. . . . " In sum, the actual importance or seriousness of a problem may be less significant for influencing public attitudes than its "mediated reality" (Nimmo and Combs, 1983).

The second factor that seems important for influencing general public attitudes is the nature of the issue that the media are addressing. Certain issues receive fairly consistent treatment by journalists. Their place on the news media's agenda of interests may be higher or lower at different times, but they regularly tend to be the object of reportorial scrutiny. Examples include news about crime, governmental waste and corruption, and corporate windfall profit making. Borrowing from terminology used in a somewhat different context, we call these topics "recurring issues" in the news

(Walker, 1977). Investigative stories about recurring issues have lower impact potential. Media effects are limited by the routine discussion of such issues in news stories, creating an information blur that may obscure the transmission of even unique disclosures. Further, as information is accumulated about a particular issue over time, the effect of subsequent communication tends to diminish (Saltiel and Woelfel, 1975; Downs, 1972). Thus, the impact of investigative reports about rape, toxic waste, and police brutality in Chicago may have been circumscribed by their appearance in the midst of a recurring stream of news events on these subjects.

On the other hand, issues that become subject to breakthrough news reports have a greater opportunity to produce effects. The home health care report provides an example of a "nonrecurring issue" in the news, one that has received infrequent or no prior attention from journalists. Investigative news stories about such issues have higher impact potential because they reveal matters that may be relatively unknown before their publication. The public's lack of accumulated information on these issues may increase its susceptibility to investigative media messages (Cook et al., 1983), although the effects may not be long-lasting (Watt and van den Berg, 1981; Saltiel and Woelfel, 1975; Downs, 1972).

We would suggest that news media investigative reports with the maximum ability to produce attitude change are those that involve unambiguous presentations of nonrecurring issues. This may explain why the home health care investigation, which spotlighted an "undiscovered" problem by showing greedy agency directors victimizing the elderly and handicapped, had the strongest public impact of the four case studies. Conversely, ambiguously presented reports on recurring issues, like the rape series and toxic waste investigation, have the least opportunity to change public attitudes. . . .

Explanations for the effects of news media investigations on policy elites and on policy are more complex and less well understood. Two of the four cases showed effects on elites, and in all four cases, policymaking effects occurred. A review of the four case studies suggests that many factors may influence the nature and extent of governmental responses to investigative reporting. These factors include the timing of the publication in relation to political exigencies, the extent of journalistic collaboration with policymakers, the level of general public and interest group pressures, and the availability of cost-effective solutions to the problems disclosed.

In the toxic waste series, the proximate cause of the initial governmental response was the involvement in the policymaking process of the Channel 5 correspondent. The level of involvement was sufficient to prompt an immediate effort to correct the specific problem at the University of Chicago. Likewise in the home health care case, the policy impact (legislation hearings and proposals for change) resulted from the active collaboration between journalists and policymakers (i.e., high-level staff members of the Senate Permanent Investigations Subcommittee).

In the other two cases, journalists did not orchestrate the policy impacts. In the rape study, we found that the series provided a platform for those already pushing for reform of rape legislation. Policymakers who already had proposals and programs to recommend before the series made their announcements soon after publication of the series, using the investigative report as a backdrop for their announcements.

In the police brutality study, the series also provided a platform but in a different way from that described above. The investigative report's results were used by Chicago mayoral challenger Harold Washington as ammunition against incumbent Mayor Jane Byrne, who had appointed the police superintendent. When elected, Washington was responsible for many of the policy changes in the police department.

Do investigative reports always result in some form of policy response? Investigative reports uncover problems in the social fabric of society. Officials directly responsible for the particular domain in which a problem is uncovered may feel obligated to take some action to show they are "responsive" and "responsible." Since our cases are small in number and are not necessarily representative of all investigative reports, we cannot generalize. However, the results to date suggest that investigative reports may have more influence than previously thought. The evidence that such reports present about social conditions serves to put policymakers on the defensive. They must either attempt to justify the problem or act to solve it. Actions—symbolic, individualistic, or substantive—are the responses seen in the cases analyzed here.

Note

1. Symbolic acts have been described as "dramatic in outline and empty of realistic detail" (Edelman, 1964:9). Here we use the term to describe policy "changes" that are largely rhetorical. Thus, when a public official responds to a media exposé by making speeches about the problem, by convening governmental hearings, or by announcing as news previously approved legislation, we call these acts symbolic. Conversely, "substantive" reforms are tangible regulatory, legislative, or administrative changes that occur after an investigative story is published. In making this distinction, we do not mean to suggest that substantive reforms are necessarily more likely than symbolic reforms to lead in the long run to the *correction* of the problem disclosed by the media.

References

Cook, F. L., T. R. Tyler, E. G. Goetz, M. T. Gordon, D. Leff, and H. L. Molotch (1983). "Media and agenda-setting: Effects on the public, interest group leaders, policy makers, and policy." *Public Opinion Quarterly* 47:16-35.

Cook, T. D., and D. T. Campbell (1979). *Quasi-Experimentation: Design and Analysis Issues for Field Settings.* Chicago: Rand McNally.

Downs, A. (1972). "Up and down with ecology: The 'issue attention cycle.' " *Public Interest* 28:38-50.

Edelman, M. (1964). *The Symbolic Uses of Politics.* Urbana: University of Illinois Press.

Erbring, L., E. Goldenberg, and A. Miller (1980). "Front-page news and real-world cues: A new look at agenda-setting by the media." *American Journal of Political Science* 24:16-49.

Leff, D., D. Protess, and S. Brooks (1986). "Changing public attitudes and policymaking agendas." *Public Opinion Quarterly* 50:300-314.

MacKuen, M. B. (1981). "Social communication and the mass policy agenda." In M. B. MacKuen and S. L. Coombs, *More Than News; Media Power in Public Affairs.* Beverly Hills: Sage.

McCombs, M., and D. L. Shaw (1972). "The agenda-setting functions of the mass media." *Public Opinion Quarterly* 36:176-187.

McLeod, J. M., L. B. Becker, and J. E. Byrnes (1974). "Another look at the agenda-setting function of the press." *Communication Research* 1:131-166.

Molotch, H., D. Protess, and M. T. Gordon (1987). "The media-policy connection: Ecologies of news." In D. Paletz (ed.), *Political Communication: Theories, Cases, and Assessments.* New Jersey: Ablex.

Nimmo, D., and J. Combs (1983). *Mediated Political Realities.* New York: Longman.

Protess, D. L., D. R. Leff, S. C. Brooks, and M. T. Gordon (1985). "Uncovering Rape: The watchdog press and the limits of agenda-setting." *Public Opinion Quarterly* 49:19-37.

Saltiel, J., and J. Woelfel (1975). "Inertia in cognitive processes: The role of accumulated information in attitude change." *Human Communication Research* 1:333-344.

Shaw, D. L., and M. E. McCombs (eds.) (1977). *The Emergence of American Political Issues: The Agenda-Setting Function of the Press.* St. Paul: West Publishing Company.

Tipton, L., R. Haney, and J. Baseheart (1975). "Media agenda-setting in city and state election campaigns." *Journalism Quarterly* 52:15-22.

Tyler, T. R., and F. L. Cook (1984). "The mass media and judgments of risk: Distinguishing impact on personal and societal level judgments." *Journal of Personality and Social Psychology* 47:693-708.

Walker, J. L. (1977). "Setting the agenda in the U.S. Senate: A theory of problem selection." *British Journal of Political Science* 7:423-445.

Watt, J. H., Jr., and S. van den Berg (1981). "How time dependency influences media effects in a community controversy." *Journalism Quarterly* 58:43-50.

30

JOHN L. HESS AND THE
NURSING HOME SCANDAL

Robert Miraldi

Editor's Note

*The relationship between reform-minded journalists and political reformers is
symbiotic. As this essay demonstrates, they need each other to succeed.* New York
Times *reporter John L. Hess could not have exposed a nursing home scandal in
New York and sparked nursing home reforms without the aid of a local politician.
Hess wrote the stories and alerted his political confederate to wrongdoings that he
had discovered. His ally had the resources to pursue the leads, garnering
favorable publicity for himself and creating fresh story material for Hess.*

*The essay illustrates how thin the borderline is between objective reporting and
political advocacy. Hess's precarious balancing along this fine line raises
questions about where the limits lie and ought to lie and what the consequences
are for politics and journalism when the rules of objectivity are breached. This
case study also sheds light on the ups and downs of investigative journalism, such
as the lucky leaks from official sources that advance the journalist's goals and the
threats of libel and defamation suits that act as deterrents.*

*At the time of writing, Robert Miraldi was associate professor of journalism at
the State University of New York at New Paltz. As a reporter for the* Staten
Island Advance *during Hess's crusade, he wrote dozens of stories about the
nursing home scandal. The essay comes from "Objectivity and the New
Muckraking: John L. Hess and the Nursing Home Scandal,"* Journalism
Monographs *115 (August 1989): 1-25. Several notes have been omitted.*

... Over a ten-month period, from October 1974 to July 1975, Hess
wrote nearly 150 stories in the *Times.* He was eventually joined by the rest
of the New York media in a crusade to reform what New York's special
nursing home prosecutor called "squalid, sometimes inhuman conditions

---

and sinister financial manipulations" in the state's 650 nursing homes where 90,000 people lived.[1] Hess's work led to a number of developments including a nationwide inquiry into this $10-billion industry,[2] a political scandal that implicated a score of high-ranking New York officials and Vice-President Nelson Rockefeller, the criminal indictment of two hundred nursing home owners for stealing millions of dollars and billing taxpayers for personal items ranging from a Renoir painting to trips to Europe, the return to the public of millions of dollars falsely charged to the federal-state system of Medicaid, the revamping of New York's nursing home reimbursement system, and the establishment in New York of a permanent prosecutor to deal with nursing home violations. . . .

Unraveling a Scandal

The nursing home industry, which had only been receiving federal money for a decade, was almost entirely a creation of public policy. Congress created an incentive for nursing home construction in 1965 when it created Medicaid (medical aid for the poor) and Medicare (government insurance for the elderly), including in its coverage reimbursement to states for long-term care of the sick and poor in private institutions. Nursing homes, 90 percent of which are operated for profit, changed from family enterprise to big business. Seeing the chance for government-subsidized health care and enormous profit, hundreds of entrepreneurs with no experience in health care entered the field. . . .

Two books had been written in the spring about abuses in the nation's nursing homes (Hess had not seen either one), and a U.S. Senate Subcommittee had held hearings on institutional care of the elderly.[3] But there was no organized reform movement when Hess's four-part series appeared in the *Times* in October. Hess's first article on October 7, "Care of the Aged a Growing Scandal," appeared on page one. The story was neither "hard" nor "soft" news; it was more of an overview of the nursing home industry with tantalizing hints of scandal. The article included charges that would repeat for months: exorbitant profits, incompetent and overpaid administrators, fraudulent billing, a shortage of nurses, and bad food ("a cat could not eat it," a dietitian told Hess).[4] On day two, Hess's story, placed on page 48, used dozens of government records and interviews with sources of witnesses to document high profits. Hess focused on Eugene Hollander, an owner whose homes had been cited for years for deficiencies. Many months later, Hollander pleaded guilty to fraud totaling $1.4 million and was forced out of the industry.[5]

On day three, Hess wrote in dramatic detail about a national "syndicate" headed by sixty-six-year-old Bernard Bergman, whom he described as a "large benign man . . . rather resembling Sydney Greenstreet."

Bergman, the central figure in the ensuing nursing home scandal, purportedly controlled nearly a hundred nursing homes which, investigators said, he traded with relatives and business associates to increase his Medicaid reimbursement. Bergman told Hess for his October 9 story: "I happen to be involved in a couple of operations." Hess cited a state document that put Bergman's income from health care at $19 million. Eventually, Bergman pleaded guilty to charges that he defrauded $2.5 million.[6] On the final day of the series, Hess discussed alternatives to institutions, stressing, as he would for the next ten months, that philanthropic or non-profit nursing homes provided better care than profit-making ones.[7]

Pursuing Two Themes—Politics and Profits

Although Hess was no student of public opinion, he was aware that for state agencies to make changes they wanted, an aroused public would be needed.[8] "Momentum would be crucial" if reform was to occur, he said.[9] Responses by two public officials kept the story alive. The state's attorney general said the *Times*'s articles prompted his office to investigate the "interlocking syndicate of operators." [10] And a young, maverick member of the state legislature, after sending a staff member to confer with Hess on strategy, said he would begin public hearings into industry practices.[11]

Over ten months, Hess kept the scandal before the public by varying the mix of stories he wrote and by unfolding a drama. He made good use of the "events" that were produced as a result of his story—government hearings, reports, and audits, for example. And to these he added revelations from his own investigation which usually appeared when there was a lull in the official investigations. Each time Hess exposed a new aspect of nursing home corruption, the need for regulatory reform and criminal prosecution became more evident. . . .

Just as an earlier muckraker, Lincoln Steffens, focused on the "invisible government" in his work, Hess, too, showed how hidden forces aided nursing home entrepreneurs. The hidden forces revealed a connection between politics and money.[12] Hess showed how elected officials from both political parties had inquired repeatedly about the problems of nursing home owners. The officials received campaign contributions and payments for non-legislative work from nursing home owners; in return, the owners were aided by the officials.[13] Concerning money, Hess used public documents to show that salaries for owners were enormous ($158,000 for Hollander), that no-show jobs were rampant, and that taxpayers were being systematically billed for luxury items.

Despite success in uncovering the scandal, Hess seemed to despair in early December. . . . Part of Hess's despair came from his problems with the *Times*'s city desk. He felt the editors were blocking and underplaying his stories. Once, he had to threaten to resign if a story was not published.[14] Fearing the investigations would fail, Hess turned to another reporter, Jack Newfield, a well-known writer for the weekly *Village Voice*. Hess told Newfield: "Those bastards at the *Times* are cutting my stories and burying them. . . . They've held up my last piece for a week. But, believe me, Bergman is the worst. And he's held up my last piece for a week. But, believe me, Bergman is the worst. And he's going to get away with everything, unless someone like you picks up the story." Newfield did, writing fifteen stories on nursing homes over the coming months, and trading information and documents with Hess. "Our mutual objective," Newfield said, "was exposure and reform." [15] By December, much of the New York City press corps was beginning to follow the nursing home story. . . .

Watching the Reformers

The *Times*'s coverage of the scandal was extensive as it followed the seventeen state and federal investigations. In January and February [1975], Hess wrote thirty-eight stories; from January to July, he wrote nearly one hundred stories. On some days the *Times* had four nursing home—related stories.

January was a dramatic month. First, on New Year's Day, Hess revealed that in 1971, the state's attorney general and the two top leaders of the state legislature had helped Bergman open a nursing home, despite the building's structural problems and Bergman's record of fraud. The news came from a memorandum leaked to Hess from the files of a health official.[16] Angered by the leak, the official released the entire contents of his nursing home files. The files revealed Bergman's meetings with Rockefeller's secretary and with Rockefeller's successor as governor.[17]

In his first official act as governor, Hugh Carey appointed a commission to devise legislative remedies and a special prosecutor. At this point, the U.S. Senate directed Bergman to testify about his nursing homes. In an interview with a weekly newspaper, Bergman, just returned from Europe, declared: "Only God in heaven knows that I am not guilty." Before the hearing, Hess used material he had gathered for months to write a profile of Bergman. He portrayed Bergman as philanthropist and pillar of the religious community, and as a deceitful, shrewd businessman.[18] Ten days before, Bergman had filed a $1-million defamation lawsuit against Hess and the *Times*.[19]

In dramatic testimony on January 22, Bergman said the charges were "baseless and false." He compared the hearing to a Joseph McCarthy witch-hunt and said that the nursing home industry was not profitable.[20] The story was placed on page one of all the city's newspapers. In the next day's *Times,* Hess quoted state documents that showed Bergman to be worth $24 million. "The guy just lied," Hess said many years later. "I had the facts and I knew the facts were different from Bergman's testimony." [21] Bergman refused on subsequent occasions to testify in public. The Senate hearing was a turning point in Hess's coverage. He stopped pursuing Bergman and turned to, first, a chronicle of the various hearings and pronouncements taking place and, second, the matter of what type of reform should occur. . . .

Influencing the Outcome

During the ten months that New York's nursing home scandal unfolded, there were two turning points. The first came after Hess wrote his opening four-part series of articles. Hess knew that someone had to respond to his exposé to, first, investigate the illegalities and, second, give him the "news pegs" around which to build a crusade. The most important response was from, [Andrew Stein, then a Democratic assemblyman from the East Side of Manhattan]. . . . Stein was known in New York as an ambitious politician. Soon after Hess's articles appeared, a Stein aide told Hess that Stein was interested in pursuing the nursing home story. Hess was glad, for he knew that Stein would have subpoena power. Stein could keep the story alive. Hess gave Stein names of potential witnesses, names of sources, and areas that needed to be researched, laying out a blueprint for the scandal. In the ensuing months, Hess worked closely with Stein, quoting him often and feeding him information. [22]

Some editors at the *Times* were unhappy at the reporter-source relationship that developed between Stein and Hess, questioning whether a reporter should have so much influence over events. [23] Years later, Hess scoffed at such an attitude. He fully encouraged Stein's investigation. The relationship between the two may be evident from Stein's first public comments on the scandal. On October 31, Hess wrote about the "giant Monopoly game" that was taking place in real estate transfers of nursing homes. Four days later, Stein was prominently quoted as denouncing "a vast Monopoly game" in the industry. Hess cannot recall if such similarities in language were a coincidence, but he concedes that at times he "sat on Stein" to pursue certain leads. [24] . . .

The second turning point came in late January, soon after Bergman testified before a senate committee. A commission appointed by New York's governor was beginning to explore reform alternatives. A clue to the direction in which Hess wanted to see changes go can be seen in a January 12 story he wrote for the *Times*'s "Week in Review," a section that recaps the week's events each Sunday. In it, the reporter usually had more room for interpretation, and Hess used that room, writing: "Many in the industry believe that so long as it is operated for profit it will generate abuses and corruption. The problem is to replace a system that relegated the elderly to commercial depositories ... with a system of dignified care." [25] In all likelihood, Hess's bias was coming through in this story. In his news stories, he was more careful and allowed others to suggest changes. As [sociologist Gaye] Tuchman points out, the objective reporter "may remove his opinion from the story by getting others to say what he himself thinks." [26] Thus, Stein, who either agreed with Hess or was prodded into agreeing by Hess, was often quoted on the need to eliminate profit.

On February 26, in a *Times* story that Hess did not write, Stein declared: "Our elderly deserve institutions which seek to provide quality care, not which provide only profit for unscrupulous real estate investors." [27] This was, in essence, the position of Hess. On nine occasions over the next four months, Stein and others urged that profit be eliminated.... Morris Abram, chairman of the special state investigating committee, said at a news conference that he hoped hearings would establish "whether or not there is a role for the profit motive." [28] The commission's hearings, although explosive, never took up the issue. In fact, two weeks after telling reporters that he would explore this key issue, Abram apparently had already resolved it. In a letter to Governor Carey, Abram said there were no "simple panaceas," but it was clear, he wrote, that the voluntary sector could not take over the work of the proprietary sector. Hess seized on this part of Abram's letter and led his story with it.[29]

Three days later, events gave Hess a chance to focus the debate further. A New York City senior citizens groups declared that a non-profit nursing home system and expanded home support were needed; witnesses at a legislative hearing also called for expanded home care by nonprofit agencies; and Stein toured centers for the elderly, campaigning for a phase-out of profit-making homes.[30] What was shaping up—partly by Hess's creation—was a battle between Stein and Abram. Stein criticized Abram's legislative proposals, saying they did not get to "the cause of the abuses, the profit motive." Two weeks later, Hess quoted Stein making the same point.[31]

Abram had the final say. He imposed new regulations even while conceding that the rules could be circumvented. "It would not surprise me," Abram told Hess, "If we need another investigation in ten or fifteen years." [32] Hess wrote a year later, "the structure of the industry remained what it was, and the cast of characters is only slightly different." [33] The profiteers stayed in control.

Objectivity's Dilemma

At the two key junctures of the nursing home saga, Hess attempted to influence the outcome by using Andrew Stein, a source over whom he undoubtedly had some control. Was it ethical for a reporter to be so close to a source as to influence what he does and says, and then to turn around and report that source's deeds and words? There is a very fine line between a reporter prompting a source to say what the reporter needs, and the source initiating the news for a story.... Reporters cannot say what they want to see happen; they are limited under the rules of objectivity to reporting what others want or say or do. Hess was privately supplying information to would-be reformers (or at the very least suggesting where that information could be found) and then publicly writing about what they found.

For example, on November 21, Stein, accompanied by Hess, visited a Bergman nursing home in Manhattan. Hess reported the visit, and wrote that the facility had the same violations of regulations for seventeen years, that its operator was drawing another salary at another Bergman home, and that it had been the subject of twenty-nine lease and mortgage transfers over those seventeen years. All these facts were available in public documents. Hess did not need Stein to write this seventeen-paragraph story which contains only five paragraphs attributed to Stein. The rest is based on Hess's research. But the Stein visit, to a home that Hess said he had visited when he began his investigation, gave Hess a news peg. Without the Stein visit, the *Times*'s city desk might have blocked or killed Hess's story since the visit came about the time that Hess told Newfield that the desk was obstructing his crusade. Because of the rules of objectivity, Hess needed Stein just to get into the paper.[34]

Was it unethical for Hess to use Stein in this fashion? Only perhaps if there was a quid pro quo—if Hess promised Stein publicity if he visited the nursing home—or if the material eventually disclosed by the source was unreliable. Then certainly it should not be used. But reporters always have the problem of trying to ascertain whether information given by a source is credible. In the end, Hess's reporting of Stein's findings held up. The indictments of the special prosecutor and the findings of the Abram Commission were the proof. Do the ends then justify the means? Not always, but in this case, with a careful veteran reporter whose stories had to be processed by a series of editors (albeit editors who were unaware of his relationship with Stein), my conclusion is that there was no breach of journalistic ethics. It is not clear where the line should be drawn, however.

A more troubling aspect of this case is Hess's having to resort to using Stein to advocate for elimination of profit. Hess was a trustworthy and veteran reporter who had reported on this scandal for ten months. He had become an expert on the nursing home industry. And yet, when the time came for a solution to be discussed, he was unable to either advocate or strongly urge a solution. Even the *Times*'s "news analysis" format would not allow Hess to propose a solution. In that format, he was still limited to balancing alternatives suggested by others. How could he objectively continue to report if he had taken a side? So, Hess was limited to reporting what others said—Abram for reform and Stein for the elimination of profit—and the public would then have to pick a solution.... In the spring of 1975, the public needed more than stories that were the sum of opposing viewpoints. They needed to be told what one reporter had found over ten months of constant research and interviewing, research that showed a historical pattern and led to certain logical conclusions. The public needed Hess's conclusions, but objectivity—even as practiced by an activist reporter—would not allow reportorial conclusions. Hess did all he could, but it was, as he said, not all he hoped for.

Conclusions and Discussion

When John Hess began his investigation in 1974, nursing home problems were not on the public's agenda. By the time Hess finished exposing corruption in the spring of 1975, reformers ranging from the Gray Panthers to the U.S. Senate were seeking change. Hess was a catalyst, prompting reform to begin and then reporting on the efforts of the reformers. This marriage of reform and journalism occurred only because Hess used the credibility and rules of objectivity in an activist fashion to reveal corruption and force a government response....

The fact that objectivity forces reporters to maintain some measure of political neutrality ensures that the public receives reasonably unbiased news and information.[35] Objectivity, however, also has a stifling effect on the reporter's ability to show the truth behind the facts....

Notes

1. Hess was nominated for the Pulitzer Prize in local special reporting....
   Historian Bruce Vladeck calls the New York City scandal the nation's worst in
   Unloving Care: The Nursing Home Tragedy (New York: Basic Books, 1980), 4.
2. ... This is not an essay on the effects of Hess's work. However, I believe that,
   at the least, as a New York official said, "the chance for adoption of reform was
   enhanced ... by *The New York Times* investigation of the nursing home
   industry." Hess, "State Denounces Nursing Home Deals as Costing State
   Medicaid Millions," Oct. 31, 1974, p. 45. Unless otherwise noted, all
   subsequent Hess articles are from *The New York Times*.
3. Mary Mendelsohn, *Tender Loving Greed* (New York: Alfred A. Knopf, 1974)
   and Donn Pearce, *Dying in the Sun* (New York: Charterhouse, 1974).
4. Hess, "Care of the Aged Poor a Growing Scandal," Oct. 7, 1974, pp. 1, 40.
5. Hess, "Nursing Homes Use a Variety of Fiscal Ruses to Lift Profits Above the
   10% Allowed by Law," Oct. 8, 1974, p. 48. "Two Grand Juries Indict
   Hollander," July 3, 1975, pp. 1, 12.

6. Hess, "Nursing Homes Here Linked by Interlocking Leadership," Oct. 9, 1974, p. 85. The charges against Bergman are detailed in Hess, "Bergman and Son Are Indicted Here in Medicaid Fraud," Aug. 6, 1975, pp. 1, 70.

7. Hess, "Alternatives Seen to Nursing Homes for Aged Infirm," Oct. 10, 1974, p. 42.

8. One health department official said, "The media created a climate more receptive to enforcement. . . . It gave us the basis for doing what we perhaps wanted to do and what we should have been doing." Hess, "Nursing Homes Face State Fines," June 4, 1975, p. 22.

9. Interview with Hess.

10. Hess, "Two State Inquiries Ordered on Nursing Home Control," Oct. 17, 1974, p. 45.

11. Interview with Hess and with two former aides to the legislator, Andrew Stein.

12. Lincoln Steffens, *The Shame of the Cities* (New York: Hill and Wang, 1957).

13. Hess, "Nursing Home Promoters Get Political Helping Hand," Oct. 21, 1974, p. 23.

14. Interview with Hess.

15. Jack Newfield, "The Rabbi Exposed and Anti-Semitism," *The Education of Jack Newfield* (New York: St. Martin's Press, 1984), pp. 11, 13.

16. Hess, "'71 Memo Reports 3 State Officials Backed Bergman," Jan. 1, 1975, pp. 1, 75.

17. "Lefkowitz Challenged Memo Linking Him to Bergman," Jan. 4, 1975, p. 46, and "Files Detail Political Help in Bergman Medicaid Rise," Jan. 14, 1975, p. 31.

18. Hess, "Opinions on Bergman as Diverse as His Background," Jan. 21, 1975, p. 20.

19. The defamation lawsuit filed on Jan. 10 charged that Hess, Assemblyman Stein, and an assistant state attorney general had conspired to deprive Bergman of his constitutional rights by an "unremitting barrage" of false reports to the public. The lawsuit was eventually dismissed by a federal judge as having no merit. Hess feared that if it went to trial he would be asked to reveal confidential sources of information.

20. Hess, "Bergman Labels All Allegations as False," Jan. 22, 1975, pp. 1, 44.

21. Interview with Hess. Also see Hess, "Bergman Certified Worth Was Almost $24-million," Jan. 23, 1975, pp. 1, 23.

22. Interviews with Hess and two former Stein staff members who requested anonymity.

23. Interview with two *Times* editors who requested anonymity.

24. Hess, "State Denounces Nursing-Home Deals as Costing State and Medicaid Millions," Oct. 31, 1974, p. 45, and "A 'Cabal' of Real Estate Deals Adds to Nursing Home Profits," Nov. 5, 1974, p. 39.

25. Hess, "The Scandal of Care for the Old," Section 4, Jan. 12, 1975, p. 6.

26. Gaye Tuchman, "Objectivity as a Strategic Ritual: An Examination of a Newspaperman's Notion of Objectivity, *American Journal of Sociology* 77 (No. 4, January, 1972), 668.

27. "Stein for Phasing Out Profit-Making Nursing Homes," Feb. 26, 1975, p. 22.
28. Hess, "Rockefeller Faces 2 State Inquiries," March 24, 1975, p. 32.
29. Hess, "Abram Denounces Failures on Aged," April 9, 1975, p. 30.
30. Hess, "Change Is Pressed on Nursing Homes," April 12, 1975, p. 31.
31. Hess, "Stein Criticizes Abram Unit Proposals," May 4, 1975, p. 39; "Reform Plans for Nursing Homes Scored," May 17, 1975, p. 31.
32. Morris Abram of the Moreland Act Commission made this point to Hess in an interview, "Abram Denounces Failure on Aged," April 9, 1975, p. 30, and repeated it in a cover letter in a commission report, *Long Term Care Regulation: Past Lapses, Future Prospects, A Summary Report* (New York: The Commission: 1976).
33. Hess, "Nursing Homes Show Progress," Jan. 12, 1976, p. 27.
34. Hess, "State Panel, in an Unannounced Visit to Nursing Home, Finds Violations," Nov. 22, 1974, p. 78.
35. Despite the merits of objectivity, it is under attack as conservative and reinforcing of the status quo. This view can be found in Gaye Tuchman, *Making News: A Study in the Construction of Reality* (New York: The Free Press, 1978); W. Lance Bennett, *News: The Politics of Illusion* (New York: Longman, 1983); and Todd Gitlin, *The Whole World is Watching* (Berkeley: University of California Press, 1980).

31

ELITE IDEOLOGY AND RISK PERCEPTION IN NUCLEAR ENERGY POLICY

Stanley Rothman and S. Robert Lichter

Editor's Note

In their book The Media Elite: America's New Powerbrokers, *published in 1986, Stanley Rothman and S. Robert Lichter claim that the media elites have a very liberal orientation on many controversial social and political issues and that this orientation is reflected in their stories. One of these issues is nuclear energy generation. In the essay presented here, Rothman and Lichter discuss why news stories have described nuclear energy as far more risky than have the reports by health and physical scientists. The authors explain this discrepancy by pointing to the predispositions and ideologies of media elites and their reliance on sources that share their pessimistic views. Others believe that the scientists have been overly optimistic because they want to protect their business interests.*

Rothman and Lichter attribute the decline in public and governmental support for nuclear ventures to negative media stories in the U.S. press. Given the climate of apprehension about the safety of nuclear energy created by these stories, the industry has withered in the United States, while it remains vital in Europe and other foreign sites. Rothman and Lichter's views provide an interesting contrast to Timothy W. Luke's argument in Part VI. Luke contends that government sources, rather than media elites, shaped the images of the Chernobyl nuclear disaster, thereby ensuring the survival of the nuclear power industry.

Rothman is Mary Huggins Gamble Professor of Government at Smith College and director of its Center for the Study of Social and Political Change. Lichter is co-director of the Center for Media and Public Affairs in Washington, D.C., and teaches at The George Washington University. The selection comes from "Elite Ideology and Risk Perception in Nuclear Energy Policy," American Political Science Review *81:2 (June 1987): 383-404. Several tables and all notes have been omitted.*

Nuclear Energy, Ideology, and the Perception of Risk

In the 1950s, the vast majority of U.S. citizens supported the development of nuclear energy ("Opinion Roundup" 1979, 23). Today a substantial majority opposes the building of new nuclear plants. Moreover, opposition is strongest among the most articulate and politically active segments of the population. Cost overruns and the abandonment of many partially completed nuclear facilities in the United States have probably played a role in the development of negative attitudes among various leadership groups. Nevertheless, for the average person, fears about the safety are far more important (Inglehart 1984). The meltdown at Chernobyl in the Soviet Union has accentuated such fears to the point where nuclear development is not, at this time, a viable energy option in the United States.

The view that nuclear plants are unsafe is shared by a significant number of citizens in positions of social influence or responsibility. For the past several years, we have been surveying various leadership groups in the United States, including national-media journalists, science journalists, military leaders, congressional staff, partners in top corporate-law firms, creators of television and motion picture entertainment, high-level government bureaucrats, and public-interest-group leaders. The journalists were surveyed in 1979, although the follow-up questions on nuclear energy were administered in 1982. The remaining groups were sampled in 1982. The overall sample size for this analysis is 1,136 individuals. The samples were generally drawn randomly from each targeted group.

Respondents rated the safety of nuclear plants on a seven-point scale ranging from 1 (very unsafe) to 7 (very safe). We characterized scores of 5 or higher as exhibiting relative confidence in the safety of nuclear plants. The results (see Table 31-1) indicate considerable variation among the groups sampled. Thirty-seven percent of the journalists interviewed consider nuclear plants to be safe, as do only 13% of the television-entertainment elite, 14% of the motion-picture elite, and 6% of public-interest-group leaders. By contrast, 49% of the corporate lawyers believe nuclear plants are safe, as do 52% of top-level federal bureaucrats and 86% of military leaders.

How do these diverse estimates of nuclear safety accord with the scientific community's own evaluations? To find out, we sampled, in 1980, one thousand scientists drawn randomly from *American Men and Women of Science (AMWS)* supplemented by another sample of three hundred scientists who work in energy-related fields. We defined the latter group broadly, including persons in fields such as atmospheric chemistry, solar energy, conservation, and ecology. In all, we included 71 disciplines in our energy-expert subsample. In our smaller nuclear-energy-expert sample, we included experts working in such nuclear-related fields as radiological health

Table 31-1   Are Nuclear Plants Safe?

Sample groups	Percentage rating nuclear plant safety 5 or higher*	Sample size
Total leadership sample	36.8	1,203
Bureaucrats	52.0	199
Congressional aides	39.1	132
Lawyers	48.6	149
Media	36.5	156
Journalists at *New York Times* and *Washington Post*	29.4	51
Journalists at TV networks	30.6	49
Military	86.0	152
Movies	14.3	90
Public interest	6.4	154
TV, Hollywood	12.5	103
Total scientists sample	60.2	925
Energy experts	75.8	279
Nuclear-energy experts	98.7	72

* 1 = very unsafe; 7 = very safe.

and radiation genetics, as well as nuclear engineers and physicists. Seventy-four percent of the scientists sampled returned usable questionnaires.

Scientists, especially those in energy-related fields, regard nuclear energy as a necessary and relatively benign source of energy. Ninety percent of the random sample and 95% of the energy-expert sample believe that we should proceed with the development of nuclear energy. Seventy-six percent of the energy-expert sample and 99% of the nuclear-energy-expert sample believe nuclear plants to be safe....

We administered a short form of the survey to the same respondents in 1985 with almost exactly the same results. A second replication of our study in Germany [1986] reveals that German scientists agree with their U.S. counterparts (Institut für Demoskopie 1985). Engineers in energy-related fields are even more supportive of nuclear energy than are scientists (Lichter et al. 1986)....

How does one explain the wide differences in safety estimates among the various nonscientific leadership groups we have studied? ...

Nuclear Energy: Scientists Versus the Media

... One would, ... expect the public and various leadership groups to follow the lead of the scientific community on this issue. In fact the public is relatively unaware of the views of the scientific community. In a 1984 national poll, almost 6 out of 10 respondents expressed the belief that those scientists who are energy experts are evenly split as to the safety of nuclear energy or consider nuclear energy unsafe (Unpublished Cambridge Reports, February 1984).

The general public is not alone in these views. Most of the elite groups in our sample seriously underestimate scientific support for nuclear energy. For example, 70% of television producers, writers, and directors believe that fewer than 65% of those scientists who are energy experts support the further development of nuclear energy. Indeed, like the general public, most of the leadership groups we studied perceive energy experts as sharply divided on the issues of nuclear energy. And this belief is associated with their views of nuclear safety. . . .

. . . Part of the reason for erroneous public perceptions of the views of the scientific community on nuclear energy lies with the manner in which information about those views is communicated to the public by scientists themselves. The scientific community as a whole does not communicate with the general public. Rather, a somewhat smaller group of more visible scientists does most of the communicating (Goodell 1977), and this group seems skewed toward the antinuclear argument.

Our survey asked scientists both how many articles they had published in professional peer-reviewed journals and how many articles they had published on science policy questions for the more general public. . . .

On the one hand, 57% of our entire sample and 59% of our pronuclear sample had published more than 10 articles in academic or professional journals, compared to only 41% of the very antinuclear scientists. On the other hand, while only 11% of all scientists and 13% of highly pronuclear scientists have published articles on science policy in popular journals, the figure for antinuclear scientists is 36%.

More significantly, among scientists who have published on nuclear energy in professional journals, only 1 out of 10 believes that the possibility of an accidental release of radioactivity from reactors is a very serious problem. In contrast, among those who have published on nuclear energy only in popular journals, 4 out of 10 hold this view. Only 1.5 out of 10 in the professional-journal group believe that there are serious problems with the safety systems of nuclear plants, compared with 7 out of 10 in the popular-journal group. Lastly, more than 9 out of 10 in the professional-journal group are reasonably or very sure that we now possess the knowledge to solve the problems of nuclear energy, as against only 6 out of 10 in the popular-journal group. All these differences are statistically significant.

The publicly oriented group is small. One hundred and twenty scientists in our sample have published on nuclear energy. Of these, only 10 have written solely for popular journals. However, this suggests that between

Table 31-2   Support for Nuclear Energy Among Scientists and Leading Journals

Leadership groups	Score on nuclear support scale*	Number of cases
Nuclear experts	7.86	72
Energy experts	5.10	279
All scientists	3.34	741
Science journalists	1.30	42
Prestige-press journalists	1.16	150
Science journalists at *New York Times, Washington Post,* TV networks	.47	15
TV reporters and producers	−1.89	18
Public television journalists	−3.25	24

* Scores range from −9 to +9.

one and two thousand scientists listed in AMWS had written articles on nuclear energy for the general public without ever submitting their ideas to review by professional peers.

The relative skepticism toward nuclear energy of scientists who write only in popular journals may help explain why the public has a distorted view of the attitudes of the scientific community. However, this cannot be the full story. Given the absolute numbers, many more pronuclear than antinuclear scientists have published articles in popular journals. It is possible that antinuclear scientists publish in larger circulation periodicals, but our data point to another factor.

Elite journalists, including leading science journalists, are skeptical of nuclear energy. The most skeptical journalists of all are television commentators. On a "nuclear-support" scale, constructed from several survey items whose scores range from -9 to +9, scientists in energy-related fields score 5.10, while television reporters and commentators score -1.89 (see Table 31-2). Journalists employed by the national media are politically liberal, and, as with other groups, their political ideology correlates with skepticism about the safety of nuclear energy. Most importantly, these attitudes seem to be reflected in news coverage. We analyzed news coverage of nuclear safety from 1970 through 1983 in the *New York Times*, the three major news magazines (*Time, Newsweek,* and *U.S. News*), and the three commercial television networks (ABC, NBC, and CBS).

This content analysis of national media coverage found that a distinct antinuclear tilt started in the early 1970s on television and the late 1970s in print. Overall, the major print and broadcast outlets analyzed failed to report the views of the scientific community accurately. Antinu-

Table 31-3   Media Coverage of Nuclear Safety, 1970-1983 (percent)

Content	New York Times	News magazines	Television
Story slant			
Pronuclear	7	25	17
Antinuclear	10	46	42
Neutral/balanced	83	29	41
Safety judgement			
Positive	45	45	34
Negative	55	55	66
Expert sources cited			
Pronuclear	9	17	11
Antinuclear	7	40	62
Neutral/balanced	84	43	27
Number of stories	486	213	582

Note: 10% random sample for New York Times, full universe for magazines, 50% sample for television.

clear stories outnumbered pronuclear stories by two to one on television and in news magazines. Judgments of particular safety issues were primarily negative at all outlets, reaching a two to one margin on television. Among nuclear experts cited in news stories, critics outnumbered supporters by more than two to one in news magazines and five to one on television (see Table 31-3 and Lichter, Rothman, and Lichter 1986).

Additional evidence is available from other sources. The Media Institute found that antinuclear experts and groups appeared on prime-time TV newscasts during the 1970s about twice as often as pronuclear sources (Media Institute 1979). By far the most widely quoted "independent expert" source on nuclear energy on television newscasts during the period of the study was the Union of Concerned Scientists (UCS). The UCS has been very critical of nuclear energy.

The individual "expert" who received the most television exposure during the period of the Media Institute study was Ralph Nader, and the only academic scientific expert quoted in the aftermath of Three Mile Island was Dr. Ernest Sternglass, a strongly antinuclear radiologist. Neither in the eleven-year period before Three Mile Island nor during the month after were pronuclear outside experts among the 10 top-quoted sources. The only pronuclear sources in the top 10 were spokesmen for utility companies and the nuclear industry. . . . [T]he public credibility of such organizations is quite low.

As our data indicate, many independent pronuclear scientists are available. Some of them, like Hans Bethe, are both well known and active in their support of nuclear energy. The views of such people would have been far more representative of the scientific community than those of Dr. Sternglass.

Physicist Bernard Cohen recently conducted a poll of academics in the radiation health field. He found that 91% believe that public fears of radiation are excessive, and about the same proportion believe that television and the press exaggerate its dangers. When asked to evaluate the scientific credibility of 19 scientists who write or speak about radiation, these experts gave Dr. Sternglass their lowest rating (14 on a scale ranging from 1 to 100) (Cohen 1983, 258-62).

It is conceivable that antinuclear scientists are more likely to seek out the media than are pronuclear scientists. However, we found that pronuclear scientists are no more likely to refuse to be interviewed by journalists than are their antinuclear counterparts. It seems equally likely, therefore, that journalists tend to seek out antinuclear scientists. Indeed, the elite journalists we surveyed were asked to list information sources they considered reliable on nuclear energy. They selected more antinuclear than pronuclear sources by a margin of over three to two (Lichter, Rothman, and Lichter 1986).

. . . [J]ournalists are probably no different from anyone else in that, to help them understand issues that are both controversial and highly technical, they seek out sources they trust. And people tend to trust "experts" who share their own social outlooks.

During the 1950s' fluoridation controversy, the leading national media deferred to the views of the scientific establishment in ways that they no longer do. Certainly, reporters then were just as interested in disaster as they are now, and the science staffs of television or newspapers were neither larger nor better-trained than they are today. Today, however, journalists regard "antiestablishment" scientists as rather more trustworthy than mainstream scientists (Goodfield 1981).

It is hard to know to what extent media coverage actually influences the views of the larger public. In the recent past, most academic commentators have suggested that this influence is minimal. However, more recently, scholars such as Elizabeth Noelle-Neumann (1973) in Germany and Michael Robinson (1976) and Benjamin Page (Page, Shapiro, and Dempsey 1984) in the United States have begun to build an impressive case on the other side.

It is not unreasonable to ascribe erroneous elite and popular perceptions of scientists' nuclear-energy views at least partly to media coverage, and other evidence adds to the plausibility of this conjecture.

References

Cohen, Bernard. 1983. *Before It's Too Late: A Scientist's Case for Nuclear Energy.* New York: Plenum Press.

Goodell, Rae. 1977. *The Visible Scientists.* Boston: Little, Brown.

Goodfield, June. 1981. *Reflections on Science and the Media.* New York: American Association for the Advancement of Science.

Inglehart, Ronald. 1984. The Fear of Living Dangerously: Public Attitudes toward Nuclear Power. *Public Opinion* 6:41-44.

Lichter, S. Robert, Stanley Rothman, and Linda Lichter. 1986. *The Media Elite.* Bethesda, MD: Adler and Adler.

Lichter, S. Robert, Stanley Rothman, Robert Rycroft, and Linda Lichter. *Nuclear News.* 1986. Washington, D.C.: Center for Media and Public Affairs.

Noelle-Neumann, Elisabeth. 1973. Return of the Concept of a Powerful Mass Media. *Studies of Broadcasting* 9:67-112.

Opinion Roundup. 1979. *Public Opinion* 2:23-24.

Page, Benjamin I., Robert Y. Shapiro, and Glen R. Dempsey. 1984. Television News and Changes in Americans' Policy Preferences. Paper presented at the annual meeting of the Midwest Political Science Association, Chicago.

Robinson, Michael. 1976. Public Affairs Television and the Growth of Political Malaise. *American Political Science Review* 70:409-32.

VI

REGULATING AND MANIPULATING MEDIA EFFECTS

Although the scholarly community remains engaged in lively debate about the potency of mass media, governments and people everywhere treat the media as powerful political actors. Governments try to make sure that news stories will not endanger national interests or work at cross-purposes with established authorities. Public and private officials try to manipulate the news so that stories favor their causes.

This part begins with a look at the political forces that come into play in the United States when policies designed to control media power are contemplated and adopted. Since the First Amendment to the U.S. Constitution prohibits Congress from making any "law abridging the freedom of the press," many people wrongly believe that all U.S. media are free from government control. It is true that print media enjoy ample, although not unlimited, freedom to support or sabotage governmental policies and philosophies. They also can grant or deny publicity to various interest groups and viewpoints as they see fit.

The situation is quite different for the broadcast media, however. Government regulations substantially curtail the freedom of entrepreneurs in broadcast media enterprises to run their businesses as they please, although legislators and regulatory commissions explicitly deny the intent to control news content. Erwin G. Krasnow, Lawrence D. Longley, and Herbert A. Terry describe how government control invariably has thrust the broadcast media into the thick of political controversy. Their essay includes a model of the patterns of interaction among the various participants in broadcast policy making.

How free from government control are American media? A discussion of government regulation of the broadcast media may leave the impression that freedom is more of a myth than a reality. But everything in life is relative. The media and First Amendment purists may complain about government controls, but these controls are far lighter in the United States than elsewhere. Harold Evans makes that quite clear in his discussion of government controls of the press in Britain. Americans, he warns, must protect their prized status by guarding against further restriction of press liberties.

The next two essays detail how government officials try to manipulate the media. Martin Linsky describes the successful efforts of the U.S. Postal Service to generate news stories in support of postal reforms opposed by powerful interest groups. Linsky's research has convinced him that efforts to win favorable publicity are absolutely essential to effective governance. Timothy W. Luke analyzes the successful efforts of the United States, the Soviet Union, several European countries, and several nuclear power interest groups to influence the media images about a major nuclear disaster in the Soviet Union. His essay illustrates how political reality, more often than not, is created by public officials rather than by newspeople.

Issues of media control are of particular concern to foreign nations that worry about the images presented by the American press. Third world governments have claimed that controls are needed to curb the deleterious influence of Western media on third world people and politics. The essay by René Jean Ravault undermines the plea for controls by arguing that third world complaints are unjustified because they are based on the unscientific assumption of automatic media effects.

In the final selection Jarol B. Manheim focuses on communication strategies used by foreign countries that seek to control their images in the American press. Such efforts to manipulate American media are often successful because astute public relations practitioners know how to attract or discourage media coverage. Their job is particularly easy when news about foreign countries is involved. American journalists are eager to get potentially expensive news cheaply from foreign sources and often lack the expertise to judge these stories critically.

32

THE POLITICS OF BROADCAST REGULATION

Erwin G. Krasnow, Lawrence D. Longley, and Herbert A. Terry

Editor's Note

The authors of this selection discuss the major factors that shape broadcast regulation and deregulation. Technological changes are occurring at a dizzying pace, but in Congress and the executive branch it is still "politics as usual." Despite mounting pressures to scrap the Federal Communications Act of 1934, legislation tailored to modern technology and developments has not passed Congress.

One major policy issue that has made passage of a new act difficult is broadcast media regulation. Television and radio have been regulated in the past for technical reasons and because it was feared that a scarcity of broadcast channels would prevent vigorous competition. Technology has changed so that there is now more competition among broadcast media than among daily newspapers, which are unregulated. Radio has been largely deregulated, but pressure to continue television regulation remains strong because the power of the medium over the public's thinking seems awesome to many people.

If regulation continues, several existing rules need reexamination because they have proved unworkable or because they have had highly undesirable side effects. The controversy surrounding these changes ensures that the politics of broadcast regulation will continue to be exciting. The political battles yet to come will continue to provide excellent insights into the interaction of media institutions with their political environment.

At the time of writing, Erwin G. Krasnow was a communications lawyer serving the National Association of Broadcasters as senior vice president and general counsel. Lawrence D. Longley was a professor of government at

381

Lawrence University, specializing in interest group politics. Herbert A. Terry,
who has been affiliated with the National Citizens Committee on Broadcasting,
was teaching telecommunications at Indiana University. The selection is from
The Politics of Broadcast Regulation, *3d ed. (New York: St. Martin's Press,*
1982).

The Historical Context of Broadcast Regulation

Broadcast regulation, like broadcasting itself, has a history spanning just
over a half-century. There is more constancy, both substantively and struc-
turally, to that history than one might expect for so dynamic a field. For
example, the basic statute under which the FCC currently operates, the
Communications Act of 1934, is fundamentally identical to the legislative
charter given to the Federal Radio Commission in 1927. The process that
produced the 1927 and 1934 acts in fact displayed many features that
characterize the regulatory process today. Just like today, the creation of
the legislative framework involved many parties—indeed, almost the same
parties as those of the 1980s. Like today, the result was compromise—
compromise that continued to be susceptible to reconsideration and re-
interpretation. . . .

Several aspects of the early history of broadcast regulation deserve emphasis. Five key participants emerged, themselves giving rise to a sixth,
the Federal Radio Commission and its successor, the FCC. The broadcast
industry was involved in the genesis of broadcast regulation. Self-regula-
tion was attempted but proved inadequate. After that, the industry worked
actively with the executive and legislative branches of government to
shape what was viewed as legislation required to eliminate audio chaos.
Also involved from the beginning were the courts. . . . The public was involved as well, its complaints about deteriorating radio service helping advance radio legislation on Congress's agenda by 1927.

Congress and the executive branch of government are the two remaining
participant groups. . . . Disputes between the president and Congress are
reflected in the "temporary" nature of the FRC and the continuing interaction today between the president and Congress whenever an FCC member is nominated and subjected to the confirmation process. When Secretary of Commerce Hoover's regulatory activities were blocked by the
courts, the salvation of American broadcasting lay with Congress. When
Congress *did* act to establish a regulatory agency, the agency's existence
and financing were subjected to yearly congressional consideration.[1] By
giving the FRC limited financial and technical resources, Congress effectively ensured the Commission's dependence on congressional good will
and kept a firm grip on this "independent" regulatory agency.

A final distinctive feature of the federal government's early regulation of broadcast stations was the focus on licensing as a primary regulatory tool. . . . The strong emphasis on the FCC's licensing role results in part from the fact that Congress did not expressly give the Commission the power to regulate the rates or profits of broadcast stations.[2] It predetermined that there would be strongly fought battles over several aspects of licensing in the future: Should the "traffic cop" review such things as choices of content in making licensing decisions? What, in general, would be both the process and standards for getting licenses renewed? . . .

Taylor Branch has divided government agencies into two categories: "deliver the mail" and "Holy Grail." "Deliver the mail" agencies perform neutral, mechanical, logistical functions; they send out Social Security checks, procure supplies—or deliver the mail. "Holy Grail" agencies, on the other hand, are given the more controversial and difficult role of achieving some grand, moral, civilizing goal. The Federal Radio Commission came into being primarily to "deliver the mail"—to act as a traffic cop of the airwaves. But both the FRC and the FCC had a vague Holy Grail clause written into their charters: the requirement that they uphold the "public interest, convenience and necessity." This vague but also often useful congressional mandate is key to understanding today's conflicts over broadcast regulation. . . .

Former FCC Chairman Newton Minow has commented that, starting with the Radio Act of 1927, the phrase "public interest, convenience and necessity" has provided the battleground for broadcasting's regulatory debate.[3] Congress's reason for including such a phrase was clear: the courts, interpreting the Radio Act of 1912 as a narrow statute, had said that the secretary of commerce could not create additional rules or regulations beyond that act's terms. This left Hoover unable to control rapidly changing technologies. The public interest notion in the 1927 and 1934 acts was intended to let the regulatory agency create new rules, regulations, and standards as required to meet new conditions. Congress clearly hoped to create an act more durable than the Radio Act of 1912. That plan has been at least somewhat successful as it was not until about 1976 that Congress seriously began to consider a major change in its 1934 handiwork. . . .

The meaning of the phrase, however, is extremely elusive. Although many scholars have attempted to define the public interest in normative or empirical terms, their definitions have added little to an understanding of the real relevance of this concept to the regulatory process. One scholar, after analyzing the literature on the public interest, created a typology for varying definitions of the term, but in the end he decided not to "argue for adoption of a single definition, preferring instead to categorize ways in which the phrase may be used. Different circumstances . . . may employ different usages." [4] . . .

Besides providing flexibility to adapt to changing conditions, the concept of the public interest is important to the regulation of broadcasting in another sense. A generalized public belief even in an undefined public interest increases the likelihood that policies will be accepted as authoritative. The acceptance of a concept of the public interest may thus become an important support for the regulation of broadcasting and for the making of authoritative rules and policies toward this end.[5] For this reason the courts traditionally have given the FCC wide latitude in determining what constitutes the public interest. As the U.S. Supreme Court noted in 1981:

> Our opinions have repeatedly emphasized that the Commission's judgment regarding how the public interest is best served is entitled to substantial judicial deference. . . . The Commission's implementation of the public interest standard, when based on a rational weighing of competing policies, is not to be set aside . . . for "the weighing of policies under the public interest standard is a task that Congress has delegated to the Commission in the first instance." [6]

Judge E. Barrett Prettyman once expanded upon the reasons for such deference:

> It is also true that the Commission's view of what is best may change from time to time. Commissions themselves change, underlying philosophies differ, and experience often dictates change. Two diametrically opposite schools of thought in respect to the public welfare may both be rational; e.g., both free trade and protective tariff are rational positions. All such matters are for the Congress and the executive and their agencies. They are political in the high sense of that abused term.[7]

Despite the usefulness of the public interest concept in keeping up with changing means of communications and the general tendency of the courts to defer to the FCC's decisions, conflicts over the meaning of the public interest have been recurrent in broadcast history. On occasion, the vague statutory mandate to look out for the public interest has hampered the development of coherent public policy since Congress (or influential members of Congress) can always declare, "That is not what we meant by the public interest." [8] Few independent regulatory commissions have had to operate under such a broad grant of power with so few substantive guidelines. Rather than encouraging greater freedom of action, vagueness in delegated power may serve to limit an agency's independence and freedom to act as it sees fit. As Pendleton Herring put it, "Administrators cannot be given the responsibilities of statesmen without incurring likewise the tribulations of politicians." [9] . . .

Unresolved Regulatory Problems

. . . Disputes concerning legal prescriptions imposed by the Communications Act often have centered on recurring value conflicts—assumptions about what ought or ought not to be done. One such question is the extent to which broadcasting should pursue social as well as economic and technical goals. The emphasis on the social responsibilities of licensees rests on the view that "the air belongs to the public, not to the industry" since Congress provided in Section 301 of the Communications Act that "no . . . license shall be construed to create any right, beyond the terms, conditions, and periods of the license." . . . Some of these rules and policies require broadcasters to present, or refrain from presenting, content contrary to what they would choose to do on their own. How far the FCC may go in the direct, or indirect, regulation of content without violating either the Communications Act's own prohibition in Section 326 against censorship or the First Amendment to the U.S. Constitution remains unsettled. Section 326 of the Communications Act states:

> Nothing in this Act shall be understood or construed to give the Commission the power of censorship over the radio communications or signals transmitted by any radio station, and no regulation or condition shall be promulgated or fixed by the Commission which shall interfere with the right of free speech by means of radio communications.

However, as we noted above, in the same act Congress also directs the Commission to regulate "in the public interest, convenience and necessity." [10] Using that standard, the Commission has promulgated many rules and policies governing broadcast programming that would be regarded by the courts as unlawful censorship of the print media. Early court cases, however, determined that the FCC did not have to ignore content, that it could consider it without necessarily engaging in censorship;[11] later court cases have perpetuated the view that government supervision of broadcast content is somehow more acceptable than review of print.[12] Clearly broadcasting continues to be plagued by divergent views of how to balance freedom with achieving socially desired and responsible service, while still not engaging in censorship.

Complicating this controversy is the conflict between First Amendment provisions guaranteeing the right of broadcasters, like other media owners and operators, to be free of government control over the content of programming and First Amendment theories that have been developed exclusively for broadcasting and that hold the rights of listeners and viewers to receive information to be "paramount" over the rights of broadcasters.[13] The theory is that in the "scarce" medium of broadcasting, some affirmative government intervention concerning content may be needed to ensure

that the public hears diverse ideas and viewpoints. J. Skelly Wright, a
judge of the U.S. Court of Appeals, has commented:

> [In] some areas of the law it is easy to tell the good guys from the bad guys. . . .
> In the current debate over the broadcast media and the First Amendment . . .
> each debater claims to be the real protector of the First Amendment, and the
> analytical problems are much more difficult than in ordinary constitutional
> adjudication. . . . The answers are not easy.[14]

These colliding statutory ground rules governing the freedom and obligations of broadcasters have been melded into one of the law's most elas-
tic conceptions—the notion of a "public trustee."[15] The FCC views a
broadcast license as a "trust," with the public as "beneficiary" and the
broadcaster as "public trustee." The public trustee concept is a natural
consequence of the conflicting statutory goals of private use and regulated
allocation of spectrum space. Congress gave the FCC the right to choose
among various candidates for commercial broadcast licenses and left it up
to the Commission to find a justification for providing a fortunate few with
the use of a valuable scarce resource at no cost. Legal scholar Benno
Schmidt, Jr., thinks the public trustee concept was designed to dull the
horns of the FCC's dilemma: to give away valuable spectrum space, with
no strings attached, would pose stubborn problems of justification.

. . . One option exercised by the FCC to reduce controversy over its activities has been to substitute "content-neutral" or "structural" policies for
policies that involve direct review of content. . . . As an alternative to . . .
content regulation the FCC can attempt to structure the broadcast marketplace so that there are many stations with different owners and assume
thereby that diversity of opinion will result naturally and without direct
government review. Many FCC rules and policies—for example, the regulation of station ownership patterns—have been of this type. They do not,
on their surface, look normative but are in fact examples of content-neutral
means of achieving social objectives. . . .

. . . Throughout its history the FCC has had to wrestle with new problems
brought about by such technical developments as network broadcasting, FM
broadcasting, VHF and UHF telecasting, color television, cable television,
direct broadcast satellites (DBS), multipoint distribution services (MDS),
and other new or modified systems. The making of public policy in each of
these areas goes far beyond resolving technical issues. Technical issues frequently disguise what actually are economic interests vying for control of
some segment of broadcasting and related markets. The politics of broadcasting are thus present in technical as well as social controversies.

. . . [T]he FCC, like other regulatory bodies, has been subjected to considerable criticism concerning its inability to cope with change—the most

common charge being that it is concerned mainly with preserving the status quo and with favoring the well-established broadcast services. . . .

An agency's ability to respond to and foster technological change is largely a matter of how dependent the agency is on dominant industry factions—the "haves" as opposed to the "have nots." Throughout its history the FCC has lacked sufficient skilled personnel and funds to weigh the merits of new technology and has been forced to rely on outside advice and technical opinion. When faced with complex technical questions, the Commission often has taken the easy road of finding in favor of the "haves" over the "have nots." Frequently, the result is delay in the development of these technologies. . . . Throughout most of its history, the Commission (usually with the support of the "haves") sought to limit the growth of technology rather than use technological innovations as correctives to problems. Beginning in the late 1970s, however, the FCC has adopted policies designed to foster technological growth as a way of promoting greater competition in the marketplace and a greater diversity of services.

The ability of a regulatory commission to inhibit or to promote a technical innovation that challenges the regulated (and sometimes sheltered) industry is a measure of the vitality and strength of that agency. . . . [T]he FCC has not been highly successful at giving birth to new communications services. At times, in fact, it has almost destroyed them. These failures result, at least in part, from the highly political environment in which the FCC operates. . . .

Broadcast Regulation: An Analytic Review

Broadcast regulation . . . is shaped by six primary determiners—the FCC, the industry, citizen groups, the courts, the White House, and Congress. In addition there are miscellaneous participants—the Federal Trade Commission or the Commission on Civil Rights, for example—sometimes involved in specific broadcast-related issues but whose participation in the regulatory process, while important, is less constant. . . . [T]he six primary determiners rarely can accomplish much by unilateral action. The president, for example, names members of the FCC but checks out potential appointees in advance with significant interest groups (the industry and, infrequently, citizen groups). In the end, the Senate must formally approve nominations. The determiners, in other words, interact with each other in a complex fashion. Often those interactions are as important as, or more important than, what the determiners do on their own. Any attempt to understand what goes on in broadcast regulation must explain regulation as the outcome of complex interaction patterns within a dynamic system. . . .

The politics of broadcast regulation can be seen in terms of an analytical framework or model we term the "broadcast policy-making system." Such a framework can be used both to understand the regulatory process and to suggest to scholars a conceptual orientation for work in this area.

As is the case with any model, the one we are suggesting is a simplification of reality. Yet to simplify is to streamline, to strip off surface complexities in order to show the essential elements of a system. . . .

Figure 32-1 represents the broadcast policy-making system. The six recurring participants in the regulatory process . . . are the authoritative decision-making agencies at the heart of the model. The figure also charts various channels of influence among these six participants. It is significant that there is no one pathway through the core of the broadcast policy-making system, and any one of the various routes necessarily involves many participants. The key to understanding the politics of broadcast regulation lies in simultaneously analyzing the individual participants and their interactions. . . . Although outside pressure, or "inputs," and the internal politics of each of the decision-making bodies can raise issues and define alternatives, it is the political relationships of, and interactions among, the six key determiners that are truly crucial to broadcast regulation.

Three of the principals (the White House, the courts, and citizen groups) usually play a less immediate, sustained, and direct role than the other three (the FCC, Congress, and the regulated industries). Thus, the primary channels of influence, information, and contact are traced among these three most significant determiners as the outer triangle in Figure 32-1.

The system produces policy dynamically. Policy decisions—which might be called "outputs"—emerge from the interaction of some or all of the participants. Although the need for policy decisions may sometimes be stimulated by parties outside the system—for example, by an action of the Federal Trade Commission—in most instances, the functioning of the system itself generates the need for still more policy decisions. In other words, although some policy decisions may have long lives, many remain accepted and unchanged only briefly: one day's policy outputs in this system commonly become the inputs for the next day's policy making.

The policy outputs of this system are varied. They include "public" policies such as FCC rules and regulations, final court actions, laws enacted by Congress, and executive orders. An example of legislation would be the statutory requirement . . . that all television sets sold after a certain date have UHF as well as VHF receiving capacity; an example of an agency decision would be the FCC's desire that incumbent broadcast station licensees should have preferred status, in renewal proceedings, over challengers for their licenses. . . . Outputs may even take the form of decisions

Figure 32-1: The Broadcast Policy-Making System

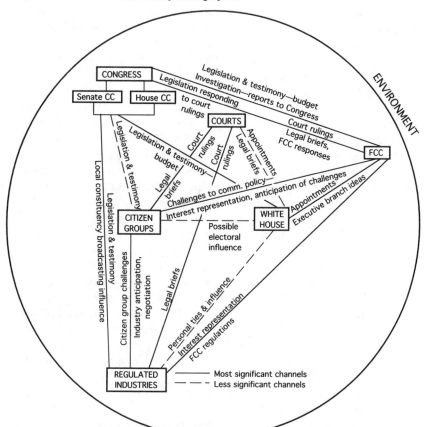

not to do something, exemplified by recent trends in "deregulation" such as the FCC decision not to supervise the number of commercials radio stations carry..., or its decision not to concern itself with the entertainment programming format those stations use.... In our model, policy outputs may even include many of the actions of the regulated industries, whose implementation of or operation under FCC rules and regulations or the Communications Act of 1934 is, in many instances, authoritative because it is unchallenged.

In most instances, such policy outputs (or authoritative decisions) bestow rewards or impose penalties on other affected interests. Reactions of those interests—or, occasionally, outside interests—stimulate the system to generate further policy output. They become, in effect, input back into the system. Some inputs are specific, such as a demand by a citizen group that a broadcast station not be permitted to change its format. Other inputs are exceedingly general, such as the mood that can be cast over an independent regulatory commission by a president or by the current public image of the agency. It is important to realize, too, that the system does more than merely respond to demands; it also molds political demands and policy preferences.

The system, of course, does not function in a vacuum. It operates in the context of an environment consisting of many factors . . . including the historical element of broadcast regulation, the basic technical and economic characteristics of broadcasting, and broad legal prescriptions. The environment outside the system also encompasses other factors, such as public attitudes toward broadcasting and government regulation and the actions of related systems—the Federal Trade Commission, for example—which may at times inspire and influence the broadcast policy-making system. It even includes actions and groups beyond the United States, for the spectrum is an international resource and U.S. broadcast networks and programs have a worldwide effect. In recent years, for example, U.S. policies toward spectrum allocation for radio and toward the location and function of communications satellites have had to be reconciled with the desires of our international neighbors. The United Nations Educational, Scientific and Cultural Organization (UNESCO) has debated policies toward a "new world information order" that, although perceived by third world nations to be important to their development, are seen by Western nations as antithetical to notions of press freedom. The major demands and supports—outputs and inputs—that determine what the system does, however, generally originate from within. . . .

One important feature of the broadcast policy-making system is that it is highly turbulent. Largely because communications is influenced by rapidly changing technology, few specific policy decisions are stable and long-lasting. The system is always responding to new or changed conditions, with consequent incessant interaction among its participants. The operation of the policy-making system in specific instances is inherently unique; each policy-making problem is likely to differ in important respects from all others. However, certain recurring patterns about the politics of broadcast regulation can be identified.[16]

1. *Participants seek conflicting goals from the process.* Pluralism and dispersion of power in policy making do not by themselves suggest that the process is inevitably a struggle for control or influence. Conceivably the participants in such a process could share certain perspectives concerning what is to be done. Such is rarely the case, however, in the

broadcast policy-making process. . . . [T]he gains of one set of participants are usually made at the cost of the interests of another. The
policy demands of different groups often conflict; they must usually
compete for scarce rewards.

2. *Participants have limited resources insufficient to continually dominate the
   policy-making process.* In a pluralistic complex such as that outlined in
   Figure 32-1, policy-making power tends to be divided. Although the
   FCC frequently initiates policy proposals, it lacks the ability to
   implement most of them single-handedly. To prevail, it must win
   significant support from other participants. Similarly, none of the other
   five participants has hierarchical control over the policy-making process,
   which is simply to say that nobody dominates the process consistently.
   In such a system policy making results from the agreement—or at least
   the acquiescence—of multiple participants, not from the domination of
   one. Coalitions of diverse participants work together and reward those
   belonging to them.

3. *Participants have unequal strengths in the struggle for control or influence.*
   Inequality among participants can arise because one party is inherently
   strong, cares more, or develops its potential more effectively. In the
   1970s, for example, citizen groups had considerably less strength than
   the Federal Communications Commission and the broadcast industry in
   their ability to influence policy concerning radio station format changes.
   Even when one federal court agreed with the views of a citizen group,
   another federal court—supported by the FCC and by broadcasters—
   prevailed. Favorable public opinion, legal symbols, congressional allies,
   and the like are all potential sources of strength that participants have
   access to in differing degrees and that they may use with varying
   success on different issues.

4. *The component subgroups of participant groups do not automatically agree on
   policy options.* Each of the six groups we have identified consists of many
   subgroups: citizen groups range from liberal to conservative; the FCC is
   organized into bureaus representing interests that may conflict, such as
   cable television and broadcasting; there is not one single court but,
   instead, a hierarchy of courts, and it is common for a superior court to
   overturn the actions of an inferior court; radio broadcasters may
   sometimes view issues differently than television broadcasters. Thus,
   while it is useful to refer to the six principal participants as if each was
   one, it is important to recognize that each group may be unable—or
   find it very difficult—to agree on a common objective or course of
   action.

5. *The process tends toward policy progression by small or incremental steps
   rather than massive change.* One means of minimizing opposition to a

policy initiative is to show its close relationship to existing and generally accepted policy. Frequently, earlier actions are cited to prove that the desired change is not unprecedented but only a logical continuation of past concerns and policies. One of the beauties of administrative law is that precedents usually can be found for almost any initiative. Although agencies are not as bound by precedent as are courts, they still hesitate to turn their backs on the past when it is pointed out to them. Such slow and gradual shifts in policy are not only strategic but probably inevitable, given the multiplicity of participants with conflicting goals, unequal strengths, and limited resources. Incrementalism tends to be at least a safe, if not necessarily the safest, course of action. As a result, however, the system is rarely bold or innovative and has a hard time responding to environmental pressures for massive change. . . .

6. *Legal and ideological symbols play a significant role in the process.* Throughout the evolution of policy a recurring theme of participants is the legal and ideological symbolism they may attach to a discussion of alternatives. In many instances policies are seen as threatening or protecting the "rights" of broadcasters or the "rights" of listeners and viewers, without refined and, most importantly, commonly agreed upon specification of the meaning of those concepts. Broadcast policy-making discussions can also become embroiled in arguments over stock, symbolic rhetoric such as "localism," the "public interest," "access to broadcasting," or "free broadcasting." The terms become symbols cherished by participants in and of themselves without careful thought, or they are not commonly understood, so that ideological rhetoric sometimes supersedes real issues and actions in importance.

7. *The process is usually characterized by mutual accommodation among participants.* Customarily, participants in broadcast policy making do not attempt to destroy one or more of their opponents. Rather, the process is characterized by consensual, majority-seeking activities. Mutual adjustment among participants may occur in a variety of ways, including negotiation, the creation and discharge of obligations, direct manipulation of the immediate circumstances in which events are occurring, the use of third parties or political brokers capable of developing consensual solutions, or partial deferral to others in order to effect a compromise. To some participants, on some issues, however, accommodation is difficult if not impossible, and on these issues policy debate is intense and the perceived stakes the greatest. . . .

Notes

1. Congress followed a similar approach with the Corporation for Public Broadcasting, which initially received funding and authorization only on an annual basis, although it eventually received some advance, multiyear support.

2. See Roger G. Noll, Merton J. Peck, and John J. McGowan, *Economic Aspects of Television Regulation* (Washington, D.C.: Brookings Institution, 1973), p. 98. Section 153(h) of the Communications Act provides that "a person engaged in radio broadcasting shall not, insofar as such a person is so engaged, be deemed a common carrier."

3. Newton N. Minow, *Equal Time: The Private Broadcaster and the Public Interest* (New York: Atheneum, 1964), p. 8.

4. Barry M. Mitnick, *The Political Economy of Regulation: Creating, Designing and Removing Regulatory Forms* (New York: Columbia University Press, 1980), pp. 278-279. See, in general, Mitnick's chapter IV, "The Concept of the Public Interest."

5. See Virginia Held, *The Public Interest and Individual Interests* (New York: Basic Books, 1970), pp. 163-202.

6. *FCC* v. *WNCN Listeners Guild,*—U.S.—, 101 S. Ct. 1266, 67 L.Ed.2d 521, 535 (1981).

7. *Pinellas Broadcasting Co.* v. *FCC*, 230 F.2d 204, 206 (D.C. Cir. 1956), *certiorari denied*, 350 U.S. 1007 (1956).

8. [An] example . . . [is] a Commission initiative to control advertising "in the public interest," which led to a stern rebuke from the House of Representatives.

9. Pendleton Herring, *Public Administration and the Public Interest* (New York: McGraw-Hill, 1936), p. 138. Vagueness, however, may also serve to protect the agency when its decisions are challenged in the courts, since the judiciary may be loath to overturn actions protected by a broad statutory mandate.

10. Congress did not uniformly use the phrase "public interest" in the Communications Act. For example, the standard of "public interest" is specified in Sections 201(b), 215(a), 221(a), 222(c)(1), 415(a)(4), 319(i) and 315; "public convenience and necessity" in Section 314(f); "interest of public convenience and necessity," Section 214(a); "public interest, convenience and necessity," Sections 307(d), 309(a), and 319(a); and "public interest, convenience or necessity," Sections 307(d), 311(b), and 311(c)(3). On September 17, 1981, the FCC recommended that Congress drop all broadcast-related mentions of "convenience" or "necessity." It called the words "superfluous. . . . To the extent the issues embodied in these terms are relevant to radio regulation, they are subsumed under Commission review of the 'public interest.' " *FCC Legislative Proposal, Track I*, September 17, 1981, p. 25 [mimeo.].

11. See *KFKB Broadcasting Association, Inc.* v. *Federal Radio Commission*, 47 F.2d 670 (D.C. Cir. 1931) and *Trinity Methodist Church, South* v. *Federal Radio Commission*, 62 F.2d 850 (D.C. Cir. 1932).

12. See *Red Lion Broadcasting Co., Inc.* v. *Federal Communications Commission*, 395

U.S. 367, 89 S.Ct. 1794, 23 L.Ed.2d 371 (1969) and *Federal Communications Commission* v. *Pacifica Foundation*, 438 U.S. 726, 98 S.Ct. 3026, 57 L.Ed.2d 1073 (1978). In *Pacifica*, at 746, the court stated: "We have long recognized that each medium of expression presents special First Amendment problems. . . . And of all forms of communications, it is broadcasting that has received the most limited First Amendment protection."

13. *Red Lion Broadcasting Co.* v. *FCC*, 395 U.S. 367, 390, 89 S.Ct. 1794, 23 L.Ed.2d 371 (1969). See also *CBS* v. *FCC*, . . . 101 S.Ct. 2813, 69 L.Ed.2d 706 (1981).

14. Quoted in Fred W. Friendly, *The Good Guys, the Bad Guys and the First Amendment: Free Speech vs. Fairness in Broadcasting* (New York: Random House, 1975), p. ix.

15. This discussion is based on a theme developed by Benno C. Schmidt, Jr., *Freedom of the Press vs. Public Access* (New York: Praeger, 1976), pp. 157-158.

16. The generalizations that follow were suggested in part by Charles E. Lindblom, *The Policy-Making Process* (Englewood Cliffs, N.J.: Prentice-Hall, 1968).

33

THE NORMAN CONQUEST: FREEDOM OF THE PRESS IN BRITAIN AND AMERICA

Harold Evans

Editor's Note

The freedom of expression that democratic societies prize comes under severest attack when it conflicts with the right of democratic governments to protect national welfare and safety. There is a power struggle between government leaders who seek to protect sensitive information in the name of major national interests and the press and its allies who try to prevent undue and harmful restraints on the flow of information. In this perennial struggle, the deck is stacked far more against the British media than their U.S. counterparts, although government attempts to throttle the press are a problem in both countries.

The major differences between the two countries when it comes to relations between the government and the press are statutory, attitudinal, and philosophical. Britain has laws that punish all unauthorized disclosures of official information, regardless of the nature of the information. U.S. laws, by contrast, require full disclosure of most government information upon request. There are only a few clearly defined exceptions. The British prefer a potential overdose of government secrecy to the dangers posed by ill-advised public revelations. Americans' preferences are the reverse. British laws rest on the assumption that information is property that belongs to its generators, while Americans regard information as a public good that must be available to all.

Unfortunately, there is no ideal middle ground between these clashing laws, attitudes, and philosophies. More careful definitions of the ground rules by which the needs for government censorship ought to be judged are well-nigh impossible because observers disagree sharply about what constitutes sensitive information and about the appropriate degree of protection. Harold Evans has experienced the British system firsthand as a former editor of London's Times *and* Sunday

Times. *In the United States Evans has served as editorial director of* U.S. News and World Report *and has taught at Duke University. The selection comes from* The Media and Foreign Policy, *ed. Simon Serfati (New York: St. Martin's Press, 1991), chap. 14.*

... Such is the feeling of communion between the British and the Americans, in blood ties, in political heritage, in the culture of a common tongue, in the comradeship of modern history's closest wartime alliance, that they often think of themselves as one society of common values. This creates a warm but misleading sentiment. For today, there exists between Britain and the United States a profound and accelerating difference, one from which both can learn. . . .

... The conflicts in the two countries between government and the press may be over similar issues. Both British and American governments have accused the press of sustaining terrorism with the oxygen of publicity. Both would prefer to conduct foreign policy without scrutiny. The issues that provoke charges of irresponsibility and countercharges of censorship are similar in all the political democracies.

But the similarities end there. The British political system is parliamentary with executive predominance. . . . There is little practical restraint from the cabinet's "collective responsibility" and less from the majority of the legislature whose members observe party discipline in a way unfamiliar to Capitol Hill. There is also in British political and social life a San Andreas fault—an underlying philosophical crack in the country's approach to freedom of the press. Britain has a half-free press and the ruling elites find nothing objectionable in that. A review of British law supports this assertion.

Official Secrets

The nomenclature is suggestive. Britain has an Official Secrets Act that punishes any unauthorized disclosure of official information. The relevant statute in the United States is the Freedom of Information Act, which stipulates that all federal government records must be provided on request to anyone unless one of nine specific conditions apply. These conditions mainly concern national defense, privacy, privileged or confidential trade secrets, and the regulation of financial institutions. The Official Secrets Act, on the other hand, makes the giving and receiving of *any* official information an offense, irrespective of whether the public interest would benefit. The British government resisted all efforts to allow a public interest defense when a "reform act" was passed in 1989. This new legislation still allows the suppression of whatever official information the government chooses to keep secret. The information may be suppressed for legitimate reasons or simply because the government finds it politically inconvenient to tell the British people what they ought and have a right to know.

The Official Secrets Act in the past has been put to both shameful and silly uses. In the 1960s it was used to conceal a series of scandals involving atomic radiation hazards. The Home Office permanent secretary warned the *Daily Express* about reporting a radiation leak at Windscale. The newspaper, fearing prosecution, refrained from disclosing the information—of indisputable immediate importance to public health and long-term nuclear policy. The public was kept unaware that the Atomic Energy Authority as constituted was incapable of ensuring the elimination of radiation leaks, an inability shown up in the 1980s revelation that the same Windscale plant had wantonly spilled plutonium into the North Sea. Successive governments have tried to misuse the act's provisions and could certainly misuse the new act. . . .

The D-Notice

. . . The D-notice is a wartime relic, a voluntary system whereby government defence and security officials, working with media representatives, agree on what subjects are off-limits to the press. In principle this makes sense. Nobody in the responsible press, even in the silly British popular press, inadvertently wants to disclose important secrets to a potential enemy. But, on the other hand, neither does anyone want to be conned into suppressing information that is really a matter of politics and not a matter of security.

The D-notice works in the following manner. There is a committee of civil servants and editors, who meet at the ministry of defence. There, the committee discusses what subjects may properly be identified to the press as sensitive and hence placed on a D-notice. Once this committee reaches agreement, the rest of the press is notified and encouraged to seek guidance from the Secretary of the D-notice committee before publishing anything covered by the one-line references in the D-notice. Editors may still choose to disregard a D-notice but they do so with the knowledge that government prosecution is likely.

The D-notice is, in effect, an institutionalized way of doing what is done in the United States through informal government-press contacts. Recently, for example, the late director of the CIA, William Casey, enlisted National Security Adviser John Poindexter and President Ronald Reagan in a successful effort to persuade the *Washington Post* to remove some information from a story on National Security Agency analyst Ronald W. Pelton. Pelton had sold the Soviet Union secrets about electronic interception techniques.

Editors who have served on D-notice committees say that it can work well. Much depends on its permanent secretary and on the government of

the day. There has to be trust and fair play. As editor of national and regional newspapers, I have both obeyed and defied D-notices. In the 1960s,
I obeyed a D-notice not to reveal the secret places where the British government would locate in the event of a nuclear war.

In another case, I took no account of a D-notice specifically reissued in
a belated attempt to discourage *The Sunday Times* from reporting on the
Kim Philby affair. The notice forbade the publication of anything regarding the past and present security service members. I disregarded it because, as the British government well knew, *The Sunday Times* had spent
more than a year investigating Kim Philby and we were about to reveal
the fact that he was a major Soviet spy who had been head of Britain's
anti-Soviet section of espionage. . . . I did so because I was convinced that
all of the information was already known to the Soviets and that the D-
notice was simply an attempt to prevent the embarrassment of certain
civil servants and politicians. . . .

Law of Confidence

In other cases, the law of contempt of court and an obscure common law
of "confidence" have been deployed to limit press freedom. Both devices
circumvent the jury system. In national security cases, as an English High
Court judge observed, the government's use of these means established a
doctrine of absolute confidentiality unknown this side of the Iron Curtain. . . . Numerous enemies of the press have resorted to it and most of
the judges who have ruled on it have succumbed to the doctrines of executive power. They have argued that ministerial decisions are prerogative
acts which preclude judicial review. This is the dangerous path.

There is not yet a law of confidence in the United States, but it is
not inconceivable that one could develop. Thus, in order to prevent its
realization in America, it is worth describing how the law developed in
Britain. . . .

It was in *Fraser v. Evans* that the contemporary law of confidence entered the jurisdiction currently affecting the press. In 1967 *The Sunday
Times* was about to disclose that the Greek colonels had bribed a British
MP, when a judge ordered the story retracted. The following week the
newspaper lost in the High Court: the document on which *The Sunday
Times'* report was based was judged the confidential property of the bribers. On appeal the newspaper won only because the bribers, the Greek
government, made the mistake of not having someone in court.

The law of confidence has been used to prevent exposure of a crooked
laundry, a property racket, and the hazardous effects of the drug thalidomide, which has maimed hundreds of mothers and children. Vice Chancellor Wood remarked once that the law of confidence could not be used to

prevent disclosure of an "iniquity." But hardly anything is judged iniquitous enough to satisfy British judges. In the thalidomide case, Mr. Justice
Talbot ruled against *The Sunday Times* and argued: "Negligence even if it
could be proved [against the drug company] could not constitute an exception to the need to maintain confidentiality." The result of this is that
. the attorney general is now able to argue that the common law of confidence applies to domestic political information as well as to glue and
drugs. The first time the government chose to rely on this law in a case of
domestic politics was when Harold Wilson's administration tried to prevent
publication of the diary of his former cabinet minister the late Richard
Crossman. The trial involved the same legal principles as the Pentagon
papers case with the exception that public interest arguments were not
allowed. The Lord Chief Justice accepted this radical extension of the law
of confidence. . . .

Consequences

The Official Secrets Act, the D-notice, the laws of contempt and of confidence are laws that have become more wide-ranging than is commonly
understood, and affect many matters of public health and happiness not
even remotely associated with the national security. The uncompensated
victims of the drug thalidomide had to suffer for twelve years due to the
blanket of secrecy imposed by contempt and confidence laws. The Franks
Committee identified sixty-one other statutory provisions which served to
conceal information of public interest. For instance, Section 26 of the
Clean Air Act makes it a criminal offense to disclose that a criminal offense
has been committed. Consequently, the owners of a factory emptying cya-
nide into a river face a maximum penalty of £100, while the river inspector
who mentions the results of his analysis to the public risks three months
imprisonment. These examples (and there are plenty more) are cited to
demonstrate how suppressive laws get out of hand.

The result of the British panoply of laws can be dramatized simply by
demonstrating that the American media never could have exposed the Watergate scandal if it had had to operate under the British legal restraints.
From the moment the famous five were charged on June 17, 1972, as from
the moment of private litigation in the case of the thalidomide children,
the certainty under British regulations of prosecution for contempt of court
would have prevented the kind of press inquiry that occurred. Nobody
knew then that the trail of wrongdoing led to the President, and even if
someone did, no public interest argument would have been allowed to affect a case before a court. Even if the press had inquired, contempt law
would have prevented publication of any of the results for years as indictment followed indictment. Under British law, revelations such as the

promise of government help for companies who contributed to Richard Nixon's campaign funds would never have occurred. More than likely, the law of confidence also would have been invoked to gag the press. Woodward and Bernstein, it will be recalled, were able to acquire and investigate the membership list of CREEP (the Committee to Re-elect the President). In Britain, that would have been stopped in the twinkling of a judicial eye. . . . The names and addresses, not merely their copyright expression, would have been "a confidence.". . .

Different Philosophies

At the heart of the differences between Britain and the United States is a distinction, insufficiently appreciated, between opinion and fact. In neither country is the coercive power of the state often brought to bear against the utterance of opinion. The teachings of Milton, Locke and Mill are embedded in everyone's consciousness. At Speaker's Corner in Britain, a beaming policeman protects hecklers who, within earshot of Buckingham Palace, incite the violent overthrow of the monarchy. And in the United States, the lawns opposite the White House are saturated with effigies of the President and banners denouncing his administration. Indeed, in both countries politicians, judges, corporate leaders, and, of course, editors pay sonorous tribute to the value of free speech. Yet, despite these similarities, significant differences exist, and they rest upon a fundamental philosophical distinction.

In America the prevailing philosophy, though it is not without its enemies, is that, in Madison's words, a popular government without popular information is but a prologue to a farce or a tragedy. The law obliges government agencies to disclose official information. The First Amendment says, significantly, "Congress shall make no law abridging the freedom of speech *or of the press* [emphasis added]." In other words, Congress should not constrain the institution which provides the facts. In Britain the comparable philosophy regarding press freedom was formulated by the great jurist Blackstone: "The liberty of the press is indeed essential to the nature of a free state; but this consists of laying no previous restraints upon a publication. Every freeman has an undoubted right to lay what sentiments he pleases before the people; to forbid this is to destroy the freedom of the press." Note the word "sentiments."

As Britain moved from monarchy, to aristocracy, to oligarchy, and finally to mass democracy, the assumption remained that the facts on which to base an opinion were available. This was always a risky assumption, but perhaps bearable in a society with very small conglomerations of power. Certainly, it was as tolerable as the classical economists' assumption of a free flow of goods and services in a perfect market. In recent periods, however, the citizen's access to knowledge has failed to keep pace with the vast expansion of state and corporate power. Yet there has been no change in the philosophy. In the thalidomide case hearing in the House of Lords, the late Lord Reid, thought the greatest judge in the land, ruled that *The Sunday Times* was entitled to publish an opinion but not the facts on which the opinion was based. This ruling, banning the thalidomide articles, had the support of all the other Law Lords.

Two attitudes seem to underlie Britain's restrictive practices. First, information is frequently considered by judges and politicians as the property of the government and not of the people. Second, in cases where free publication has been challenged, the British courts have fallen back on common law precedents rooted in property rights. There is no Bill of Rights to place personal rights in the balance. A Bill of Rights is rejected on the grounds that it would limit Parliament's supremacy. Consequently, Parliament is no longer either an effective monitor of the executive or a reliable defender of individual rights.

Today, there is substance to Jefferson's conviction that in Britain the Tory or Norman concept of rights is dominant: they are grants from the Crown. This is distinct from the Whig or Saxon concept, which holds that rights are natural to the people and that the Crown has no powers except those expressly granted. Jefferson believed that the American people's idea of popular sovereignty had its origins in the fact that their Anglo-Saxon ancestors held their lands and property in absolute dominion until the Normans came. Jefferson blamed Norman lawyers, rather than William the Conqueror, for lumbering the Anglo-Saxons with the feudal burdens which blotted out their ancient rights.

Thus, Britain and America are two societies that have diverged in questions of government and freedom in ways more significant than political structure. To miss this point and to impose British methods on the American system would be disastrous as well as unconstitutional.

In the United States there have been, of course, abridgments of the First Amendment—for example, the Sedition Act, the Espionage Act, and the Smith Act. There have been periods hostile to political dissent and fact finding. Nonetheless, the First Amendment remains a foundation of American freedom. It has been a restraining influence on the adjudications of the courts and an emboldening influence on the conduct of the press. Hence Americans should not tolerate any weakening of the First Amendment, even on the grounds of national security.

At the same time, one must recognize that no right is enhanced by its irresponsible exercise. Alexander Hamilton was wrong to doubt the value of a Bill of Rights, as history has shown, but he had a valid point when he wrote that "whatever fine declarations may be inserted in any constitution must altogether depend on public opinion and the general spirit of the people and government."

The press must behave responsibly. But it must also be cautious of gypsies bearing gifts. There are risks of confusion and contamination in seemingly helpful laws concerning journalist privilege, such as shield laws to protect sources. These seductions should be spurned because they lead to constant fiddling by the lower courts and legislators and because, as British experience demonstrates, they increase the risk of hazardous precedents that work against the public interest. Exceptions to the First Amendment have been proposed, for instance, to protect information that would cause "grave and irreparable damage to national security." This sounds reasonable enough, but portentous phrases are not a substitute for real patriotism. And real patriotism invariably requires that people who bear the sacrifice should weigh the risk. With language as vague as that regarding national security, who knows what room would be left for fact finding and debate on precisely those grave issues where they are needed? Secrecy is sometimes essential in operations and in new technology, but where policy is concealed from public scrutiny, it is commonly the handmaiden of disaster. The invasion of the Bay of Pigs, Laos and Cambodia; the fake oil sanctions against Rhodesia; the ill-controlled nuclear test explosions; the supply of arms to Iran and the diversion of funds to the Contras—were they all issues better left unexplored and undebated? As Justice Gurfein once said: "Security is defended not on the ramparts alone but in the values of a free society." America, arguably the best template for a free—and secure—society, embraces a certain set of values which find their clearest expression in the First Amendment. Even in the face of the most eloquent "patriotic" appeals, that amendment must never be sacrificed.

34

HOW POLICY MAKERS DEAL
WITH THE PRESS

Martin Linsky

Editor's Note

The book from which this selection is taken was based on a three-year study done under the aegis of Harvard University's Center on the Press, Politics, and Public Policy. The author and his associates investigated six federal policy decisions during the Nixon, Ford, Carter, and Reagan presidencies to ascertain the interplay between press and government. All senior federal policy makers during the twenty-year span encompassed by the study were surveyed by mail to discover their perceptions of government-press interactions in policy making. In addition, twenty policy makers and sixteen journalists who had been identified by their peers as particularly successful were interviewed at length.

Based on this evidence, Linsky concludes that policy makers must learn how media operate so that they can use media power to enhance important policy goals. If they fail to consider communications aspects of policy or if they mismanage them, policies are more likely to fail. The case study presented here, originally researched and written by David Whitman, involved reforms in the Postal Service and is an example of highly effective use of the media. It brought policy success when failure seemed to be in the cards. As is always true in complex situations, however, it is difficult to pinpoint the precise contribution made by the media campaign. All that can be said with certainty is that the reformers were convinced that their case would not have carried without a favorable press and an advertising blitz.

At the time of writing, Linsky was a lecturer in public policy at the John F. Kennedy School of Government at Harvard University. He had experience in government as a three-term member of the Massachusetts House of Representatives and assistant attorney general for the Commonwealth of Massachusetts.

His journalism experience includes editorship of Cambridge's Real Paper *and editorial writing and reporting for the* Boston Globe. *The selection comes from "How Policy Makers Deal with the Press," in* Impact: How the Press Affects Federal Policymaking *(New York: Norton, 1986), 148-68. Several footnotes have been omitted.*

. . . Postal reform began to emerge as a concern for federal officials in the late 1960s. The volume of mail had just about tripled since World War II, the deficit from operations had increased to $1.1 billion, and systems and equipment were antiquated. If anyone needed tangible evidence of a problem, they got it when the Chicago Post Office nearly shut down in October 1966.

[Larry] O'Brien was postmaster general at the time, and he tried to take advantage of the Chicago crisis by warning that a "catastrophe" was approaching.[1] In April 1967, he told a stunned audience from the Magazine Publishers Association that he favored turning the Post Office Department into a non-profit (and nonpolitical) government corporation. When O'Brien left the government to work for Robert Kennedy in his campaign for president, whatever momentum there was for postal reorganization went with him.

However dismal the prospects seemed, Nixon had made postal reform a campaign promise and he began to make good on his commitment early into his administration. The first step was a dramatic and unpopular one: Nixon and [Postmaster General Winton] Blount eliminated Post Office political patronage by ending the practice of allowing congressmen to name the postmasters. Republican congressmen, contemplating the fruits of recapturing the White House, were furious, but Nixon and Blount knew that with both the House and Senate controlled by Democrats, there would be no postal reform without Democratic support. If they waited until after filling available postal jobs with friends of Republican congressmen before moving on reform, they knew that the Democrats would never have taken them seriously. The second step, eventually more important but less visible for the time being, was to develop a strategy for convincing the public, and through them the Congress, of the benefits of reorganization. It was really a two-stage process: first the case had to be made that there was a serious and important problem at the Post Office; then, reorganization had to become the solution.

Blount knew that reorganization would not come about without going outside Washington: "Congress owned the Post Office and they liked that old baby just the way it was. We needed the newspaper pressure in the members' districts to shake up things."[2] He decided to set up what POD [Post Office Department] memos referred to as a "front organization" to push for reform. The idea had three enormous advantages: it provided a way to create a lobbying campaign that federal personnel were prohibited from doing directly or allocating funds for; it created a funding channel to allow those who favored reform to offset the efforts of the unions; and, most important, it permitted the public effort on behalf of the Nixon-Blount bill to be bipartisan.

The key to bipartisanship was O'Brien, the former postmaster general and former Democratic Party chairman who was already on record as favoring both reorganization and a grassroots lobbying approach. After some persuading, O'Brien agreed to co-chair the operation, to be called the Citizens Committee for Postal Reform (CCPR). The Republican half of the team was to be Thruston Morton, retired US senator and also a former national party chairman. The final step at the preliminary stage was to hire a marketing expert; Blount settled on William Dunlap, who did marketing for Procter & Gamble.

Dunlap was given an office at the POD, and two weeks to develop a full-scale plan. He remanded his public salary; P&G continued to pay him while he worked on the reorganization during 1969 and 1970. Dunlap wrote a marketing plan, he recalled, "just the way I would at Procter & Gamble. Essentially I took a packaging goods approach that you use to market a product, and applied it to the government sector." His approach was explicit, thorough, and very sophisticated. The purpose was to "stimulate the maximum amount of active support . . . and to utilize this favorable public reaction as a positive force that could be directed toward the members of Congress." [3] In the twenty-eight-page document he prepared, he laid out plans to utilize all the available media, national and local, print and electronic, in all their available slots: letters to the editor, editorials, news stories, feature articles by the postmaster general, and even appearances on entertainment television such as *The Tonight Show* and *The Joey Bishop Show*. The appeal to the media was to be based on their role as opinion makers, their self-interest as mail users, and their commitment to keep their readers and viewers abreast of the news, namely the news about postal reform. It was a saturation strategy in which press support, or at least press cooperation, was crucial.

Kick-off was set for May 27, 1969. During the preceding week, Blount and a handful of his aides gave background briefings to the editorial boards of papers in six major cities to ensure that all the coverage around the announcement was not from the highly political Washington press corps. On May 27, the president sent the reorganization message to the Congress. Nixon read a statement at the White House and Blount followed with a press briefing and a twenty-two-page press packet outlining the legislation. POD designed a special packet for editorial writers. There was a POD headquarters briefing for staff which was wired directly to three hundred top postmasters around the country. A POD publication called *Postal Life*, sent to every postal employee, explained the legislation in great detail. The Mail Users Council sent a "Memo to Mailers" presenting the reorganization proposal to sixty thousand business executives. CCPR, whose formation had been announced on May 26, issued a press release hailing the bill.

Editorial reaction to the reorganization was enthusiastic. Congressional reaction was cool in general, and absolutely frosty among the senior members of the House Post Office Committee (HPOC). Chairman Thaddeus Dulski (D-NY) had his own modest reform bill which stopped far short of establishing a government corporation to replace the Post Office Department. Senior Republicans on the committee were upset because the White House had eliminated congressional patronage in Post Office jobs. The administration had to reach all the way down to the fourth-ranking Republican Edward Derwinski (R-IL) and Democrat Mo Udall (D-AR) to find co-sponsors.

A confidential recap of a June 10 senior POD staff meeting indicated that reaching the postal employees was to be the number one short-run priority of the public relations campaign. Number two was producing favorable editorials in the home districts of congressmen on the Post Office Committee. Specific efforts toward these objectives were to be supported by continuing national coverage. During June and July, Blount appeared on *Meet the Press, Today,* and two nationally distributed radio programs; plus, he gave several dozen interviews to editorial boards, national reporters, and syndicated columnists. O'Brien and Morton testified together before Congress and appeared together before the National Press Club, drawing editorial praise for CCPR and postal reform as being "above politics." Ads soliciting support for CCPR were taken in the *New York Times* and the *Washington Post* in late June. Blount and other top officials at POD began giving background briefings for editorial boards at key papers around the country. POD press kits were mailed to virtually all of the nation's newspapers. Many newspapers used large parts of the press releases and editorials supplied by POD and CCPR. Some prestigious newspapers, such as the *Denver Post* and the *Milwaukee Journal*, were almost in front of the bandwagon, writing editorials urging Blount and CCPR to keep up the good fight against, as the *Journal* said, "the traditionalists in Congress." [4]

The activity produced coverage. As early as June 16, Dunlap counted 194 news stories, 232 editorials, 27 op-ed pieces, and 39 cartoons on the reorganization bill. At the end of June, Blount reported that 88 percent of the editorials favored the bill, now numbered H.R. 11750, with 9 percent undecided and only 3 percent opposed.

The pressure from the coverage was beginning to be felt where it counted—in the Congress. At a HPOC hearing near the end of July, Congressman Robert Tiernan (D-RI), originally opposed but thought to be wavering, referred to the "tidal wave" of local press support generated by CCPR. Testimony to Congress by union officials during the summer reflected their frustration at the success of CCPR in building support for the reorganization; they used words like "brainwashing" to describe what was happening.

By the time HPOC took its first vote in early October, there was as much support on the committee for the administration's bill as for Dulski's. In six months, Blount and his friends had taken a solution that almost no one supported to a problem that few people took seriously and made it politically salient and even compelling.

Soon after the committee vote, postal reform became intertwined with another issue dear to the hearts of postal employees: a pay raise. Udall agreed to support a pay raise bill which was far in excess of what the administration said it would accept, and the Udall pay raise bill was rushed through the House on October 14, despite the threat of a presidential veto. . . .

While the president and the unions were facing each other in this standoff during the fall, CCPR went back to the streets. The press campaign was more or less put on hold; something of a saturation point had been reached and there was no coming event to provide hard news coverage. . . .

CCPR began to gear up the media campaign as the Senate began its hearings on postal reform in November. The unions attacked CCPR: "One of the smoothest and most massive attempts at public brainwashing since the German glory days of Joseph Paul Goebbels," said NALC [National Association of Letter Carriers] President James Rademacher on November 25,[5] while simultaneously taking a page out of the CCPR success story and starting a media campaign of his own.

The objectives of the NALC campaign were to break the connection between reorganization and the pay raise, and to pressure the president into signing the pay raise bill when it reached his desk. It was a three-part initiative. First, ads were run in four hundred newspapers and on three hundred radio stations seeking support for the pay raise bill, and urging people to write to the president. Second, just to make sure the message was received, letter carriers, the ladies' auxiliary, and several unions distributed a total of six million pre-addressed cards with requests that they be filled out and sent to the White House. If Nixon still vetoed the bill, part three of the plan would be implemented: a march on Washington by 15,000 letter carriers, and a television broadcast responding to the veto message. Within a week of the beginning of the NALC marketing blitz the White House received three million pieces of mail in support of the pay raise. . . .

With the assistance of Udall, Colson and Rademacher hammered out a compromise in early December, trading substantial collective bargaining provisions and pay raise support, for ending union opposition to the government corporation concept. Rademacher says that he made the deal because he "saw the handwriting on the wall," [6] but he had made a huge tactical error in not involving the rival postal union, the UFPC [United Federation of Postal Clerks], in the White House negotiations. As a result, Rademacher's union was the only one to support the compromise. . . .

Rademacher and Blount met the press and tried to claim that the victory was in everyone's interest, but the New York postal union locals were not convinced. A strike vote was taken on March 17, and on the next day all mail service was halted in New York City as the first postal strike in the nation's history was underway. . . .

Finally, after several weeks of hard bargaining, a package was worked out which provided for an immediate and retroactive pay hike, with a larger hike to take effect when reorganization was signed into law. The reorganization agreed to was in all essential respects the same as the one reported by HPOC. George Meany, who was by then speaking for the unions, hailed it as "a tremendous step forward" because postal employees had won the right to collective bargaining.[7]

The bill passed the House overwhelmingly on June 18. On the Senate side, eight of the twelve members of the Senate Post Office Committee were up for re-election in the fall and didn't want the blood of another postal strike on their hands. David Minton, then counsel to the committee, says that "reform was a high visibility item in the media following the strike and that had a very influential role in pushing reorganization through." [8] The Senate passed the bill in essentially the same form as it had come over from the House. When the House approved the conference committee report on August 6, reorganization was on its way to the White House, where, not surprisingly, the information folks at POD had prepared an elaborate bill-signing ceremony that received enormous and favorable press coverage.

The Impact of the Press

Assessing the impact of the press in the enactment of postal reorganization is complicated. What was produced in the media by the POD and CCPR press strategies went far beyond news coverage, and included commentary, editorials, and advertisements. In addition, there were other elements which played important roles, such as the grassroots organizing and the pressure it generated on members of Congress and the strike. White House support was obviously important. Winton Blount's tenacity was crucial. In the view of Congressman Derwinski, "What got postal reform through was that Blount was an unusually determined, able man who just bulldogged it." [9] Blount himself sees the campaign to win the support of the public and the local media as central to their success, although not solely responsible for it. "There is no key force or event that created postal reform; it was a lot of forces and events working together. . . . The campaign to draw media support was enormously important; that's the way you move the Congress and if we had not had the media support we would have had a bad time. I don't remember specific incidents where a Congressman would cite editorial support in his home district as his reason for changing his position, but you could see that their changes corresponded to periods when public support for reorganization was voiced. . . . If the public had been 'ho-hum,' fifty-fifty, I don't think we would have reorganized the Post Office." [10]

Assessing the impact of the press is further complicated by the understandable tendency to separate news coverage from editorials and both of them from paid advertisements. One of the insights behind the Blount strategy is that all those pieces of the media play a role and have an effect. Advertisements are public relations, not press coverage, but Blount and his allies understood that each element of the media has its own constituency and influence, and that all were important in putting reorganization on the agenda, framing the issue, putting pressure on the Congress, and eventually passing the bill. When it comes to advertising, the press is just a conduit. In the Post Office case, officials were able to get news coverage and editorial support for reorganization that was almost as unfiltered as their ads. It is challenging enough to examine what role in general the press played. The task becomes impossible if it has to include distinguishing impacts among different types of newspaper copy. It also becomes irrelevant, because the point is that the POD and CCPR set out to use the mass media, in all its formats, to help achieve their policy goals and they succeeded. The question is how much credit does the entire media campaign deserve for their success.

When the bill was filed in May 1979, the outlook for its passage was bleak. Postal reform was not a salient issue for the editorial writers, never mind the general public. It was a priority for the Nixon administration, but there was strong opposition from powerful unions, a Democratic Congress, Republicans angered by the patronage shutoff, and those beloved letter carriers who delivered the mail.

Then for a few months, the pro-reorganization forces had the field to themselves. The opposition was there, but asleep. During that period, most of whatever appeared in the newspapers about reform was there at the initiative of CCPR and the POD. When the opposition awoke in September, their advantage had been almost completely dissipated. What looked almost impossible in May now appeared to be about to happen.

The unions had wanted a pay raise and wanted to keep their future in the friendly hands of the Congress. By mid-September, it appeared that they might get the worse of both possible worlds, no pay raise and a reorganization bill out of their beloved House Post Office Committee. During the interim, the POD and CCPR had been able to achieve two huge objectives. First, they had taken an issue, postal reform, and put it on the national political agenda. That was no mean feat, and it was aided enormously by the willingness of the president to climb aboard and stay there. Without the press strategy it seems very unlikely that, absent an unforeseen external intervening event such as another Chicago-type crisis, reorganization would have ever gained its momentum in the Congress in general or in HPOC in particular. The second great achievement during that period, besides putting reorganization on the front burner, was to frame the administration's bill in such a way as to give it the best shot at success. The framing had three pieces to it: whatever were the grievances with the Post Office, whether they be late mail or underpaid letter carriers, reorganization was an answer, if not *the* answer; support for the proposal was bipartisan; and the administration bill was the only real reform. While the unions and their supporters in the Congress were talking with each other, these three messages were being systematically trumpeted all over the land in a multimedia spectacular aimed directly at the press and the public, and only indirectly to the legislators themselves. When the music stopped, there was a sense out there that the problems in the POD were real, that the Nixon bill was a positive response to them, and that this was an issue above partisanship.

The unions recognized this and responded with their own press campaign, which stemmed the tide, not by directly countering any of those three messages, but by adding two of their own. The first was the CCPR, which was not what it appeared to be; the second was that the only real issue for the postal employees was pay. The unions appear to have understood that the clear field had given the POD and CCPR the opportunity to put reorganization on the political agenda and to frame it in a way that made the union opposition rhetoric on the merits no longer credible to journalists and editorial writers following the issue. By their own positive campaign, the unions were able to salvage the most they could: reviving the pay raise issue as a high congressional priority, and putting the CCPR and its campaign for reorganization temporarily on the defensive.

There was a third great press campaign in this story: the effort of the White House to try to create a climate during the strike which would help to ensure that whatever happened, reorganization would not be hurt by the walkout. As the strike spread, the White House developed a strategy with four objectives, as recalled by Ehrlichman: "Nixon . . . wanted us to paint the strikers as outlaws who were doing something illegal; . . . to convey to the American public how to use the post office during the strike; . . . to use the strike to sell postal reform; and finally, he wanted to make sure that he came out of this looking like a strong leader." [11]

The program was straightforward and well executed. Under the direction of H. R. Haldeman, a game plan was prepared to convey these messages through a variety of means, including saturating television talk and news shows with administration spokespeople and friendly members of Congress. Herb Klein sent fact sheets to three hundred editorial writers and nine hundred radio and television news directors. Handling the combination of messages was tricky; too much strong leadership and strike-baiting might backfire. Letter carriers were generally among the most popular of public employees, and the polls showed that there was substantial sympathy for the postal workers and their specific grievances. The administration did not want to encourage other unions to join the postal workers, or to encourage the most militant among their number to take control.

This campaign, too, was successful, although once again helped significantly by the firm commitment in the White House to sticking with the issue during the hard bargaining which produced the combined pay-and-reform package that eventually was enacted.

The press campaigns played a major role in the outcome of this policy-making. Campaign is not used casually here; these were not one-time efforts, such as a single press conference or individual leak. They were well planned, complicated, continuing, multifaceted, and well executed. Most important, they worked. One moral of the tale is that Ronald Reagan did not invent the concept of press management, but anyone who remembers Franklin Delano Roosevelt's fireside chats knows that anyway.

Notes

1. David Whitman, "Selling the Reorganization of the Post Office (A)," Kennedy School of Government, case C14-84-610, pp. 2-4.
2. Ibid., p. 9.
3. Ibid., pp. 11-12.
4. Ibid., p. 20.
5. Senate Post Office and Civil Service Committee, Postal Modernization, Hearings, 91st Congress, 1st session, 1969, page 800.
6. Ibid., p. 38.
7. Post Office Department transcript of Winton M. Blount/George Meany press conference, August 5, 1970, pp. 1 and 2.
8. Whitman, Post Office Sequel case, p. 7.
9. Ibid, pp. 7-8.
10. Ibid, pp. 8-9
11. Ibid, p. 4.

35

CHERNOBYL: THE PACKAGING OF TRANSNATIONAL ECOLOGICAL DISASTER

Timothy W. Luke

Editor's Note

All governments seek to control media images, hoping that their policies and actions will create favorable impressions among the public. When a disaster strikes, like the 1986 explosion at Chernobyl in the former Ukraine, government officials try hard to control damaging publicity. By taking an exceptionally broad sweep through news stories from the former Soviet Union, the United States, and several European countries, Timothy W. Luke is able to demonstrate that control efforts are universal. In fact, the efforts of governments to interpret the story so that it supports their ideological stances are supplemented by similar efforts by private groups, such as nuclear power firms and the antinuclear movement.

Luke claims that damage control was effective. By depicting Chernobyl's problems as an isolated instance, occurring in a climate of bureaucratic inefficiency in an obsolete nuclear power plant, it was possible to convince much of the public that the disaster did not reflect on the safety of nuclear power. Hence nuclear power generation could proceed unhampered. Luke's conclusion conflicts with Rothman and Lichter's view in Part V that media coverage has seriously damaged the nuclear power industry. It should be kept in mind, however, that Luke deals with governmental efforts to control coverage of a single dramatic disaster, whereas Rothman and Lichter examine long-range coverage of the nuclear power industry broadly and systematically.

Luke has published widely in the areas of political thought, international relations, and comparative politics. At the time of writing, he was associate professor of political science at Virginia Polytechnic Institute and State University. The selection comes from "Chernobyl: The Packaging of Transnational Ecological Disaster," Critical Studies in Mass Communication 4 (1987): 351-75.

On Saturday April 26, 1986, an unprecedented event happened. At 1:24 a.m., two large explosions tore apart nuclear reactor No. 4 at the Chernobyl atomic power station in the Ukraine, killing two people and releasing fissionable materials into the environment. Chernobyl is so shocking because it is that unlikely statistical improbability suddenly become an immediately real, transnational, ecological disaster. It starkly contradicts images of technical precision and positive cost-benefit comparisons with coal, oil, or gas consumption that the nuclear power industry usually packages into its image advertising. The catastrophic meltdown that experts had predicted could happen only once in 10,000 years took place less than 10 years after the first unit at the Chernobyl power station went on line. . . .

. . . The Soviet and American governments used the Chernobyl accident to forestall new criticisms of their commitment to nuclear energy. Antinuclear activists in contrast played upon Chernobyl to demystify the serious risks involved in nuclear power as well as its intrinsic ties to nuclear weaponry. None of Chernobyl's many meanings, then, exists as such. Instead, they have had to be manufactured in both the East and West to define the experience of Chernobyl for a diverse range of mass publics. As they are produced, the broader reception of such meanings is rarely clean, clear, or complete.

Against the backdrop of the events in the reactor itself, and their ongoing secondary implications on the economies and ecologies of Western and Eastern Europe, the meaning of Chernobyl has been remanufactured by Moscow, the news media, the nuclear power industry, anti-nuclear activists, and the OECD (Organization for Economic Cooperation and Development) nations to convey many ideological meanings. In this regard, Chernobyl is an excellent example of how spectacles develop and are managed in advanced industrial societies. . . .

The news of Chernobyl has fit well within the ideological mechanisms in both the East and the West. State agencies and technocratic experts have drawn on widely available cultural stories such as Faust, the sorcerer's apprentice, and Frankenstein to transform a specific social and historical event into a tale of technological inevitability. . . .

. . . Newsweek's issue on Chernobyl, for example, stated, "so nuclear power turns out to be a bargain with the Devil," and "the Devil always sets his own fee" (Martz, Miller, Greenberg, & Springen, 1986, pp. 40, 49). According to one version of these official fables, post-Hiroshima humanity has made a fateful wager. In order to enjoy the immense but dark powers of the atom, nuclear society either has made a pact with Mephisto for its soul or has created an evermore threatening servant that can easily evade human control. Even General Secretary Mikhail Gorbachev felt the need to repeat these myths. During his May 14 television address to the Soviet Union, he implied that humanity directly confronted the nuclear power monsters it has created as an afterthought from the larger monster of nuclear arms. "For the first time ever, we have confronted in reality [at Chernobyl] the sinister power of uncontrolled nuclear energy" (Greenwald, Jackson, & Traver, 1986, p. 32). Therefore, as Weinberg (1986, p. 57) claims, "in this Faustian bargain, humans in opting for nuclear energy, must pay the price of extraordinary technical vigilance if they are to avoid serious trouble."

Such mythologies stress the strengths of the status quo, glossing over the accident that has torn only a small, temporary hole in the conventional order. These stories represent realities and forces that are beyond the control of ordinary individuals. By reducing the Chernobyl disaster to the work of "alien, reified forces," the media presentations of Chernobyl reveal what Tuchman (1978, p. 214) sees as two familiar effects of the news. First, they affirm "that the individual is powerless to battle either the forces of nature or the forces of the economy." Second, they "soothe the news consumers even as they reify social forces. . . . If experts look into a 'freak accident,' it is to ensure that a similar disaster could never happen again." As a freak mishap, any failure easily can be assigned to the Chernobyl reactor operators' or designers' technical blunders. As a result, the nuclear magic basically remains sound; the disaster came only from inept magicians, and they rightly paid their price in serious trouble for lacking technical vigilance. On April 30, 1986, for example, a *New York Times* editorial reaffirmed the myths: "The accident may reveal more about the Soviet Union than the hazards of nuclear power. . . . Behind the Chernobyl setback may lie deeper faults of a weak technology and industrial base" ("Chernobyl's Other Cloud," 1986, p. A17, A19). When presented in these terms, the immediately visible images of Chernobyl can be taken as meaning something in themselves without contradictions, because they reassuringly link up with existing Western mythologies about the Soviet Union as an industrial power. Given this ideological spin in the West, all the correct myths thereby are revalidated: the nuclear bargain was not flawed, the Soviet Union simply was too weak for Mephisto; Chernobyl was merely a setback, revealing nothing about the growing hazards of atomic energy; the deeper fault was in Soviets, who lack a firm industrial base and strong technology; or, Soviet nuclear sorcerers lack adequate magic, so their atomic apprentice ran amok. Moreover, the atomic Frankenstein monster was unleashed *only* in the Soviet Union. Western nuclear sorcerers are much more crafty, just as a *Los Angeles Times* story on April 30, 1986 claimed: "Minimum safety standards . . . clearly have not been met in the Soviet Union, where most nuclear reactors—apparently includ-

ing the ill-fated plant at Chernobyl—do not have containment structures
of the sort that are almost universal outside Russia" (Dorman & Hirsch,
1986, p. 56).

When deployed in this context, such mythologies usually acquire an
ugly ideological cast. As Alan Krass, an analyst with the Union of Concerned Scientists, noted, American officials "have an incentive for making
the accident worse than it is—just as the Soviets have an incentive to make
it better. There's no way to keep these things out of the propaganda war"
(Levin, Charles, Winslow, Burton, Austen, & McKenzie, 1986, p. 26). . . .

The East

In the Soviet Union, on one level, Chernobyl enabled Moscow to reit-
erate the common Faustian mythologies of "Humanity Tragically Trapped
by·its Own Runaway Technology." General Secretary Gorbachev's May
14, 1986 address clearly was guided by such myths in explaining to the
world and the Soviet Union one meaning of Chernobyl. On another level,
however, Chernobyl served Gorbachev by expressing his personal break
with the cultural and political stagnation of the Brezhnev era. It is unclear
if Gorbachev chose this *glasnost* for himself or if the crisis forced *glasnost*
upon him. Still, Chernobyl eventually was packaged in Moscow, first, as a
subtle sign of Gorbachev's goal of cleaning out the Brezhnev era bureaucracy in the national and union republic bureaucracies and, second, as an
indicator of Gorbachev's commitment to frankness, openness, and effective
publicity. . . .

Although Gorbachev did not directly criticize Chernobyl's management
of local officials in his May 14 address, *Pravda* reported on June 15 that
the party organization at the Chernobyl site was "sharply condemned" by
the local territorial apparatus (Hoffman, 1986, p. 35; Marples, 1986, pp.
32-35). The plant director and chief engineer were discharged for irresponsibility, inefficiency, poor discipline, and inadequate leadership,
while the shift supervisors and plant foremen were described as still being
on the defensive. Moscow, therefore, shifted the blame for the accident,
the delay in evacuations, inefficient relief reports, and tardiness in reporting the accident for three days on to the Brezhnev appointees in the local
and regional party apparatus. . . .

This concern with cleaning house and punishing lax workers was affirmed in March 1987, and the policy of *glasnost*, or the new openness of
the Soviet state to popular opinion and the use of modern publicity techniques, has continued since the accident. In March 1987, the chairman of
the State Committee for Atomic Energy told a visiting Nuclear Regulatory
Commission (NRC) delegation that the persons responsible for Chernobyl
would be put on trial soon in Kiev (Bohlen, 1987a, pp. A17, A19). Mem-

bers of the delegation also visited the Chernobyl power station and were shown its operating units and the two under construction or development. But *glasnost* was not total. The team learned some minor details, but basically the NRC was told "nothing really new since Vienna" (Bohlen, 1987a, p. A19). Since the accident, many people inside and outside of the Soviet Union have complained that *glasnost* has not gone nearly far enough. In March 1987, Viktor Afanasyev, the editor of *Pravda*, complained that many state agencies still were giving his reporters scanty information and then only reluctantly ("Soviet Editor," 1987, p. A27). The Soviet press, however, continued to expose official blunders during the Chernobyl crisis, charging local officials with most of the blame (Bohlen, 1987c, pp. A1, A38). . . .

In seeking to package Chernobyl at home and abroad in the new look of *glasnost*, Gorbachev has been somewhat more successful (Bohlen, 1987b, pp. A21, A26). During his May 14 speech, he stressed the "accuracy" of Soviet accident reports versus the "veritable pack of lies" in the Western press and official commentary. Whereas he portrayed his regime's more open press policies on the Chernobyl disaster as frank and truthful, Gorbachev noted how it was overshadowed by false Western reports of "thousands of casualties, mass graves of the dead, desolate Kiev, [and] that the entire land of the Ukraine has been poisoned" (*Daily Report: Soviet Union*, 1986, p. L1-L4). At the same time, he linked Chernobyl to the danger of nuclear arms, calling for a summit with President Reagan to negotiate a test moratorium and announcing a continuation of suspended Soviet nuclear testing (Greenwald, Jackson, & Traver, 1986, pp. 32-33). By lashing back at overdrawn Western criticism, Gorbachev sought to cast the Soviet Union in the most favorable light as an honest, open, great power wrestling with the unknown mysteries and sinister forces of nuclear energy. He recounted why the accident happened, admitting to 13 deaths and 299 hospitalized casualties. He also emphasized that Soviet scientists had contained the threat and were capable of meeting the formidable technical challenges ahead. To prove he was serious about *glasnost*, Gorbachev apparently approved greater access to Chernobyl for the Soviet press, permitting unprecedented on-site interviews, dramatic close-up television footage of reactor No. 4, and critical reporting on the local authorities' response to the crisis. . . .

In repackaging Chernobyl, the Soviet Union stressed its progressiveness as a nation fearlessly facing new technological frontiers with a new international openness. Even though it failed miserably to warn or assist its Eastern European allies and Western European neighbors in coping with Chernobyl's nuclear and economic fallout, the Soviet Union has gotten away with such negligence, perhaps because these behaviors were almost expected from Moscow. Gorbachev's packaging, to a degree, has pinned this aspect of Chernobyl on "the old regime" of Brezhnev appointees, while he holds out a promising image of himself and Raisa spurring the Soviet Union toward a more open future of prosperity, reform, and peace. . . .

. . . Despite the negative aftershocks from the crisis, Chernobyl clearly has produced some positive fallout for the international image makers in Moscow.

The West

In the OECD nations, Chernobyl also soon acquired mythic dimensions.
. . . [T]he Chernobyl accident was used to assign fresh sources of meaning to the commonly circulated images of the Soviet Union as, first, a barbaric slave state with little regard for human life, and, second, as new evidence of the Soviet Union's continuing backwardness as an industrial power.

. . . Secretary of State George Shultz " 'bet $10' that the deaths were 'far in excess' " of the two initially reported by Moscow. Kenneth Adelman, head of the U.S. Arms Control and Disarmament Agency, also decried Soviet casualty reports as "frankly preposterous" (Dorman & Hirsch, 1986, p. 54). In the seesaw of superpower arms negotiations, the accident also was portrayed as meaning Washington could not trust Moscow to verify nuclear treaties because of the Soviets' inadequate disclosure about Chernobyl. A May 1 *New York Times* editorial argued, "Gorbachev cannot win confidence in his pledges to reduce nuclear weapons if he forfeits his neighbor's trust over the peaceful uses of nuclear energy" ("Mayday! and May Day," 1986, p. A26). President Reagan also used Chernobyl to cast doubt on Soviet credibility at the Tokyo economic summit, while *Time* (Greenwald, Aikman, & Traver, 1986, p. 46) reported one American official as saying, "Imagine what they do to national security items if they handle themselves like this with just a civilian power plant." In a similar vein, *The Times* of London stated editorially, "Soviet standards in nuclear power are lower and the risks of disaster consequently higher. . . . Plain self-interest may persuade the Soviet rulers to insulate nuclear energy policy from general Soviet paranoia and open its plants to international inspection" ("The Soviet Interest in Cooperation," 1986, p. 13). Thus the image of the Soviet Union as a totalitarian monolith with little regard for individual human life gained new meaning in the Chernobyl afterglow. Although Soviet government, military, and party leaders displayed great concern for the local citizens of Pripyat and Chernobyl and although individual firemen, technicians, and helicopter pilots displayed incredible personal sacrifice in containing the reactor fire, the bureaucratic confusion between

Kiev and Moscow practically verified such cynical Western packaging of Chernobyl.

The Soviet Union clearly deserves no credit and little praise for its handling of Chernobyl. As Hoffman (1986, p. 36) concludes, "Any government, socialist or capitalist, that withholds from its citizens information about the dangers of nuclear energy or fails to help citizens protect themselves ... before and after a nuclear accident at home or abroad diminishes its legitimacy and effectiveness." Nevertheless, as Bernstein (1986, p. 40) states of American nuclear information policies from the Manhattan Project to Three Mile Island, Americans must recognize that "their own government, at various levels, has sometimes suppressed information and deceived its own citizens about the safety and purposes of the U.S. nuclear program."

Chernobyl also was employed as a fresh citation to the Soviet Union's deepening technological backwardness. . . . White House Press Spokesman Larry Speakes announced that poor Soviet design and engineering were at fault in the crisis. To forestall comparisons with U.S. reactors, he assured the world that "ours are quite different from the Soviet system and have a number of redundant safety systems built in" (Greenwald, Aikman, Duffy, & McGeary, 1986, p. 43). Even though such claims were somewhat false, numerous Western experts came forward to assure the public that the Soviet reactor was antiquated, poorly designed, and lacked a containment structure. In Donald Regan's assessment, Soviet industrial backwardness was to blame, *not* atomic energy itself: "Nuclear power is a good thing for the future of many nations, including our own—we shouldn't throw out the baby with the bath water and condemn all nuclear power plants because of this" (Hawkes et al., 1986, p. 161).

To reinforce this picture of Soviet industrial inefficiency and incompetence, the Nuclear Energy Agency (NEA) of the OECD met 12 days after Chernobyl to assess the accident's meaning for the West. The NEA decided it should study how to improve cooperation in future nuclear accidents. It concluded, however, that because Western reactor types were quite superior to Soviet designs (Soviet reactors could not even be licensed in the West), no reconsideration of OECD nuclear energy programs was necessary. Since 30% of Western Europe's, 16% of the United States', and 20% of Japan's electricity is nuclear generated, the Tokyo economic summit affirmed the OECD's joint support of "properly managed" Western nuclear power (Fischer, 1986, pp. 47-48). . . .

The American media, in particular, actively participated in packaging Chernobyl in terms of Soviet callousness and backwardness. In its typical style, the *New York Post* ran headlines, lifted from a New Jersey Ukrainian weekly, that bellowed "MASS GRAVE—15,000 reported buried in

Nuke Disposal Site" (McGrath, 1986, p. 31). More reputable news operations did not do much better. For days, on the basis of an unconfirmed report from Kiev, UPI, AP, NBC, ABC, CBS, *The New York Times*, and *The Washington Post* used the figure 2,000 deaths with varying degrees of qualification in reporting on Chernobyl. When put in context with official Soviet reports of 2 to 31 deaths, these news reports implicitly exposed the Soviet Union as the lying, untrustworthy dictatorship it always was. For most of the week following the accident, news reports consistently overestimated casualties, claimed two or even more reactors might be on fire, and suggested the rescue and cleanup were going very slowly. Reports of Western aid, like the West German robots, Swedish technical consultants, and the American bone marrow transplant team, also were highlighted to stress the Soviet Union's technical inabilities in coping with the disaster. Yet, beyond buying SPOT or LANDSAT photos for visual confirmation of their dire dispatches, most news organizations relied on Western officials and handouts for most of their copy rather than any on-the-spot reporting.

This tendency undoubtedly was accentuated by the unusual press access to officials afforded by President Reagan's Far East tour leading into the Tokyo summit. Overall, as Dorman and Hirsch (1986, p. 55) observe:

> The initial Soviet statements turned out to be largely correct on a number of significant concerns—for example, the number of casualties, the number of reactors on fire, and whether or not the fire had been contained—while those of the Reagan administration, which were taken by journalists at face value, proved not to be.

The American press also was remarkably slow about correcting its earlier sensational and inaccurate packaging of Chernobyl. By May 19, 1986, *The New York Times* and *The Wall Street Journal* ran stories reporting that the Soviet Union had built substantial containment structures in its reactors after Three Mile Island and that American complacency about U.S. reactor designs was unwarranted (Diamond, 1986, pp. A1, A6; Taylor, 1986, p. 4). Yet these insights were mainly drawn from an NRC briefing nearly two weeks earlier on May 8 and NRC Commissioner James Asseltine's testimony before the House on May 5. While titillating inaccuracies were given front-page first column spreads in late April, the sober realities were tabled for two or three weeks only to end up later as minor sidebars or back-page, second section fillers. In the end, both the Western press and Washington flatly claimed that if some media reports were inaccurate, "this was the inevitable result of the extreme secrecy with which the Soviet authorities dealt with the accident in the days following it" (Greenwald, Jackson, & Traver, 1986, p. 32).

Beyond the Western nations, the most highly motivated Western group, working to redefine the meaning of Chernobyl, was the American nuclear power industry. A White House official echoed their interests in *Time*: "we don't want the hysteria building around the Soviet accident transferring over to the American power industry" (Greenwald, Aikman, Duffy, & McGeary, 1986, p. 43). Given the American nuclear power industry's political problems at Indian Point, Seabrook, Shoreham, Browns Ferry, Zion, Diablo Canyon, Palo Verde, Three Mile Island, as well as the TVA and WPPSS (Washington Public Power Supply System) reactor programs, such concerns were quite significant.

. . . Chernobyl's meaning in the packaging of the Western nuclear power industry was simple: it had "no meaning" because the RBMK [Russian Graphite-Moderated Channel tube] reactor was so radically different from all Western reactors. The Atomic Industrial Forum (1986, pp. 1-3) sent out mailings claiming that Chernobyl had no containment structure and that all American reactors had the extensive steel and concrete protective barriers that most Soviet units lacked. A public relations blitz mounted by the Electrical Power Research Institute also claimed that Chernobyl was poorly designed because it lacked steel and concrete containments common in the United States (Dorman & Hirsh, 1986, p.55). The Edison Electric Institute simply stated, "We have not and will not have a Chernobyl-type plant accident here" (Hawkes et al., 1986, p. 16). With no orders for new plants since 1978, the American nuclear companies were correctly worried. Before the accident, some experts foresaw offers for new plants by 1991 or 1996, but Chernobyl threatened to pull the plug on America's dying nuclear technology industry.

Subsequent revelations about Chernobyl's design, as well as those of American reactors, underscored the importance of assigning a negative, irrelevant meaning to the Soviet accident when it was headline material in the United States (Paul, 1987, p. 63). By May 1986, it was revealed that the United States was operating two graphite-moderated reactors, one water cooled and one gas cooled, in Washington and Colorado (Stoler, 1986, p. 59). Contrary to the Edison Electric Institute's claims, a Chernobyl-type graphite-fire accident theoretically could occur in either trouble-plagued unit. Moreover, the graphite-moderated N-reactor in Hanford, Washington as well as four other units in Savannah, Georgia, which are producing plutonium and tritium for the Department of Energy's nuclear weapons program, lack adequate containment structures (Hawkes et al., 1986, pp. 163-164). . . .

Conclusion

In the last analysis, the packaging of Chernobyl in both the East and the West basically has proven effective. Within days after the accident, it was clear that many of its threatening meanings had been contained. Even though they were not entirely neutralized, Chernobyl really has not called the future of nuclear power into question. Instead, the mythologies of advanced industrial ideology used Chernobyl to reaffirm the impossibility of future human progress without *more* nuclear power.

... In certain respects, the ideological reprocessing of Chernobyl by the Soviet Union, the Western media, the leadership of the OECD nations, and the Western nuclear power industry was interconnected. Each of them, working in its own fashion, sought to reaffirm the legitimacy of high technology and the authority of technological competence from an episode of high-tech disaster and clear technological incompetence. Otherwise, the anti-nuclear, ecological opposition might gain more ground in its struggle against nuclearization. Chernobyl flashed "transmission interruption," "technical difficulties," or "broadcast interference" across the screens of scientific-technological power. It had to be repackaged as a warning to everyone "not to adjust your sets." Those powerful elites with access, competence, and control of the technological codes were stalling the mass publics without access, competence, or scientific code command, reassuring them "to remain calm and await further instructions" rather than increase their growing resistance to the dominant ideology's endorsement of nuclear energy.

Despite these elites' best efforts, however, the nature of these images' reception is open to question, given the growing popular resistance to nuclear power and nuclear weaponry. In some smaller nations, such as Sweden, New Zealand, Australia, Denmark, Austria, Greece, and Luxembourg, an anti-nuclear consensus already has taken hold. For the ecological opposition, Chernobyl served well as its dire prophecies of nuclear disaster fulfilled in deadly fact....

... Apparently, the ideological repackaging of Chernobyl, like many costly advertising campaigns, simply reinforced already existing attitudes, providing new reasons for individuals to continue holding on to their anti-nuclear or pro-nuclear stances.

References

Atomic Industrial Forum, Inc. (1986, May). *Multiple barrier containment: Significant differences between U.S.-Soviet reactors: AIF background info* [Publicity leaflet].

Bernstein, B. (1986). Nuclear deception: The U.S. record. *Bulletin of the Atomic Scientists*, 42 (7), 40-43.

Bohlen, C. (1987a, March 14). Chernobyl personnel to go on trial, U.S. delegation visits plants, finds radiation level "very low." *The Washington Post*, pp. A17, A19.

Bohlen, C. (1987b, April 26). Chernobyl was first test of Gorbachev's policy of openness. *The Washington Post*, pp. A21, A26.

Bohlen, C. (1987c, June 11). Soviet article charges local officials hid Chernobyl risks. *The Washington Post*, pp. A1, A38.

Chernobyl's other cloud. (1986, April 30). *The New York Times*, p. A17, A19.

Daily Report: Soviet Union. (1986, May 15). Text of 14 May Gorbachev television address. III, No. 94 Supp. 95 pp. L1-L4. Foreign Broadcast Information Service, Springfield, VA.

Diamond, S. (1986, May 19). Chernobyl design found to include safety plans. *The New York Times*, pp. A1, A6.

Dorman, W. A., & Hirsch, D. (1986). The U.S. media's slant. *Bulletin of the Atomic Scientists*, 42 (7), 54-56.

Fischer, D. A. V. (1986). The international response. *Bulletin of the Atomic Scientists*, 42 (7), 46-48.

Greenwald, J., Aikman, D., Duffy, M., & McGeary, J. (1986, May 12). Deadly meltdown. *Time*, pp. 39-44, 49-50, 52.

Greenwald, J., Aikman, D., & Traver, N. (1986, May 19). More fallout from Chernobyl. *Time*, pp. 44-46.

Greenwald, J., Jackson, J. O., & Traver, N. (1986, May 26). Gorbachev goes on the offensive. *Time*, pp. 32-33.

Hawkes, N., Lean, G., Leigh, D., McKie, R., Pringle, P., & Wilson, A. (1986). *Chernobyl: The end of the nuclear dream*. New York: Vintage Books.

Hoffman, E.P. (1986). Nuclear deception: Soviet information policy. *Bulletin of the Atomic Scientists*, 42 (7), 32-37.

Levin, B., Charles, K., Winslow, P., Burton, J., Austen, I., & McKenzie, H. (1986, May 12). The fear of nuclear chaos. *Macleans*, pp. 26-34.

Marples, D. R. (1986). *Chernobyl and nuclear power in the USSR*. New York: St. Martin's Press.

Martz, L., Miller, M., Greenberg, N. F., & Springen, K. (1986, May 12). There's a price to be paid for atomic energy, and it could be a high one. *Newsweek*, pp. 40-41, 44, 49.

Mayday! and May Day. (1986, May 1). *The New York Times*, p. A26.

McGrath, P. (1986, May 26). Did the media hype Chernobyl? *Newsweek*, p. 31.

Paul, B. (1987, March 18). Electric utility analysts almost never discuss financial impact of accidents at nuclear plants. *The Wall Street Journal*, p. 63.

Soviet editor tells reporters to change. (1987, March 15). *The Washington Post*, p. A27.

Stoler, P. (1986, May 12). Bracing for the fallout. *Time*, p. 59.

Taylor, R. E. (1986, May 12). Soviet workers trying to seal reactor's core. *The Wall Street Journal*, p. 4.

The Soviet interest in cooperation. (1986, May 2). *The Times*, p. 13.

Tuchman, G. (1978). *Making news: A study in the construction of reality*. New York: Free Press.

Weinberg, A. M. (1986). A nuclear power advocate reflects on Chernobyl. *Bulletin of the Atomic Scientists*, 42 (7), 57-60.

36

INTERNATIONAL INFORMATION: BULLET OR BOOMERANG?

René Jean Ravault

Editor's Note

In 1977 the UNESCO-sponsored McBride Commission, named after its chair-man Sean McBride, investigated ways to create a New World Information Order. The purpose of the Order would be to protect mass communication systems in the third world from domination by major Western powers. Third world nations had complained that Western news agencies, with the blessing of their governments, use their virtual monopoly on news dissemination to vilify the third world. Western newspeople were accused of ignoring positive developments, swamping the third world with information supporting Western imperialism, and raising false expectations and dangerous demands among the peoples of the developing world. Accordingly, the McBride Commission recommended curbs on the uncontrolled flow of information from the West to the third world and greater government control over the activities of the press.

The passage of time has done little to abate the controversy. Most Western observers refute the charges and denounce the proposed remedies as muzzles on a free press; observers in the third world, joined by socialist critics elsewhere, hold to the contrary, asserting that liberty without restraint amounts to license, damaging the third world.

René Jean Ravault approaches the controversy from an empirical basis. He argues that news does not have the hypodermic effects claimed by the proponents of the New World Information Order. Audiences transform the meaning of the news to suit their own purposes. Ravault also contends that Western news benefits the third world. Conceding a point to third world critics, he urges Western media to focus more on economic and political development issues.

Trained in sociology at the Sorbonne (Paris) and in mass communication at the University of Iowa, Ravault at the time of writing was a professor in the

From *Political Communication Research: Approaches, Studies, Assessments*, ed. David L. Paletz, pp. 246-265. Reprinted with permission of Ablex Publishing Corporation.

Communications Department at the University of Quebec (Montreal). The selection is from "International Information: Bullet or Boomerang?" in Political Communication Research: Approaches, Studies, Assessments, *ed. David L. Paletz (Norwood, N.J.: Ablex, 1987), 246-65.*

During the last 10 years, international communication has more and more captivated the attention of a growing number of social scientists throughout the world. This increased interest in the subject seems to parallel the appearance, growth, and expansion of the demand from Third World countries, especially the non-aligned nations, for a *New World Information Order*. This demand has been progressively shaped and articulated at UNESCO meetings dealing with either transnational cultural problems or international information issues including, more recently, the implantation of new transborder telecommunication technologies (Hamelink, 1983, pp. 56-72).

While this demand for a *New World Information Order* has been the source of tumultuous debates both within UNESCO and in the industrialized Western World, especially by the commercial media which firmly oppose it, most scholars and researchers seem to support it, document it, reinforce it, and do their best to publicize it to a large educated audience.

... [C]ritics seem to agree on the necessity to denounce and debunk the reigning international information structure. To them, this structure is grossly imbalanced and benefits only the multinational corporations and transnational banks of the Western World, instead of contributing to the socio-economic and cultural development of the Third World countries.

Their analysis, paralleling, inspiring, and reflecting the analyses made by the spokespersons of the non-aligned countries, suggests that there is a strong relationship between the economic domination of the North over the South and the cultural domination of the First World over the Third World. According to them, as well as many spokespersons of the developing countries, the implementation of the *New World Information Order* should go along with the implementation of the *New World Economic Order*. Often getting more radical then most Third World's spokespersons, these researchers are proposing a *New World Information Order* in which economic and cultural dissociation of the developing countries from the West seems to be the ultimate solution or panacea.

Taking issue against this extremely radical solution ... this paper contends that the cultural dissociation proposal is based upon a victimizing view of the communication process in which the receiver is considered to be passive and totally receptive to the "messages" broadcast or diffused by powerful producers or senders.

This victimizing view of the communication process has been notoriously referred to by Wilbur Schramm as the "Bullet Theory."

... During the last 30 years, the "Bullet Theory" has progressively been considered as ill-founded and abandoned by communication researchers, as Schramm (1971, pp. 6-11; emphasis added) puts it:

> ... Communication was seen as a magic bullet that transferred ideas or feelings or knowledge or motivations almost automatically from one mind to another. . . . In the early days of communication study, the audience was considered relatively passive and defenseless, and communication could *shoot something into them*. . . . But scholars began very soon to modify the Bullet Theory. It did not square with the facts. The audience, when it was hit by the Bullet, refused to fall over. *Sometimes, the Bullet had an effect that was completely unintended*. . . .

Contrary to the obsolete "Bullet Theory," the "Boomerang Theory" does not consider the receiver as a passive target, but gives him or her a power to respond to one-way communications in stronger and more efficient ways. According to the "Boomerang Theory," the receivers, even deprived of diffusion means, can use information provided by the "cultural dominator" to their own advantage. They can even use this information in order to make decisions and elaborate military, diplomatic, political, and economic strategies totally unintended by the sender and sometimes quite detrimental to the "dominating sender."

Dissociating Third World countries from transnational communication networks would put them in the situation of their "dominators" who, while talking instead of listening, have not been able to foresee and react properly to decolonization, the uprise of national and ethnic minorities all over the world, the growing economic competition of newly industrialized countries, and almost all of the geopolitical and economic changes which have been taking place lately. . . .

Amazingly enough, excellent illustrations of the "Boomerang Theory" are provided by several of the experts and critical researchers whose postures were questioned in the preceding part of this article.

Eudes' argumentation in the last two chapters of his book [The Conquest of Minds] concludes in a way which strongly contradicts the general impression of effectiveness of the U.S. cultural export machinery:

> In most situations, poverty and oppression tend to generate a systematic rejection of the ruling elites who, then, are considered as "denationalized" through their consumption of foreign cultural products. In such situations the practice of the American culture is mainly perceived as a sign of treason. Conversely, the national culture becomes a strategic agent in the resistance to the implantation of "interdependence" (Eudes, 1982, p. 252).

The contribution of the media and advertising to this "Boomerang" process is further emphasized by Hamelink who suggests that: "As a result of this bombardment by advertising, the elite sectors, with higher incomes, tend to be integrated increasingly into the international economy, while the poor, spending scarce resources on unneeded things, lag farther behind in essentials such as health and education. This creates a widening gap between the rich and poor and contributes to an explosive social disintegration" (Hamelink, 1983, p. 16).

In such situations, one could wonder what happens to the cultural "integration," "homogenization," and "synchronization" that the present international information structure is supposed to generate? In fact, instances of this kind of situation can be found in many places during this century of decolonization and national as well as ethnic revival. The most striking and recent case is certainly Iran. "There, an indigenous information system, Shi'ite Islam, discovered itself intact at the end of a decade or more of vigorous importation of Western culture and on the crest of a wave of oil prosperity. The whole quest for modernization was rejected along with the Shah and the electronic culture, technically advanced though it was, was suddenly seen to have been an excrescence, an imposition, a conflict-bearing overseas culture which appealed to a particular Western-leaning elite, but which had not and could not penetrate the entire culture" (Smith, 1980, p. 59).

Similar backlash or "Boomerang" situations seem to be present in many countries of Latin America and more especially, Central America. While Cuba and Nicaragua have expelled their Americanized or "Gringoized" urban elites and middle classes, conflicts between these classes seem to rage in other countries where American culture is omnipresent within the local media. . . .

In many instances, mass media have provided colonized audiences with a clear understanding of their dominator's views of the world. This knowledge of their enemy's expectations and values helped them to elaborate shrewd strategies of resistance which successfully led them to independence.

> . . . [D]evices introduced by the French, such as the radio, were adapted as a means of internal communication in the movement of independence from France. A similar phenomenon occurred [in Chile] during the rule of Allende. In the working class district of Santiago, North American television series were viewed with close attention; the symbols, however, were interpreted in accord with the prevalent resistance to North American influences (Hamelink, 1983, p. 31).

This awareness of the possibility for exported cultural products to generate a backlash against the exporting country rather than supporting it is not so new.

In the early days of Hollywood exporting there was some anxiety in Washington as to its possible unfortunate consequences for the American reputation abroad. From time to time such anxieties have again surfaced; some surveys have shown that familiarity with Hollywood products does not necessarily induce love of the United States. Occasionally foreign regimes—including those of Hitler and Stalin—have used careful selections of especially unsavoury Hollywood films, deliberately to reflect discredit on the USA (Tunstall, 1977, pp. 271-272). . . .

Many other examples could be mentioned to point out that, indeed, the "Bullet Theory" is "full of holes." In many instances, the receiver using his or her own cultural and experimental background can, to a large extent, control the meaning that a foreign message has for him or her. Through the "Boomerang Theory" the function of communication can no longer be limited to the function intended by the producer or sender, it can have an adverse or perverse effect. As in the case of Iran, foreign cultural imports can contribute to the revival of a cultural and ethnocentric background, according to which, eventually, international communications are interpreted and evaluated. . . .

What, then, seems to be most needed for all countries involved in a world in which "escaping interdependence" seems to be a genuine utopia is not a return to pre-World War II economic and cultural dissociation of the have-not countries, which may very well lead us back precisely to what the United Nations Organization and UNESCO have been established to stand against; but rather a genuine opening of Western countries that, so far, have been legally and, worse, psychosociologically closed to most foreign (and more especially Third World) culture and communication products.

Indeed, because of the fact, briefly noted by Hamelink (1983, p. 81), that "the Federal Communications Commission in the United States has placed severe restrictions on the entry of foreign broadcasting into its territory," as well as the self censoring behavior of American audiences who seem to believe that America is the "top Banana" country in the industrialized and technologized world [, Americans] consequently believe that they do not have anything to learn from foreign cultures. . . .

America is suffering from "linguistic and cultural myopia," which "is losing" her "friends, business and respect in the world" (Fulbright, 1979, p. 15).

The core countries of capitalism are seriously disadvantaged by their inability to comprehend adequately, not only what is going on in the world, but, most important, how foreign decision-makers perceive and make sense out of what is going on in the world and, consequently, will act or react to it. Then, being almost always "taken by surprise," the core countries of capitalism seem to demonstrate an increasingly dangerous tendency to overreact in a rather brutal fashion. These reactions having often taken the form of direct or disguised military interventions, they, some-times, manifest themselves through unilaterally decided financial reforms or monetary measures which may very well end up jeopardizing the whole, so painfully elaborated, international monetary order, as we are witnessing nowadays.

If the *New World Information Order* based upon a balanced communication traffic (instead of cultural dissociation), as originally proposed and supported by a good number of Third World countries, were implemented, it would be able to make the core countries of the industrialized and tech-nologized world better informed about how different social and ethnic strata of different nations in the world do perceive and make sense out of what is going on. Then, tremendous progress in the wisdom and welfare of all the people involved in this new and balanced communication process could be accomplished. . . .

References

Eudes, Y. (1982). *La Conquête des Espirits, l'appareil d'exportation culturelle americain.* Paris: Maspero.

Fulbright, J. W. (1979). "We're Tongue-Tied." *Newsweek* (July 30), 15.

Hamelink, C. J. (1983). *Cultural Autonomy in Global Communications.* New York: Longman.

Schramm, W. (1971). "The Nature of Communication Between Humans." In W. Schramm and D. Roberts (Eds.), *The Process and Effects of Mass Communication* (Revised ed.). Urbana, IL: University of Illinois Press.

Smith, A. D. (1980). *The Geopolitics of Information.* New York: Oxford University Press.

Tunstall, J. (1977). *The Media Are American, Anglo-American Media in the World.* London: Constable.

37

STRATEGIC COMMUNICATION

Jarol B. Manheim

Editor's Note

Journalists' power rests largely in their ability to select news for publication and frame and feature it as they choose. The many people in and out of government who want media publicity, or a respite from media attention, try to influence these media choices. These media clients are increasingly turning to professional public relations experts to help them control media coverage.

In recent decades foreign countries have joined the crowds of publicity seekers or avoiders that try to manipulate the nation's media to their advantage. Jarol B. Manheim explains the motivations behind these efforts, discusses commonly used tactics, and assesses the results. His work is based on systematic comparative analysis of a large sample of nations that contracted for the services of U.S. public relations firms. Manheim's study shows that it is indeed possible for foreign countries to guide their news coverage in the American press. By generating newsworthy events that enhance their image or by making access to news difficult, countries can increase the amount of favorable coverage they receive and reduce the number of potentially harmful stories.

At the time of writing, Jarol B. Manheim was professor of political communication and political science at George Washington University. He also directed its political communication program, which has since become the National Center for Communication Studies. The selection comes from his book All of the People All the Time: Strategic Communication and American Politics *(Armonk, N.Y.: M.E. Sharpe, 1991), chap. 6.*

The use of strategic communication (and lesser forms of political public relations) by foreign governments—as judged by the number of contracts and client countries—has roughly doubled since the 1970s. The most recent report of the attorney general—listing clients, contractors, and ser-

Reprinted by permission of M. E. Sharpe, Inc., Armonk, New York 10504.

vices—numbers several hundred pages, and the total value of the contracts each year runs well into eight figures. The client countries over the years have included a veritable Who's Who of folks with an interest in American foreign policy—the Philippines, of course, but also the Shah's Iran, the Soviet Union, South Africa, Israel, South Korea, Canada, Turkey, and many others. And the list of companies serving their needs has been equally distinguished—Hill & Knowlton, Burson-Marsteller, Edelman International, Ruder and Finn—in short, all of the biggest names in public relations and many of the lesser lights as well. They are joined by a bevy of Washington law firms, trade consultants, and general lobbyists like Arnold and Porter, a law firm whose list of clients includes corporations and governments from around the world. . . . Many employees of [these] firms are former government officials whose principal asset is a simple one—who they know.[1]. . .

What kinds of services do these companies provide for their clients? One set falls under the general rubric of lobbying. If public affairs firms are hired for who they know—for the access they have to Washington decision makers—then using their access is an important part of what they do. . . .

Perhaps more interesting to us in the present context, however, is a second group of services, those relating to communications with the press and public. Here, a great deal of what is produced—particularly by firms that came to the business from the media rather than the political side—takes the form of the traditional bells and whistles that we commonly associate with the practice of public relations. Truckloads of newsletters, news releases, fact files, glossy photographs, books, pamphlets—multicolored, multifaceted, but totally obvious propaganda—are produced and distributed. The propaganda goes to news organizations, libraries, college professors, and a variety of other target audiences. And when it arrives, most if not all of it finds its way rather quickly—indeed, as if powered by unseen forces—into the nation's sanitary landfills.

When journalists and members of the public think about the public relations activities of foreign governments—if they ever do—this is the stuff they think about, and it is small wonder that they discount its importance or potential influence. As William Safire put it a few years back, "The whole business smacks of rainmaking, and it seems to be about as effective." [2]

What our research suggests, however, is that there is something else going on here—something of far greater significance. For in addition to all the flackery and puffery and pap that they distribute, some of the more sophisticated strategic communication firms also provide their clients with some useful kinds of advice, advice as to how best to package their policies in order to gain approval in the United States, how and when to control access to news and information so that they appear to best advantage in the American press, and how to communicate with and through the American news media. Specifically, these companies teach governments what to say about their policies and activities. They train embassy and other personnel in how to talk to American journalists about such thorny problems as antiregime activity or human rights violations. They help governments to control access to information, potential news makers, and events, and to stage media events. And more generally, they anticipate and employ to their clients' advantage the predictable tendencies of journalistic behavior. In short, they do for their foreign clients very much what they do for their domestic ones.[3]

A case in point was the visit to the United States by Japanese prime minister Yasuhiro Nakasone in early 1985. At the time, as for a long time before and after, the imbalance of trade between the two countries was an issue of some importance. Indeed, anti-Japanese sentiment among Americans was growing, nurtured by resentment over what was perceived as a Japanese pattern of closing markets to American goods, especially agricultural goods for which there was presumed to be considerable demand. In advance of the Nakasone visit, viewers of local newscasts around the country saw reports showing American produce on its way to Japan. Mike Mansfield, United States ambassador to Japan, appeared on the report saying, "Japanese markets aren't as closed as we might think." Timely? You bet. Prominent issues and personalities? You bet. Good film? You bet. News? Well, what the audience was not told was that this report—in whole or in part, depending on the station—had been produced for the Japanese government by Gray and Company [a Washington-based powerful public relations firm].[4] For a professional image-slinger, it was just another notch on the old '45.

Even network news operations can be susceptible to such appealing video packaging. In the same year as the Nakasone visit, for example, Gray and Company scored another coup. CNN ran a feature in which former Washington news anchor Meryl Comer interviewed King Hasan II of Morocco, who advised the United States not to worry about his recently concluded treaty with President Reagan's erstwhile nemesis, Muammar Quaddafi of Libya. "Any harsh reaction from the West," said Comer, "must be tempered with the acknowledgment that Morocco is strategically important to the United States, and that in this part of the world, strong pro-American leaders are hard to find. This is Meryl Comer reporting from the palace in Marrakech." What CNN and local stations that picked up the report did not know was that the piece was prepared and distributed by Gray—which apparently neglected to label it as required by law—and that Comer herself was a vice president of the company.[5]

Added to services like these, those firms that have access to officials of the United States Congress and government—principally the Washington-based lobbying firms—sell it, or, more accurately, rent it out. Advice. Assistance. Access. It is an altogether enticing package for a government with policy needs in the United States and a little cash to burn.

The results? We see them every day: . . .

• Mark Siegel—former executive director of the Democratic National Committee and later presidential aide in the Carter White House—conducted what he described as a "political campaign" in his orchestration of the 1989 visit to Washington of newly elected Prime Minister Benazir Bhutto of Pakistan. Siegel set out to present the emergence of democracy in Pakistan as a triumph of American political values, and planned a five-day media blitz around this theme. He carefully controlled media access to the prime minister, favoring those he thought most likely to pursue the central theme of cooperation among the world's democracies, and avoiding those he thought might ask other "distracting" questions. In advance of the visit, Bhutto appeared on CBS's "60 Minutes" and PBS's "MacNeil/Lehrer NewsHour," and was interviewed by Connie Chung, then of NBC. During the visit, she was interviewed by Peter Jennings of ABC and appeared on NBC's "Today."

Siegel saw these interviews as the equivalent of free media in a campaign—seeking to control them indirectly just as a candidate for office might do—while he treated the focal events of the visit as paid media whose scripting could be more directly managed. These included an appearance before a joint session of Congress: "We sacrificed a part of our lives and bore the pain of confronting tyranny to build a just society. We believe in ourselves, in our cause, in our people and in our country. And when you believe, then there is no mountain too high to scale. That is my message to . . . America . . . and to its people." Delivering the commencement address at her alma mater, Harvard University—"Democratic nations should forge a consensus around the most powerful political idea in the world today: the right of people to freely choose their government. Having created a bond through evolving such a consensus, democratic nations should then come together in an association designed to help each other and promote what is a universal value: democracy." And at a state dinner at the White House: "I didn't know until tonight that Yale ever produced a charming man, and I'm glad I've met the only one." [6] The result? An increase in American aid to Pakistan at a time when many foreign assistance programs were being reduced, dropping of the American demand that Pakistan pledge not to enrich uranium above 5 percent, and final approval of a long-pending shipment of sixty F-16 aircraft to Bhutto's country.[7] . . .

We can look at the process from the other side as well—that of the client countries. Some examples:

- Canada. In recent years, the Canadians have taken a comprehensive approach to their image and policy concerns in the United States. In addition to working through Michael Deaver to combat acid rain, which they attribute largely to emissions from utilities in the American Midwest, the Canadians launched a large-scale, and ultimately success-ful, lobbying effort to extract a free-trade agreement with the United States—an effort which, in the end, proved more difficult to conclude in Ottawa than in Washington. Concerned about tourism as well as trade policy, they commissioned Market Opinion Research—Robert Teeter's Detroit-based firm—to conduct a nationwide poll measuring images of Canada south of the border. What did they discover? That, despite its proximity to the United States—what country, after all, is more proximate?—its cultural affinity, and its status as a major United States trading partner, most Americans did not think about Canada very much, one way or the other.[8]

- South Korea. Korean corporations and industry associations have long been major clients of American public relations and lobbying firms, while the Korean government and a variety of cultural and educational foundations have developed an extensive program of exchange visits similar to the Fulbright Program operated by the United States Informa-tion Agency. The Korean approach to protecting its interests in the United States, like that of many foreign countries, is to focus on elite-level contacts. And in selecting consultants, the Koreans tend to favor lobbyists over communicators. One exception to this was the effort to generate maximum favorable publicity in the course of promoting the 1988 Summer Olympics in Seoul, for which Korea selected the public relations firm of Burson-Marsteller. Interesting enough, the Koreans made this selection through elite channels as well—on the advice of former National Security Advisor Richard V. Allen, whose consulting company assists Korean industries on matters of international trade.[9]

- South Africa. The apartheid regime in South Africa has long pursued relations campaigns and lobbying efforts in the United States. In 1979, twenty-two agents represented South African interests; five years later, the number had increased to thirty-one, nine of whom represented the government in one way or another. . . . Altogether, in the decade from 1974 through 1984, South African interests paid some $7 million to American lobbyists and consultants. At one point in the 1970s, a scandal arising from South African efforts to buy influence in the United States, which included a secret loan to finance the purchase of the *Washington Star* (now no longer published), forced the resignation of Prime Minister John Vorster.[10]

Again, these are but a few of the more prolonged and noteworthy efforts.

There are two general strategies available to countries seeking to bolster their images and influence in the United States. One of these—the what-you-see-is-what-you-get style of public relations . . . with its fancy books and mass mailings—focuses on raising the visibility of the client, getting more attention from the news media and the public. One of the more un-usual promotional efforts of this type was that undertaken by Saudi Arabia at the time of the 1984 Summer Olympics in Los Angeles. The Saudis spent an estimated $2 million producing and airing on network television a series of commercials designed to enhance their national image in the United States. A more common form of promotional effort—familiar to any reader of such newspapers as the *New York Times,* the *Washington Post,* or the *Wall Street Journal*—is the placing of large advertising supplements, typically four to eight pages in length, in the most influential newspapers of the United States and other countries. Such advertising is usually in-tended to promote industrial development or tourism, but sometimes it is placed simply for the purpose of bragging. One study found that the most active countries placing such advertisements included (in order of magni-tude) France, India, the United Kingdom, Mexico, Japan, Greece, Switzer-land, Italy, and Spain, with many others trailing behind. Altogether, during the eleven years studied (1970 through 1980), 114 countries purchased such advertising.[11] Extrapolating from the study, we can estimate that the two United States newspapers that were included, the *Times* and the *Wall Street Journal,* carried more than 10,000 advertisements from foreign gov-ernments during this period.

The second approach to political public relations available to these countries is a more subtle, low visibility approach much like the one the Bush campaign employed in the period leading up to the 1988 presidential primary season. It takes the form of news management and information control, and is intended less to persuade than to manipulate perceptions. Such a strategy can be very effective—indeed, more effective when ap-plied in foreign affairs than in domestic. This is the case for several rea-sons.

First, the issues and participants in foreign affairs are remote. Members of the public—and, importantly, journalists—are unlikely to have any di-rect experience with them. Most, if not all, of what we know about, say, Namibia, we have learned from the media. . . . Unlike our contacts with the domestic scene, . . . when it comes to foreign affairs, we are entirely dependent on the cameras, microphones, and word processors of the world press. We know only what they tell us. We are vulnerable.

Second, the media themselves are limited in both their ability to cover foreign affairs and their inclination to devote staff and resources to that purpose. . . . As a result, only an elite few—the networks, the prestige press, the wire services—make any serious effort to gather information abroad, and even those efforts they do put forward are limited. Reporters whose responsibilities include two, three, or ten entire countries—think about trying to present an accurate picture of the United States, Canada, and Mexico from a one-person bureau based in Mexico City. Stringers who work part time for news organizations and rush to the scene of an event after the fact to provide us with the news. Journalists who don't speak the language, know the history, or understand the culture of the country they are portraying. They know only what is happening on the surface, and sometimes precious little of that.[12] We are vulnerable.

Third, in foreign affairs, even public officials can have a hard time gathering information, so even they may be dependent on the media for some portion of their understanding of events. . . . At times, even central players can be dependent on the media. In describing early attempts by the Reagan administration to measure the level of political violence in El Salvador, for example—a task required in order to provide Congress with a certification of progress toward ending that country's civil strife— Thomas Enders, at the time the State Department official in charge of the assessment, said in an interview on PBS's "MacNeil/Lehrer News Hour" that principal among the indicators he used to measure violence was the number of violent incidents reported in the press.[13] And more recently, the likelihood is that most people in our government and others, even at the highest level, received at least as much information about the June 1989 massacre in Beijing's Tiananmen Square from media reports as from diplomatic or intelligence sources. They know little more than we know. We are vulnerable.

Putting all of this together, it is clear that foreign governments—and other foreign interests—have both a motive to influence American opinion and policy, and an opportunity to do so. The question is: How effectively do they do it? Have strategic communications efforts on behalf of these governments improved their standing among the people, the press, and the policy makers of the United States? . . .

With respect to the success of systematic efforts to influence portrayals of foreign countries in the United States press, we do have a growing body of evidence. Let us consider that evidence at some length.[14] . . .

What does a successful effort at influence look like? The initial answer is: It depends on the circumstances. We must begin asking ourselves: What does a given country's news image look like at the time it sets the wheels of strategic communication in motion? In particular, it is useful to differentiate between two aspects of news coverage of the client country— visibility and favorability—and to characterize initial images in these terms. Visibility refers to the amount of coverage a country or government (or anyone else) gets in the press. Favorability is a measure of how positive or negative, on average, its portrayal is. Putting these together yields four different settings, or communication environments, in which countries might be motivated to engage in strategic communication efforts, each of which might lead to a very different communication strategy.

The first setting is that of a country that is very much in the news—and consequently prominent in the public mind—but has a generally negative image. . . . The news image of South Africa over the last several years is typical of a high visibility, high negative country. . . . For countries in this situation, it frankly does not make much sense to engage in a promotional blitz that can do little more than call attention to the country and, perhaps, even heap ridicule upon it. . . .

. . . [Such] governments often conclude that they must restrict the access to news makers and events that they afford to journalists, especially foreign journalists. They cut back on the amount and type of information issued by the government itself. They impose censorship. They create visa problems, satellite transmission problems, staffing problems, and a host of other woes for foreign journalists—moves that play directly to the existing disincentives for news organizations to cover foreign news in the first place. It is the home-court advantage with a vengeance. Sometimes—and South Africa is an extreme case in point—governments outlaw news coverage altogether, or so restrict it as to make the journalists' job all but impossible. They arrest and intimidate journalists, or, more conveniently, their sources; they openly follow them, tap their telephones. They beat—and occasionally murder—perceived media troublemakers, or make clear their intention to do so, as the Chinese army did to photographers in the aftermath of the Tiananmen debacle.[15] No more Mister Nice Guy. It isn't pleasant, or pretty, or smooth. But, bit by bit, they squeeze their way out of the news. Bit by bit, they disappear from public view. We don't hear so much about the troubles now, do we? Indeed, a Canadian government study has found that news coverage of South Africa on American networks declined by two-thirds within a year after December 1986, when very stringent press controls were implemented.[16] Things must be getting better. . . . The news was still substantially negative, but there was a lot less of it.

That, in fact, describes the second of our four communication settings, one in which coverage is generally negative, but visibility is relatively low. . . . Countries with low visibility and negative images—indeed, the lower their visibility, the more this is true—have an opportunity to engineer for themselves a much more favorable portrayal in the press. This is the case because—given their near invisibility in the media—neither journalists nor members of the public are thinking much about them. To put it bluntly, they are just not very important. As a result, the guards of these two groups are lowered, and they will be unlikely to resist positive messages—so long as those messages are subtle and do not directly call attention to the fact that a persuasive effort is underway. The objective of the strategic communicator in this situation, then, is to improve the favorability of the country's portrayal *without calling attention to the effort and without raising its visibility in the news.* . . .

The third and fourth settings in which communication efforts may be undertaken are quite different in that, in each instance, the client country has, not a negative image, but a positive one. There is no need to change people's minds or to distract them. Rather, the objective is to draw their conscious attention to the good thoughts they are already thinking, and to find ways of reinforcing and extending them. . . .

It is in situations like these that promotional efforts . . . and advertising supplements like those placed by so many countries in the *Times* and the *Wall Street Journal* can be expected to pay dividends. Where images are positive but visibility low, the objective is to build recognition. Where visibility is already high, the objective is to firm up support. Social psychologist William McGuire has likened this to inoculating patients to protect them from disease.[17] Here, however, the disease is wrongheaded thinking, and the vaccine is a large dose of positive reinforcement. Promote. Promote. Promote.

For all of its evident national-ego-gratifying appeal, however, promotion is not the only—nor necessarily the most effective—form of inoculation against slippage in a favorable image. Another device is that of encouraging those with favorable views of a country to espouse them publicly—to go on the record with their support. Over the years, for example, Israel has been a particularly effective practitioner of this technique, especially in applying it to members of Congress. The idea is that once a person has made a public proclamation of support, the psychological cost of changing his or her mind—in the form of the public embarrassment that inevitably accompanies the admission of error—is simply too high to bear. The result? A friend for life. To assess the effectiveness of this device, compare the treatment of Israel in the American press and public opinion during the period of the *Intifada*—the uprising of resident Palestinians—with the treatment of the governments of South Korea, China, or the Philippines when confronted with, and responding to, similar antiregime activities. Please pass the vaccine.

All of that, at least, is the theory. . . . Does this actually happen? Do countries with high visibility and high negatives that hire American consultants, in effect, succeed in getting out of the news? Do countries with low visibility and high negatives that hire American consultants actually achieve a more positive image as their visibility bottoms out? And so forth. The answer, in a nutshell, is yes. There are some factors that limit the effectiveness of these efforts to manipulate news images, but by and large, they do succeed.

To arrive at that conclusion, we [Manheim and Albritton] analyzed news coverage of a number of countries in the *New York Times* over a period of years. In each instance, we were able to determine from the Department of Justice records that a contract with an American public relations adviser had been signed, and when it took effect. We then measured the amount and favorability of coverage of each client country for several time points during the year immediately before the contract date and the year immediately after. Comparing these two periods—and adjusting for events, trends, and other factors that might have influenced the results—we ascribed any differences we observed in a given country's news image between the precontract and postcontract years to the efforts of the consultants. What we found was a consistent pattern that resembled very closely the situation-specific objectives of strategic communication set forth above. Our conclusion? Systematic efforts at manipulating news images work. . . . They work when applied to the *New York Times,* which publishes more foreign news than any other American newspaper, is far less dependent on wire service and other outside sources in gathering that news, and is as well equipped—by virtue of the skill of its journalists—as any American news organization, and better than most, to defend itself against such efforts. If these techniques are effective on the *Times,* they must be even more so when directed at the general run of American news media, which are far more vulnerable. . . .

Notes

1. Phil McCombs, "Inside the Power House," *Washington Post,* 28 June 1984, pp. D1, D9; Phil McCombs, "The Connection Makers," *Washington Post,* 29 June 1984, pp. C1, C6; and Stuart Auerback, "Foreigners Hiring Reagan's Ex-Aides," *Washington Post,* 16 February 1986, pp. A1, A14, A15.

2. William Safire, "An Excess of Access," *Roanoke Times & World News (VA),* 19 February 1986, p. A7.

3. Jarol B.Manheim and Robert B. Albritton, "Changing National Images: International Public Relations and Media Agenda Setting," *American Political Science Review* 78 (1984), pp. 641-57; and Richard S. Tedlow and John A. Quelch, "Communications for the Nation State," *Public Relations Journal* 37 (1981), pp. 22-25.

4. Jeanne Saddler, "Public Relations Firms Offer 'News' to TV," *Wall Street Journal,* 2 April 1985, p. 6.

5. Mary Battiata, "What's News? Well, There's a Gray Area," *Washington Post*

National Weekly Edition, 15 April 1985, p. 11.

6. Information about the Bhutto visit is drawn from a personal interview with Mark Siegel, July 1989; the official texts of the prime minister's statements; and Donnie Radcliffe and Martha Sherrill, "Bhutto, Back at the White House," *Washington Post*, 7 June 1989, pp. C1 and C8.

7. For a more complete discussion of the Bhutto visit see Jarol B. Manheim, "Coming to America: Head of State Visits as Public Diplomacy," paper presented at the Annual Meeting of the International Communication Association, Dublin, Ireland, June 1990.

8. Personal discussion with Norman T. London, Academic Relations Officer, and Harry F. Adams, Counsellor, Embassy of Canada, 1986.

9. Jarol B. Manheim, "Political Culture and Political Communication: Implications for U.S.-Korean Relations," paper presented at the Annual Meeting of the American Political Science Association, Washington, D.C., August 1988; Jarol B. Manheim, "Rights of Passage: Elections, Olympics, and the External Communications of the Republic of Korea," paper presented at the World Congress of the International Political Science Association, Washington, D.C., August 1988; and personal interview with Daryl Plunk, vice president, Richard V. Allen company, 1989.

10. Rick Atkinson, "Law Firm's Split Airs S. African Lobbying," *Washington Post*, 12 March 1984; Greg Goldin, "The Toughest Accounts," *Mother Jones*, January 1985, pp. 28-29; and "Pittsburgh Forces Hand of Pretoria Lobbyists," *Africa News*, 19 March 1984, pp. 6-8.

11. Odekhiren Amaize and Ronald J. Faber, "Advertising by National Governments in Leading United States, Indian and British Newspapers," *Gazette* 32 (1983), pp. 87-101.

12. For some examples see John Weisman, "Ignorants Abroad," *TV Guide*, 28 May 1983, pp. 2-8.

13. The interview was broadcast on January 21, 1983.

14. Portions of the discussion that follows are based on Manheim and Albritton, "Changing National Images," *American Political Science Review*.

15. For other examples, see John Weisman, "Intimidation," *TV Guide*, 23 October 1982, pp. 4-10.

16. Cited in "South Africa's Toughest Censor," *Columbia Journalism Review*, July/August 1988, p. 6.

17. "Inducing Resistance to Persuasion: Some Contemporary Approaches," *Advances in Experimental Social Psychology* 1 (1964), pp. 192-202.